UNCOMMON DEMOCRACIES

September 1990

To Bruce

With best regards
and in friendship

T.J

This book is based on a conference sponsored by the Joint Committees on Japanese Studies and Western Europe of the American Council of Learned Societies and the Social Science Research Council, and the Japan Society for the Promotion of Science. Support for the activities of the Joint Committees was provided by the Ford Foundation and the National Endowment for the Humanities.

Uncommon Democracies

The One-Party Dominant Regimes

Edited by

T. J. PEMPEL

CORNELL UNIVERSITY PRESS

ITHACA AND LONDON

First published 1990 by Cornell University Press.

International Standard Book Number 0-8014-2367-8 (cloth)
International Standard Book Number 0-8014-9696-9 (paper)
Library of Congress Catalog Card Number 89-22111
Printed in the United States of America
Librarians: Library of Congress cataloging information
appears on the last page of the book.

⊖ The paper used in this publication meets the minimum requirements of the American National Standard for Permanence of Paper for Printed Library Materials Z39.48–1984.

Contents

Preface

This book, like many others in politics, grew out of a mixture of intellectual trends and contemporary events. Although every effort has been made to create a truly comparative study, the project began with Japan, and concerns about events in that country and explanations for them led to examination of other one-party dominant states. Within the community of Japan specialists, many prevailing notions about the country were being reassessed during the late 1970s and early 1980s. Some scholars challenged the expectations and consequences of Japan's high economic growth policies. Some expressed concern that the power of the national bureaucracy had perhaps grown so great as to pose a threat to the links between elections, parties, and popular sovereignty. For others, growing evidence suggested that the links between the Liberal Democratic party (LDP), certain interest groups, and the national bureaucracy had become so institutionalized as a consequence of the long-term rule by the LDP as to be a parallel threat. Others considered the likelihood that the ever-dwindling electoral support for the LDP might lead to a coalition government or to rule by the opposition parties.

Most important by far was an increased awareness that dealing with such questions about Japan would best be done in comparative terms. Despite the frequent assumptions about Japanese uniqueness, many political scientists began to recognize that questions being asked about Japan were similar to those being asked by comparativists in many other industrialized countries—questions about party-bureaucratic and/or state-society relations; about the possibly diminishing relevance of elections and parties for understanding the key decisions being forced on industrialized democracies in the late 1970s and early 1980s; about the integration of some or all social interests into governing coalitions; about the creation of regimes and ideological biases; and a host of others.

But with what nations should Japan be compared? The standard reference point for many studies had been the United States, the country of origin of most Western scholars of Japan. Yet the two countries share so little in political history, political structures, and political philosophy that most such comparisons concluded by simply reinforcing preexisting notions about Japanese uniqueness. Only as Japan specialists became more familiar with European politics did it become clear that more often than not it was the United States, not Japan, that was unique among industrialized democracies. In this broader universe, what emerged as particularly striking to many of us was the unusually long period of conservative rule in Japan. For an understanding of the causes and consequences of this long-term rule, the experiences of Sweden, Israel, and Italy became particularly compelling.

Just as Japan in the late 1970s had faced a possible loss of dominance, so these other three nations experienced similar threats to long-term rule. The Social Democrats in Sweden had just been replaced by a bourgeois coalition after forty-four years of uninterrupted rule; the Labor party in Israel had been defeated in 1977 after being in control since the formation of its predecessor, Mapai, in 1930; and in Italy, the Christian Democratic party, in many ways remarkably similar in its history and support base to the LDP, appeared to be in similar electoral trouble.

The logical academic response—a conference to bring together scholars whose primary work had been on one or more of these countries—was facilitated by the collaborative efforts of the Committee on Japanese Studies and the Committee on Western Europe of the Social Science Research Council. Various members of the group met in New York City; Ithaca, New York; Kona, Hawaii; and Oxford, England, over a period of several years to refine their specific topics and the group's overall agenda.

Scholars who had become convinced that they understood the general preconditions for, or consequences of, long-term rule because of their experience with the country they studied were suddenly confronted by evidence from other countries in which presumed causes and consequences were different. As the search for general principles proceeded, moreover, it was clear that not all of the countries under study behaved similarly at all times. The question arose as to why these four one-party dominant regimes succeeded and regimes that seemed at one point in history to have had similar potential for long-term dominance ultimately gave way to coalition government or opposition-party rule—countries such as Norway, Denmark, Britain, West Germany, Australia, New Zealand, and France.

At least two competing and complementary agendas emerged: how to identify the most appropriate comparisons both inside and outside the universe of one-party dominant regimes; and, within the comparative framework, how to find patterns while remaining true to the specific cases we knew best. This volume is the result. We hope that we have shed light both on the specific countries we have studied and on general problems in comparative politics.

In addition to the Social Science Research Council, numerous organizations and individuals provided help in this project. At Cornell University, the Center for International Studies, the East Asia Program, the Department of Government, and the Western Societies Program all provided financial and administrative assistance. Extremely useful reportorial services were given by H. Richard Friman, Shoko Tanaka, Elizabeth Arms-Wirls, and Lynn Wozniak. Within the Department of Government, thanks for typing and other organizational assistance are due to David Anderson, Arline Blaker, Michael Busch, and Dolores Robinson. Gratitude is owed to Laurie Damiani of the East Asia Program, who handled with unfailing patience and efficiency the lion's share of the administrative and liaison tasks for most phases of the project.

Our conference in London was made possible by the assistance of the Nissan Institute for Japanese Studies at Oxford University. Its director, J. A. A. Stockwin, was a most cordial host and an ever-challenging intellectual participant.

In addition to the authors in this book, several other scholars attended one or more of the conferences that preceded this volume. Ronald Aqua, Theodore Bestor, Bo Bjurulf, John C. Campbell, Mitsutoshi Itoh, Peter J. Katzenstein, Masataka Kosaka, Yoichi Masuzoe, Seizaburo Sato, and Martin Shefter all contributed to the development of our ideas through their participation. Several individuals provided stimulating and often penetrating readings of various drafts of the manuscript. Francis Castles, David Cameron, Peter J. Katzenstein, Andrei Markovits, Richard J. Samuels, and two anonymous readers deserve appreciation for their many generous suggestions, helpful corrections, and enthusiastic encouragement.

Holly Bailey and Roger Haydon at Cornell University Press have been unfailingly helpful and efficient in their efforts to make this a better book.

Thanks finally to Coraleen Rooney, who for several years has struggled through more Swedish, Japanese, and Italian phrases and footnotes, not to mention diverse handwriting samples, and has typed more about one-party dominance than I'm sure she ever deemed possible when she first agreed to take on the task.

T. J. PEMPEL

Ithaca, New York

Contributors

Myron J. Aronoff is Professor of Anthropology and of Political Science at Rutgers University, New Brunswick, New Jersey

Giuseppe Di Palma is Professor of Political Science at the University of California, Berkeley

Gøsta Esping-Andersen is Professor of Sociology at the European University Institute, Florence, Italy

Takashi Inoguchi is Professor of Political Science in the Institute of Oriental Culture at Tokyo University, Tokyo, Japan

Ellis S. Krauss is Professor of Political Science at the University of Pittsburgh, Pittsburgh, Pennsylvania

Michio Muramatsu is Professor of Public Administration in the Faculty of Law at Kyoto University, Kyoto, Japan

Hideo Otake is a Professor in the Faculty of Law at Tohoku University, Sendai, Japan

T. J. Pempel is Professor of Government and Adjunct Professor of Business at Cornell University, Ithaca, New York

Jon Pierre is Assistant Professor of Political Science at the University of Goteborg, Goteborg, Sweden

Jonas Pontusson is Assistant Professor of Government at Cornell University, Ithaca, New York

Michael Shalev is Professor of Sociology and of Political Science at the Hebrew University of Jerusalem, Israel

Sidney Tarrow is Maxwell M. Upson Professor of Government at Cornell University, Ithaca, New York

Introduction. Uncommon Democracies: The One-Party Dominant Regimes

T. J. PEMPEL

The vast majority of the nation-states in the world could be characterized as one-party states. Virtually all of the Eastern bloc countries restrict electoral competition to official Communist parties. Many authoritarian regimes of the ideological right mirror the Eastern bloc by recognizing only one party as legitimate. And by far the vast majority, though by no means all, of the so-called less developed countries, when they allow political parties to function at all, are typically governed by a single party.

The advanced industrial democracies provide a stark contrast. By far the largest number are governed by coalitions that shift periodically, as in the Netherlands, West Germany, Denmark, and Belgium. A few, such as Britain, Austria, West Germany, and the United States, typically have governments that periodically alternate between two major parties. The changeable nature of voters and the ability to switch governing parties, rewarding appealing promises or "throwing the rascals out," has long been a keystone of electoral democracy and a hallmark of politics in these countries. Indeed, such periodic changes in government have come to be identified in the popular mind, and in much scholarly analysis, with democracy itself.

Yet as with most broad sociohistorical patterns, there are noteworthy exceptions, which by their unusual character force a reexamination of many of the generalizations about the meaning and basis of political democracy. These exceptions are the presence, within the group of industrialized democracies, of one-party dominant states. In these countries, despite free electoral competition, relatively open information systems, respect for civil liberties, and the right of free political association, a single party has managed to govern alone or as the primary and ongoing partner in coalitions, without interruption, for substantial periods of time, often for three to five

1

decades, and to dominate the formation of as many as ten, twelve, or more successive governments.

This phenomenon has been subject to very little analysis, in part because we lack a clear definition of what constitutes single-party dominance, agreement on which countries are the principal examples of such dominance, and appreciation of the analytic significance of this phenomenon. This volume represents an effort to address these problems in ways that will shed light not only on the phenomenon of single-party dominance narrowly conceived but also on the broader interrelationship among parties, social groups, and the state within industrialized countries. Unifying all of the chapters is an underlying belief that it is only in this broader context that single-party dominance is of analytic interest.

This introduction sketches the key themes addressed throughout the volume. The first section attempts to sharpen our understanding of dominance per se and to identify the key examples of one-party dominance within the industrialized democracies. An examination of why the phenomenon is particularly interesting subsequently isolates several key puzzles that one-party dominance presents for students of advanced democracies. The problem of single-party dominance is then situated within the broader context of political parties in industrialized democracies. It shows the importance of treating parties not simply as electoral machines but also as the organizers of coalitions among broad socioeconomic sectors, as the formulators of governments, and, in this role, as the implementing agents of public policies that can profoundly affect the strength of the party's socioeconomic support base. Following this discussion is a comparative exploration of the interaction of these interwoven roles for dominant political parties. The causes and consequences of long-term political dominance in Sweden, Israel, Japan, and Italy are examined and compared with other similar countries that had the potential for such dominance but never secured comparable long-term single-party rule, a situation we have labeled "failed dominance." Finally, the introduction closes by offering a very brief overview of the chapters that follow.

Identifying Dominance

The literature on dominance among the industrialized democracies is marked by vagueness in definition and disagreement on cases. Thus Maurice Duverger speaks only briefly of dominant parties, citing as examples Switzerland before the introduction of proportional representation and the post–Civil War U.S. South. His discussion of dominance is vague, resting heavily on unspecifiable assessments by the mass public: "A party is dominant when it is identified with an epoch, when its doctrines, ideas, methods, its style, so to speak, coincide with those of the epoch. . . . A dominant party is that which public opinion *believes* to be dominant."[1] Jean Blondel, using no more clear-cut criteria, focuses on more recent cases, listing as examples Denmark, Sweden, Norway, Italy, Iceland, Chile, Israel, India, Venezuela, and Colombia.[2] Two studies devoted primarily to comparing dominant parties (or dominant party systems) also fail to provide any explicit definition of what is meant by dominance, although few would challenge their selection of cases.[3] Giovanni Sartori, preferring the term *predominant party system,* uses it to refer to politics in which one party "outdistances all the others." In such cases, he notes, "this party is dominant in that it is significantly stronger than the others."[4] This definition is no less unsatisfactory than others. The real problem, as Sartori is quick to note, is that very little attention is given to operationalizing the notion of dominance or predominance. Ronald H. McDonald, writing in the context of Latin America, does offer an explicit definition of the single-party dominant system as one in which "a minimum of 60 percent of the seats . . . are controlled by one political party."[5] This definition, though perhaps practical in some Latin American cases, would almost never be met in industrialized countries and would exclude most cases, such as those cited by Blondel, that come instantly to mind when one speaks of dominant or predominant parties. Furthermore, although the 60 percent cutoff might be met in a single election or two, it is rarely sustained over any substantial period of time.

What, then, is meant by single-party dominance? Four dimensions seem crucial. First, a party must be *dominant in number;* it must win a larger number of seats than its opponents. It makes very little sense to speak of the second or third most popular vote getter as dominant; only a party that receives at least a plurality should qualify as a dominant party. Second, a party must enjoy a *dominant bargaining position;* to stay in government on a regular basis, it must hold a position within the party system that enables it to bargain effectively with other, smaller parties in the formation of governments. Thus even if a party does not itself enjoy a parliamentary majority, to dominate it must be in a strategic position that makes it highly unlikely for any government to be formed without its inclusion. Third, a party must be *dominant chronologically.* It must be at the core of a nation's

1. Maurice Duverger, *Political Parties: Their Organization and Activity in the Modern State* (New York: Wiley, 1963), pp. 275–80, 308–9.
2. Jean Blondel, *Comparing Political Systems* (New York: Praeger, 1972), pp. 99–102.
3. Asher Arian and Samuel Barnes, "The Dominant Party System: A Neglected Model of Democratic Stability," *Journal of Politics* 36, no. 3 (1974): 592–614; Ariel Levite and Sidney Tarrow, "The Legitimation of Excluded Parties in Dominant Systems: A Comparison of Israel and Italy," *Comparative Politics* 15 (1983): 295–327.
4. Giovanni Sartori, *Parties and Party Systems,* vol. 1 (London: Cambridge University Press, 1976), p. 193.
5. Ronald H. McDonald, *Party Systems and Elections in Latin America* (Chicago: Markham, 1971), p. 220.

government over a substantial period of time, not simply for a few years. Finally, a dominant party must be *dominant governmentally*. Because of its long-standing presence at the core of government, the dominant party carries out what many would call a historical project, a series of interrelated and mutually supportive public policies that give particular shape to the national political agenda. In short, the dominant party must dominate the electorate, other political parties, the formation of governments, and the public policy agenda. Parties that combine these features fit most commonsense notions of a dominant party or of politics within a dominant party system.

These conditions are met in relatively few instances, but Japan offers a clear-cut case. There, the Liberal Democratic party held unambiguous majorities in both houses of parliament, providing all the prime ministers and virtually all the cabinet ministers, from its formation in 1955 until 1989.[6] Indeed, if one includes the predecessors of the LDP, conservative party dominance began in 1947. Since then Japan's governments have committed themselves to a consistent agenda of alliances with the United States and high economic growth. For similarly long periods, both Israel (preindependence and/or from 1948 to 1977) and Sweden (1932 to 1976) were also functioning democracies in which a single party continually won electoral pluralities and dominated the executive branch of government (although with less totality than the LDP in Japan). Israel's ruling party carried out an agenda of rapid national development and the realization of a Jewish state; Sweden became the prototype of the social welfare state. Likewise, the Christian Democratic party has been the largest party in Italian politics since immediately after World War II, controlling the prime ministry, providing the bulk of all cabinet members until 1980 and remaining the plurality party and the key to cabinet formation since then. It followed a foreign and domestic agenda similar to Japan's—high growth and anticommunism but with heavier overlays of social security, Christianity, and patronage politics.

As one looks at shorter time periods, examples come more easily to mind. The Gaullists might be said to have dominated France for the period 1956–81 if one includes the dubious case of Valéry Giscard d'Estaing. In Australia, from 1949 to 1972 a coalition of the Liberal and Country parties held sway, forcing the larger Labour party into semipermanent opposition. In West Germany, the Christian Democratic Union/Christian Socialist Union (CDU/CSU) controlled governments from the end of the war until the formation of the Grand Coalition in 1966. Labour predominated in New Zealand from 1935 to 1949, holding absolute parliamentary majorities

6. The literature on the LDP and its role in Japanese politics is enormous. See my discussion in *Policy and Politics in Contemporary Japan: Creative Conservatism* (Philadelphia: Temple University Press, 1982). A recent study in Japanese is Sato Seizaburo and Matsuzaki Tetsuyo, *Jimintō Seiken* [LDP Power] (Tokyo: Chūō Kōronsha, 1986).

throughout that period. Other democracies such as Norway, Canada, and Ireland have seen relatively long, although occasionally interrupted, periods of one-party rule.

The Puzzles of Dominance

Though several such instances of long-term rule by a single political party can be cited, the phenomenon remains rather rare in the industrialized democracies. Unusual, however, does not automatically equal interesting. What makes long-term rule by a single political party among the industrialized democracies an enticing puzzle is not just that it is rare but that it is not supposed to happen. And the puzzle becomes more tantalizing the longer the period of uninterrupted single-party rule lasts.

Long-term rule by a single political party is not difficult to comprehend in countries where social stagnation and rule by a limited oligarchy prevail.[7] Nor is it perplexing in authoritarian regimes where the sole legal party serves as a key element in a broad arsenal of rigid state controls.[8] It is also not perplexing as the historical remnant of anticolonial movements that papered over social diversities as a means of achieving national independence, as was true in many regimes formed during the period following World War II.[9]

But the industrialized democracies are not socially stagnant; they are not characterized by authoritarian controls; they are countries that typically were built on the recognition, rather than the denial, of social diversity.[10] As a consequence, most theories of voting behavior or party systems are unequipped to deal with the regular and unswerving return of one party to

7. Examples would include the Falange under Franco in Spain, the National Popular Action of Salazar in Portugal, and the Democratic party of the Jim Crow U.S. South.

8. Franz Neumann, *Behemoth* (New York: Harper, 1942); Franz Shurman, *Ideology and Organization in Communist China* (Berkeley and Los Angeles: University of California Press, 1966); Samuel P. Huntington and Clement Moore, eds., *Authoritarian Politics in Modern Societies: The Dynamics of Establishing One-Party Systems* (New York: Basic Books, 1970); Juan Linz, "An Authoritarian Regime: The Case of Spain," in Erik Allardt and Stein Rokkan, eds., *Mass Politics* (New York: Free Press, 1979), pp. 251–83; Linz, "Totalitarian and Authoritarian Regimes," in Fred Greenstein and Nelson Polsby, eds., *The Handbook of Political Science* (Reading, Mass.: Addison Wesley, 1975).

9. See David Apter, *The Politics of Modernization* (Chicago: University of Chicago Press, 1965), chap. 6; Samuel Huntington, *Political Order in Changing Societies* (New Haven: Yale University Press, 1968); Aristide R. Zolberg, *Creating Political Order: The Party States of West Africa* (Chicago: Rand McNally, 1966); Zolberg, *One-Party Government in the Ivory Coast* (Princeton: Princeton University Press, 1964); Robert E. Scott, *Mexican Government in Transition* (Champaign: University of Illinois Press, 1957); and Pablo Gonzales Casanova, *Democracy in Mexico* (New York: Oxford University Press, 1970).

10. See, e.g., Dankwart Rustow, "Transitions to Democracy: Toward a Dynamic Model," *Comparative Politics* 2 (April 1970): 337–64.

office decade after decade in vigorous industrial democracies. Fluidity and party change among voters are far more frequently their key ingredients.

One-party dominance is also puzzling from the perspective of organizational theory. One of the most well-established theorems in that field, dating back to the works of Robert Michels, is that organizations will find it difficult to adapt to changing external circumstances.[11] Rather, argue Michels and his successors, organizations over time come to adopt their members' and their leaders' particularistic interests rather than the more general goals and interests to which they were originally pledged. Correspondingly, an organization's activists and leaders tend to stand firmly against adaptations that, though good for the organization as a whole, might be bad for them personally. Thus the history of organizations generally and political parties specifically is far more rife with examples of stagnation and marginality resulting from failure to adapt than it is of successful and ongoing adaptations to fluctuating sociopolitical conditions. Failure to adapt is particularly noteworthy among organizations that appear to be successful in achieving their goals. The temptation not to fix it if it ain't broke makes it far harder to imagine adaptation by parties in power than by those recently and roundly defeated.

Therefore, a central puzzle for single-party dominance within the industrialized democracies is how or why it occurs under situations of social dynamics and political openness. How does a single party come to retain a plurality or a majority of a relatively free vote by a dynamic and fluid citizenry decade after decade? Why don't at least some of its supporters desert it? Why, with demographic changes, don't other voting blocs become more numerous, thereby reducing it to minority status? Why don't other parties or coalitions find it sufficiently desirable and possible at least once or twice to organize an alternative government?

Another aspect of one-party dominance is whether it makes much difference in a nation's behavior. Long-term rule by a single party may not be logical in industrialized democracies, and understanding the causes behind the rare exceptions may provide some important insights into the relationship between social changes, elections, and formation of governments. But a broader concern is whether long-term rule by a single political party makes countries that have experienced such long-term rule different from those that have not.

If one assumes that long-term rule by a single political party involves simply the stringing together of electoral victories, there would be a prima facie case for assuming that such rule was largely irrelevant in any systematic way, except perhaps in the tactics of electoral mobilization. But long-term rule involves more than simply electoral victories; it provides one political party with a continuous opportunity to pursue its historical agenda. More-

---

11. Robert Michels, *Political Parties* (New York: Free Press, 1962).

over, as Angelo Panebianco has observed, it gives a party the opportunity to shape its own following.[12] And the longer a party is in power, the greater the opportunity it has to use state resources to shape and reshape its following. In addition, the longer a party remains in power the more compelling the pressures for social groups, even those initially hostile to the party, to accommodate to its seemingly unshakable control. As will be explored in the chapters in this book, as well as in the conclusion, this capability to dominate a nation's policy agenda and to use that agenda to recreate and reconstitute the dominant party's own following may be one of the most important but least analyzed aspects of long-term single-party dominance in government.

Finally, at a broad theoretical level, the experience of long-term dominance by a single political party raises profoundly troubling questions about the "trueness" of a nation's democracy.[13] The ability of citizens to change their government is taken as a major hallmark of democracy. But when governments seem not to change, how genuine is a country's democracy? When a party in government can use the resources of the state to reshape society in its own image, to reward its adherents, and to deny such rewards to its opponents, it has the potential to make semipermanent minorities out of certain portions of its citizenry. Such a situation requires either a rethinking of whether one-party dominant regimes can be democratic or a rethinking of many existing notions about the links between elections, democracy, and alterations in government. Viewed slightly differently, a democracy predicated on the ability to "throw the rascals out" is far less convincing when it exists only in the abstract than when it is backed up by periodic examples of rascals actually flying through the doors.

In these senses both the causes and the consequences of single-party dominance are of interest. The causes are puzzling because one-party dominance is at variance with most expectations about voting behavior in complex and changing societies. It is also at variance with expectations of organizational behavior by both the dominant party and its opponents. Both such literatures suggest the improbability of a single political party remaining uninterruptedly at the core of government for three or four decades.

The consequences of one-party dominance are also interesting. Long-term rule by a single party shows that political parties are of consequence not simply in their electoral, vote-getting mode, but also in their governing and policy-formulation modes. Long-term rule by a single party affords an opportunity to view parties in both veins simultaneously, winning elections and governing, and in ways that reinforce each other.

12. Angelo Panebianco, *Political Parties: Organization and Power* (Cambridge: Cambridge University Press, 1988), p. 4.
13. A particularly interesting discussion of this problem is found in Alan Ware, *Citizens, Parties, and the State* (Princeton: Princeton University Press, 1987), esp. chaps. 1 and 2.

Parties and the Comparison of Industrialized Democracies

During the 1950s and 1960s, the study of political parties and party systems was integral to many of the more influential analyses of industrialized democracies.[14] As Peter Lange and Hudson Meadwell put it,

> the party system was seen as the central institutionalized form of interest organization, representation, and mediation, and party representatives were important—if not crucial—sources of political leadership. The party system was a central arena for raising and settling issues among social interests and was the mechanism by which political leaders were held accountable. Finally, parties were socializing agents, providing the electorate with relatively enduring, affective, and cognitive orientations on political issues. In short, the party system was assumed to be the basic structuring principle for democratic politics.[15]

Parties played an essential role in the pluralist paradigm that dominated the analysis of the industrial democracies. Variations in party systems and among political parties in turn were presumed to provide key insights into the broader exploration of comparative politics.[16]

Political parties and party systems continued to attract their share of research attention, but such studies moved away from questions of societal and state power. Instead, they increasingly took for granted assumptions about the rationality of voters and their control over government, focusing instead on the internal dynamics of party organization, candidate selection, party popularity, program generation, and the like.[17] Parties came to be treated largely as competitive electoral machines with little attention given to their other key roles. As Klaus von Beyme has put it, "Party research saw its function for a long time as examining the *input* from society to the decision-making process. Studies concentrated on what parties put into the political system in the way of mobilization, socialization and elite recruit-

14. Several of the more impressive works in this body are Samuel Beer, *British Politics in the Collectivist Age* (New York: Knopf, 1967); Robert A. Dahl, *Polyarchy* (New Haven: Yale University Press, 1971); Dahl, ed., *Political Oppositions in Western Democracies* (New Haven: Yale University Press, 1966); V. O. Key, *Politics, Parties and Pressure Groups* (New York: Crowell, 1958); Joseph LaPalombara and Myron Weiner, eds., *Political Parties and Political Development* (Princeton: Princeton University Press, 1966); Sigmund Neumann, ed., *Modern Political Parties* (Chicago: University of Chicago Press, 1956). For further citations, see the bibliography in LaPalombara and Weiner, eds., *Political Parties*, pp. 439–64.

15. Peter Lange and Hudson Meadwell, "Typologies of Democratic Systems: From Political Inputs to Political Economy," in Howard J. Wiarda, ed., *New Directions in Comparative Politics* (Boulder, Colo.: Westview Press, 1985), p. 93.

16. Arendt Lijphart, "Typologies of Democratic Systems," *Comparative Political Studies* 1 (1968): 3–44; Blondel, *Comparing Political Systems*; LaPalombara and Weiner, eds., *Political Parties*; Peter H. Merkl, ed., *Western European Party Systems: Trends and Prospects* (New York: Free Press, 1980).

17. See, e.g., Leon B. Epstein, *Political Parties in Western Democracies* (New York: Praeger, 1967); Angus Campbell et al., *The American Voter* (New York: Wiley, 1960); Anthony Downs, *An Economic Theory of Democracy* (New York: Harper, 1957).

ment; far less attention was devoted to the question of how far the *output* of the system, expressed in political decisions and material policies, depended on the activities of political parties."[18]

As the analytic study of parties moved away from many of the core questions about the distribution and control of power, serious empirical questions were being raised about the importance of parties and party systems. Two sets of challenges were particularly important: a decline in the perception that parties provided meaningful alternatives or determined key policy outcomes and the corresponding realization of the important roles played by various nonparty actors and phenomena. A number of the principal presuppositions behind the pluralist assumptions about the relationship between parties and democracy came in for widespread criticism.[19]

By the mid-1960s and into the 1970s, political parties in much of the industrialized world seemed to offer more limited choices to the electorate. Increasingly they mimicked one another in their appeals to an ever-more-homogenized constituency occupying a presumed ideological middle ground. Otto Kirchheimer highlighted this phenomenon as the "waning of opposition" and the rise of the "catchall party."[20] Others pointed to the real or imagined "end of ideology" and in particular to the decline in "oppositions of principle."[21] As R. M. Christenson later phrased it, "it [became] ever more difficult to distinguish the policies and goals of socialist and non-socialist parties. Dealing with common problems and appealing for majority support, both [found] it necessary to offer roughly similar programs."[22]

The choices offered to voters in the decades since World War II, and particularly in many of the more prominent party systems, did shrink. In the United States, the choice was often dismissed as that between Tweedledum and Tweedledee; in Britain, Butskellism became the electoral and policy watchword; in West Germany, the Grand Coalition was tangible evidence to many of the waning differences among the major parties. Even in once polarized Sweden conservatives seemed increasingly to accept the Social Democratic agenda. Consequently, in much of Europe, North America, and

18. Klaus von Beyme, *Political Parties in Western Democracies* (New York: St. Martin's, 1985), p. 335.

19. Some of the more interesting critiques can be found in Wiarda, ed., *New Directions in Comparative Politics.* See also William E. Connelly, *The Bias of Pluralism* (New York: Atherton, 1969); Richard Rose, *Do Parties Make a Difference?* 2d ed. (London: Macmillan, 1984).

20. Otto Kirchheimer, "The Transformation of the Western European Party Systems," in LaPalombara and Weiner, eds., *Political Parties;* and Kirchheimer, "The Waning of Opposition," in Roy C. Macridis and Bernard E. Brown, eds., *Comparative Politics* (Homewood, Ill.: Dorsey, 1964).

21. Daniel Bell, *The End of Ideology* (New York: Free Press, 1960); Seymour M. Lipset, *Political Man* (Garden City, N.Y.: Doubleday, 1960).

22. R. M. Christenson et al., *Ideologies in Modern Politics* (London: Nelson, 1971), p. 274, as quoted in Francis G. Castles, "Introduction: Politics and Public Policy," in Castles, ed., *The Impact of Parties* (Beverly Hills: Sage, 1982), p. 6.

Australasia the outcome of elections and the behavior of political parties seemed more and more divorced from variations in governmental behavior.

Paralleling this apparent decline in the political impact of parties was the growing awareness of alternative explanations for power distribution and political choices. Arendt Lijphart, in his study of several small European democracies, demonstrated the importance of elite consociationalism as a device for circumventing some of the otherwise fractious consequences of the party systems in these countries.[23] Even though several of these societies were fragmented religiously, ethnically, and sometimes linguistically, and even though the party system reflected these divisions, the political systems held together, he argued, because party and government elites were amenable to compromise over the heads of the parties' separate constituents. Thus compromise among elites could circumvent the more centrifugal tendencies of the party and electoral systems.

Theodore J. Lowi's analysis of interest group liberalism and Robert Presthus's study of elite bargaining focused attention on key processes that had little to do with parties per se and reinforced the sense of their irrelevance.[24] In a similar vein, works by Philippe C. Schmitter, Gerhard Lehmbruch, Leo Panitch, and others within the broad rubric of corporatism identified ways in which many of the industrialized democracies had institutionalized the policy-making roles of interest associations.[25] In numerous areas of labor-management relations, social welfare policy, and macroeconomic steering, the bargaining among such interest associations had become legitimated as the primary procedure for setting national policy, thereby removing numerous important policy decisions from the whimsicality and fractiousness of electoral politics. Johan Olsen showed how certain states were highly responsive to demands well beyond the broad and institutionalized social groups usually analyzed and were governed instead by ready accommodation to a wide range of much narrower and relatively unstructured interests.[26] Corporatism thus emerged in many industrialized democracies as a paradigmatic alternative to pluralism.[27] Parties in turn seemed increasingly irrelevant to real, rather than symbolic, politics.

23. Arendt Lijphart, *The Politics of Accommodation* (Berkeley and Los Angeles: University of California Press, 1975).

24. Theodore J. Lowi, *The End of Liberalism* (New York: Norton, 1979); Robert Presthus, *The Organizational Society* (New York: Vintage, 1962).

25. Philippe C. Schmitter, "Interest Intermediation and Regime Governability in Contemporary Western Europe and North America," in Suzanne Berger, ed., *Organizing Interests in Western Europe* (Cambridge: Cambridge University Press, 1981), pp. 287–330; Schmitter, "Still the Century of Corporatism?" *Review of Politics* 36, no. 1 (1974): 85–131; Schmitter and Gerhard Lehmbruch, *Trends towards Corporatist Intermediation* (Beverly Hills: Sage, 1979); Gerhard Lehmbruch, "Liberal Corporatism and Party Government," *Comparative Political Studies* 10 (1977): 91–126; Leo Panitch, "The Development of Corporatism in Liberal Democracies," *Comparative Political Studies* 10 (1977): 61–90. The last two essays are reprinted in Schmitter and Lehmbruch, *Trends towards Corporatist Intermediation*.

26. Johan P. Olsen, *Organized Democracy* (Oslo: Universtetsforlaget, 1983).

27. This point is made most explicitly in Schmitter, "Still the Century." It is also developed in Peter J. Katzenstein, *Corporatism and Change* (Ithaca: Cornell University Press, 1985).

The increasing role played by the media in advanced democracies also undercut the importance attributed to parties. By providing a direct link between candidate and citizen, the media in many countries shunted parties and party organizations into subsidiary roles in the electoral process. And as constant monitors and articulators of public opinion, they simultaneously undercut the importance of the party as a link between parliamentarian and constituent.

A rather different body of explanations also downplayed the importance of political parties. Scholars such as Barrington Moore, Peter Gourevitch, Thomas Ferguson, Theda Skocpol, and others pointed out how key historical compromises led to the forging of coalitions among major socioeconomic blocs in different countries.[28] Bankers, exporters, farmers, industrial workers, landlords, and other such economically based blocs, they argued, had relatively specific interests, and the combinations they forged at key historical junctures took on broad powers to shape the character of the different regimes, particularly in the nexus of each country's specific public policy choices. In many instances, such coalitions formed without regard to party label; in many others, the party system was at most tangential to effecting the dominant coalition's goals.[29] In few cases did political parties or the party system appear particularly momentous for the broad political outcomes analyzed; politics appeared in other guises.

Studies of the international arena also suggested the limited importance of parties and elections. War and commerce played their dual roles in reshaping nation-states in ways that often left political parties and elections as little more than bystanders before these supranational forces.[30] The oil shocks of 1973 and 1979 reoriented the domestic politics of many industrialized democracies in suprapartisan ways. So did the economic decisions made in the European Economic Community (EEC), the International Monetary Fund (IMF), and the General Agreement on Tariffs and Trade (GATT).[31] The

28. Barrington Moore, *Social Origins of Dictatorship and Democracy* (Boston: Beacon, 1966); Peter A. Gourevitch, *Politics in Hard Times* (Ithaca: Cornell University Press, 1985); Thomas Ferguson, *Critical Realignment* (New York: Oxford University Press, forthcoming); Ferguson, "From 'Normalcy' to New Deal: Industrial Structure, Party Realignment and American Public Policy in the Great Depression," *International Organization* 38, no. 1 (1984): 41–94; Theda Skocpol, *States and Social Revolutions: A Comparative Analysis of France, Russia, and China* (Cambridge: Cambridge University Press, 1979).

29. This theme is particularly developed in Ferguson, "From 'Normalcy' to New Deal."

30. Robert Gilpin, *U.S. Power and the Multinationals* (Princeton: Princeton University Press, 1975); Kenneth N. Waltz, "The Myth of National Interdependence," in Charles Kindleberger, ed., *The International Corporation* (Cambridge, Mass.: MIT Press, 1970). See also Waltz, *Man, the State and War* (New York: Columbia University Press, 1959), in which he treats domestic influences as a "second image." Cf. Peter A. Gourevitch, "The Second Image Reversed: The International Sources of Domestic Politics," *International Organization* 32 (1978): 881–912; Robert O. Keohane and Joseph S. Nye, *Power and Interdependence* (Boston: Little, Brown, 1977).

31. An interesting discussion of the mutual interplay between domestic partisan politics and international pressures treats the two as interrelated two-level games. See Robert D. Putnam, "Diplomacy and Domestic Politics: The Logic of Two-Level Games," *International Organization* 42, no. 3 (1988): 427–60.

realities of such international influences exposed the narrowness of any perspective, and surely that on parties, that began from an insular domestic view of policy formation.

The growing skepticism about the importance of parties and party systems was furthered when in many countries the single-issue movements that emerged in the 1960s and 1970s seemed to defy the broad assimilative tendencies of major parties. Environment, abortion, race, immigration, peace, divorce, nuclear power, and a host of other issues emerged throughout the industrial democracies, catalyzing the formation of citizens' movements typically outside of and challenging the existing party systems.[32] By attracting widespread popular support, these movements frequently left the established parties trying futilely to recapture control of the national political agenda and with it the votes of growing numbers of single-issue adherents.

As another delimiter over the parties and party systems, the state was "brought back in."[33] The basic model of pluralist democracies had often treated the state and its instruments as relatively passive regulatory agents subject to the dictates of the party in power: electoral winners formed governments and ran the state in accord with their intentions and programs.[34] In one common image, the state was but a cash register tallying up the competing demands of societal interests; by simple addition and subtraction it could conclude what policies were due. In fact, empirical study of the state and its agencies—army, police, tax collectors, educators, public corporations, civil bureaucracy, and the like—revealed independent state interests that transcended or bypassed party and electoral politics. Rather than being the passive instrument of electorally successful parties, these state agencies and the state itself were shown to be active, interested, and determined actors in their own right.[35] This too reduced the analytic weight given to parties and party systems.

32. Helmut Norporth, "The Parties Come to Order," *American Political Science Review* 73 (1979): 724–36; L. J. Sharpe, ed., *Decentralist Trends in Western Democracies* (Beverly Hills: Sage, 1979); Arthur Marsh, *Protest and Political Consciousness* (Beverly Hills: Sage, 1977); Charles R. Foster, *Comparative Public Policy and Citizen Participation* (New York: Pergamon, 1980); Margaret McKean, *Environmental Protest and Citizen Politics in Japan* (Berkeley and Los Angeles: University of California Press, 1981).

33. Peter Evans et al., eds., *Bringing the State Back In* (Cambridge: Cambridge University Press, 1985).

34. Some of the more interesting interworkings of parliaments and higher civil servants in advanced industrialized democracies can be found in Ezra N. Suleiman, ed., *Bureaucrats and Policymaking* (New York: Holmes and Meier, 1984); and Suleiman, ed., *Parliaments and Parliamentarians in Democratic Politics* (New York: Holmes and Meier, 1986).

35. See, e.g., Theda Skocpol, "Bringing the State Back In: Strategies of Analysis in Current Research," in Evans et al., eds., *Bringing the State Back In*, pp. 3–43; Peter Flora and Jens Alber, "Modernization, Democratization, and the Development of Welfare States in Western Europe," in Flora and Arnold J. Heidenheimer, *The Development of Welfare States in Europe and America* (New Brunswick, N.J.: Transaction, 1981). See also Charles Tilly, ed., *The Formation of National States in Western Europe* (Princeton: Princeton University Press, 1975).

The cumulative picture emerging from both scholarly analysis and public perception was that many political arrangements and power structures short-circuited the party system to a usually greater, though sometimes lesser extent among some or all of the industrialized democracies. It was unrealistic to presume that political parties and the party system were the sole, or even the main, aggregators and articulators of interests within a country, even one purportedly based on popular sovereignty and in which elections served as the principal basis for transferring government power. Vital political choices were frequently shaped elsewhere in disregard for party differences or electoral politics. At the extreme, parties came to be seen as perhaps amusing anachronisms to be trotted out for high school civics classes but not to be taken seriously by anyone genuinely interested in identifying the real loci of power. Pluralism and its assumptions emerged as demonstrably naive. As a consequence, the importance attached to parties and party systems declined.[36]

Even as the more extreme oversimplifications of pluralism were being undercut, however, other scholars were demonstrating that party influence could not be completely dismissed. Douglas A. Hibbs, Jr., for example, showed that strong social democratic parties were positively associated with greater labor peace.[37] When organized labor had gained political influence by putting social democrats into government office, its leverage in the marketplace was increased. When bargainers on both sides of the labor-management table knew that organized labor had important allies controlling the key offices of government, the recourse to strikes and lockouts was significantly reduced. David R. Cameron found similar results in regard to policies related to inflation, unemployment, and social welfare, as well as strikes.[38] Similar findings emerged from studies by Walter Korpi and Michael Shalev, Manfred Schmidt, John D. Stephens, and others.[39] Industrialized democracies with strong organized labor organizations and powerful social democratic parties were found, as one might expect, to have been historically more prolabor in their public policy mix than countries in which both were weak. Surely parties were essential vehicles in working out such a prolabor nexus.

36. A good counter to this trend is Castles, *The Impact of Parties*.

37. Douglas A. Hibbs, Jr., "On the Political Economy of Long-Run Trends in Strike Activity," *British Journal of Political Science* 8 (1978): 153–75; Hibbs, "Industrial Conflict in the Advanced Industrial Societies," *American Political Science Review* 70 (1976): 1033–58.

38. David R. Cameron, "Social Democracy, Corporatism, Labour Quiescence, and the Representation of Economic Interest in Advanced Capitalist Society," in John H. Goldthorpe, ed., *Order and Conflict in Contemporary Capitalism* (New York: Oxford University Press, 1984), pp. 143–78.

39. Walter Korpi and Michael Shalev, "Strikes, Industrial Relations and Class Conflict in Capitalist Societies," *British Journal of Sociology* 30 (1979): 164–87; "Strikes, Power and Politics in the Western Nations, 1900–1976," in Maurice Zeitlin, ed., *Political Power and Social Theory* 1 (1980), pp. 301–34; Manfred Schmidt, "The Role of the Parties in Shaping Macroeconomic Policy," in Castles, ed., *Impact of Parties*, pp. 97–176; John D. Stephens, *The Transition from Capitalism to Socialism* (Urbana: University of Illinois Press, 1979).

A different ideological interpretation was added to the debate in several works by Francis G. Castles and others.[40] Castles argued that among the major industrial democracies it was primarily the power of the right to inhibit left-of-center initiatives, rather than the strength of the left to generate them, that was critical to policy outcomes. Thus he argued that the Scandinavian right, fragmented into three or more parties, was relatively powerless to oppose the more concentrated Social Democrats, whereas in New Zealand and Australia, strong labor movements and strong social democratic parties confronted more organizationally cohesive conservative forces, thereby frustrating any social democratic agenda. Here too one could see broad-gauged historical significance for the policy-making influence of political parties.

Analogous logic formed the underpinning of Peter Katzenstein's work on the smaller democracies of Western Europe. Differentiating these countries from their larger counterparts, primarily on the basis of relative economic vulnerability to international forces, he pointed out that all of them had developed policy-making mechanisms to facilitate agreements aimed at adjusting to rapidly changing international economic conditions. In some cases these mechanisms bypassed or leapfrogged the party system, but for the most part the mixture and balance of power between parties of the left and the right gave preponderance to one policy adjustment over another. Gerhard Lehmbruch in several studies of corporatism also recognized the importance of parties as structuring mechanisms for corporatist bargaining.[41]

All of these diverse studies redirected attention to the important historical role of parties as systematic integrators of broad socioeconomic interests. In all cases, of major interest was the relationship between the ideological balance of power among the major parties, their key socioeconomic blocs, the policy-making structures that were introduced to blunt the extremes of such ideological clashes, and the resulting public policy mix that came to characterize different countries. The key feature of the party system that emerged from such studies was less their electoral role and more the way they forged and shaped socioeconomic coalitions, policy-making structures, and public policies. This is also the assumption of the current volume.

The real key to understanding and differentiating among the industrialized democracies would appear to lie less in choosing between parties and other factors as explanations and more in locating the collective intersection among them. In what ways do political parties and the party system

40. Francis G. Castles, *The Social Democratic Image of Society* (London: Routledge & Kegan Paul, 1978); Castles, *The Working Class and Welfare* (Wellington: Allen & Unwin, 1985); and Castles and Robert D. McKinlay, "Does Politics Matter: An Analysis of the Public Welfare Commitment in Advanced Democratic States," *European Journal of Political Research* 7–8 (1979): 169–86.

41. Gerhard Lehmbruch, "Liberal Corporatism and Party Government," in Schmitter and Lehmbruch, *Trends towards Corporatist Intermediation.*

connect, either causally or consequentially, to the other state and societal forces that shape and differentiate public policies within the industrialized democracies? In what way are parties and the party system nested in a country's power structure? As Miriam Golden formulated the problem with regard to interest groups: "Modern interest groups, like modern democratic states, are intimately intertwined with parties and party systems. Party systems set historical boundaries on the political workings of interest groups and their interactions with the state. Parties are, moreover, frequently active participants in the process of building bridges of cooperation, however fragile, between interest associations and state actors."[42] Her point can be broadened to include socioeconomic blocs, state institutions, often single-issue movements, and the like. Parties and election systems function in a much more complicated manner than is suggested in the more simplistic models of pluralism. They are frequently the pivotal bridging and shaping mechanisms among broad socioeconomic groups within the industrialized democracies. They are typically the creators and driving forces behind specific governments. Their actions in government frequently determine how cohesive, or short-lived, various socioeconomic alliances will be. Just how they play these roles, and with what degree of centrality, remain essential questions in the analysis of advanced democracies.

It is in this context that single-party dominance emerges as a potentially fruitful area of investigation. The permanent or semipermanent governance by a single party, alone or at the heart of a coalition, provides a potentially extreme case of one party that is the glue in a political regime.[43] The dominant party serves many functions, some of them reinforcing, others occasionally contradictory. At what is typically labeled the input side of politics, the party mobilizes social blocs and individual voters in its support. (This support, of course, goes well beyond the simple expedient of gaining a specific number or percentage of votes on election day; it includes financial, ideological, organizational, and policy support.) In this capacity the party exists largely as an agent of combat with other parties organized around competing support bases.

If the party wins a plurality but not a majority, it must endeavor to take advantage of whatever strategic position it holds to form a government in conjunction with other parties. But once in government, the party acts to implement a policy agenda reflecting its own and its supporters' historical program. In making this effort, it must keep not only its own supporters but also its coalition partners sufficiently happy that it retains the ability to govern. It is in these guises of relations with voters and other parties that political parties are most often recognized and analyzed.

42. Miriam Golden, "Interest Representation, Party Systems, and the State: Italy in Comparative Perspective," *Comparative Politics* 18, no. 3 (1986): 298.
43. A useful treatment of the notion of regime is found in David Easton, *A System Analysis of Political Life* (New York: Wiley, 1965), chap. 5.

A substantial part of any party's agenda, however, will also serve the concrete goals of keeping its existing supporters content, isolating political opponents, and attracting additional support. Public policy, in other words, can serve not only to approximate a party's promised electoral platform and to make or change laws, but also to make changes that will simultaneously serve the organizational imperatives of the party and government that carries them out. Its success may well determine its fate in subsequent elections, which, in turn, will influence its future ability to reward its real and potential followers and to refurbish its socioelectoral base.

In other words, politics is an ongoing game, and any successful political party constantly eyes the interplay of many mutually reinforcing goals. The dominant party is the one that plays this game well enough to keep itself in power long enough so that it can continue enacting and implementing policies that reinforce its power base. If it plays this complex game particularly cleverly, it may unleash a "virtuous cycle" that will propel it into semipermanent governance. Such virtuous cycles are most evident in the four countries that are the focal point of the subsequent chapters—Sweden, Israel, Japan, and Italy. They all show to varying degrees the combined interaction of dominance in socioeconomic mobilization, intraparty bargaining, public policy, and longevity.

The Virtuous Cycles of Dominance

A dominant party must gain at least an electoral plurality, which means dominance in socioeconomic mobilization. It must also enjoy or create a bargaining advantage vis-à-vis other political parties so it remains at the core of any coalitions that are formed. Then, it must remain in office long enough to implement its historical agenda. Finally, while in office it must be able to implement that historical program and use the instruments of state so as to isolate its opposition and strengthen its own electoral position. Dominance thus involves an interrelated set of mutually reinforcing processes that have the potential to beget even more dominance. It is this interrelationship that I have called a virtuous cycle of dominance. The interplay among these relations becomes evident in the four countries when each is compared with a parallel case of failed dominance. A comparison of cases that looked historically similar but resulted in dominance in one and failure to dominate in the other reveals the complex interrelationships among mobilization, strategy, payoffs, and long-term dominance.

Two Patterns of Dominance by the Left: Sweden and Israel

The Social Democratic party in Sweden followed the classic left-of-center scenario in gaining power. At the end of the nineteenth century, well-entrenched conservative political forces in Sweden faced a proparliamentary and prosuffrage movement spearheaded by both the Liberal and Social Democratic parties. Equal manhood suffrage in local and parliamentary elections was granted in 1918 because conservatives conscious of the revolutionary events in both the Soviet Union and Germany reluctantly abandoned their opposition. Yet ties to the developing labor movement and success in mobilizing citizens anxious to secure the right to vote gave the Social Democrats a substantial mass base similar to those of other labor and social democratic parties throughout Europe at that time.[44]

Following the 1932 elections, with the Socialdemokratiska Arbetar Partiet (SAP) or Social Democrats as the largest party in the Riksdag, the Swedish party system took on the major outlines that have continued until today. The Social Democrats were the party of labor and the left; to their left was a small Communist party. On the political right were the Conservatives (later the Moderates), the Liberals, and the Agrarian party (later the Center party). This pattern remained relatively fixed for the next five decades, helped in large measure by the 4 percent cutoff for parliamentary representation that kept smaller parties from gaining a foothold, particularly to the left of the SAP.

Before the Social Democrats' ascension to power in 1932, the Confederation of Trade Unions (Landsorganisationen, LO) had grown approximately in parallel to unions and union federations throughout Europe. But in 1938 with the Saltsjöbaden Agreement, the country instituted centralized bargaining between capital and labor, thereby confirming the overall authority of LO over member unions and providing an additional stimulus to union membership. Under continued SAP rule and the implementation of a series of prolabor policies, unions penetrated the work force at levels unparalleled in other industrial countries, with approximately 90 percent of workers unionized in many sectors. As Jonas Pontusson makes clear in Chapter 2, from 1956 onward, the Social Democratic party has obtained at least 69 percent of the votes of industrial manual workers and more often closer to 80 percent.[45] Cooperatives, too, were created throughout Swedish society, providing an additional base for party mobilization by SAP.

In addition to this large working-class base, the SAP benefited from its ability to attract support from two other important segments of society at critical junctures in its history. First, it was able to garner support from the agricultural sector during its earliest periods of rule (the so-called red-green coalition) by policies that blended protectionism and unemployment insurance to reward farmers and workers. Then in the late 1950s with the debate over pensions policy, the agricultural sector was essentially jettisoned in

44. Reinhard Bendix, *Nation-Building and Citizenship* (New York: Anchor, 1969), chap. 3; Walter Korpi, *The Democratic Class Struggle* (London: Routledge & Kegan Paul, 1983); Stein Rokkan, *Citizens, Elections, Parties* (Oslo: Universitetsforlaget, 1971).

45. Richard Scase, *Social Democracy in Capitalist Society* (London: Croom Helm, 1977), pp. 319, 327–28.

favor of an appeal to white-collar wage earners, which invigorated the SAP.[46] In short, the party demonstrated an ability to use public policies and thereby to transcend its initial base of power and to attract more politically valuable support without losing its blue-collar core.

At the same time, other major sectors of society were mobilized by the remaining "bourgeois" parties in relatively fixed ways that provided for some limited movement by supporters of one or another of them within this bourgeois bloc but made virtually impossible any significant movement across the two competing camps. As both Gøsta Esping-Andersen and Pontusson make clear in their chapters, continued governance by the SAP and its ability to implement its political agenda reinforced this cleavage line and gave it important weapons for defusing the appeals of these parties, while reinforcing the mobilization of labor into LO and the SAP, as well as rewarding other SAP supporters. More important, it forced the business sector to accommodate to a version of capitalism that became compatible with the emerging social welfare state. Finally, long-term rule gave the SAP an important advantage in socializing subsequent generations of Swedish voters so that much of its once controversial agenda gradually took on the air of "common sense," and the Swedish "middle way."[47]

The logic of the Social Democrats' dominance was made most clear in the late 1970s. They lost control of the cabinet following the 1976 and 1979 elections in part as a result of failure to deal successfully with parliamentary issues, as Ellis S. Krauss and Jon Pierre demonstrate. Even so, the Social Democratic party remained the largest in parliament, with nearly twice as many seats as its closest rival. Policy from 1976 to 1982 seemed even more social democratic than before; for example, in six years the bourgeois government nationalized more industries than the Social Democrats had in forty-four years. Even out of government, the Social Democrats were in a sense dominant because the programs they had initiated had become institutionalized. Their return to office in 1982 and reelection in 1985 and 1988 proved a testimonial to the benefits of the virtuous cycle of dominance they had created and from which they benefited, just as it revealed the inability of the opposition bourgeois government to provide a compelling alternative.

Social Democrats in neighboring Denmark have had parallel but less striking success. In Denmark, the Social Democratic party (SD) was the largest single party from the 1913 elections until 1924. During the 1930s it was the leading partner in a majority coalition with the Radical Liberals, and many expected it to emerge after the war and the German occupation with a clear parliamentary majority. It seemed to have more potential for long-term rule than did the Swedish SAP.

---

46. Gøsta Esping-Andersen, *Politics against Markets: The Social Democratic Road to Power* (Princeton: Princeton University Press, 1985).

47. Marquis Childs, *Sweden: The Middle Way on Trial* (New Haven: Yale University Press, 1980).

The Danish labor movement never became as strong as that in Sweden, however, and membership in the Social Democratic party began to fall sharply after 1948.[48] More important, the party failed to attract new and younger members, and, unlike its Swedish counterpart, showed no capacity for altering its electoral support base.

Because the electoral system had no major threshold for parliamentary representation, the party also lost any claim to ideological hegemony over Denmark's political left. First, the hitherto banned Communist party gained parliamentary seats in 1945. Then in 1960 the Socialist People's party gained strength. The SD was consequently relegated to a position more in the center of the spectrum, its flank eroded by new parties able to thrive within the fluid Danish electoral system.

Meanwhile, Denmark's bourgeois parties showed a greater capacity for cooperation than those of Sweden. In Denmark they formed a coalition government without the Social Democrats immediately after the war and again in the early 1950s, thereby denying the Social Democrats the continued rule and the potential to introduce a prolabor agenda such as was being introduced at the same time by the SAP in Sweden. Even though the SD remained the largest single party in the Danish Folketing, it did not enjoy the favorable bargaining power of Sweden's SAP. Heavily outflanked on its left and unable to prevent a coalition on its right, the Danish SD had no power to dominate the formation of all coalitions. The Radical Liberals, Agrarian Liberals, and Conservatives formed a government coalition in 1968. The relative stability of the party system that had prevailed since the early 1920s was drastically upset in the 1973 election, when five new or previously unrepresented parties, backed by over one-third of the electorate, joined the existing parties in parliament. The Social Democrats now held under 30 percent of the seats in parliament. Although they regained some strength in the next election, thereafter they were reduced to being but one element in a series of minority coalition governments.

Thus although the Social Democrats in Denmark enjoyed many of the same early successes as their Swedish counterparts, they never had a similar long-term dominance. At least three points seem worthy of attention.[49] First, the Danish SD never was able to penetrate and mobilize the working force as effectively as the SAP did. Being periodically out of government exacerbated this difficulty. Second, the SD was never able to maintain the same degree of ideological hegemony and tactical bargaining power over the left, partly because of the low threshold for parliamentary representation under the Danish electoral system. Third, the political right in Denmark was far more capable than that in Sweden of reaching political accords that

48. Alistair Thomas, "Social Democracy in Denmark," in William Paterson and Thomas, eds., *Social Democratic Parties in Western Europe* (London: Croom Helm, 1977), pp. 240–92.
49. A far more detailed comparison is found in Esping-Andersen, *Politics against Markets*, passim, but esp. chap. 4.

periodically interrupted Social Democratic rule. The SD was thus denied the capacity to carry out its policy programs over a sustained period of time, which undercut its mobilization efforts and eventually shut it out of government completely. Though often the largest party in parliament, the SD has never come close to the tactical, policy, or longitudinal dominance enjoyed by the SAP in Sweden. Consequently, it has never been able to set in motion and thereby benefit from the virtuous cycle of strength, rule, and further strength enjoyed by the Swedish SAP.

Though nominally a labor party, the Israeli Mapai emerged from a set of historical circumstances rather different from those in Sweden. Unlike Sweden, which was a country marked by old traditions and social cleavages, Israel was a new society in the sense that the term is used by Louis Hartz.[50] Moreover, as Michael Shalev notes in his chapter in this volume, the political economics of Sweden and Israel were vastly different. Israel was a country of immigrants, who arrived in a series of waves from 1882 until 1947. The earliest group, who came from 1882 to 1903, consisted primarily of refugees from eastern Europe. They were offered cheap land and were able to rely largely on cheap Arab labor, and they engaged in profitable agricultural production. A second and much larger wave from 1904 to 1915 was made up largely of Russian intellectuals strongly influenced by the socialist traditions that had been developing in that country before and during the revolution. A third wave, largely from eastern Europe, and similarly socialist, took place from 1919 to 1923. Two final waves in the years before independence were made up predominantly of petit bourgeoisie, largely from Europe.

Despite the social and historical differences from Sweden, in particular the greater ethnic heterogeneity and the greater reliance on agriculture, Israel resembled Sweden in that there was, during this period of population growth, a massive mobilization of labor. By 1926 some 70 percent of all laborers were members of the Histadrut labor organization, which became the dominant support base for Mapai when that party was formed in 1930. Because labor was so well organized and so closely linked to the political party structure, subsequent immigrants were readily absorbed into Mapai (later Labor) through the Histadrut. But unlike the workplace mobilization of LO in Sweden, one of the keys to the successful integration of these immigrants was that the party controlled the immigration certificates granted by the government and could use these to bolster the party's support and curtail that of potential opponents. Jobs, housing, and other social benefits were distributed to the immigrants through the party machinery. The center-right suffered the drawbacks of smaller numbers and later arriv-

50. Louis Hartz, *The Founding of New Societies* (New York: Harcourt, Brace and World, 1964).

al in the country, and these parties were late to attempt mobilization. Their members came predominantly from more prosperous immigrants, who joined them primarily as free-floating individuals rather than as members of poorer classes drawn like the immigrants in American cities by the benefits of a patronage machine. A strong socialist ideology characterized the immigrants, particularly those who arrived from 1904 until 1924.[51] As a result, from the early 1930s, Israel had a substantial mass-based political party on the left that dominated its opposition in the prestate elections allowed by the British; the party used this dominance to reinforce its electoral base.[52] When Israel achieved statehood in 1948, Mapai had already dominated electoral and government politics for nearly twenty years and continued in this preeminent position for nearly thirty years thereafter.

The success of Mapai/Labor in Israel was clearly a result of its ability to mobilize the successive waves of immigrants. It was a mobilization based more on patronage than on a strong ideological and class appeal. The apparent strength of the left in Israel was also a function of the weakness of the right. Not only had potential supporters of the right been later in arriving in large numbers and slower to mobilize, but the right was divided within itself and lacked a strong economic base, as Shalev demonstrates in Chapter 3. In addition, as Ariel Levite and Sidney Tarrow in an earlier piece[53] and Aronoff in Chapter 8 have well documented, the main political forces on the right, Herut, then Gahal, and later Likud, were systematically delegitimized for much of the period of Labor's rule. The right was associated with prestate terrorism and therefore was excluded from participation in government from 1948 until 1967, when it joined as a junior partner in an emergency government of national unity. Likud's exclusion was even more striking in light of the right's strong electoral base and Mapai's (and later Labor's) continued need for coalition partners.[54] Yet conscious political efforts by Mapai, Labor, and especially Labor's leader David Ben-Gurion succeeded in tainting the main parties of the right with the brush of illegitimacy and in sustaining public doubts about the right's commitment to the rules of the parliamentary game. Participation in the government of national unity in 1967, a growing proximity between the foreign policy positions of Labor and the Likud following the 1967 war, and the growing popular support base of the Likud all combined over the next decade to eradicate this stigma while at the same time undermining Labor's claims to governmental exclusivity. Labor failed to use government resources and the power of office to continue mobilizing new immigrants and reinforcing its support base. The eventual result was that the Israeli right gained sufficient

51. Eva Etzioni-Halevy, *Political Culture in Israel* (New York: Praeger, 1977), pp. 5–11.
52. Noah Lucas, "A Centenarian at Thirty: The State of Israel, 1978," *Political Quarterly* 19, no. 3 (1978): 298.
53. Levite and Tarrow, "The Legitimation of Excluded Parties in Dominant Party Systems."
54. Ibid., p. 301.

electoral support to topple the weakened Labor Alignment, which not much earlier had seemed invincible and integral to the political functioning of the country. Subsequently, as Aronoff points out, the Likud showed signs not only of having toppled Labor from its long-standing dominance but of having achieved a position that would enable it to continue its rule long enough and under a new format of political and religious symbolism so that it could become a dominant party. Strong as Israel's Mapai/Labor had been, it was incapable of fully institutionalizing its rule as had Sweden's SAP.

The early success of the left in Israel contrasts sharply with the relative failure of the left in two other "new" societies that achieved respectable levels of industrialization and democratization, New Zealand and Australia. Like Israel, both countries were formed largely through immigration, although mostly from more culturally homogeneous England rather than from throughout Europe and Asia. As Richard H. Rosecrance notes, the Australian immigrants were not "the outpourings of the poor-houses and the unions of the United Kingdom" but were "largely a homogeneous group of city folk of humble economic and social origins," who were unable to migrate to more attractive regions such as the United States or Canada.[55] A high proportion of these immigrants brought with them the political attitudes of the British lower classes and unionist supporters, providing a strong base for the political left in both countries. Thus labor organization preceded industrialization.[56] Consequently, in both of these countries at the end of the nineteenth and the beginning of the twentieth centuries, labor and the organized left were widely recognized as ahead of their European counterparts in successfully organizing and influencing public policies of the national and local governments. In 1910 the Australian Labour party formed a majority government with a level of support that was not matched by any other social democratic party until the success of SAP in Sweden in 1940.[57]

Along with the potential radicals who entered New Zealand and Australia came large numbers of middle-class agriculturalists. But the middle-class attitudes prevalent in this "squattocracy" never reached the pretentiousness of the European gentry, and their political beliefs were always diluted by the radicalism of their immigrant status and the values of their fellow immigrants from the working class. Potentially conservative industrialists never achieved the levels of class-bound reaction that developed among conservatives in Europe. Squaring off against a relatively radical opposition from political positions much weaker than those of European conservatives, the Australian and New Zealand industrialists never were

---

55. Richard N. Rosecrance, "The Radical Culture of Australia," in Hartz, *Founding of New Societies*, p. 280.

56. James G. Murtagh, *Australia: The Catholic Chapter* (New York: Sheed and Ward, 1959).

57. Castles, *The Working Class and Welfare*, p. 21.

able to prevent the left from achieving parliamentary democracy, union rights, or social benefits. Instead, conservatism in Australia and New Zealand necessitated the early acceptance of many of labor's classic demands. Labor, in turn, never adopted the more extreme positions of the First or Second International, rejecting, for example, the demand for nationalization of industry and readily accepting compulsory bargaining. The ideological extremes that separated labor and capital in Europe were thus less polar in Australia and New Zealand in the early twentieth century. Certainly the political right in these countries never had to overcome the stigma of illegitimacy faced by the right in Israel.

Still, the political left in the two Australasian outposts was in a strong position to make a bid for permanent power in the early twentieth century, much as Mapai did in the 1930s. As Castles has noted, the right was divided, lacking a unified base in the old, established, landed class and with a moderate industrial segment not inclined to side with agriculture against labor.[58] Meanwhile the institutional barriers to working-class parties had been eliminated, there was a strong organized labor movement, and the tactical position of the left was favorable. Yet in 1908 in Australia and during the 1920s and early 1930s in New Zealand there was a successful countermobilization by conservative forces as the country parties and those of urban conservatives joined together against the strong working-class parties. Both cases involved the fusion of protectionists and free traders: landowners and manufacturers united against the domestic and international demands of labor.

The right in both countries was helped by the electoral system's peculiar preference ballot, which allowed each to compete independently but then to unite against labor. Australia saw three decades of conservative rule as a result. Labour in New Zealand held power from 1935 to 1949, but from 1950 to the late 1970s, in both countries, the political right was preeminent. Parties of the left were virtually excluded from government. From 1950 to 1980, despite an average vote for these parties that was comparable to, or in excess of, that for the Social Democratic party of Sweden and well above that of Israel's Labor party, the left was in government for only three years in Australia and six years in New Zealand; comparable figures for Sweden and Israel were twenty-six and twenty-seven years respectively. (In this respect the contrast between Australia and New Zealand on one hand and Israel on the other mirrors the situation of British and Swedish labor analyzed by Pontusson in Chapter 2.)

Clearly, Swedish and Israeli successes in gaining left-of-center dominance rested primarily on an ability to mobilize large numbers of the working class and to hold control of a wide portion of the ideological left. But as the cases of New Zealand and Australia indicate, early successes in mobilization and ideological turf alone are insufficient to ensure dominance. At least as crit-

58. Ibid., pp. 62–69.

ical is a disunited, far less mobilized, and, at least in the Israeli case, delegitimized political right plus the ability of the left to hold office long enough
and use its powers cleverly enough to reconstitute its support base on an
ongoing basis. Political parties are the central instruments in the laying out
of these dynamics. To the extent that the political right enjoys organizational unity, or at least the ability to coalesce periodically, dominance by the
left will be correspondingly difficult to gain or maintain, a point made also
by Giuseppe Di Palma in his analysis of the dilemmas of the left's efforts to
dominate in Spain, Portugal, and Greece. Hence even in states that had one-
party dominance by parties of the left, namely Sweden and Israel, to the
extent that the right can coalesce, this dominance remains highly problematic. And if the left cannot hold on to and reinforce its ideological
hegemony and its electoral base, as happened in Denmark, it may also lose
ground. Hence although in Sweden the SAP was able to return to power
following a short interlude by a conservative coalition, its counterparts in
Denmark or Israel have found such a return much more difficult. Indeed, in
the Israeli case, by getting through the government of national unity intact
and eventually gaining a monopoly in foreign policy and over the loyalties
of new immigrants, and finally over national symbols, Likud and the right,
as Aronoff argues, were well poised to institute a comparably long period of
rightist rule, perhaps analogous to that of Australia and New Zealand.

Dominance by the Right: Italy and Japan

Unlike Sweden and Israel, which for long periods experienced ideological
hegemony on the left and center-left and fragmentation on the center-right,
in Italy and Japan one sees fragmentation on the left and relative unity on
the right. The well-mobilized labor movements in Israel and Sweden are
paralleled by fragmented labor movements and relatively unified manufacturing, financial, and agrarian sectors in Italy and Japan. Whereas coalitions
with agriculture were effected through the party system by the Swedish and
Israeli lefts, in Italy and Japan agriculture was captured by parties on the
right, much along the lines of the business-agriculture fusions in Australia
and New Zealand. Many of these differences are the result of the different
patterns of historical development in Japan and Italy, which allowed the
political right to coalesce and stimulated the fragmentation of the left in
ways that would have been unthinkable in Swedish or Israeli history. Such
conditions, however, were not unique to Italy and Japan. In many respects,
they were paralleled by political developments in Germany and to a lesser
extent in France. Yet, just as the left in Denmark, Australia, and New
Zealand never realized any potential it might have had for left-of-center
dominance, so too France and Germany did not experience the conservative
party dominance that prevailed in Italy and Japan during the bulk of the

postwar period, a point that is explored in detail by Giuseppe Di Palma in Chapter 5.

Suffrage and parliamentary democracy came relatively early and remained free and democratic in Israel and Sweden (as well as in Denmark, Norway, Australia, and New Zealand). In contrast, universal suffrage for men was not introduced into Italy until 1913 (women did not get the vote until 1945), and opposition from the Vatican to its loss of temporal power led to a decree that Catholics should abstain from participation in the public life of the new nation, further constraining voter turnout and circumscribing the meaningfulness of elections. Parties were essentially made up of the landowning gentry and the professional middle class.[59] Although a socialist party was formed in the late nineteenth century, its role was circumscribed by the strict suffrage restrictions, while its hostility toward parliamentary politics kept it on the fringes of Italian political life. With the rise of Mussolini's fascist government in 1924, this embryonic left was crushed, and parliamentary supremacy was precluded. The Italian left burgeoned during the Resistance, but it was not until the postwar elections that political parties of the left had the opportunity to contest meaningful elections in the context of universal suffrage.[60]

This situation was paralleled by conditions in Japan. Manhood suffrage was introduced in 1925 (again women did not gain the vote until after World War II). But as in Italy, elections to parliament did not provide the major criterion for the formation of governments. Only during a brief period in the 1920s was the winning of a parliamentary majority the primary consideration in the creation of a cabinet.[61] The parties contesting elections were largely representative of agrarian interests and those of the emerging urban industrial and middle class. Parties of the left and labor unions enjoyed minimal success during the late 1910s and 1920s; in the 1937 election, for example, parties on the left secured only 10 percent of the popular vote. But the formation of the Imperial Rule Assistance Association, which merged all parties into one official organization, and the domestic impact of the Pacific war short-circuited even the limited political role played by elections, parliament, and political parties. Their effect on Japan's political left was even more devastating. Thus in both Japan and Italy, it was only after the war that the left had the opportunity to organize freely and to contest elections for a politically relevant parliament.

It is instructive in this context to compare the situation to that in the other member of the Axis. In Germany suffrage was introduced in 1867, and the left was well organized and a major electoral force before the ascension of

59. P. A. Allum, *Italy: Republic without Government?* (New York: Norton, 1973), p. 5.
60. Giorgio Galli and Alfonso Prandi, *Patterns of Political Participation in Italy* (New Haven: Yale University Press, 1970), chaps. 1–3.
61. See, for example, Peter Duus, *Party Rivalry and Political Change in Taisho Japan* (Cambridge, Mass.: Harvard University Press, 1965).

Hitler. Although Nazi rule put an end to free elections and parliamentary sovereignty, under the Weimar Republic the Social Democratic party (SPD) effectively contested elections and gave many indications of being a growing and potentially major source of power within the country. It emerged from the war as a radical but powerful factor in the Federal Republic, gaining nearly 33 percent of the parliamentary seats in the 1949 elections.[62]

If the left was slower in organizing in Italy and Japan, it quickly became a political force in the years immediately following World War II. In Italy, the combined vote and the number of parliamentary seats of the Partito Communista Italiano (PCI) and the Partito Socialisto Italiano di Unità Proletaria (PSIUP) exceeded that for the Christian Democrats (DC) in the 1946 election. But in 1948, the DC outdrew the PCI by 305 seats to 183, and with the emergence of the PSI in the 1953 elections, the gap between DC and PCI grew even wider. (This gap began to narrow once again and in 1975 and 1983 was only about 4 percent.)

In Japan, the left has been divided between the communists and the socialists since the first elections of the postwar era, but between them they garnered over 20 percent of the parliamentary seats in the 1946 election while the two major conservative parties divided a bare majority of seats. And in the 1947 elections the socialists were sufficiently strong to form a minority government. Hence in both Italy and Japan, as well as Germany, the reactions to authoritarian rule, combined with initial organizational successes by labor unions and the parties of the left, set up a situation in which it was not unreasonable to expect rapid growth for the left and the eventual demise or at least checking of the more conservative forces of politics. Yet in Italy and Japan, resurgent conservative parties dominated parliament and the cabinet for periods soon after the end of the war. And in West Germany, the CDU/CSU remained in control until 1966. What explains such conservative dominance?

The left in all three countries was weakened by the wartime governments but emerged with the renewed zest of liberation and U.S. encouragement. But with the outbreak of the Cold War, U.S. policies changed, and support for domestic conservatives in all three countries became the political order of the day. Because of America's leading role, particularly its occupation of Germany and Japan but also its economic and strategic dominance of the agendas in Italy, Japan, and West Germany, it revitalized the right and weakened the left in all three.[63]

The role of the United States and its foreign policy cannot be discounted in analyses of the resurgence of the right in Italy, Japan, and West Germany, but domestic forces also aided the conservative parties. In Italy and Japan,

62. Lewis J. Edinger, *Politics in West Germany* (Boston: Little, Brown, 1977), p. 172.

63. A good summary of the interplay of U.S. domestic politics and its impact on the left and right in Europe is Charles Maier, "The Politics of Productivity," in Peter J. Katzenstein, ed., *Between Power and Plenty* (Madison: University of Wisconsin Press, 1978), pp. 23–49.

the labor movements lacked historical and organizational depth and were internally fragmented. Different political parties competed for the left-of-center vote and the support of the union movement. Moreover, in neither country was more than 33 percent of the work force unionized. In Italy, the conservative DC attracted the institutionalized support of a portion of the fragmented labor movement, making it even more difficult for labor to gain control. Meanwhile, the DC gained the continued social support of the Catholic church, which provided it with an important social base, particularly in the rural, southern, and more provincial areas. The LDP in Japan gained strong and comparable support from Nokyo, the organized cooperative movement that enrolled 99 percent of Japan's farming population. DC provided a united electoral front in Italy throughout the postwar period, and following the unification of the Liberals and the Democrats into the LDP in 1955, conservatives in Japan had a comparably unified electoral vehicle.

Both conservative parties developed extensive mass bases, and both used their long-term rule to benefit farmers and small shopkeepers thus shoring up their electoral base through public policies of patronage, as Takashi Inoguchi, Michio Muramatsu and Ellis Krauss, and Sidney Tarrow all demonstrate in their respective chapters. These conservative bases were never as strong as those among the working-class parties and the unionists in Israel and Sweden, but the DC and LDP came to represent two of the most numerically extensive conservative parties in the industrialized world.

In both Italy and Japan, finally, conservatives could claim an element of ideological and policy hegemony that resulted from their continued control of government. Not only did they enjoy tactical bargaining positions that allowed them to control an entire component of the ideological spectrum in their countries, much as the SAP did in Sweden or Labor did in Israel, but their association with their countries' economic growth and national traditions reinforced their support bases and became part of the dominant ideologies. In Japan, as Inoguchi shows, threats to conservative continuance in the late 1970s were blunted by government tax changes designed explicitly to shore up the LDP's electoral base. As Muramatsu and Krauss point out, in Japan groups once hostile to the conservatives had to deal with the LDP and the national bureaucracy as LDP rule continued or face the prospect of permanent marginality. And as Krauss and Pierre demonstrate, the LDP was able to use its parliamentary position to defuse the potentially destabilizing issues raised by the opposition parties during its moments of greatest weakness. And as Tarrow and Di Palma respectively note with regard to Italy, despite the DC's ideology of confrontation with the left and especially the PCI, it was by the 1960s and 1970s far more open, flexible, and accommodative. It was able to use this position to outflank its opponents and enhance its own electoral support base to remain in office into the 1980s.

In some respects the situations were comparable in West Germany and, under the Gaullists, in France. But in neither Germany nor France was the right as electorally unified as in Japan or Italy. Indeed, the higher levels of industrialization in the former countries made it extremely difficult for conservative parties to make the agrarian–petit bourgeois appeals that the LDP and DC used so successfully.[64] The social and electoral bases of conservatism in both countries were not as strong as in Japan and Italy. Finally, French conservatives enjoyed the symbolic benefits of being the first to govern in the new Fifth Republic, but that was hardly akin to being the forces restoring the national economies after the wartime destruction in Japan, Germany, and Italy.

Equally important, particularly in Germany, and to some extent France, the left was never as thinly rooted and vulnerable to charges of illegitimacy as in Japan and Italy. In France during the Third and Fourth Republics various left-of-center parties had been in power and the country had survived. In Germany, the SPD had participated democratically in Weimar. Moreover, in agreement with Hideo Otake's analysis, the postwar foreign and defense policies of the French and German left were not so radically critical of ties with the United States as were those of the left in Japan and Italy, leaving the former parties far less marginalized on security questions. More important, following the Gödesberg program, under which the most radical elements of the SPD's party platform were scrapped, the party presented a moderate democratic socialist image to the German public. Its entry into the Grand Coalition with the CDU/CSU further weakened the potential impact of any charges that it was irresponsible or illegitimate and also broke the CDU/CSU's hold over the formulation of public policies. In short, neither country witnessed absolute, fixed, and mutually hostile patterns of political mobilization and party competition. Neither country's right could shut out its left; in both the left was strong enough to challenge and moderate conservative attempts at hegemony. Once conservative monopoly was checked, state actions to shore up the conservative base were also stymied.

In Japan and Italy, in contrast, the foreign policies of the conservative governments, in particular the ties to the United States and the anti-Soviet strategies, were initially subjected to harsh criticism from the left. The PCI took steps to moderate its image during the 1960s and 1970s, but the Japan Socialist Party (JSP) continued into the late 1980s to oppose Japan's ties to the United States, to refuse to accord legitimacy to the Self-Defense Forces, and to declare itself a party of revolution which espoused a dictatorship of the proletariat. The left's limited experiences with government in both countries were so brief as to be negligible, making it even harder for these parties to forestall questions about their commitment to maintain democratic forms

64. See Suzanne Berger, "Regime and Interest Representation: The French Traditional Middle Classes," in Berger, ed., *Organizing Interests in Western Europe*, pp. 83–101.

of government and existing foreign and domestic policies for which there appeared to be widespread public support. Both were hard-pressed to present themselves as suitable alternative bases for governance or as potential coalition partners, and out of office they found it difficult to use state policies to broaden their support. Consequently, in both countries the left spiralled into greater and greater marginality.

Hence in many respects the situation in Italy and Japan mirrors, on the other side of the ideological spectrum, the cases of Sweden and Israel. A strong and united right confronted a divided and multiparty left. Ideological hegemony, reinforced through long-term governance, became the property of the conservatives. An aura of legitimacy and automaticity became associated with conservative rule in both countries, just as it had with social democratic rule in Sweden and Israel. The PCI and the political left in Italy, however, have always been more important and successful than their Japanese counterparts. Ideological dominance by the DC was always compromised by its practicality, patronage, and smaller vote totals, as Tarrow points out. Indeed, by the late 1970s it was compelled to bring the PCI into the cabinet. In Japan, following the 1983 elections, the LDP finally accorded a cabinet post to a non-LDP parliamentarian (from the small conservative New Liberal Club [NLC], an offshoot of the LDP subsequently reabsorbed into the party). But in 1986 it won stunning victories that eventually led to the NLC's reabsorption into the LDP. LDP dominance was never seriously challenged by the Japan Socialist party or the Japan Communist party (JCP) until 1989. Its hold on the political right in that country and on the reins of government seems to be far more secure than is the case for the DC in Italy. In this respect, it may well emulate the long-term dominance of the SAP in Sweden, whereas the DC, in its future inability to dominate, may well be closer to the Labor party in Israel.

Consequently, important as the ideological and socioeconomic similarities are between Sweden and Israel on one hand, and Japan and Italy on the other, there are also major differences. Perhaps the most important is that socialism has never been as immutable in Israel as it has in Sweden, nor has conservatism been as potent in Italy as in Japan. Though the roots of dominance may make Japan look like Italy, and Israel look like Sweden, the *extent* of dominance may well make Italy and Israel appear more similar, and Sweden and Japan exhibit the most vivid manifestations of dominance.

Studying One-Party Dominance

Hypothetically, there are many possible approaches to the study of one-party dominance. From what has been said so far, however, two major considerations should be preeminent. First, several countries have experienced conditions similar in many respects, including the potential for one-party dominance, to those in Italy, Japan, Sweden, and Israel. Several of the other Scandinavian countries, for example, resemble Sweden. At the end of World War II, Japan, Italy, West Germany, and perhaps France all bore important similarities. Italy shares traits with other Mediterranean states in the 1970s and 1980s, and in the late 1950s and 1960s Italian Christian Democracy looked to many to be similar to Gaullism in France. Israel resembles a number of other new states though it is more advanced economically than most and has experienced democratic transfers of power. In short, the universe of one-party dominant democracies does not have sharp and unmistakable boundaries, and dominance is often a matter of degree. The similarities suggest comparisons between regimes that experienced long-term single-party dominance and those that historically seemed similar but did not have one-party rule.

The second point follows from the earlier discussion suggesting that long-term dominance means more than a series of successful electoral campaigns. The study of one-party dominance must be less concerned with parties and party systems and more attentive to regimes in which a single party has been dominant for a long period of time. Consequently, the essays in this volume focus less on the results of specific elections, public opinion, or internal party organization. More central are matters related to the dominant party and its relationship to socioeconomic support groups, interest associations, and the state apparatus. The study also relates to changes in the socioeconomic roots of a party's supporting coalition, the dominant party and symbol manipulation, and patterns of governance under one-party dominance.

The chapters that follow have largely been organized by the extent to which they concentrate principally on the establishment of dominance or the challenges to and maintenance of dominance. Chapter 1 by Gøsta Esping-Andersen examines the roots of Social Democratic hegemony in Sweden, comparing the conditions there to those of neighboring Norway and Denmark. Chapter 2 by Jonas Pontusson also examines Sweden, comparing it with Britain to show why, despite relatively comparable levels of mobilization of the laboring sector, the SAP has been far more dominant as a party than its British counterpart.

In Chapter 3 Michael Shalev examines the broad political economy of Labor dominance in Israel. This is followed by Hideo Otake's essay, which compares the German and Japanese lefts, concentrating particularly on the period following World War II. The German SPD, he argues, was tactically more flexible than the JSP, and the leadership was far freer from ideological pressures by grass-roots members so the party was never as marginalized on issues of security and defense as was the left in Japan. He considers dominance by the LDP and the inability of the CDU/CSU to enjoy similar dominance as much a consequence of the strategies of the opposition parties as it is of the actions of the two conservative parties.

In Chapter 5 Giuseppe Di Palma takes up the broad problem of dominance and democracy within countries emerging from authoritarian governments. One might expect parties of the left to do especially well as countries rebound from tight-fisted right-of-center rule, but in a comparison of seven countries, he shows that this did not happen. Rather, somewhat more right-of-center parties, especially in Japan and Italy, were better able to blend respect for democratic procedures with long-term continuity of their own rule and thus were most likely to merge democratic institutions with postauthoritarian single-party dominance.

During the 1970s worldwide economic shocks toppled most of the major governments in the industrialized democracies, including the long-term ruling parties in Israel and Sweden. Japan was an exception. There, though the LDP came close to being defeated, it remained in power and continued its rule. Takashi Inoguchi explores this situation in Chapter 6 and shows how Japan's conservatives cleverly used the power of office to solidify and broaden their support base and to make their response to the international economic downturn less cataclysmic for the incumbent party than was the case elsewhere.

The same period is of concern to Ellis Krauss and Jon Pierre, who compare the parliamentary tactics of the dominant parties in Sweden and Japan. They show how missed opportunities by the SAP led to its defeat in 1976, while far more clever adaptations by the LDP led to the reinvigoration of its support.

In the Swedish and Israeli elections of 1976 and 1977, although the SAP was defeated it was never fully replaced by Sweden's bourgeois coalition. It was returned to office in 1982 with much of its previous agenda untouched. In Israel, by contrast, once Labor was out of office, many of its policies were systematically dismantled by Likud. Myron Aronoff examines this phenomenon in the context principally of Labor's loss of symbolic control of the Israeli political agenda and its replacement by a Likud party adamantly hostile to Labor's policies, symbols, and actions. Using very different religious symbols than Labor, the Likud began systematically to marginalize Labor and reconstitute its own base in ways that through the late 1980s seemed to have led to its continued electoral success, even though, as Aronoff suggests, the party still is not close to enjoying the hegemony once held by Labor.

Michio Muramatsu and Ellis Krauss in their treatment of interest groups in Japan show conclusively how the LDP absorbed certain of the groups that were once its strong opponents. In this regard LDP hegemony was very different from the exclusionary hegemony of Israel's Labor party. Opposition groups were forced to deal with the LDP as the length of its rule increased, but although the LDP enjoyed almost a two-to-one electoral margin over its nearest opposition, it also grew into a party of broad ideological scope. With time it welcomed new socioeconomic interests into its fold, albeit with far fewer benefits than were accorded to its core constituency.

This same pattern can be found with the Italian DC, as Sidney Tarrow shows. In contrast to the attempted "hard hegemony" of conservatives in France, the DC ruled with a "soft hegemony" that left it far more able to respond tactically to its opponents and to changing political opportunities than the DC's more rigid French counterparts.

My concluding essay attempts to tie the chapters and case studies together by examining three central questions: What are the necessary conditions for the establishment of one-party dominance? What conditions seem to cut across all the cases? How can one examine the commonalities that seem most important among the four major cases? In this context, I examine the means by which a single party gains and maintains power as well as the specific difficulties encountered in maintaining or changing the party's socioeconomic base while still holding electoral office. I also argue that long-term rule can be used to impose an agenda that makes continued rule more likely. In this sense, the conclusion focuses both on the causes and consequences of dominance. It argues essentially that the two feed each other and that long-term dominance by a single party involves clever tactics of electoral mobilization, ideological positioning, and governance. When blended skillfully, these are mutually reinforcing and suggest that one-party dominance is an art far more than it is an inevitability.

1. Single-Party Dominance in Sweden: The Saga of Social Democracy

GØSTA ESPING-ANDERSEN

The Swedish Social Democratic party (SAP, or Sveriges Socialdemokratiska Arbetarparti) must be examined in any explanation of one-party dominance in democratic polities. It is, worldwide, the party that has governed longest and most consistently over the past five decades. This achievement is the more astounding because it is explicitly a (democratic) socialist party.

After a number of aborted efforts, the SAP came to power in 1932 and remained the governing party for the next forty-four years. In 1976, it was forced into opposition for two successive election periods but was then returned to office in 1982, 1985, and 1988. It is thus the longest governing democratically elected party in the Western world. If we consider the six-year period of opposition as a de facto continuation of Social Democratic politics under a center-right label (as I do), the dominance of the SAP within Swedish politics is even more overwhelming. Indeed, Sweden arguably has experienced one-party hegemony.

The conventional theory of competitive democracy is difficult to reconcile with the unique degree of electoral stability that marks Swedish social democracy. From one election to another, the party has hardly deviated more than two or three points from its average of about 46 percent of the electorate. On two occasions, its share surpassed the magic 50 percent mark; first in the unusual 1940 wartime election and then in 1968 (with 50.1 percent). Its worst performances since 1932 occurred in 1956 (with 44.6 percent) and

A large part of the description and analysis presented in this chapter is based on Gøsta Esping-Andersen, *Politics against Markets: The Social Democratic Road to Power* (Princeton: Princeton University Press, 1985). An earlier version was presented to the Social Science Research Council working group on One-Party Democracies at Cornell University in April 1984. I thank T. J. Pempel for his generous comments and patience.

in 1976 (with 42.8 percent). Following both these losses, the party was able to recuperate its habitual electoral position.

Dominance, to say nothing of hegemony, is obviously not a question of electoral returns alone; it must assume a capacity to shape policy making and, more generally, to structure society in accordance with a party's priorities. It is this quality that most sharply demarcates the SAP from its socialist brethren in Scandinavia and elsewhere and that underpins the argument that the SAP is one of the few examples of party hegemony worldwide. Sweden does not just happen to harbor the world's strongest socialist movement; decades of labor movement influence have rendered Sweden itself social democratic.

The 1930s were a watershed for social democracy in Scandinavia as a whole. The Swedish Social Democratic party evolved, came to power, and consolidated its position pretty much in tandem with its Danish and Norwegian counterparts. The model was largely identical: both the parties and their affiliated trade unions grew very rapidly after World War I, adopted a reformist political line, and managed to obtain governing majorities on the basis of an alliance with the Agrarian party. In all three nations, the postwar era has been essentially identified with social democracy. Until World War II, the Danish party was broadly regarded as the leading force of the Scandinavian labor movements. Subsequent developments, however, led to sharply divergent trajectories. While Swedish Social Democracy established its hegemonic status, the Norwegian and especially the Danish parties began to decay from late 1960s onward. Indeed, the two latter became incapable of maintaining their accustomed role as the natural parties of governance, their capacity to control governments slipped, and they were confronted with both a growing leftist opposition and the eruption of populist rightist anti-welfare-state movements.

These contrasting profiles are evident in the parties' electoral shares. In contrast to the Swedes' extraordinarily stable 44 to 46 percent, the Danes slipped badly in the 1960s and even more in the 1970s; the Norwegians paralleled the Danish fate in the 1970s (see Table 1.1).

Table 1.1. Average electoral shares of the Scandinavian Social Democratic parties, 1950s, 1960s, and 1970s (percentages)

	Denmark	Norway	Sweden
1950s	41	47	46
1960s	38	45	48
1970s	34	38	44

Source: Gøsta Esping-Andersen, *Politics against Markets: The Social Democratic Road to Power* (Princeton, N.J.: Princeton University Press, 1985), pp. 327–29.

None of the three parties has escaped the fate of being ousted from office, but the experience of each was quite different: the Swedes returned from their six-year opposition status with their accustomed strength; the Norwegians were ousted in the mid-1960s and were never again able to assert themselves as the natural governing party; and the Danes shuttled in and out of government throughout the postwar era with the need to forge increasingly difficult and precarious coalitions. In Denmark, the nonsocialist parties came to dominate the cabinets of the 1970s and 1980s, and the Social Democrats slipped to an average 32 percent of the vote in 1981–84.

One of the most significant contrasts has to do with challenges to the parties from either left or right. Again, the Swedish case is unique. As early as the 1930s, Swedish Social Democracy effectively emasculated the competition from the left (in the form of the Communist party), and the right has been chronically unable to forge a united front against Social Democracy (despite presiding over a numerical majority on numerous occasions). Even during the period 1976–81, the "bourgeois coalition" splintered repeatedly and was forced to continue in the end as a minority cabinet. In contrast, both Danish and Norwegian Social Democratic parties have suffered from the right's superior ability to coalesce and present itself as an effective governing force. In Denmark, especially, the Social Democratic party became increasingly squeezed between a strong (noncommunist) left (averaging 10 to 12 percent of the vote in the 1970s and 1980s) and an electoral move toward the right.

If we examine the social bases of voting, the variable performances of the three social democracies becomes even more pronounced. As is often argued,[1] a basic problem facing socialist parties is to hold on to their traditional working-class base while simultaneously mobilizing among other electorates. Available data paint a clear picture of Swedish Social Democracy's unique capacity to override this dilemma. Its sustained electoral stability is clearly owing to its ability to maintain the loyalty of workers while simultaneously making major inroads into the new salaried strata; the party's weakness in the late 1970s was related to a marginal drift of both groups to the right. Crucial to the Swedish party's long-term strength is its continual ability to mobilize newly entering young voters.

The Danish case is an extreme contrast. Over the 1970s, the Danish party lost large sections of blue-collar voters to both the left and the right, and it has been only marginally successful in mobilizing the new salaried groups (who, interestingly, are a prominent part of the New Left's clientele). Perhaps the most serious symptom of the party's decomposition in Denmark is its growing inability to attract younger voters. It is rapidly becoming a party of old-age pensioners.

1. Adam Przeworski, *Capitalism and Social Democracy* (Cambridge: Cambridge University Press, 1985); Esping-Andersen, *Politics against Markets*.

These contrasts illustrate the basic point that, despite common origins, the Swedish Social Democratic party commands an exceptional status in a Scandinavian as well as a global context. The question is why? What are the causes of Swedish Social Democracy's extraordinary performance?

An answer to this question would be impossible if our inquiry were limited to the Swedish case study. There would be too many contending variables to account for. A comparison with the other Nordic countries offers a way to reduce the number of possible explanations substantially: a host of historical and sociological factors can quickly be dismissed because they would obtain more or less equally for Norway and Denmark as well.

Nonexplanations

It would be tempting to search for an explanation of Swedish Social Democracy's success in the country's history of industrialization and democratization, as have numerous scholars.[2] Sweden's gradualist and nonviolent path toward a modern capitalist democracy is not unusual, however. In addition to Denmark and Norway, this route was also shared by the Swiss, the Dutch, and a host of other nations. A unique feature of Scandinavia was the early decay of absolutist rule and reactionary aristocratic forces, as well as the early collaboration between farmers and the working class in the struggle for full democracy. But, again, these conditions were shared by both Denmark and Norway. Indeed, Denmark was the pioneer, Sweden the follower. The early experience with a popular red-green alliance of farmers and workers was decisive for social democracy's breakthrough in the 1930s in Scandinavia at large but does not differentiate Sweden.

In all the Nordic countries, the process of industrialization came late and rather gradually. The cataclysmic, disruptive, and polarizing consequences experienced in many European nations were largely absent in Scandinavia. It is true that Swedish industrialization has unique features that single it out from its Nordic neighbors: it was, at once, highly concentrated and geographically decentralized. This is an important issue that will be examined later in this chapter.

The literature frequently cites social and cultural homogeneity in contributing to the success of social democracy. There is no doubt that Sweden appears extraordinarily homogeneous in language, religion, ethnicity, and cultural tradition, in contrast to Norway's linguistic and center-periphery cleavage structure, but Denmark is also homogeneous.

Characteristics of the political system are a third factor often invoked in

2. Seymour Martin Lipset, *Political Man* (New York: Doubleday Anchor, 1960); Stein Rokkan, *Citizens, Elections, Parties* (Oslo: Universitets Forlaget, 1972).

the explanation of cross-national differences in political parties' performance. Thus it can be argued that a system of strict proportional representation, as exists in Sweden, is conducive to a multiparty competitive system in which the individual parties are encouraged to develop distinct sociopolitical profiles and strong internal organization. This is certainly the case in Sweden, but it is equally so in many other nations. All three Nordic countries are remarkable in the degree to which the social classes and interests are directly represented in the party system, with a distinct Agrarian party and labor party mobilizing and representing essentially the entire underlying clientele. But there is nothing distinctly Swedish in this respect. Indeed, another property of multiparty systems—the difficulty for any single party to mobilize an absolute majority alone—seems to have been superseded in the Swedish case and provides another instance of the extraordinary performance of Swedish Social Democracy.

Sweden has a somewhat higher threshold for party representation (5 percent of the vote) than Denmark and Norway (2 percent). A higher threshold helps stall the formation of new parties and the splintering of parties. Yet it would be difficult to regard this as a cause of single-party dominance. Other nations with high thresholds (such as West Germany) have seen new parties emerge and upset the position of the existing parties. And in Sweden, the 1988 elections brought about the entry of a new Green, ecological party with roughly 6 percent of the vote. But in contrast to Germany, the Swedish Greens seem to rob votes from and destabilize the right rather than the Social Democrats. They certainly did not impair SAP's capacity to govern yet another term. Characteristics of the political system alone cannot explain SAP's relative success.

In sum, in explaining single-party dominance in Sweden we can largely ignore many of the standard textbook arguments. To account for Swedish Social Democracy's dominance, we will first have to distinguish the issue of how the SAP came to power from the question of how it stayed in power. Clearly, long-term dominance is difficult to predict from the process of power attainment; maintenance of power requires consolidation and concurrent reproduction of the conditions that fuel power.

Second, we must identify the causes of SAP's dominance within the comparative framework of Scandinavian social democracy because this will allow us to single out specifically Swedish circumstances. As I shall argue, there are three factors that make Swedish conditions peculiar: the social structure within which Social Democracy emerged and matured; the party's ability to forge critical cross-class political alliances; and the SAP's unusual capacity to institutionalize and invigorate its own power bases through its reformist policies. The latter factor is of particular importance. Yet the final explanation cannot be based on the added impact of these three factors but only on the way they came to interact and reinforce each other in Sweden.

The Origins of Swedish Social Democratic Ascendance

In classical socialist thought, the long-term power of socialist parties was assumed to follow from the process of proletarianization: as workers became the majoritarian class, the socialist parties would be able to command majority power via the ballot box. The theoretical revisionism of Eduard Bernstein[3] turned out, however, to be closer to the truth. By and large, strictly working-class majorities failed to materialize.

As the socialists began to realize this logic of class structural development, they faced the choice between a continued strict adherence to the working-class party model, which would conceivably lock the party into a perennial minority status, or an alliance strategy of collaboration across the class structure to compensate for the numerical shortcoming. Choosing the latter option would almost certainly compel the party to dilute its orthodox programmatic tenets.

Still, of course, the tensions resulting from the absence of clear working-class numerical majorities can be lessened by the degree to which the available working-class clientele can be effectively unified and mobilized under the social democratic banner. Similarly, the ease with which a party can forge necessary cross-class coalitions depends on the social character of potentially allied classes. Hence the nature and composition of the underlying social structure defines the conditions under which social democracy can mobilize, gain, and sustain majorities.

Social structural conditions have been favorable for Swedish Social Democracy. Paradoxically, its rise to power in the 1930s and 1940s was based not so much on the working class as on the rural classes.

The process of industrialization in Sweden had a number of internationally peculiar characteristics. Centered around iron ore mining, hydroelectric power, and timber, it was from the start dominated by large industrial concerns but was scattered across a geographically vast nation. The industrial establishments were located in small, remote, and isolated rural localities, not, as elsewhere, in burgeoning cities. This geographical factor had profound effects on political and organizational development. First, it helped smooth the process of "proletarianization"; local, rural-based industries helped absorb the peasantry into industrial life without the social trauma of massive population movements.

Well into the twentieth century, the Swedish economy was dominated by a mass of poor and economically unviable farms. Emigration to the United States was considerable. The decentralized mode of industrialization, however, helped absorb substantial rural labor surpluses; the result was the rise of a peasant-worker class with blurred class divisions and a strong traditionalist, local-based solidarity.

3. Eduard Bernstein, *Evolutionary Socialism* (1899; rpt. New York: Schocken Books, 1971).

Geographical dispersion meant that the emerging labor movement's strategy for mobilization had to be based on centralization. Concerted industrial action, bargaining, and strikes could be effective only under conditions of strong centralized coordination. This is one reason why the Swedish trade union movement rapidly moved in the direction of industrial unionism and national-level representation. A second reason is the absence of a strong skill- and craft-exclusive tradition; the Swedish working class has always been comparatively undifferentiated.

Thus, to a degree not found elsewhere, the Swedish union movement was favored by homogeneity and a capacity for centralized, national unification. Organizational growth was rapid in the 1920s and 1930s.[4] By 1940, trade union organization exceeded 1 million, or 50 percent of wage earners; by the 1960s, about 90 percent of blue-collar and close to 70 percent of white-collar workers were unionized, the former in the central LO (Landsorganisationen) federation, the latter in the independent TCO (Tjanstemannens centralorganisation) federation.[5] Compared to many other nations (Denmark excluded), Sweden did not experience sagging unionization in the 1970s and 1980s.

The homogeneity, organizational density, and centralism of the labor movement had profound effects on SAP's fortunes. As in Denmark and elsewhere, the independent strength of the union movement helped move the socialist party away from ideological orthodoxy toward practical reform politics. It was thus comparatively easy for the Swedish socialists to shelve ideological orthodoxy, move out of the traditional working-class ghetto, and embrace the broader and electorally more rewarding popular reform strategy.

The Swedish Social Democrats have always been more theoretically inclined than other Scandinavians. The party was, in fact, fairly radical during the 1920s. Its election campaign in 1927 was devoted to economic socialization (far-reaching inheritance confiscation). On the other hand, its ideological elasticity can be seen from the swiftness with which it abandoned the orthodoxy of socialization when faced with indifference or outright opposition from both outside and within the working class. The trade unionists played an important role in moving the party from Marxism to Keynesianism in the crucial period of the 1930s.

The organizational power of the Swedish trade unions is unparalleled elsewhere and, as we shall see later, it has become a key factor in the postwar strength of Social Democracy. But it was not a significant cause of the party's rise to power. The LO suffered a major defeat in the 1909 general conflict, and membership growth subsequently grew slowly. In the 1920s and 1930s, the Swedish union movement was weaker than the Danish, albeit more unified. More important, Swedish industrial relations in

4. Nils Elvander, *Skandinavisk Arbetarrörelse* (Helsingborg: Liber, 1980).
5. Esping-Andersen, *Politics against Markets*, pp. 57–70.

that period were unusually tumultuous, boasting some of the world's highest strike rates.[6]

Indeed, before the war it was not the unions' strength that catapulted SAP to power, but the opposite: full trade union recognition and the stabilization of Swedish industrial relations had to await the affirmation of Social Democratic governance in the late 1930s.[7]

The key to Swedish Social Democracy's ascent to power thus lies not in the labor movement but in the class structural mix that prevailed before the war. On one side, the party's capacity to mobilize working-class votes was vastly aided by its homogeneity, complemented by the pervasive sense of social solidarity that not only characterized the Swedish working class but society at large. On the other side, the party's rise to power could only be premised on some form of accord with the rural classes, who were the numerical key to a parliamentary majority required for consolidation of power.

Sweden was, until World War II, the most rural of the Nordic countries. But its rural structure was peculiar. Genuinely viable family farming was limited to the south; the vast majority of the people were fragile peasants and/or wage workers. The former group was parallel to those in Denmark, although numerically relatively smaller. The latter was a strata peculiarly Swedish in that its economic interests and needs were often the opposite of those of the larger farmers but convergent with those of industrial workers. In short, the rural economy was dualistic. Since World War I, the wealthier farmers had been effectively organized and politically represented by the Agrarian party; large sections of the rural "quasi-proletariat" were potential recruits to Social Democracy. This was a situation that both favored and threatened the SAP when in the 1930s, the Depression pauperized agriculture.

For Social Democracy, then, the creation of a cross-class coalition was a necessity; the rural structure made it objectively possible. Yet neither necessity nor objective potential could have resulted in a viable political coalition were it not for two critical conditions: the nineteenth-century experience of cooperation in the struggle for full democracy and the ability to develop a common program that would override perceived conflicts between workers and farmers.

Sweden before World War II was rent with three axes of fundamental class conflict: the tumultuous and unsettled conflict in the labor market between the unions and employers' organizations; conflict between industry and farmers on issues such as tariffs and protectionism; and chronic antagonism between farmers' organizations and the labor movement. Facing de-

6. Walter Korpi and Michael Shalev, "Strikes, Power and Politics in the Western Nations, 1900–1976," in Maurice Zeitlin, ed., *Political Power and Social Theory* 1 (1980), pp. 301–34.

7. Walter Korpi, *The Working Class in Welfare Capitalism* (London: Routledge & Kegan Paul, 1978).

clining food prices and severe economic problems, Swedish farmers saw unionism as a major cause of their deteriorating profitability; in contrast, workers naturally opposed higher food prices. During the Depression, Swedish farmers began to drift toward Nazi sympathies.

The Swedish Social Democrats, having followed the political events in Europe, saw the pacification of the farmers as a precondition for stable democracy as well as for coming to power. Yet, unlike many European countries, the presence of a deep conflict between farmers and industrial interests precluded the formation of a reactionary, rightist alliance. It was this combination of factors which in Sweden helped launch the red-green coalition of workers and farmers in 1933.

The prelude to the Red-Green alliance was not especially auspicious. The SAP took office in 1932 with no clear parliamentary majority. Deep conflicts over food prices seemed to preclude the possibility of support from the Agrarian party, and the SAP thus faced the prospect of governing without the power to implement its program for restoring employment and introducing long-delayed welfare state reforms. The turning point came in the wake of a parliamentary crisis in 1933, when the nonsocialist parties vetoed SAP's (rather modest) Keynesian employment policies. The SAP negotiated a package deal with the Farmers party, providing for agricultural price supports in return for agrarian backing of SAP's deficit-financed economic revitalization policies. Once established, the coalition with the farmers permitted the SAP to build its position as the dominant political force for the long-range future. But it is difficult to interpret the conditions that allowed its establishment as such as a major cause of SAP's five decades of dominance. More or less similar conditions prevailed in Denmark and, a little later, in Norway. It can be strongly argued that the Red-Green coalition was a necessary stepping-stone to power. But in and of itself, it would certainly hold no guarantees, as subsequent developments in Denmark illustrate.

The Social Bases of Postwar Dominance

Single-party dominance over a span of half a century requires an extraordinary capacity to adjust to changing social structure. The postwar era was, by any yardstick, one of massive social change. Was there any factor particularly favorable to Social Democracy in light of Sweden's process of modernization?

At first glance, one would probably answer in the negative. As everywhere else, the rural population diminished rapidly, the relative size of the industrial working class was stagnant and even declining, and the new white-collar middle strata became increasingly dominant. Concurrently, educational levels increased, birth rates declined, and the population was aging. On none of these counts does Sweden stand out especially.

At second glance, however, it is possible to locate a critical source of SAP's strength in the way these universal processes unfolded, in the process of social class formation, organization, and unification. The Swedish social structure is uniquely capable of nurturing strong social organization; Swedish Social Democracy has benefited from this capacity and has nurtured its conception.

To understand this situation, we have to return to the mix of conditions inherited from the nineteenth century. Sweden was, until the beginning of the twentieth century, an isolated, industrially backward, and poor nation. It was relatively insulated from foreign influences, culturally homogeneous, and with a simple conflict structure. The matrix consisted of a small, albeit powerful, bourgeoisie, an emasculated landed aristocracy, a sizable but not dominant class of independent farmers, and a mass of small quasi-proletarianized peasants. Industrialization coincided with the struggle for democracy and liberalization, a struggle that pitted the rural classes, the urban liberals, and the embryonic labor movement against industry and aristocracy, the latter strongly associated with the conservative party. The class confrontation was more apparent than in other nations because of the concentration of ownership within a small and highly visible group of powerful families.

The capacity of the peasantries and working classes to struggle effectively was aided by their high level of literacy and education, and thus by their ability to articulate and represent political demands, and by their capacity to unify and organize in collective organizations such as agricultural cooperatives and trade unions. The combination of geographical dispersion and cultural homogeneity was then and has been subsequently a chief inducement to the centralization and national coordination of interest representation. Within the respective social classes and strata, mobilization was made easier; free-rider problems were less important than elsewhere. More crucial for Social Democracy and the trade unions were the homogeneity and unity of their base. The unions never had to struggle seriously with internal divisions between craft segments, skilled, and unskilled workers; the party was never seriously wrought with ideological dissension, polarization, or fragmentation.

The traditional, preindustrial mechanisms of social integration were crucial for Social Democracy's ascent. Equally important, the way they were transplanted into modern industrial society favored the labor movement considerably. SAP's ability to count on an extraordinary level of loyalty, compliance, and social solidarity today has its roots in nineteenth-century Sweden, a society that was insulated from influences from abroad, organized around small, localistic, and cohesive communities in which solidarity and conformity not only came naturally but were strictly enforced. In large measure, the Swedish labor movement could employ this culture of preindustrial solidarity in its mobilization efforts during much of the twentieth century because urbanization came exceedingly late and the natural inclination toward social conformity was carried on from generation to generation. Traditionalist consensus mechanisms were easily transposed into a social democratic framework, and when combined with the structure of class-organizational affiliation, resulted in an extraordinary level of collective identity formation. Thus both the level of working-class identification and party identification are substantially higher in Sweden than in either Denmark or Norway.[8]

The blend of these sociocultural characteristics marks Sweden as a special case in Scandinavia and in Europe at large. They are imperative for understanding the rise of Sweden's extraordinary organizational network, without which it is difficult to imagine persistent Social Democratic hegemony.

The LO is closely linked to the SAP (the TCO is independent) and has since the war been a key power resource for the party in attaining finances, party membership, and voter mobilization. Sweden is one of the few countries in which trade union members collectively affiliate with the labor party. Partly as a consequence, membership in the SAP was, and remains, unusually high. At the eve of World War II, SAP claimed 14 percent of all eligible voters; in 1976, the ratio stood at 25 percent. These figures contrast sharply with those in Denmark, where the party membership ratio dropped from 37 to 13 percent in the same period.[9]

Parallel to the organizational density of trade unionism and the party, Swedish Social Democracy has managed to erect an organizational empire that penetrates most of Swedish society, ranging from the cooperative movement, tenant organizations, and pensioner associations to education and leisure societies. As critics of Swedish Social Democracy argue, the labor movement has more or less organized the entire country.[10] That is, of course, an exaggeration, but the point is that such a degree of penetration serves as a powerful resource for political mobilization, cultivation of Social Democratic ideals, and reproduction of social solidarity. Although quantitative comparisons are difficult to make, there seems no doubt that activity and participation rates in the Social Democratic empire are much stronger than in either Denmark or Norway.

The link between organizational mobilization and party strength is evident and can be tapped in various ways. First, the societal penetration of the labor movement (and other interest organizations) helps maximize electoral participation. In fact, Sweden consistently boasts one of the world's highest rates of electoral participation. Voter turnout is positively related to SAP's

8. Diane Sainsbury, "Scandinavian Party Politics Re-examined: Social Democracy in Decline." *West European Politics* 7 (1984): 84–88.
9. Gunnar Sjoblom, "The Role of Political Parties in Denmark and Sweden," in Richard Katz, ed., *The Future of Party Government: European and American Experiences* (Berlin: De Gruyter, 1987), pp. 169–70.
10. Erik Anners, *Den Socialdemokratiska Magtapparaten* (Boraas: Askild and Karnekull, 1976).

electoral performance, the bivariate correlation being .498 for the period 1918–81. Electoral turnout explains 20.6 percent of the variance of the party vote (T = 2.44).

A second and more important link has to do with the organizations' role in directly mobilizing party votes. The overwhelming majority of LO trade union members support the SAP, although in the 1970s a decline set in (75 percent supported SAP in 1970, 68 percent in 1979). Among the white-collar TCO unionists, the percentage of SAP support is lower but also more stable (about 38 percent). Indications are that the decline in unionist support was reversed after 1979.[11]

A third phenomenon of profound importance for SAP's sustained dominance is its ability to mobilize optimally among both its traditional working-class clientele and "allied" classes. Of special significance has been its success in shifting from rural white-collar mobilization when, in the 1950s and 1960s, changing social structure compelled such a shift. Thus the SAP has been able to count on possibly the world's highest score of class voting among manual workers while simultaneously increasing the white-collar share. Until the party slipped in the mid-1970s, it could normally rely on about 70–75 percent of blue-collar votes and about 48–52 percent of white-collar (lower and middle-level) votes. Again, this contrasts with Denmark and Norway, where the decline in blue-collar support has been sharp since the 1960s and white-collar support has been stagnant and, in Norway especially, declining. The stability of class political allegiances is, of course, a mirror image of SAP's stable political record.

Nevertheless, the social structural and organizational conditions that facilitate Social Democratic mobilization have only limited explanatory power unless it can be demonstrated that the party, through its political alliance strategies and policies, is able not only to mirror and formulate mass demands but also to cohere potential or real interest differences. This is especially so because the SAP has never been able to rely solely on traditional working-class support but has perennially faced the necessity of presenting a political package that can mobilize across the class structure. The relative size of the manual working class (including agricultural workers) has been a rather stable 50 percent of the labor force, declining markedly in the last two decades. If we additionally posit that the SAP can realistically hope to capture up to 80 percent of its votes, the conclusion is clearly that the party is chronically captive to the logic of coalition building.

Formation of Political Alliances and Social Democratic Power

In a multiparty system such as the Swedish, parties tend to represent distinct clienteles. In Scandinavia, where the degree of interest organization

11. Sören Holmberg, *Svenska Valjara i Forandring* (Stockholm: Liber, 1984); Sainsbury, "Scandinavian Party Politics Re-examined."

among the various social groups and classes is so strong, the likelihood that the parties directly mirror an underlying and well-identified collectivized social stratum is additionally enhanced.

Thus, from the cradle of democracy until today, the party system has been pretty much a replica of the social structure. The conservative parties represent business and industry; the farmers' parties represent farmers; the liberal parties, urban professionals and the middle class; and the social democratic parties came, naturally, to represent the working classes. Since no particular stratum is numerically dominant, the result is that either minority or coalition cabinets prevail.

The Swedish Social Democratic party has, since the early 1920s, been the largest party. But except for two extraordinary occasions (1940 and 1968), its electoral share has never surpassed the magic 50 percent mark. From a European perspective, there is nothing unusual in this, nor is SAP's high share of the total vote (and parliamentary seats) unique; a more or less similar share has been maintained by the Austrian socialists.

What is uniquely Swedish is the terrain for the formation of political alliances. In part because of class structural circumstances, and in part historical fate, the Nordic countries in general, and Sweden in particular, rendered a broad conservative-dominated social coalition difficult. In the nineteenth century, the urban liberals (often in liaison with the farmers) were pitted against the conservatives; in the early twentieth century, as the socialist movement rose, conflicts among the nonsocialist parties remained so strong that they were unable to unify against the socialist threat even when they tried. This failure to unify juxtaposes Scandinavia to most of the continental European nations and helps explain the ease with which Social Democracy could come to power, as well as the immunity of the Nordic countries to reactionary and fascist responses during the 1930s.

Over the postwar era, the nonsocialist bloc was unable to replicate the European model of broadly based, conservative mass parties such as the CDU in Germany, DC in Italy, or the Gaullist alliance in France. Instead, the prewar matrix of a fragmented center and right remained pretty much intact.[12] Thus the Scandinavian Social Democratic parties were uniquely positioned to play the Machiavellian and, being the single largest parties, remained the only really plausible contenders to power. A decisive difference between Sweden, on one hand, and Denmark and Norway, on the other, is that in the two latter nations, the bourgeois parties managed to forge a more united front from the mid-1960s onward.

There is no doubt that the SAP in Sweden has benefited enormously from the chronic inability of the nonsocialist bloc to govern in unison. SAP's six years in opposition confirm this tendency, as the "bourgeois" coalition first broke on the issue of nuclear power and, in its second term, on taxation. In subsequent elections, the coalition's incapacity to unify has been recon-

12. Francis Castles, *The Social Democratic Image of Society* (London: Routledge & Kegan Paul, 1978).

firmed; during virtually every electoral campaign, including the 1988 campaign, the three nonsocialist parties have been preoccupied more with combating one another than with attacking the Social Democrats. In contrast, both in Denmark and Norway bourgeois coalitions fared well in the late 1960s and in the 1970s and 1980s.

It would misrepresent reality, however, to argue that SAP's political dominance occurred by default. Social Democracy has played an active role in nurturing rightist divisions, and its dominance has been possible because of its own coalition strategies. Social Democracy could not have held power for half a century on the basis of rightist splits alone.

A common Scandinavian characteristic is the historical legacy of cross-class alliances for democracy in the nineteenth century and for an anticrisis policy package again in the 1930s. The postwar evolution of this alliance took different forms in the Nordic countries. In Denmark, the Social Democrats failed to gain dominance precisely because the Agrarian party (Venstre) was too strong; in Norway, the Social Democrats became preeminent, but only under the condition that their policies remained favorable to the needs of the rural and fishery-based interests in the peripheries. In Sweden, in contrast, the SAP found itself compelled to reinvigorate the red-green alliance during the 1950s as the only means of staying in power. The SAP was the overwhelmingly dominant partner in the alliance (unlike Denmark), but the Agrarian party nevertheless came to dictate the limits of permissible reform. This constraint, paradoxically, favored Swedish Social Democracy's future.

The SAP emerged from the war with a fairly radical and ambitious welfare state—cum—full-employment program that clearly superseded the limited accord made with the Farmers' party in the 1930s. The SAP's electoral success in the 1940s would have seemed to warrant a dashing and aggressive program. Yet postwar circumstances swiftly eroded these conditions, and the party slipped back to its 46 percent level. The necessity of a continued alliance with the farmers meant that the SAP's reformist zeal was seriously dampened in the 1950s, which seems to have weakened its electoral fortunes.

It was the interrelation of class structural change and the increasingly burdensome alliance with the farmers that reversed SAP's fortunes. Political realignment crystallized with the conflict over pension reform in 1957 to 1959. In part, the realignment occurred because the farmer and peasant population shrank dramatically during the 1940s and 1950s as Sweden embarked on a wave of urbanization and because the Farmers' party refused to support the LO-SAP pension reform bill. Most important was SAP's understanding that long-term power would have to rest on its ability to mobilize the growing white-collar strata. The pension issue was uniquely tailored for a political realignment that entailed a break with the farmers and an opening toward the new middle classes. The SAP, unlike its Nordic brethren, was thus in a position to transform itself from the old "peoples" party to the new "wage earner" party model. A parallel realignment was not feasible in the other two countries, in Norway because a confrontation with the periphery interests would seriously harm any party, be it left or right and in Denmark because the farmers' interests remained politically dominant well into the 1960s.

A peculiar characteristic of the SAP's shift from a farmer to a middle-class coalition is that the rising white-collar class (although increasingly unionized) was largely unaffiliated with any given party. Aside from upper-echelon professionals and civil servants, who traditionally cast their loyalties with the conservatives, and the lowest ranks of routine white-collar occupations, who had a tradition of supporting Social Democracy, the new class was politically up for grabs. Only the small centrist Liberal party could make any real claim to representing the middle classes. In this context, the coalition-building strategy would turn from the tradition of parliamentary alliances between parties to that of mobilizing the middle-class vote internally.

Although the SAP never made a clear decision on these two alternatives, subsequent events were decisive. The pension conflict, combined with SAP's highly successful attempt to appeal to the middle strata, resulted in a major rise of electoral support and party membership during the 1960s. Indeed, the SAP came to enjoy single-party majority status in 1968. As a reciprocal effect, SAP's success meant that the nonsocialist parties' chances to mobilize the critical new middle-class electorate were stalled.

The new middle-class realignment of Social Democracy was evident not only in party electoral fortunes but also in the country's organizational matrix. Although retaining their formal political independence, the basically white-collar TCO unions were moving closer and closer to the LO as well as to the SAP's policies. And the heavily public sector bias in the growth of white-collar jobs strengthened the ties of that group to Social Democracy. Yet the middle-class coalition that appeared so successful in the 1960s proved to be somewhat fragile. A number of factors conspired to stall its full institutionalization. First, issues such as aggressive income and status equalization became an Achilles' heel for Social Democracy because they were strongly demanded by SAP's traditional base yet faced widespread opposition among the middle strata. Second, New Left issues such as the environment and nuclear power (which the SAP promoted) pulled the middle strata toward the reconstituted and "intellectualized" small Communist party and the Center party. Third, the economic democracy plan for collective wage earner funds that SAP promoted in the 1970s was far from popular among white-collar groups (or even workers).

The result was that SAP's potential for mobilization eroded in the 1970s; the party's capacity to forge a sufficiently viable middle-class alliance internally was thwarted. One can view the SAP's decision to incorporate the

Communists as an unofficial alliance partner after 1973 as a functional equivalent to single-party rule on the basis of a worker–middle-class mix; yet as long as the nuclear power issue remained, SAP's ability to govern continued to erode. The relegation of the nuclear power question to a popular referendum in 1980 helped remove it as a Social Democratic Achilles' heel.

It would be incorrect to say that the SAP's middle-class coalition collapsed during its opposition years, 1976–82. The party's losses to the right included both workers and white-collar groups (although the latter were more likely to shift); more to the point, the electoral shift was by no means a landslide. The return of both workers and the middle classes in the 1980s suggests that the long-run coalitional status of white-collar groups remains uncertain. Their return to Social Democracy can be interpreted as a disenchantment with the failed right. This suggests a weak case for SAP's mobilizational capacity, or it can be interpreted as a new enthusiasm for Social Democracy in light of its convincing performance in bringing the Swedish economy out of its severe difficulties in the 1980s. It is still too early to judge. Yet a scrutiny of SAP's policies and their electoral impact should aid us considerably in understanding the party's short- and long-term mobilizational capacity.

The Institutionalization of Power through Policies

In the final analysis, for several reasons, party dominance is a function of successful policies. First, voters may be persuaded by ideological promises for a period—but not in the long haul. Labor parties, in particular, are expected to satisfy demands for social and economic betterment, security, and equalization. They must be able to improve material conditions.

Second, social reforms are never neutral but have long-term implications for social stratification and the balance of political power. Policies may be motivated by immediately pressing problems, and their implementation helps institutionalize interests. Thus social policies may solidify class and status differences; or they may stigmatize and foster dualisms; or they may cultivate universalism and broad solidarity. As we shall see, a precondition for Social Democratic dominance is its ability to institutionalize universalism. Its success in this area helps secure broad popular solidarity behind the welfare state and, as a consequence, shelters it against tax resistance.

Third, the coalitional necessity that Social Democracy continuously faces means that it must be capable of presenting positive-sum policy packages, that is, a policy mix that benefits both workers and the potentially allied classes in a Pareto-optimal way.

Swedish Social Democratic dominance rests ultimately on its capacity both to launch and to institutionalize a social democratic society via reforms. The SAP succeeded, as nowhere else, in creating a universalistic welfare state, and it managed to install a general consensus behind full employment in large part because that goal was secured without incurring substantial economic costs. On one hand, class structural and coalitional conditions were favorable for full employment; on the other, the causality is reversed: SAP represents a case in which policies have facilitated electoral mobilization and have reproduced Social Democracy's power. A survey of its policy record since the 1930s will illustrate this point. The discussion will hinge on SAP's combined social and economic policy achievements.

As we have seen, the 1930s provided the stepping-stone for social democratic power in the Nordic countries. But as events in Denmark and Norway suggest, this alone offered no guarantees for the long run. Was there anything unique about SAP's performance? The answer is both yes and no. A number of conditions existed that were especially advantageous for Swedish social democracy. First, in comparison to Denmark and Norway, the issues of democratic and social stability were less settled in Sweden between the wars. Social democracy's consolidation of power in the 1930s helped put an end to industrial strife and labor market unrest, reaffirmed social democracy's image as the ultimate guarantor of democracy, and, above all, the red-green alliance affirmed the party's status as a party of the people, not of a class. To quote the party leader, Per Albin Hansson, the party became the carrier of the "Peoples Home" (Folkhemmet).[13] As such, SAP was a consensus builder, a party committed to the national interest, a party capable of rising above sectionalism and narrow class egoism.

Second, the SAP was privileged by inheriting a clean slate with regard to policies. The legacy of social reform from previous administrations was extraordinarily thin. Indeed, if Sweden today ranks as the world leader in welfare statism, its status in the 1930s was that of an international laggard. Unlike in other nations, the Swedish conservatives and liberals had not embarked on the strategy of preempting and stalling labor militancy with "social pacifist" reforms. In Sweden, therefore, a political platform based on social policy and full employment was thus a response to exceptionally dire need, expecially in light of the 1930s Depression. The promotion of unemployment insurance and employment creation programs in combination with agricultural relief became a rallying point of substantial electoral promise.

Third, Swedish Social Democracy profited tremendously from pure and simple good fortune. With the formation of the Red-Green alliance, the party succeeded in implementing its chief reform objectives: unemployment insurance, employment creation, farm subsidies, and its internationally vanguard countercyclical stimulation policies. The SAP adopted the Keynesian

---

13. A. L. Berkling, *Fraan Fram till Folkhemmet: Per Albin Hansson som Tidningsman och Talare* (Falkoping: Metodica, 1982).

prescription before the *General Theory* had been published. In reality, the deficit-financed expansionary program was modest and cannot account for Sweden's rapid economic recovery in the 1930s.[14] On one hand, economic conditions were favorable even before SAP came to power because Sweden had gone off the gold standard in 1931 and the currency remained undervalued. On the other hand, the rapid decline in unemployment after 1933 occurred mainly because of the rapid rise of Swedish exports, which were predominantly targeted to Hitler's vast rearmaments drive. The paradox is that Swedish Social Democracy benefited from the Nazi dictatorship.

Nevertheless, SAP reaped electoral benefits from its policies. It was spared the trauma of cutting back existing welfare measures, as the German socialists and the British Labour party were forced by the Depression to do, and it was instead in the position of implementing vast improvements. The resurgent economic growth improved industrial profits, farm prices, employment, and incomes. Social Democracy had proven itself capable of governing and, with rising popular support (it gained more than 4 percent in the 1936 election), had confirmed its status as a party likely to remain in office. Thus industry was forced to move from its traditional oppositional stance toward one of accommodation.

Thus emerged another key element in SAP's subsequent dominance, the social accord between capital and labor in the 1930s. This accord consisted of two more or less officially sanctified agreements: the famous Saltsjobaden accords between the LO and the Employers' Association, which de facto put an end to industrial strife and secured a long era of regularized and peaceful collective bargaining; and the results of negotiations between labor leaders and industrialists, which fostered mutual trust.[15] The bourgeoisie came to accept the idea of equalization via the welfare state; labor promised to honor the sanctity of private property rights.

Swedish Social Democracy's performance in the 1930s was therefore more auspicious than elsewhere from the point of view of harvesting long-term political dividends. Yet there is nothing globally unique in this success; the legacy of Franklin D. Roosevelt in the United States appears in many respects even more spectacular. The question turns to how the SAP succeeded in reproducing the position it had gained in the 1930s.

The period that followed invited serious problems. During the war, Swedish neutrality meant that the labor movement could not (as in Norway) harvest sympathy and loyalty on the basis of heroic resistance to Nazism. Indeed, the SAP coalition government compromised its ideals by allowing German troop transports across Swedish territory.

---

14. Lars Jorberg, "Industrialization in Sweden," in Carlo Cippola, ed., *The Economic History of Europe* (London: Fontana, 1976); Erik Lundberg, *Instability and Economic Growth* (New Haven: Yale University Press, 1968); Assar Lindbeck, *Svensk Ekonomisk Politik* (Stockholm: Bonniers, 1975).

15. Sven Anders Söderpalm, *Direktörsklubben* (Stockholm: Raben & Sjögren, 1976).

In addition, in 1944 the party launched a major program revision that consolidated its status as a reformist party focused on welfare reform and full employment while, concomitantly, promoting a fairly radical model of economic planning. The latter had to be shelved soon after the war.

Yet the welfare state–cum–full-employment promise soon presented the party with difficulties. Although most of the ambitious welfare reforms (especially pensions) could be financed by reducing defense spending, the commitment to full employment soon confronted the classical Phillips curve dilemma; by 1948–49, wage pressures and inflation severely threatened the balance of payments and economic growth. SAP's response, as in Britain, was to impose a two-year wage freeze on the trade unions. This freeze helped stabilize the economy, but it severely jeopardized political stability. The trade unions were unwilling to accept further political measures that influenced income and feared a likely future scenario of stop-go policies. In other words, the SAP government faced a zero-sum problem.

The solution came from the trade union movement in the form of the now world-famous Rehn model for an active labor market policy. The adoption of this model ensured Social Democratic capacity to govern over the next decades by sparing the party (government) from having to intervene frequently in wage negotiations and thereby avoided serious tensions between unions and the party.

The Rehn model, named for its architect, Gösta Rehn, a trade union economist, was a brilliant positive-sum solution to the Phillips curve problem: based on the assumption that the unions pursue an aggressive and equalizing wage policy, the model called for government-sponsored programs of mobility and retraining so as to absorb labor made redundant in declining industries and transfer it to dynamic growth sectors. In brief, the model assured both equality and efficiency: it promoted equality and full employment, and it helped promote industrial rationalization and restructuring without costs to individual workers. Even skeptics of the social democratic model acknowledge the success of the Rehn model in promoting balanced economic growth during the postwar decades.[16]

The active labor market policy became Swedish Social Democracy's answer to the perennial efficiency-equality dilemma that confronts labor governments. The party could present itself as an effective guarantor of both ideals.[17] The political opposition, in consequence, was prevented from claiming that socialist policies would destroy the economy.

Nevertheless, the SAP's electoral performance began to slip during the 1950s. It suffered a marked loss in the 1956 elections. The reasons were not immediately identifiable, but, in hindsight, the problem was SAP's continued reliance on its farmer allies, which prevented it from pursuing some

16. Lindbeck, *Svensk Ekonomisk Politik.*
17. Theodore Geiger and Frances Geiger, *Welfare and Efficiency* (Washington, D.C.: National Planning Commission, 1978).

of its more ambitious social reforms (health reform was delayed by many years, for example) and forced upon SAP a noticeable ideological and programmatic caution and even lethargy. To its supporters, the SAP would have appeared increasingly bland, technocratic, and tired. The turning point came with the proposal for a major pension reform. If the active labor market policy was the cornerstone for SAP's power in the economic arena, the pension policy came to occupy the same position in the social arena.

At first, the issue would appear relatively uncontroversial; it involved the introduction of an earnings-related second-tier pension system. Yet it soon became one of the most conflictual issues in postwar Sweden. Urged by the trade unions, SAP presented in 1957 a bill for a supplementary pension (usually referred to as the ATP pensions). This bill would hardly have provoked conflict were it not for its design and radical implications. First, in line with SAP's traditional social policy model, it called for compulsory and universal membership—a principle explicitly designed to foster broad national solidarity and equality of status. Second, in contrast to the employers' counterproposal, it was to be legislated (and thus not a voluntary, private occupational plan) and financed with publicly controlled pension funds. The method of funding was undoubtedly the key issue because the employers as well as the nonsocialist parties correctly saw the hugely funded system as a shift of capital control from private to public sector authority.

The lines of conflict over the ATP pension issue were drawn very sharply between left and right. But the pension issue invoked far more than a question of pensions and credit markets; it became a question of Sweden's future political power balance. The issue forced the SAP to break with its erstwhile farmer allies but offered it a unique opportunity to mobilize the rising white-collar strata, which increasingly came to favor the SAP's pension proposal as the conflict dragged on in the late 1950s. The ATP pension issue was a political turning point for Social Democracy.

This is not the place to review the long pension conflict. It involved both the resignation of a government and a national referendum and was finally resolved with a one-vote majority in favor of the SAP in 1959.[18] The important point is that it fostered a coalitional realignment at the most opportune time, just when the historical importance of the farmers had decayed and the new middle classes began to assert their electoral clout. Not surprisingly, the SAP underwent a substantial programmatic and ideological reorientation. Its traditional populist Peoples Home image was shelved in favor of a new image as a wage earner party. Its electoral success during the 1960s bears witness to its new-found ability to attract white-collar votes.

The SAP was invigorated by its policy achievements. It had proven itself capable of synthesizing economic efficiency and social equality concerns; it had succeeded in coalescing the working class and white-collar groups; and it presided over an economy that became internationally celebrated for its

18. Björn Molin, *Tjänstpensionsfragan* (Lund: Akademisk Forlag, 1967).

ability to ensure sustained full employment, welfare, equality, social peace, international competitiveness, and material growth.

This positive policy record was lacking in both Danish and Norwegian Social Democracy; Danish Social Democracy was the least capable of securing a similar positive-sum solution. Although Danish Social Democrats proposed policies almost identical to those of their Swedish brethren, Denmark's political conditions were such that they were systematically stalled. In economic management, there was nothing equivalent to the active labor market policy; instead, the Social Democrats were continuously compelled to intervene with incomes policies, which alienated the trade unions. On the social policy front, they were unable to pass a supplementary pension; the result was proliferating and highly inegalitarian private pensions. The net effect in Denmark was that Social Democracy had little capacity to win over the new middle classes and thus even less capacity to succeed with its reform intentions.

An irony of Swedish Social Democracy is that its celebrated model began to unravel exactly when the SAP harvested its electoral dividends. By the early 1970s, the positive-sum formula was gradually turning negative-sum. The signals appeared everywhere: industry faced declining profits, and investment levels began to fall, jeopardizing the commitment to full employment; workers were increasingly unwilling to participate in the active manpower policy system because it often meant unwanted geographical relocation; the equalizing wage-bargaining system faced growing resistance from the worker "aristocracies," who saw that their wages were slipping relatively; and with a slowdown of economic growth, higher inflation, and welfare state consolidation, tax rates grew very rapidly in the early 1970s. The formula that had so successfully carried Social Democracy through the postwar era had become contradictory. And it is this turnabout that accounts for SAP's losses during the 1970s.

The SAP's immediate responses actually aggravated the problems. Escalating wage costs and demand pressures began to jeopardize exports and competitiveness; SAP's response was to manufacture a relatively severe recession from 1971 to 1973, which, in turn, led to acute overloading of the active manpower programs, which had to absorb rising unemployment; and it led to a subsequent wage explosion. By 1974–75, the economy was in acute imbalance; public expenditures grew tremendously as did wages and, of course, taxation. And with the onset of the international economic crisis after 1973, the government's chief concern came to be focused on maintaining full employment.

The means available for maintaining full employment were limited to the absorptive capacity of the active manpower programs, expansion of public sector employment (in welfare state services), and industrial subsidies. The government did succeed in retaining full employment but at enormous public budgetary costs.

Social Democracy's lack of a convincing policy alternative in the face of these accumulated problems may not directly explain its substantial electoral losses in 1976. But it undoubtedly furnishes the backdrop. There were two ad hoc issues that clearly weakened the party in the 1970s. One was the controversy over nuclear energy. The trade unions and the SAP had been strong supporters of a nuclear power buildup in Sweden and were unprepared for the rising popular backlash. When it came (led by the leftist Communist party and the erstwhile Agrarian party, now the Center party), SAP was vulnerable and lost considerable votes on the issue in the 1976 elections. Second, the Swedish LO had developed a plan, written by Rudolf Meidner, for economic democracy through collective wage earner funds as a means to salvage its commitment to wage equalization and as a new thrust toward democratization of the economy. The economic democracy issue came to a head in the 1976 election because of its controversial nature and the abjectly clumsy way it was handled. Because economic democracy became the key issue of the 1970s and 1980s, that issue requires some explanation.

Economic democracy was of double importance to the trade unions. First, the unions had, since the 1960s, demanded greater control over investments and greater democratic control of the economy in general. The Meidner plan intended to tax a percentage of profits to be reallocated in investment funds collectively owned by workers; indeed, it was designed so that, over four or five decades, workers would control a majority share of Swedish enterprise. In other words, the plan called for a creeping socialization of the economy. Second, the economic democracy proposal served labor's more immediately pressing problems of collective bargaining, especially the resistance to continued wage equalization among large sections of the labor force, who saw that their wage moderation fueled excessive profits. LO's intention was to preserve wage equality while granting workers, as a collectivity, an indirect compensation in the form of share ownership.

It is not difficult to see that the economic democracy plan explicitly broke with the social accord of the 1930s. Its incursion into the prerogatives of private ownership implied that labor demanded a renegotiation—one that clearly invoked terms unacceptable to employers. The immediate response of the employers was, of course, extremely hostile. The LO passed the plan on to the SAP for legislative consideration in the middle of the 1976 electoral campaign, and the political focus was naturally shifted toward the Social Democratic party. This tactical clumsiness accentuated SAP's weakness in the elections, and the issue was expertly exploited by the nonsocialist parties, which could successfully rally on the slogan of "socialism or freedom."

The 1976 elections gave the SAP only 42.8 percent of the vote, in Swedish terms a painful loss. The loss cannot be ascribed to one single issue—electoral survey data suggest that party shifts were caused by a variety of factors, among which nuclear power and economic democracy certainly figured prominently.[19] Growing skepticism about Social Democracy's capacity to manage the economy was clearly evident, and a majority of voters began to believe that the nonsocialist parties would be better able to guarantee continued full employment.[20]

At first, the 1976 elections may have appeared to terminate Swedish Social Democratic dominance, especially when, in the 1979 elections, the SAP was not returned to power. The 1976 elections were the first in which the bourgeois bloc was able to unify and take office. But the two terms the SAP spent in opposition did little to alter its de facto political dominance.

The nonsocialist coalition proved itself incapable of sustained unity; it broke apart both in its first and its second terms, resulting in weak minority cabinets. After the coalition's first term, 1976–79, SAP's electoral share increased moderately; following its second term, SAP returned to its normal 45 to 46 percent share, and it retained this level in the 1985 elections. In the 1988 elections, SAP declined by 1 percent, but with implicit Communist party support and the bourgeois parties as divided as ever (and further emasculated by the emergence of the Green party), SAP's grip on government power remains as solid as ever. Hence, viewed in electoral terms, the six years in opposition would appear as a temporary and transitory experience. What is more important is the nonsocialist coalition's policy performance while in office.

The bourgeois coalition was clearly captive to the hegemony of the Social Democratic agenda. It took office in the midst of the economic crisis and was forced to expend the lion's share of its attention on the maintenance of full employment. To this end, it continued—by and large—Social Democracy's previous, albeit questionable, policies; the accent was on massive subsidization of industries and jobs. Concomitantly, it was both unwilling and unable to cut welfare state programs. The result was, predictably, escalating budget deficits and growing imbalances in the economy. Thus it was Social Democracy which, in the end, could win elections by persuading the electorate that it was the only political force capable of responsible economic management. After the nonsocialist bloc's second term in office, the voters faced an odd political choice between efficient and inefficient social democracy; that they opted for the latter is not surprising.

Conclusion

The account given thus far in this chapter seems to suggest that SAP's return to power in 1982 was largely by default. In a superficial sense, there is some truth to this argument: its opponents were unable to present an

19. Olof Petersson, *Valjarna och Valet 1976* (Stockholm: Liber, 1977).
20. Ibid.; Esping-Andersen, *Politics against Markets*.

attractive or even convincing alternative. And SAP's return in 1982 was not founded on a workable and consensual new political formula with which to build a viable class coalition and thus launch itself on a new era of undisputed party dominance.

The SAP was brought back in office because its capacity to manage the economic difficulties was more credible, not because the party had anything new to offer. Granted, the 1982 elections included the controversial economic democracy proposal (in a significantly watered-down version), but this is certainly not what accounts for its reinvigoration. All accounts indicate that the proposal remains fairly unpopular among the party's working-class base and much more so among the white-collar strata.[21] It distinctly alienates the employers.

The considerably modified economic democracy plan was passed in parliament with support from the small Communist party in December 1982. In the new version, the plan has a built-in maximum limit to capital accumulation in the wage earner fund, and it stipulates that the fund's investments take place in the open, private market. The past years' experience with economic democracy does not suggest that it has had a significant electoral or coalitional dividend; nor has it brought major changes to the Swedish economic system.

Instead, SAP's return to political dominance rests by and large on its respectable economic policy performance along conventional policy parameters: it has been able to calm wages and inflation, and Swedish international competitiveness has been restored. The huge deficits have been transformed into surpluses.

Why was Swedish Social Democracy able to continue to rule even under a bourgeois flag, discredit the opposition, and then return seemingly unchallenged? The real answer has not to do with marginal electoral shifts or party credibility but with how Sweden became thoroughly social democratized over a period of many decades. The answer must, in the end, be found in the interplay of the three factors examined in this chapter: Sweden's social structure, the mobilization of citizens and political coalitions, and SAP's ability to institutionalize its power by enacting reforms. These three factors have come to interact in such a way that Social Democratic power is virtually impossible to break.

Social Democracy's policies became the nexus around which this favorable interaction emerged. The critical question is not SAP's day-to-day, or year-to-year, political management of the social economy but its policies' lasting influence on shaping social structural evolution and on coalition building. The key is SAP's consistent adherence to the principle of universalist inclusion. Its welfare state empire is one in which virtually every single program embraces and benefits more or less the entire populace. The wel-

21. Sören Holmberg, *Svenska Valjara* (Stockholm: Publica, 1981).

fare state thus actively constructs a social structure in the image of social democracy: it overrides cleavages, dualisms, and differentials by cementing equal status of citizenship across a very broad array of vital human needs. The welfare state, in turn, is assured optimal support because virtually everyone benefits directly and because the welfare of the majority is directly dependent on it. This explains why Sweden, the most extreme case of welfare state expenditure and taxation, has yet to experience even a modest tax revolt. Even a marginal tampering with welfare programs in Sweden will immediately unleash mass furor, as the bourgeois coalition experienced in its last term.

The Swedish social democratic welfare state is, unlike welfare states almost everywhere else, a consensus-building institution. It not only supplements the citizenship of equal legal and political rights; it is viewed as actively reinforcing them. In this sense, it has become an indispensable collective good and a definitional part of Swedish nationhood. It is the Swedish equivalent of the Italian mamma.

Nevertheless, the spread of universalism alone would clearly not suffice to explain Social Democratic dominance. Over the past two or three decades, and for many to come, SAP's position depends on middle-class support. Thus the public benefits must be attractive to the discriminating tastes of high-income groups as well as to workers. It was this issue that came to the fore with the conflictual ATP pension controversy in the late 1950s and which Social Democracy successfully solved. The SAP managed, in brief, to build a welfare state that, at once, pleased workers and the middle classes. It did this by synthesizing the principle of adequate benefits (through earnings-graduated benefits and high-quality services) and equality (through universal and equal rights and status). Powerful middle-class solidarity behind the welfare state and social democracy is not surprising when we realize that its distributional consequences are advantageous to the better-off.[22]

In summary, Swedish Social Democracy's extraordinary political dominance rests on its capacity to count on a very broad social solidarity; and it is able to do so because the SAP itself largely constructed it. Accordingly, we reach a conclusion that sounds tautological: Swedish Social Democracy is dominant because Sweden has become thoroughly social democratized. But the tautology disappears when we disentangle historical forces of social democratization; these do not refer just to party power and election victories but to the interaction effect of structural properties inherent in Swedish society, the organizational features of political mobilization, especially coalition building, and the institutional characteristics of policy development.

22. A. C. Stahlberg, *ATP Gynnar Hoginnkomsttagarna* (Stockholm: Institute for Social Research Reprint, 1981).

2. Conditions of Labor-Party Dominance: Sweden and Britain Compared

Jonas Pontusson

Among reformist labor parties operating in advanced capitalist societies, Sweden's Social Democratic party clearly stands out as the most successful. From 1932 to 1976, Sweden had but three prime ministers, and they were all Social Democrats. The party's share of the popular vote slipped in the 1970s, but only slightly. Following six years of coalition government by the "bourgeois" parties, the Social Democrats restored their claim to be the "natural party of government" by winning three consecutive elections in the 1980s (1982, 1985, and 1988). Their share of the popular vote in these elections ranged between 44 and 46 percent, as compared to an average of 46.7 percent for nine parliamentary elections from 1944 to 1970.[1]

Arguably, Sweden represents a limiting case of labor reformism in advanced capitalism. A great deal has been written about what the Swedish Social Democracy has or has not achieved in income redistribution, welfare provision, employment, control of investment, and other areas. In this chapter, I pursue a different question: how and why did Social Democracy come to assume such a dominant role in Swedish politics? The existing literature tends to answer this question by describing the political ascendancy of Swedish Social Democracy. A more adequate answer presupposes a system-

I rewrote this chapter while on a grant from the German Marshall Fund of the United States, and I wish to acknowledge its support. For comments on earlier drafts, I thank Miriam Golden, Geoffrey Garrett, Peter Hall, Peggy Kahn, Peter Katzenstein, Leo Panitch, T. J. Pempel, Michael Shalev, Sven Steinmo, Sidney Tarrow, Vincent Wright, and anonymous reviewers.

1. The Social Democrats' best postwar election was 1968, when they polled 50.1 percent of the vote, and their worst postwar election was 1976, when they polled 42.7 percent. (The election of 1968 was exceptional, occurring less than two weeks after the Soviet invasion of Czechoslovakia in 1968.) Following Swedish convention, the term *bourgeois parties* is here used as a collective label for the three parties to the right of the Social Democrats: the Center party, the Liberals, and the Conservatives. Also, it should be noted that the Social Democratic tenure in government was interrupted for about three months in 1936.

atic comparison with countries in which reformist labor parties have been less successful. In the preceding chapter, Gøsta Esping-Andersen tries to specify the determinants of Social Democratic dominance by focusing on the features that distinguish the Swedish case from the Norwegian and Danish cases. The following analysis conforms to a similar logic but instead uses Britain as the foil shedding light on the political success of Swedish Social Democracy.

From a strictly social structural point of view, the British Labour party has enjoyed more favorable circumstances than any other party purporting to represent the interests of workers as a class. For no other country ever became as thoroughly proletarianized as Britain, the first nation to industrialize. Whereas manual workers accounted for 69 percent of the gainfully employed population of Britain at the time of the 1951 census, the corresponding figures for Sweden were 41 percent in 1930 and 39 percent in 1965.[2]

If Swedish Social Democracy could become the "natural party of government," then surely British Labour should have been able to assume this role as well. Britain seemed slated for one-party dominance in the wake of Labour's landslide victory in the election of 1945, but the Tories returned to power in 1951. The Labour governments of 1964–70 and 1974–79 also failed to create the conditions for durable Labour rule. The Labour party's share of the popular vote dropped precipitously from 1966 (48.1 percent) to 1983 (27.6 percent) and recovered only slightly in 1987 (31.5 percent). After three consecutive defeats at the hands of Margaret Thatcher, it is an open question whether Labour will ever again be able to form a majority government.

There are two possible interpretations of the divergent fortunes of Swedish Social Democracy and British Labour. One interpretation would be that the divergence dates to the 1970s (or late 1960s) and derives from more favorable economic circumstances and/or more competent leadership in Sweden. According to this view, a similar welfarist/Keynesian consensus was established in both countries after the war. In the face of economic adversity, the consensus broke down in Britain but survived in Sweden. Alternatively, one might argue that Sweden's "postwar consensus" was quite different from Britain's and that this accounts for its greater endurance. Britain's commitment to an overvalued pound precluded a consistently Keynesian approach to economic management; more important, postwar Swedish governments went beyond the liberalism of Keynes and Beveridge to promote economic efficiency and social equality.

2. Figures from Perry Anderson, "Problems of Socialist Strategy," in Perry Anderson and Robin Blackburn, eds., *Towards Socialism* (London: Fontana, 1965), p. 248, and Göran Therborn, "The Swedish Class Structure," in Richard Scase, ed., *Readings in the Swedish Class Structure* (Oxford: Pergamon, 1976), p. 155. The British figure includes those self-employed engaged in manual labor.

Table 2.1. Voting support for left parties among different categories of wage earners: Sweden and Britain compared, 1964 and 1979 (in percent)

	Britain		Sweden*	
	1964	1979	1964	1979
Salariat	20	22	8 (8)	27 (20)
Routine nonmanual	31	36	47 (46)	41 (37)
Manual	70	55	77 (72)	71 (66)

Sources: Anthony Heath, Roger Jowell, and John Curtice, *How Britain Votes* (Oxford: Pergamon Press, 1985), pp. 32–33; and Walter Korpi, *The Democratic Class Struggle* (London: Routledge & Kegan Paul, 1983), pp. 241–42.
*The first Swedish figures refer to votes cast for the Social Democratic and Communist parties; the figures in parentheses refer to votes cast for the Social Democratic party.

Proponents of the latter interpretation might justifiably speak of Sweden as an instance of labor "hegemony" in capitalist society. The notion of labor hegemony is a slippery one, however, I shall not try to nail it down here. Elsewhere, I have tried to demonstrate that the Swedish labor movement has been able to determine the issues on the political agenda and set the terms of public policy debate to a far greater extent than its British counterpart.[3] Table 2.1 brings out a related point: it shows that Sweden's two socialist parties have together mobilized a significantly larger share of the votes cast by both blue-collar and white-collar voters than the British Labour party.[4] For manual (blue-collar) and routine nonmanual voters, this was true in 1964 as well as 1979.

The British Labour party relies more heavily on the votes of manual workers than does the Swedish left and has been more adversely affected by the decline of the manual working class relative to the electorate as a whole. Nevertheless, the Labour party's share of the blue-collar vote dropped sharply in the 1970s. The British Labour party seems to have been caught in the dilemma stipulated by Adam Przeworski and John Sprague: reformist socialist parties must appeal to nonworkers to gain an electoral majority, yet such appeals undermine their support among workers.[5] As Table 2.1

3. Jonas Pontusson, *Swedish Social Democracy and British Labour* (Ithaca: Western Societies Occasional Papers, Cornell University, 1988), chap. 2.
4. It seems appropriate to include votes cast for the Swedish Communist party in this comparison. The party is considered part of the labor movement and has invariably voted for legislation proposed by Social Democratic governments whenever a unified bourgeois opposition would otherwise have prevailed. The Communists' share of the total vote averaged 5.2 percent from 1944 to 1970.
5. Adam Przeworski and John Sprague, *Paper Stones* (Chicago: University of Chicago Press, 1986).

indicates, the Swedish left also gained white-collar votes at the expense of blue-collar votes in the period from 1964 to 1979, but the trade-off appears to have been less steep. At any rate, it should be clear from the table that the combination of strong working-class support and cross-class appeal constitutes the key to the electoral strength of Swedish Social Democracy.

The electoral mobilization capacity of Swedish Social Democracy can be treated as a cause as well as a consequence of its control of the political agenda. In postwar Sweden, electoral competition has primarily revolved around the support of the white-collar strata. Whereas the Social Democrats' hold on the blue-collar vote has never been seriously challenged, the bourgeois parties have had to respond to Social Democratic initiatives to defend their core constituencies. In Britain, by contrast, the Labour party has been on the defensive by virtue of its weaker hold on the blue-collar vote.

Esping-Andersen's analysis emphasizes the role of government policy in the "virtuous cycle" of Social Democratic dominance in Sweden. Essentially, Esping-Andersen argues that the reform policies implemented by the Swedish Social Democrats in the postwar era enabled them to avoid the electoral "decomposition" experienced by the Danish Social Democrats as well as the British Labour party in the 1970s.[6] Depending on how it is organized, the welfare state may accentuate or attenuate conflicts of interest within the electoral base of Social Democracy. The potential for conflict between taxpayers and welfare recipients is reduced to the extent that the welfare state benefits all citizens by providing a high level of coverage on a universal basis. Furthermore, the welfare state promotes working-class solidarity to the extent that it decommodifies labor power (i.e., to the extent that it provides services rather than cash benefits and/or severs the link between consumption and income from employment). The contrast between the Swedish and British welfare states on these scores would seem to be even sharper than the Swedish-Danish contrast presented by Esping-Andersen.[7]

In a similar vein, one might argue that the policies of Social Democratic governments have enhanced the organizational resources of the Swedish labor movement. While Social Democratic governments have directly and indirectly promoted unionization, the unions affiliated with LO have played a crucial role in mobilizing the blue-collar vote for the Social Democrats, and there is a definite correlation between union membership and socialist voting among white-collar as well as blue-collar strata. More subtly, the

6. Gøsta Esping-Andersen, *Politics against Markets: The Social Democratic Road to Power* (Princeton: Princeton University Press, 1985), and Chapter 1 in this volume.

7. Cf. Andrew Martin, "Is Democratic Control of Capitalist Economies Possible?" in Leon Lindberg et al., eds., *Stress and Contradiction in Modern Capitalism* (Lexington, Mass.: D. C. Heath, 1975); Norman Furniss and Timothy Tilton, *The Case for the Welfare State* (Bloomington: Indiana University Press, 1979); and Mary Ruggie, *The State and Working Women* (Princeton: Princeton University Press, 1984).

system of press subsidies introduced by the Social Democrats in 1969 has largely (though not exclusively) served to support daily newspapers owned by the labor movement.[8]

The political dominance of Social Democracy in Sweden might thus be conceived as a virtuous cycle involving three essential features: capacity to mobilize voters, control of the political agenda, and control of the government. Each feature can be said to explain the others, and beyond that, it is difficult to say anything definitive about the causal relations among them. Accepting the notion of one-party dominance as a phenomenon that tends to reproduce itself, the following discussion explores external conditions that might explain how this virtuous cycle is established and sustained over time. Esping-Andersen's analysis of the feedback effects of government policy invites the obvious question, Why have some labor parties been able to wield government power in such a way as to reproduce their political dominance and others have not? Esping-Andersen argues that the economic and political strength of the petit bourgeoisie has constrained the exercise of political power by labor in Denmark, but social structure clearly does not explain the success of Swedish Social Democracy relative to British Labour.

Economic circumstances would seem to provide a more compelling explanation. Arguably, rapid postwar growth enabled the Swedish Social Democrats to implement reforms that would pay off politically and to avoid the problems associated with incomes policy in Britain. Sustained economic growth was undoubtedly a necessary condition for the political success of Swedish Social Democracy, but the postwar growth rate of the Swedish economy was by no means exceptional, and the difference between Sweden and Britain on this score was not so great. The Swedish economy grew at an average annual rate of 3.0 percent and the British at 2.4 percent in the 1951–73 period, as compared with 4.4 percent for France, 4.8 percent for Germany, and 5.5 percent for Italy.[9] An economistic account of the contrast between our two cases would presumably focus on the competitiveness of export industries and the peculiar vulnerability of the pound sterling by virtue of its traditional role as a reserve currency (rather than aggregate growth rates). Without denying the importance of such factors at any given conjuncture, the following discussion emphasizes political variables. As Stephen Blank argues, Britain's industrial decline should not be seen as a predetermined, inexorable process; the politics of economic policy has mattered throughout.[10] We should not presume that more vigorous efforts to

8. See Pontusson, *Swedish Social Democracy*, pp. 26–27, for a more extensive discussion. With union members accounting for roughly 85 percent of the work force, Sweden is by far the most thoroughly unionized of the capitalist countries.

9. Figures from Peter Hall, *Governing the Economy* (New York: Oxford University Press, 1986), p. 26.

10. Stephen Blank, "Britain," in Peter Katzenstein, ed., *Between Power and Plenty* (Madison: University of Wisconsin Press, 1978).

reform British capitalism by postwar Labour governments would necessarily have failed.

I shall first address the significance of different electoral systems as an explanatory variable and then consider the nature of the opposition faced by labor parties in the two countries. The interests and organization of capital as well as the parties of the right will be discussed. In the course of this discussion, I shall try to build a case for looking at the politics of labor. The Swedish labor movement has enjoyed more favorable circumstances than the British in several respects, but it has also been more able to take advantage of favorable circumstances. In other words, I shall argue that strategic choices by labor matter. When such an argument is made, strategic choices are commonly treated as discrete and more or less fortuitous. By contrast, I shall argue that the Swedish labor movement possesses a certain strategic capacity that the British labor movement has always lacked and that this capacity is embedded in the organizational structures of the labor movement.

The oft-noted contrast between the fragmented structure of British unions and the centralized structure of Swedish unions is of secondary importance in this context. My discussion of the politics of labor will instead emphasize the integration of union and political activities in Sweden and the essentially political orientation of the Swedish union movement, that is, its willingness to subordinate short-term economic gains to long-term political goals. These features, rooted in the formative experiences of the Swedish labor movement, stand in sharp contrast to the instrumental relationship between the Labour party and the unions in Britain and the "economism" of British unions.

Comparing the Swedish experience to that of the other Scandinavian countries, Esping-Andersen argues that "the key to Swedish Social Democracy's ascent to power . . . lies not in the labor movement but in the class structural mix." My comparison of Swedish Social Democracy and British Labour yields the opposite conclusion. The choice of comparative reference points clearly matters a great deal to our understanding of the Swedish case. But Esping-Andersen's and my own analyses are by no means mutually exclusive; quite the contrary, they could easily be integrated within a broader comparative discussion of conditions of labor-party dominance.

Electoral Systems

From 1944 to 1970, the Swedish Social Democrats averaged 46.7 percent of the popular vote in nine parliamentary elections, and the British Labour party averaged 46.0 percent in eight elections. The Swedish Social Democrats controlled the government for the duration of this period, but the

British Labour party held office less than half the time. It is tempting to conclude that the contrast between these two cases hinges on the effects of different electoral systems, proportional representation in Sweden versus winner-take-all in Britain. The comparison of aggregate voting shares is somewhat misleading, however, for it ignores the Communist party's contribution to the electoral strength of the Swedish labor movement as well as Britain's more favorable social structure. The only reason the British Labour party did relatively well in aggregate terms was that manual workers constituted a greater proportion of the British electorate. As indicated in Table 2.1, the British party's ability to mobilize the blue-collar vote was distinctly inferior.

Nonetheless, the argument that proportional representation explains the ability of the Swedish Social Democrats to stay in power and to reproduce their political dominance deserves attention. One version of the argument would hold that control of the government matters more than the particular policies a party pursues in government. In a slightly different vein, Sven Steinmo argues that the Swedish Social Democrats have been able to approach policy making in a different manner from the British Labour party because they have been virtually assured of at least a share of government power. Above all, they have been more able to pursue long-term policy objectives.[11]

On the assumption that the distribution of votes between socialist and nonsocialist parties would remain the same, an electoral system modeled on the British would have enhanced the political power of the Swedish Social Democrats, but Steinmo challenges this assumption. The electoral strength of the Swedish left is itself a product of proportional representation, he argues. Whereas the British system of winner-take-all elections forces left critics of Labourism to remain within the Labour party, proportional representation has enabled the left wing of the Swedish labor movement to survive as a separate political force. According to Steinmo, the absence of a strong left wing within the party has enabled the Swedish Social Democrats to appeal more effectively to swing voters in the center of the political spectrum.

I am persuaded by Steinmo's argument that electoral systems have a profound impact on patterns of policy making, but I am *not* persuaded by his argument that electoral systems explain the political dominance of Swedish Social Democracy and the failure of British Labour to become equally dominant. For one thing, Steinmo speculates about the effects of electoral systems on the size of the left electorate without any reference to their effects on the size of the right electorate. One could just as well argue that a winner-take-all system would undermine the ability of Sweden's

---

11. Sven Steinmo, "Taxes, Institutions and the Mobilization of Bias" (Ph.D. dissertation, University of California, Berkeley, 1986).

bourgeois parties to appeal to swing voters in the center of the political spectrum. The fragmentation made possible by proportional representation has enabled these parties to appeal to a wide range of voter preferences. In the 1970s, the Conservatives appealed to antitax, antiwelfare sentiments, the Center party appealed to environmentalist concerns, and the Liberals sought to distinguish themselves by advocating increased aid to developing countries and equal rights for women and immigrants.

Steinmo's argument about the connection between electoral arrangements and the electoral appeal of the left raises two distinct issues: factionalism and radicalism. Internal party unity is indeed an outstanding feature of Swedish Social Democracy from a comparative perspective and clearly distinguishes Swedish Social Democracy from British Labour. But is it true, as Steinmo implies, that British Labour has been more leftist than Swedish Social Democracy? It is clear that a significant proportion of British voters came to perceive the Labour party as extremist in the early 1980s, but polling data do not provide an answer to the question here, for voters' perceptions and preferences may well vary independently of party policy. Under some circumstances, voters may perceive nationalization measures, for instance, as extremist; under others, they may not.

The idea of British Labour as more leftist than Swedish Social Democracy has some validity if we compare party rhetoric in the early 1980s, but it becomes untenable if we extend the time frame of the comparison and consider not only what these parties have said they would do but also what they have done when in power. One would be hard put to argue that the electoral promises made by Harold Wilson in 1964, 1966, 1970, and 1974 were, on balance, more radical than those of the Swedish Social Democrats in the corresponding period (and the same is true for the electoral promises of James Callaghan in 1979). In power, the Labour party has each time abandoned its reformist ambitions in the face of balance-of-payments difficulties, demonstrating a marked penchant for "calling upon its keenest supporters for the greatest sacrifices."[12] Meanwhile, the Swedish Social Democrats have conceived and implemented a series of far-reaching reforms, pertaining to industrial democracy as well as public welfare provision and education. And the so-called Meidner Plan adopted by LO in 1976 would have entailed a more far-reaching collectivization of ownership than any proposal put forth by the left wing of the British Labour party in the 1970s.[13]

The absence of factionalism within the Swedish Social Democratic party might be linked to Social Democratic control of the government as well as

12. James Cronin, *Labour and Society in Britain, 1918–1979* (London: Batsford, 1984), p. 13.

13. The Meidner Plan became a source of intense ideological controversy in 1978–82 and was never implemented. The debate over wage earner funds illustrates the limits of Social Democratic control of the political agenda in postwar Sweden. See Jonas Pontusson, "Radicalization and Retreat in Swedish Social Democracy," *New Left Review* no. 165 (1987): 5–33.

proportional representation. At the leadership level, the party has largely become a party of careerists, and the promise of power has served to integrate potential dissidents. By the same token, I would argue that factional strife within the British Labour party should be seen as a symptom of the crisis of Labourism rather than its cause. It is surely not an accident that the most intense factional struggles have occurred when the Labour party has been out of office.

From a broader comparative perspective, proportional representation clearly does not provide a sufficient explanation for the political success of Social Democracy in Sweden. After all, several West European countries have proportional representation, and in only a few has Social Democracy come to assume a dominant position. Wedding proportional representation to rapid economic growth does not seem to yield much greater explanatory power.

Bourgeois Parties

With Britain as his principal reference point, Francis Castles argues that the dominance of Social Democracy in Sweden (and the other Scandinavian countries) is a product of the fragmentation of the right.[14] At the same time as the Swedish Social Democrats have been able to mobilize working-class support by invoking the ideology of class struggle, they have been able to play the bourgeois parties against each other and to strike compromises with either or both parties of the center, the Agrarian/Center party and the Liberals.

The differences between the party-political constellations opposed to labor in our two cases are clearly related to the differences between their electoral systems. Whereas the electoral ascendancy of the Labour party served to marginalize the Liberals in Britain, proportional representation enabled several bourgeois parties to survive in Sweden. Indeed, one might argue that proportional representation encouraged these parties to maximize electoral support in the short run, at the expense of a long-term hegemonic project. (This argument is quite different from Steinmo's.)

Though reproduced by proportional representation, the fragmentation of the right must, as Castles argues, ultimately be explained in terms of preindustrial class relations.[15] Swedish feudalism was characterized by a relatively weak nobility and an independent peasantry. The commercialization

14. Francis Castles, *The Social Democratic Image of Society* (London: Routledge & Kegan Paul, 1978). Esping-Andersen develops essentially the same argument in *Politics against Markets* and in his contribution to this volume.

15. Cf. also Timothy Tilton, "The Social Origins of Liberal Democracy," *American Political Science Review* 68 (1974): 561–71. Tilton and Castles both approach the Swedish case from the comparative perspective of Barrington Moore, Jr., *Social Origins of Dictatorship and Democracy* (Boston: Beacon Press, 1966).

of agriculture diverged from the modal patterns of England and Prussia. While the nobility gradually became transformed into a royal urban bureaucracy, the enclosure movement in the first half of the nineteenth century consolidated a distinct class of farmers with small-to-medium-sized holdings. The politics of the bicameral parliament established in 1866 initially revolved around conflicts of interest between farmers, whose representatives (Agrarians) dominated the Second Chamber, and the urbanized nobility, whose representatives (Conservatives) dominated the First Chamber. By contrast, the commercialization of agriculture in England, which occurred much earlier, transformed the nobility into a capitalist landowning class, and the reconstituted Conservative party of the late nineteenth century spanned the urban-rural divide.

The political unity of Swedish farmers disintegrated over the issue of democratic reform, but the tradition of independent farmer politics remained. The Agrarian party was formed in the wake of World War I. Initially leaning toward the right, the party was distinguished by its concern with the immediate interests of a well-defined constituency and its lack of a strong ideological profile. This pragmatism made possible the "cow trade" of 1933, whereby the Agrarian party supported the Social Democratic government's public works program in return for higher agricultural tariffs, and subsequent Red-Green coalition governments (1936–40 and 1951–57).

The pension reform of 1959 might be characterized as a second breakthrough for Swedish Social Democracy. As Esping-Andersen has emphasized, the reform enabled the Social Democrats to mobilize new support among white-collar strata and thus weather the defection of the Agrarian party.[16] Divisions among the bourgeois parties again played a critical role in this realignment. The Agrarian party objected to the pension reform proposal put forth by the Social Democrats (known as ATP) but refused to back the alternative advocated by organized business and the opposition parties. Instead, it presented its own proposal for pension reform in the advisory referendum of 1957. Although a majority of voters supported the other two proposals, the ATP proposal received a large plurality (45.8 percent).

The Agrarian party left the government shortly after the referendum, and the extraordinary elections of 1958 resulted in a tie between the proponents and opponents of ATP in the Second Chamber (i.e., between the socialist and the bourgeois parties). Having lost badly in the elections, the Liberals began to reevaluate their opposition to the ATP proposal. The Social Democrats and the Liberals failed to reach a compromise, but a Liberal member of parliament abstained when the ATP proposal was finally put to a parlia-

16. Cf. also John Stephens, *The Transition from Capitalism to Socialism* (London: Macmillan, 1979). See Hugh Heclo, *Modern Social Politics in Britain and Sweden* (New Haven: Yale University Press, 1974), for the most detailed treatment of the politics of the ATP reform available in English.

mentary vote in 1959. The ATP system, commonly considered the center-piece of the modern Swedish welfare state, was thus introduced by a one-vote majority. The Liberal party endorsed the reform once passed, and by the late 1970s the ATP system had become a sacred cow with which no party dared to tamper.

The fragmentation-of-the-right thesis is quite apposite, but several qualifications are in order. To begin with, the critical importance of the coalition with the Agrarian party for the breakthrough of Swedish Social Democrats in the 1930s does not reveal why the British Labour government of 1929 failed to adopt a Keynesian response to the Depression. The Red-Green coalition in Sweden was necessary because of the continued importance of small farmers in Sweden, and it entailed significant concessions by the labor movement. Britain's greater proletarianization should, in principle, have made it easier for labor to break with the orthodoxy of deflation. Moreover, the Labour government did not confront a united bourgeois front in 1929–31. Quite the contrary, the idea of expansionary spending was the center-piece of the Liberal party's platform in the election of 1929, and Ramsay MacDonald could have chosen to ally with the Lloyd George Liberals rather than the Tories.[17]

With respect to the Swedish case, we should not lose sight of the limits within which the Social Democrats have been able to play the bourgeois parties off against one another. Whenever the Social Democrats have broached issues pertaining to the fundamentals of capitalism, as in the debate over planning in the immediate postwar period and the recent debate over wage earner funds, the bourgeois parties have joined forces in opposition.

Also, the Agrarian party and the other bourgeois parties together held a majority in the Second Chamber of parliament on only one occasion between 1937 and 1976, briefly in 1957–58, and even then the socialist parties held a majority in joint voting by the two chambers. Plausibly, the Social Democrats could have stayed in power without any compromises with the bourgeois parties. To be sure, greater reliance on Communist support might have entailed electoral risks, but the point here is simply that the Social Democrats have been able to exploit divisions among the bourgeois parties because they have bargained with them from a position of strength.

The fragmentation of the right can be seen as a consequence as well as a cause of Social Democratic dominance. As suggested earlier, the cross-class appeal of the Social Democrats has placed the bourgeois parties on the

17. See Peter Gourevitch, *Politics in Hard Times* (Ithaca: Cornell University Press, 1986), chap. 4; and Margaret Weir and Theda Skocpol, "State Structures and the Possibilities for 'Keynesian' Responses to the Great Depression," in Peter Evans, Dietrich Rueschemeyer, and Theda Skocpol, eds., *Bringing the State Back In* (Cambridge: Cambridge University Press, 1985).

defensive: these parties have had to respond to Social Democratic initiatives to defend their core constituencies. This was most obviously the case with the Liberals in the pension reform debate.

The Organization and Interests of Capital

It would be wrong to conclude from the preceding discussion that the opposition to labor has been weaker in Sweden than in Britain, for party politics constitute but one dimension of the balance of class forces, and there is, in both cases, a curious asymmetry between party politics and industrial relations. In the arena of party politics, the Swedish case is characterized by Social Democratic dominance and fragmentation of the right, but in the arena of industrial relations, it is characterized by exceptionally strong employer as well as labor organizations. British industrial relations are, by contrast, characterized by organizational fragmentation on both sides. It is instructive to consider how the organization and interests of capital have affected the fortunes of Swedish Social Democracy and British Labour.

It is not necessary, for our purposes, to describe the differences between Swedish and British business organizations in any detail. Suffice it to note that the collective bargaining and lobbying activities of Swedish business have been coordinated by two comprehensive and centralized peak organizations, the Swedish Employers' Association (SAF) and the Federation of Industry (the latter being a trade association). The Employers' Association was created in 1902 and from the beginning sought to bargain directly with unions. Indeed, the institutionalization of industrywide bargaining in the early 1900s and the economywide bargaining in the 1950s was largely imposed upon the unions by the employers. The Confederation of British Industry (CBI), established in 1965, is far less representative and far less centralized than its Swedish counterparts and has always avoided direct involvement in collective bargaining.

The organizational cohesion of capital as well as labor has facilitated the institutionalization of class compromise, and this in turn appears to have facilitated Social Democratic dominance. Specifically, employer organization has facilitated the exercise of wage restraint by the unions and enabled the Swedish labor movement to avoid the internal tensions associated with incomes policy in Britain. Though essential to the success of labor reformism, wage restraint becomes an intractable problem for unions if employers offer wage increases that exceed what the unions have secured through collective bargaining. To a greater extent than in Britain, employers' organizations in Sweden have shared responsibility for enforcing wage restraint.

At the same time, corporatist relations between business organizations and the government have weakened the position of the opposition parties in

Sweden. During the 1950s and 1960s, government and business representatives met regularly to discuss matters of economic policy. Such meetings seldom entailed direct bargaining, but they did legitimize government policies, making it difficult for the bourgeois parties to claim that Social Democratic rule was bad for the country.

Geoffrey Ingham argues persuasively that the pattern of industrialization explains the organizational cohesion of Swedish employers and the lack of such cohesion in Britain.[18] Sweden industrialized much later and more rapidly than Britain. Being latecomers and lacking a significant domestic market, Swedish industrialists from the very beginning had to contend with world competition. Most firms pursued niche-oriented marketplace strategies based on a narrow range of products. Consequently, they seldom competed with each other, but their dependence on export markets made it imperative to resist wage increases. At the same time as the commonality of interests among employers has been greater in Sweden than in Britain, the relatively small number of employers in each industry, because of the country's small size as well as a more concentrated industrial structure, has facilitated employer coordination.

The Swedish business community is distinguished from its British counterpart not only by a higher level of organization and organizational centralization but also by the hegemony of export-oriented manufacturing capital, as opposed to finance capital. Arguably, the failure of the Labour party to impose its own policy priorities when in government is related to the prominent role of the City of London (i.e., the financial community) in the British political economy.

It is a commonplace that the first Wilson government's commitment to maintain an overvalued pound effectively torpedoed its attempt to break with the pattern of stop-go policy and to institutionalize tripartite collaboration to promote industrial development. As deflationary measures were imposed in response to the sterling crisis of 1965, planning turned out to be little more than a rhetorical exercise, and the government came to rely on wage restraint as the centerpiece of its strategy to restore international competitiveness.

Clearly, it was the City and its clients that benefited most from the policy of defending the value of the pound. Stephen Blank argues that it is nonetheless false to see the failure to devalue as an expression of the City's political influence. According to Blank, Wilson and most, if not all, members of his cabinet very much believed in the policy of defending the pound. But why was there such a strong consensus around the defense of the pound? In his

18. Geoffrey Ingham, *Strikes and Industrial Conflict* (London: Macmillan, 1974). For a critique of Ingham, see Peter Jackson and Keith Sisson, "Employers Confederations in Sweden and the U.K. and the Significance of Industrial Structure," *British Journal of Industrial Relations* 14 (1976): 306–23. Jackson and Sisson rightly criticize Ingham for ignoring the significance of the political realignment of the 1930s for the decline of strike activity, but explaining variations in strike activity is not my concern here.

effort to demonstrate that direct pressures from the City did not alter the government's policy in the 1960s, Blank misses the hegemony of the City in the arena of foreign economic policy, a hegemony that was institutionalized in the nineteenth century and confirmed by the return to the gold standard in 1925.[19] In view of the close links between the City, the Bank of England, and the Treasury, it seems problematic to treat the City as a pressure group standing outside the state and then to inquire whether it has influenced state policy.

To characterize the contrast between Sweden and Britain in terms of the dominance of manufacturing as opposed to finance capital is somewhat misleading, however, for it is really the merger of industrial and finance capital that distinguishes the Swedish case from the British. Again, the differences between the two cases derive from the timing and pattern of industrialization.

By comparison with later industrializers, Britain industrialized relatively slowly, and early industrial entrepreneurs enjoyed very high rates of profit. Consequently, British industry has traditionally relied on retained profits and equity markets to finance new investment. The City of London never engaged in industrial finance; rather, it financed commercial transactions and became a conduit for the export of British capital. By contrast, Sweden and other late industrializers had to mobilize large amounts of capital quickly, and banks assumed a key role in the finance of early industry.[20] The banks became actively involved in the affairs of their corporate clients, and the intimate relationship between finance and industry was cemented by overlapping ownership. Each of the big commercial banks remains the organizational nexus of a distinctive constellation of industrial firms and capitalist families.

These differences in the relationship between industrial and financial capital correspond to basic differences in the structures of the British and Swedish economies. Imported goods account for a very large proportion of gross national income in both cases. But Sweden has paid for its imports with revenues derived from manufacturing exports, whereas Britain has relied on the return on investment abroad and an invisible trade surplus (income from international banking and shipping services) to make up for a chronic deficit in the balance of visible trade. The commonality of interests between labor and capital has been greater in Sweden than in Britain by virtue of the manufacturing basis of the economy as a whole and the export

19. See Frank Longstreth, "The City, Industry, and the State," in Colin Crouch, ed., *State and Economy in Contemporary Capitalism* (New York: St. Martin's, 1979); and Geoffrey Ingham, *Capitalism Divided* (London: Macmillan, 1984).

20. It is hardly necessary to point out that this argument follows the logic of Alexander Gerschenkron, *Economic Backwardness in Historical Perspective* (Cambridge, Mass.: Harvard University Press, 1962). The structure and organization of capital is an area in which the existing literature (including the Swedish-language literature) on the Swedish political economy is very weak.

dependence of manufacturing industry. From this perspective, centralized union and business organizations may be necessary but do not represent a sufficient condition for the institutionalization of class compromise.

Policy Innovation

The Swedish Social Democrats have enjoyed more favorable economic and political circumstances than the British Labour party, but they also seem to have been more able to take advantage of favorable circumstances. Policy innovation would appear to be an important consideration here. In Andrew Shonfield's judgment, "Sweden offers the solitary instance in the postwar capitalist world of a trade union movement which has made a significant intellectual contribution to the development of the system." By contrast, the British Labour party displays, in Göran Therborn's words, "a striking lack of initiative, imagination and capacity."[21] Perhaps the innovative capacity of the Swedish labor movement accounts for its political dominance. If so, how is this innovative capacity to be explained? Let us briefly examine the two most famous instances of Social Democratic policy innovation: the adoption of an active employment policy in the 1930s and the postwar strategy to reconcile full employment and price stability, known as the Rehn-Meidner model (the latter being the contribution to which Shonfield refers).

Economic historians have shown that the public works program introduced as part of the "cow trade" of 1933 played only a minor role in the economic recovery of the 1930s. Going a step further, Nils Unga challenges the conventional wisdom that the recovery program on which the Social Democrats campaigned in 1932 was informed by the writings of Keynes and that the Social Democrats, once in power, proceeded to apply the principles of Keynesian economics in a conscious and consistent manner.[22] Unga demonstrates that the Social Democratic leadership perceived deficit spending as an extraordinary crisis measure, a necessary evil, rather than a means to stimulate economic expansion. Although unemployment among union members did not drop below 10 percent until the onset of the war, the government made no attempt to combat unemployment through deficit spending after 1933. In fact, it strove to repay the crisis loans of 1933 ahead of schedule on the grounds that social reforms presupposed the return to a balanced budget.

Unga argues that the Social Democrats' break with the orthodoxy of deflation was a response to the concrete concerns of organized labor rather

21. Andrew Shonfield, *Modern Capitalism* (Oxford: Oxford University Press, 1965), p. 200; Göran Therborn, "Britain Left Out," in James Curran, ed., *The Future of the Left* (London: Polity Press, 1984), p. 123.
22. Nils Unga, *Socialdemokratin och arbetslöshetfrågan, 1912–34* (Lund: Arkiv, 1976).

than the result of new theoretical insights. A system of public relief works, paying well below market wages, had been established in the 1920s. At the outset, the unions supported the policy of below-market wages, for it meant that more unemployed could be put to work. The competition for jobs in the open market could thus be reduced, but this presupposed that relief works did not reduce the level of regular employment in the public sector. LO's support for the policy of below-market wages became untenable as the pool of truly extraordinary public works was exhausted and the definition of relief works was extended in the course of the 1920s. In response to pressure from relief workers as well as public sector unions, LO changed its position in 1928 and called for the replacement of the system of relief works with public works of a productive nature, paid at market wages. The Social Democratic party in turn adopted this position.

Unga's analysis suggests that innovative thinking by party leaders is *not* the key to the different responses to the Depression of the labor parties in Sweden and Britain. Rather, the divergence seems to hinge on the responsiveness of party leaders to union concerns. In proposing to cut unemployment benefits, Ramsay MacDonald and Philip Snowden completely disregarded the views of the Trades Union Congress (TUC). But why were Swedish party leaders more responsive to union concerns? The strategic choices made in 1929–31 must be understood against developments in the preceding decade.

In Sweden, union membership grew steadily in the 1920s. The membership of unions affiliated with LO nearly doubled, increasing from 280,000 in 1920 to 553,000 in 1930, and the rate of unionization among nonagrarian blue-collar workers increased from 31 percent to 52 percent. The Social Democrats made substantial gains in the elections of the early 1920s, but their share of the popular vote dropped from 41.1 percent in 1924 to 37.0 percent in 1928. In Britain, by contrast, electoral support for the Labour party continued to increase through the 1920s, peaking at 37.1 percent in 1929. Yet the membership of unions affiliated with the TUC dropped from 6.4 million in 1920 to 3.7 million in 1930, and the rate of unionization among blue-collar workers dropped from 51 percent to 26 percent. Most of this decline in union membership actually occurred before the disastrous general strike of 1926 (the rate of unionization was 31 percent in 1925).[23]

Swedish unions entered the Depression in a much stronger position than the British unions, and their leverage vis-à-vis the Social Democratic party leadership was undoubtedly strengthened by the party's electoral difficulties. But to explain divergent strategic choices in terms of the balance of power between the two wings of the labor movement is not entirely satisfactory. For reasons to which I shall return, party-union relations in the two

23. Unionization figures are from Anders Kjellberg, *Facklig organisering i tolv länder* (Lund: Arkiv, 1983), pp. 269, 299.

cases have always differed qualitatively. As Lewis Minkin argues, the Labour party is distinguished from Social Democratic parties by two seemingly contradictory features: it is more purely a trade-union party, yet the party leadership from the very beginning enjoyed a greater degree of autonomy vis-à-vis the "movement."[24] Arguably, the coincidence of electoral growth and union decline in the 1920s, and the outcome of the general strike, enhanced this autonomy.

The second case of policy innovation also brings out the importance of the organizational makeup and internal politics of the Swedish labor movement. The basic elements of what came to be known in the 1960s as the Rehn-Meidner model were first presented in a report to the LO congress of 1951 written by Gösta Rehn and Rudolf Meidner, two academic economists hired by LO when it established a research department a few years earlier.[25] The model was conceived as an alternative to the wage freeze of 1948–50. Against the background of this experience, Rehn and Meidner argued that unions could not prevent wage increases that employers were able and willing to pay and that the unity and strength of the labor movement would be undermined if the unions tried to assume this role. Instead, the government had to assume responsibility for price stability.

Rejecting the "pure" Keynesianism of the immediate postwar period, Rehn and Meidner argued that selective measures to sustain full employment should be combined with a restrictive fiscal policy that would keep the lid on corporate profits and thereby enforce employers' resistance to inflationary wage increases. For their part, the unions should pursue a solidaristic wage policy, coordinating their wage bargaining with the objective of eliminating wage differentials caused by variations in corporate profitability and imposing a wage structure based on the principle of equal pay for equal work. This wage structure would be more acceptable to workers and thereby reduce inflationary wage rivalries. It would also promote productivity growth through a selective profits squeeze and thus make it possible to reconcile high wages with price stability.

Although it restrained the wage demands of workers in the most efficient firms or sectors, solidaristic wage bargaining would raise the wage of the least efficient firms or sectors and force them to rationalize production or go out of business. To deal with the unemployment generated by the squeeze on the profits of inefficient firms or sectors, the government should develop an active labor market policy designed to promote labor's adjustment to structural changes in the economy. In short, the Rehn-Meidner model pre-

24. Lewis Minkin, "The British Labour Party and the Trade Unions," *Industrial and Labor Relations Review* 28 (1974): 7–37.
25. Subsequent reports by the LO research department elaborated further on various components of the Rehn-Meidner model. For a comprehensive treatment of the evolution of LO's strategy and the relationship between theory and practice, see Andrew Martin, "Trade Unions in Sweden," in Peter Gourevitch et al., eds., *Unions and Economic Crisis* (London: Allen & Unwin, 1984).

scribed a policy package consisting of a tight fiscal policy, active labor market policy, and solidaristic wage policy.

The Rehn-Meidner model was never completely implemented, but it did provide the labor movement with a coherent approach to wage bargaining and economic policy. Although its significance as the intellectual foundation of labor's postwar strategy can hardly be exaggerated, the Rehn-Meidner model has all too often been treated as a more or less fortuitous, and essentially theoretical, achievement by a couple of individuals. The elaboration and implementation of the Rehn-Meidner model must be understood in the context of internal politics and external circumstances of the Swedish labor movement.

Taken separately, the basic elements of the Rehn-Meidner model were not particularly original. What was innovative about this intellectual construction was the way it combined a number of ideas that had long been discussed and were broadly accepted within the labor movement. Invoking the egalitarian ideals of the labor movement, low-wage unions put forth the idea that LO should collectively pursue a "solidaristic" or socialist wage policy at several LO congresses in the interwar period. At the same time, most union leaders were predisposed in favor of rationalization and structural change by virtue of the economy's exposure to international competition. The idea that real wage increases depended on productivity increases prevailed among union leaders long before the Rehn-Meidner model was elaborated.[26] In addition, several public commissions of inquiry in the 1930s and 1940s advocated government intervention to promote labor mobility.

While combining preexisting ideas, the Rehn-Meidner model addressed the immediate concerns of the labor movement, and did so in a way that obviously suited the unions. For the model treated inflation as a result of capital being inefficient rather than wages being too high and shifted the political burden of fighting inflation from the unions to the government.

Significantly, the report presented to the 1951 congress did not immediately convince the LO unions to begin practicing solidaristic wage bargaining. Rather, LO's pursuit of a solidaristic wage policy evolved in piecemeal fashion, in response to external pressures from the employers and internal pressures from the low-wage unions.[27] Though solidaristic wage policy implied some form of economywide coordination of wage bargaining, LO only reluctantly agreed to direct negotiations with the Employers' Associa-

26. See Axel Hadenius, *Facklig organisationsutveckling* (Stockholm: Raben & Sjogren, 1976).

27. See Peter Swenson, *Fair Shares* (Ithaca: Cornell University Press, 1988), and Hugh Heclo and Hendrik Madsen, *Policy and Politics in Sweden* (Philadelphia: Temple University Press, 1986), chap. 3. Arguing that the "Swedish model" represents an ex post facto justification for policies that the labor movement adopted in response to immediate problems, Heclo and Madsen provide an important corrective to conventional interpretations, but they go too far in the opposite direction.

tion in the second half of the 1950s. For the employers, such negotiations represented a means to enforce wage restraint. The centralization of wage bargaining in turn strengthened the position of low-wage unions within LO. These unions in effect refused to go along with central agreements unless they contained provisions to reduce wage differentials.

Arguably, LO would have had to pursue a solidaristic wage policy even if the Rehn-Meidner model had never been conceived. But the model served to facilitate this outcome by identifying the long-term interests of the labor movement as a whole with the "selfish," short-term interests of the low-wage unions. In the end, the Rehn-Meidner model prevailed as the unifying strategy of the labor movement because the low-wage unions, in alliance with the LO research department, prevailed within LO, and because LO prevailed within the labor movement.[28]

Again, the innovative capacity of the Swedish labor movement seems to turn on the interaction between its different components rather than the intellectual qualities of labor leaders or policy advisers. This discussion introduces a new perspective on the contrast between Swedish Social Democracy and British Labour, for it suggests that we are not simply comparing two more or less similar labor movements operating in different circumstances. The labor movements themselves are different.

Labor Movements

As indicated above, LO has played a very important role in the success story of Swedish Social Democracy. But it is not adequate to characterize the differences between the Swedish and British labor movements—the dominance of the unions in one case and the dominance of the party in the other. After all, the unions control the vast majority of votes at Labour party conferences and can effectively dictate party policy if they agree among themselves. At least formally, the LO unions have much less leverage over "their" party. What truly distinguishes the Swedish labor movement from the British is a more political, class-oriented unionism and closer integration of party and union activities.[29]

As many authors have argued, the formation of the Labour party in 1906 did not represent a break with the essentially economistic orientation of British unions.[30] For the unions, the decision to organize a third party was,

28. The Rehn-Meidner model became a source of conflict between LO and the government in the 1950s; see Gösta Rehn, "Finansministrarna, LO-ekonomerna, och arbetsmarknadspolitiken," in Jan Herin and Lars Werin, eds., *Ekonomisk debatt och ekonomisk politik* (Stockholm: Norstedts, 1977).

29. Cf. Winton Higgins, "Political Unionism and the Corporatist Thesis," *Economic and Industrial Democracy* 6 (1985): 349–81.

30. See Tom Nairn, "The Nature of the Labour Party," in Anderson and Blackburn, eds., *Towards Socialism;* James Hinton, *Labour and Socialism* (Brighton: Harvester, 1983); and Leo Panitch, *Working Class Politics in Crisis* (London: Verso, 1986), chap. 1.

in the first instance, a response to a series of court decisions (Taff Vale in particular) that threatened to curtail their immunity from tort actions and hence their ability to engage in strikes. The unions' dissatisfaction with the Liberal party's inaction on this score undoubtedly extended to other issues as well, but the crucial point is that the unions turned to independent political action primarily as a means to secure legislation that would protect or enhance their ability to pursue the interests of their membership through collective bargaining. The unions' conversion to the idea of political action as an alternative to industrial action, that is, as a means to satisfy working-class interests directly, was slow and incomplete.

A fairly clear-cut division of labor between union and party leaders became institutionalized in the Labour party's formative period. So long as their activities as unions were not directly affected, the unions allowed the party leadership great autonomy in formulating party policy and setting political priorities. As Perry Anderson puts it, "the organizational nexus tying the trade-union and parliamentary institutions of labourism together did not mean any practical unification of industrial and political struggles. Quite the reverse: they were rigidly separated in the ideology of the movement, each wing defining its arena of activity as off-limits to the other—in the familiar duo of economism and electoralism that came to define Labourism."[31] Relations between the Labour party and its union affiliates have changed significantly since the early 1960s, of course, but the separation of union and party spheres remains more pronounced than in any other West European country.

The way collective affiliation has been organized illustrates the different nature of union-party relations in Britain and Sweden. In the British case, union members are affiliated with the Labour party through their national unions, and each union casts the votes of its affiliated members as a single bloc vote at party conferences. National union leaders stand between the party and the bulk of its membership. Indeed, the party headquarters does not even have the names and addresses of collectively affiliated members.

In the Swedish case, by contrast, union branches affiliated with party organizations at the local level until the party abolished collective affiliation in 1987. Collectively affiliated members had the same status as individual members, and their votes were cast by the representatives of local party organizations at party congresses. Leadership positions in union and party organizations at the local level frequently overlapped, and this pattern will undoubtedly continue. Whereas the formal-organizational link between party and unions occurs at the level of the national party convention in Britain, the link occurred at the local level in Sweden, and relations between the unions and the party at the national level have been almost entirely informal.[32]

31. Perry Anderson, "The Figures of Descent," *New Left Review* no. 161 (1987): 52. Cf. Minkin, "The British Labour Party and the Trade Unions."
32. Since collective affiliation was not an instrument of union influence over party policy,

The differences in the structure of party-union relations are closely related to differences in the strategic outlook of the unions. Swedish unions have been much more inclined to think in terms of political exchange; that is, they have been willing to restrain the exercise of power in the marketplace to achieve political objectives perceived to benefit the long-term interests of the working class as a whole. Equally important, Swedish unions have been less willing to let government policy become the exclusive purview of party leaders. Herein lies the significance of the Rehn-Meidner model. At the same time as it assigned pivotal importance to wage bargaining as a means to promote income equalization and structural change, the model specified very clearly the kinds of policies that the government had to pursue for the unions to be able to assume this role.

Virtually all the major policy initiatives of the Social Democrats in the postwar period were proposed—or at least very actively supported—by LO. This is true, most notably, of the supplementary pension reform of 1959, the development of an active labor market policy from the late 1950s onward, the "industrial policy offensive" of the late 1960s, the industrial democracy reforms of the early 1970s, and, most recently, the idea of wage earner funds. As Winton Higgins and Nixon Apple stress, it is LO rather than the Social Democratic party that has kept up the momentum of labor reformism.[33]

The political orientation of Swedish unionism manifests itself in rank-and-file attitudes as well as the statements and actions of union leaders. In a 1971 interview survey of workers in two comparable British and Swedish factories, Richard Scase registered markedly different responses to the question, "What do you think should be the major aim of trade unions?" He found that 42.6 percent of the Swedish respondents suggested improved social justice or socialism, 39.4 percent mentioned economic factors, and 9.8 percent wanted improved working conditions; the corresponding figures for the British respondents were 1.6 percent, 55.9 percent, and 23.6 percent.[34]

Swedish unions became more politically active in the postwar period, but I argue that this development represents a natural outgrowth of earlier experiences. The dominance of industrial unionism helps explain the politi-

---

the decision of the 1987 Social Democratic party congress to abolish collective affiliation is unlikely to alter the relationship between the party and the unions. Curiously, a thorough study of the organization and internal politics of the Swedish Social Democratic party has yet to be undertaken. For a brief, journalistic account, see Martin Linton, *The Swedish Road to Socialism* (London: Fabian Tract no. 503, 1985).

33. Winton Higgins and Nixon Apple, "How Limited Is Reformism?" *Theory and Society* 12 (1983): 603–30. The TUC did, in LO-like fashion, develop its own economic policy agenda in the 1970s; see Stephen Bornstein and Peter Gourevitch, "Unions in a Declining Economy," in Gourevitch et al., eds., *Unions and Economic Crisis.*

34. Richard Scase, *Social Democracy in Capitalist Society* (London: Croom Helm, 1977), p. 137.

cal orientation of Swedish unions, and industrial unionism is in turn a related consequence of the pattern of industrialization. Being a late industrializer, Sweden skipped over the early, craft stages of industrial production, and Swedish industry quickly adopted advanced forms of production technology and organization. Except in a few industrial sectors, organizing skilled workers in defense of craft privileges was a much less viable strategy in Sweden than in Britain. But industrial unionism must also be seen, in part, as a political choice that early union organizers made, a choice informed by socialist ideology. Whereas the unions organized the Labour party in Britain, the Social Democratic party organized the unions in Sweden.

Related to the question of the timing of economic and political development, the struggle for equal and universal suffrage played a critical role in the formation of the Swedish labor movement and helps explain the features that distinguish the Swedish labor movement from the British. As in imperial Germany (and other Continental countries), the struggle for democratic reform served to politicize union activities and thus produced what might be termed class unionism. The demand for universal suffrage figured prominently in early union organizing, and the LO unions staged a three-day general strike in support of universal suffrage in 1902. In response to employers' efforts to cut wages, the unions' attention shifted to the industrial arena in the following years. As collective bargaining became institutionalized, union and party activities became more differentiated, but this differentiation occurred within the framework of a common political project.[35] In the face of a cohesive and aggressive employer movement, the weakness of the unions' marketplace power, as revealed most notably in the disastrous general strike of 1909, curtailed the development of economistic thinking among the unions.

While the Social Democrats and the Liberals allied at the parliamentary level, the struggle for democratic reform came to serve as a point of convergence among the "popular movements" (*folkrörelser*) that had emerged in the late nineteenth century.[36] The major popular movements were the labor, temperance, and nonconformist movements. Like the labor movement, the temperance and nonconformist movements mobilized the lower strata of society against hierarchy and privilege. They appealed primarily to farm laborers and poor farmers but also gained support among workers in the mill towns that provided the social setting of early industrialization. Overlapping membership between the labor movement and other popular movements was common.

35. See Donald Blake, "Swedish Trade Unions and the Social Democratic Party," *Scandinavian Economic History Review* 8 (1960): 19–44.

36. See Sven Lundkvist, "Popular Movements and Reforms, 1900–1920," in Steven Koblik, ed., *Sweden's Development from Poverty to Affluence, 1750–1970* (Minneapolis: University of Minnesota Press, 1975).

The alliance with the Liberals and the broad popular coalition behind the demand for universal suffrage undoubtedly enhanced the legitimacy of the Social Democratic party and of the labor movement more generally. Perhaps more important, this experience in coalition politics shaped the strategic outlook of the labor movement. As Steven Koblik suggests, its interaction with other popular movements enabled the Swedish labor movement to escape the "class ghetto" that isolated the German and Austrian labor movements from the petit bourgeoisie and from society at large.[37]

The British labor movement was never quite so insular, and it certainly interacted with nonconformist movements. But other popular movements were less significant in Britain, and there did not exist any overarching issue, like universal suffrage, around which such movements could converge with the labor movement. Whereas the Swedish Social Democrats proclaimed themselves a "party of the nation" in 1910 and explicitly sought to appeal to new voting groups in the election of 1911, the British Labour party did not open its ranks to "workers by brain" until 1918. (It actually rejected a proposal to this effect in 1912.)

I do not mean to imply that the Swedish Social Democrats opted to become a national party and the British Labour party opted to remain a class-pure party. Leo Panitch argues persuasively that the political strategy of the Labour party was from the beginning premised on the idea of serving the nation.[38] But the Labour party accepted the national interest as essentially given, and the unions affiliated to it remained representatives of sectional interests. In a sense, the key to the hegemony of Social Democracy in Sweden is its ability to avoid this juxtaposition of national and sectional interests. On one hand, the Swedish labor movement has subordinated sectional interest to class interest; on the other, it has wedded class interest to national interest. The way the Rehn-Meidner model combines considerations of equality and efficiency represents the most obvious illustration of the latter point, but the earlier, vaguer, and more all-encompassing idea of the "people's home" (*folkhemmet*) linked class interest and national interest in a similar fashion.[39]

If my analysis is correct, the ability of the Swedish labor movement to avoid becoming caught in the juxtaposition of sectional and national interests is not simply a matter of fortuitous circumstances; it is, in large measure, a product of the organization and politics of the labor movement itself and, in particular, a product of what might be termed class unionism.

Furthermore, the coincidence of the struggle for democratic reform with the formation of the labor movement helps explain the electoral strength of

37. Steven Koblik, in ibid., p. 466.
38. Leo Panitch, *Social Democracy and Industrial Militancy* (Cambridge: Cambridge University Press, 1976).
39. See Seppo Hentilä, "The Origins of *Folkhem* Ideology in Swedish Social Democracy," *Scandinavian Journal of History* 3 (1978): 323–45.

Swedish Social Democracy. In Britain, most male workers gained the right to vote in 1867, and the Liberals, in particular, had established a strong electoral base within the working class before the formation of the Labour party. In Sweden, by contrast, the Social Democratic party predated the Liberal party by a decade and could appeal to first-time working-class voters on the basis of its vanguard role in the suffrage struggle. Whereas the Social Democrats effectively controlled the working-class vote from the party's inception, the Labour party had to win over working-class electoral support from the other parties. Furthermore, the struggle for democratic reform enabled the Social Democrats to project themselves as a national party and to appeal to lower-class strata other than industrial workers.

Conclusion

The Swedish labor movement emerged from the struggle for universal suffrage and parliamentary government with a hegemonic disposition, by which I mean that it was inclined to set priorities for long-term political objectives and had learned to consider building alliances with other social and political forces. The British labor movement never acquired a hegemonic disposition in this sense.

By now, at least a few readers will already have formulated the following objection: the early dominance of industrial unionism and the formative role of the struggle for political democracy clearly distinguish the Swedish labor movement from the British, but the formative experiences of the Swedish labor movement are hardly exceptional from a broader comparative perspective. The struggle for political democracy played a pivotal role in the formation of most labor movements on the Continent; yet German, French, or Italian labor parties, to mention only the most obvious examples, have never assumed a dominant position comparable to that of Swedish Social Democracy. In other words, the argument that I have developed is subject to the same objection I raised with reference to the economistic explanation of the contrast between the two cases: it does not represent a *sufficient* explanation of the political dominance of Social Democracy in postwar Sweden.

It thus becomes necessary to distinguish between labor's ability to generate a hegemonic project and its ability to realize such a project. Arguably, the German, French, and Italian labor movements also developed a hegemonic disposition in their formative period, but they failed to become dominant because of unfavorable circumstances. Two basic background conditions set the Swedish case apart from late-industrializing countries on the European continent. First, Sweden industrialized more thoroughly than other late industrializers: self-employment and small business became more marginalized, and the industrial working class assumed greater numerical importance.[40] Second, there were no significant religious, ethnic, or linguistic cleavages in Sweden.

On both these counts, the British labor movement also enjoyed more favorable circumstances than its Continental counterparts. At this level of generalization, one could perhaps characterize the British case as having favorable circumstances but no hegemonic disposition, the Italian case as one of hegemonic disposition but unfavorable circumstances, and the Swedish case as hegemonic disposition and favorable circumstances. (The United States is the most obvious case of no hegemonic disposition and unfavorable circumstances.)

As we have seen, however, the Swedish labor movement has also enjoyed more favorable circumstances than the British labor movement in several respects—second-order favorable circumstances, as it were. First, its opponents in the realm of party politics have been divided, for reasons that have to do with preindustrial class cleavages and proportional representation. Second, the manufacturing basis and organizational cohesion of Swedish capital, rooted in the timing and pattern of industrialization, have facilitated the institutionalization of class compromise. Third, the economic margins for social reforms have been wider in Sweden than in Britain by virtue of the greater international competitiveness of the Swedish economy.

To avoid the charge of historicism, let me emphasize that I do not believe that the origins of a phenomenon constitute an explanation of its continued existence. I hope that it is clear from my analysis in the last section that the hegemonic disposition of the Swedish labor movement has persisted because it has been embedded in the organizational structures and political practices of the labor movement. By virtue of their comprehensive and centralized character, Swedish unions have been more able to pursue a coherent set of wage-bargaining objectives and have effectively been forced to consider political exchange.

Similarly, the feedback effects of government policy identified by Esping-Andersen are crucial to understanding how Social Democratic hegemony has been reproduced over time. Although welfare reforms have provided a material foundation for the ideology of solidarity, government policies have enhanced the mobilizational capacity of the labor movement by promoting unionizaton and subsidizing the labor movement press.

40. Cf. Przeworski and Sprague, *Paper Stones,* p. 35.

3. The Political Economy of Labor-Party Dominance and Decline in Israel

MICHAEL SHALEV

Mapai: A Dominant Party

Simplistically defined, dominant parties are those that head governments over long periods (on a scale of the number of decades rather than of cabinets), continuously or with only ephemeral interruption. They are not necessarily majority parties, but they always enjoy a plurality of the popular vote. Until 1977, Mapai (the Hebrew acronym for Palestine Workers' party) and its successor the Israel Labor party, which since 1969 has run in electoral "alignment" with smaller labor parties, eminently fits this description. In fact, Maurice Duverger's notion of one-party dominance was for many years a leading paradigm of Israeli political sociology.[1]

Mapai was formed in January 1930 by a merger of the two leading labor

The themes of this chapter and a number of related issues that could not be dealt with here are elaborated in my forthcoming volume *Labour and the Political Economy in Israel* (Oxford: Oxford University Press). Readers curious about my intellectual debts will find them described in that book. I wish to record here my gratitude to the editor of the present collection for his tireless patience and assistance under trying circumstances and for arranging my participation in two stimulating and convivial conferences. I am also very grateful to Lev Grinberg and Gershon Shafir for contributing several ideas developed in the chapter and to Michael Barnett, Joel Beinin, Adam Seligman, Gershon Shafir, and Sidney Tarrow for commenting on draft versions.

1. See Maurice Duverger, *Political Parties: Their Organization and Activity in the Modern State* (London: Methuen, 1964), pp. 307–15, 417–18. Several prominent Israeli scholars have employed the notion of dominance as a party system to analyze Israel under Mapai. In particular, see the work of Yonathan Shapiro, *The Party System and Democracy in Israel*, unpublished English version of the author's *Democracy in Israel* (in Hebrew) (Ramat Gan: Massada, 1978); and Asher (Alan) Arian and Samuel H. Barnes, "The Dominant Party System: A Neglected Model of Democratic Stability," *Journal of Politics* 36 (1974): 592–614. The internalization of this paradigm by other observers is evident in an article by Yaakov Reuveni, "The Political Economy of the Likud, 1977–1984: A Diagnostic Examination" (in Hebrew), *Rivon L'Kalkala* 126 (1985): 237–47.

parties of the Yishuv (the Hebrew term for the twentieth-century Jewish "settlement" in Palestine before Israel's attainment of sovereignty in 1948). In two major electoral contests only a year after its foundation, Mapai signaled the growing political strength of organized Jewish labor. The party received 40 percent of the votes for the Elected Assembly of the Yishuv and 60 percent of the Palestinian ballots cast for delegates to the international Zionist Congress. By 1933 Mapai had won a substantial electoral edge over the other camps in the world Zionist movement, and from 1935 its leader, David Ben-Gurion, served as chairman of the Zionist Executive. Ben-Gurion subsequently became prime minister of Israel, and his successors remained at the head of every government formed in Israel until the late 1970s.

Despite profound changes in the size and composition of the electorate in the years following Israel's creation, Mapai's share of the vote remained extraordinarily stable for almost two decades. Although typically it garnered only about one-third of the popular vote, until the mid-1960s the party consistently commanded well over twice the support enjoyed by any one of its rivals on the left or right. Because of the wide ideological gulfs between these rivals, no other party could feasibly contemplate forming a government without Mapai, and Mapai was able to play off a variety of alternative coalition scenarios.

In the decade or so before what is known in Israel as the "political upheaval" which unseated Mapai/Labor, the party's electoral standing deteriorated; but it succeeded in partially redressing these losses by forming alliances with other labor-oriented groups. Nevertheless, since the major parties of the right also entered into a series of electoral partnerships, the distance separating the rival blocs (which came to be known as the Labor Alignment and the Likud) narrowed. This trend continued in the historic elections of May 1977, when a "flash" centrist party (the Democratic Movement for Change) succeeded in siphoning off nearly a third of the Labor Alignment's supporters, thereby overturning the traditional balance of parliamentary forces and terminating more than four decades of continuous governance by Mapai-led coalitions.[2]

The remarkable length and continuity of Mapai's political dominance was not merely a matter of its ability to sustain a clear plurality of the popular vote in the face of relatively weak and divided competitors. Mapai could be described as a hegemonic party in other, deeper senses. The party's positions on key issues represented the center of a far-flung consensus; it enjoyed the power to direct and coordinate a highly ramified institutional complex; and its power reached out across the entire spectrum of political action.

2. Election results for the Yishuv period are furnished by Dan Horowitz and Moshe Lissak, *Origins of the Israeli Polity: Palestine under the Mandate* (Chicago: University of Chicago Press, 1978), pp. 90–91, 101–3. For a summary of trends since 1948, see Nathan Yanai, *Party Leadership in Israel: Maintenance and Change* (Ramat Gan: Turtledove, 1981), chap. 1.

Ideologically, Mapai's interpretation of Israel's national mission, its military and geopolitical strategy, and its principal domestic policy commitments were internalized by the vast majority of Jewish citizens. It is true that during the first few decades after sovereignty, political debate on domestic issues was formally conducted in contested terms (such as capitalism versus socialism) on which Mapai's official position was well ahead of the electorate at large and even of the views of its own supporters.[3] Nevertheless, the principal lines of the social and economic policies actually pursued by Mapai—full employment, generous state subsidy of both consumers and producers, and the mixed private-public economy—were widely regarded (in Jewish eyes) as appropriate to the country's foremost tasks: attracting and absorbing immigrants, promoting economic infrastructure and growth, and encouraging national solidarity. In practice, the debate between the political blocs on domestic issues revolved around *cui bono*—the political consequences of the role of the state, not the nature of that role per se.

Institutionally, Mapai's capacity to govern was greatly enhanced because the party's sphere of influence was not limited to the political executive. It also controlled both the other major arms of the state (the army and the bureaucracy) and the great centers of quasi-state power inherited from the Yishuv era (the Jewish Agency and the Histadrut labor organization).

Beyond the ideological and institutional realms of dominance, there lies the arena of the extraparliamentary politics of protest and pressure groups. Here too Mapai enjoyed noteworthy success. At its peak, the party successfully installed itself as mediator among the most important organized interests and between them and the state. Simultaneously, it managed to prevent the emergence of "disorganized" interests as credible political challengers.[4]

Toward a Fresh Departure

Mapai clearly embraces, indeed epitomizes, all of the functional hallmarks of one-party dominance: a routinized monopoly over the formation of governments, the ability to preempt or control nonparty forms of political action, and a high degree of legitimacy in the eyes of most of the mass public. But the particular structures of dominance, and the historical trajec-

---

3. Alan Arian, *Ideological Change in Israel* (Cleveland: Case Western Reserve University Press, 1968).

4. The gap between Mapai's positions and the attitudes of its supporters was studied by Arian, *Ideological Change*. For discussions of Mapai's control of the army and of government bureaucracies, see respectively Yoram Peri, *Between Battles and Ballots: Israeli Military in Politics* (Cambridge: Cambridge University Press, 1983), and Yaakov Reuveni, *The Israeli Civil Service* (in Hebrew) (Ramat Gan: Massada, 1974). Peter Y. Medding, *Mapai in Israel: Political Organisation and Government in a New Society* (Cambridge: Cambridge University Press, 1972), reviews Mapai's role vis-à-vis organized interests in the 1960s, and Eva Etzioni-Halevy, "Protest Politics in the Israeli Democracy," *Political Science Quarterly* 90 (1975): 497–520, has analyzed the state's "absorption of protest" under Labor.

tory of the emergence and reproduction of dominance, are if anything even more nationally distinctive in Israel than they are in each of the handful of other Western polities in which a single party has enjoyed long-term preeminence. On the surface, the most striking points of resemblance between Israel under Mapai/Labor and other one-party dominant regimes are those with Sweden under Social Democracy. Although the SAP has typically garnered a substantially larger share of the popular vote than Mapai, for both parties decades of unbroken governance rested on successful coalition building and a fragmented opposition. Like Mapai, the Social Democrats were the "natural party of government" in more than electoral terms. Above all, both Sweden and Israel were dominated by labor movement parties—not only in the weak sense of parties belonging to the Socialist International but, more important, in their heavy reliance on a broad-based and highly centralized peak labor organization for financial backing, mobilization of voters, and the legitimation of government policy.[5]

The difficulty in analyzing the Israeli case through the prism of social democracy is that the ethos and evolution of Israel's labor movement depart strikingly from the European experience in a number of important respects. Historically, the key organizations of the Jewish working class opted for national exclusivism in preference to class solidarity and treated class struggle objectives as secondary to the Zionist project of national revival and political sovereignty. Unlike the SAP and other successful parliamentary socialist parties, Mapai's mass base has rested as much (and in many periods, even more) on mobilization of the middle strata as on the working-class vote. Finally, as I will argue more fully at the close of this essay, the labor movement's dominance in Israel was in many respects founded on elements (nationalism, "opportunism," machine politics) commonly identified with strong parties of the right. The only way these apparent anomalies can be made comprehensible is to place them firmly in context. Particularly needed is an appreciation of the institutions of the Israeli labor movement and the historical conditions in which they emerged and developed.

Any case study that attempts, as this one does, to make sense of more than half a century in a nation's political history must avoid three pitfalls. One is to retell a story that is already well known. A second is to tell everything unselectively. And a third is to preempt theory by description and thus to neglect insights of more universal import. This essay attempts to

5. In addition to essays in this volume, see Walter Korpi, *The Working Class in Welfare Capitalism: Work, Unions and Politics in Sweden* (London: Routledge & Kegan Paul, 1978), and Francis G. Castles, *The Social Democratic Image of Society* (London: Routledge, 1978), for influential accounts of Swedish Social Democracy. On the formal similarity between the Histadrut-Mapai relationship and the pattern characteristic of European social democracy in general, see Shmuel Bahat, "Structural Relations between Trade Unions and Labor Parties—A Comparative Study" (in Hebrew) (M.A. thesis, Tel Aviv University, 1979). The most comprehensive discussion of this relationship in the Israeli context is Rachel Tokatli, "Political Patterns in Labor Relations in Israel" (in Hebrew), (Ph.D. dissertation, Tel Aviv University, 1979).

combat these dangers by drawing inspiration from an analytical paradigm that has been widely implemented in the literature on the democratic capitalist societies of the West but has hardly touched the extensive scholarship devoted to Israeli politics and society. The perspective in question is the revival of macro political economy in comparative studies of politics and public policy. Among the central themes in this literature[6] which are of particular relevance to the phenomenon of one-party dominance, the following may be singled out:

1. The role of class and other economy-based interests and cleavages in shaping mass political mobilization;

2. The importance of political control of the economy and effective political management of distributional conflicts for the success of governing parties, especially parties of the left;

3. The impact on the domestic political economy of its economic and political connections to the international system.

Despite a certain amount of theoretical and methodological pluralism, most of the literature on Mapai has in common a rather pronounced evasion of these issues.[7] Political processes have been treated largely in voluntaristic terms, as a function of the will of political elites. Debate has been confined to the subsidiary question of why these elites were so successful— was it because of ideological commitment, inspired consensus building, or skillful manipulation? Cultural and institutional explanations have dominated the literature, with the economy viewed as exogenous to political processes rather than as a motive force for political action and an integral parameter of governance. Finally, the limited *manifest* role of class and class conflict in Israeli politics has been interpreted by most scholars as tantamount to their actual irrelevance, especially in comparison with national and ethnic conflict and solidarity, which have in turn been viewed as largely autonomous from economic forces.

This essay is not premised on a wholesale rejection of previous scholarship, but rather on the conviction that it suffers from biases badly in need of correction. I propose to supply such a corrective by asking questions

6. Some influential and representative collections are those edited by John H. Goldthorpe, *Order and Conflict in Contemporary Capitalism* (Oxford: Oxford University Press, 1984); by Thomas Ferguson and Joel Rogers, eds., *The Political Economy: Readings in the Politics and Economics of American Public Policy* (Armonk, N.Y.: M. E. Sharpe, 1984); and by Leon N. Lindberg and Charles S. Maier, eds., *The Politics of Inflation and Economic Stagnation: Theoretical Approaches and International Case Studies* (Washington, D.C.: Brookings Institution, 1985).

7. Significant and representative studies are those of S. N. Eisenstadt et al., *Stratification in Israel* (in Hebrew) (Jerusalem: Akademon, 1968); Medding, *Mapai in Israel;* Yonathan Shapiro, *The Formative Years of the Israeli Labour Party* (London: Sage, 1976); and Horowitz and Lissak, *Origins of the Israeli Polity.* For an inspired if unduly harsh radical critique, see Shlomo Swirski, "Remarks on the Historical Sociology of the Yishuv Period" (in Hebrew), *Machbarot Lemechkar Ulebikorat* 2 (1979): 5–41.

about what did not happen as well as what did and by suggesting hypotheses that are well grounded from a political economy perspective but have been conventionally bypassed. The organization of the chapter is chronological. The major emphasis is on the emergence of one-party dominance and its perpetuation over two eras, prior and subsequent to World War II. More focused attention will then be addressed to the decline and apparent demise of labor-party dominance since the 1970s.

In the formative period of dominance the peculiarities of the process of working-class mobilization which gave birth to Mapai resulted from the economic plight of Palestine's propertyless Jewish settlers. Competition in the labor market between Jews and Arabs led the former to champion Jewish nationalism and exclusivity and to forge a lasting alliance with the Zionist movement. The resulting "socialist-Zionist syntheses" did not offer a complete solution to the settlers' deprivations. But the Histadrut's distribution of Zionist subsidy to Jewish workers was sufficient to furnish the labor movement with an impressive mass base. It was the combination of Jewish working-class mobilization with the limited and fragmented socioeconomic basis for political mobilization on the right and labor's essential role in realizing the perceived national interests of the Jewish community as a whole which propelled Mapai to hegemony.

The transformations wrought by World War II and then by sovereignty ended a long-standing disjuncture between the political suzerainty of the labor movement and its limited power in the economic arena. The unprecedented impact of the state on the economy, as both a client and a regulatory agency, awarded veteran Jewish workers unprecedented bargaining power and diminished the role of private capital in determining national prosperity. Through its control of economic enterprises linked to the Histadrut and policies of generous government subsidy of private and Histadrut business, Mapai succeeded in steering capital formation and mobilizing public support in ways that strengthened the party's preeminence. Yet the success of this model of political management of the economy was dependent on two broad contingencies. The first was a steady supply of massive and unobstructed gift capital from foreign governments and sympathizers. The second was the continued viability of political ties (between Mapai and both workers and capitalists alike), which had their roots in economic dependency. The demise of these preconditions provides a persuasive political-economic explanation for Mapai's eclipse as a dominant party.

The Era of Ascendancy

The Zionist Labor Movement

To grasp the meaning of the long-run trajectory described in this chapter and to appreciate the distinctiveness of the Israeli case, it is essential to place the origins of the Zionist labor movement in historical context. Some half a million Jewish settlers arrived in Palestine between 1900 and Israel's creation in 1948. Most of them fled Europe and Russia in the wake of rising nationalism and anti-Semitism and shrinking economic opportunities; they turned to Palestine because other destinations were closed to them. In the decade preceding World War I, a small wave of immigrants arrived whose ranks included the architects and many of the future leaders of the labor movement. These newcomers were self-styled pioneers who saw their move both as a means of personal redemption and as part of a political project, to defend and "normalize" the Jews as a nation by resettling them on their own historic territory, ultimately as a politically autonomous entity. Many regarded themselves as socialists, but they rejected the predominant view in Jewish-socialist circles that the "Jewish problem" would be solved in Europe in the universal context of class struggle. Rather, it was up to the Jews themselves to transform their class composition and create the good society in their *own* land.[8]

In addition to this ideological common ground, the newcomers of the pioneering era shared common economic traits: they had little or no financial means (even though in many cases the parents they left behind were petit bourgeois), and such human capital as they possessed (a fair number were well educated) was of nugatory economic value in Ottoman Palestine. The lands of Zion were too expensive for independent settlement, and the limited market for manual labor among Jewish employers was fully supplied, in most cases by Arabs, whose labor was considerably cheaper than that of the immigrants. Jewish settlers thus faced problems of sheer survival which for all but a small minority were so overwhelming that they either returned home or sought alternative destinations. As Gershon Shafir demonstrates in an important new study,[9] it was the economic plight of the pioneers in the first few decades of the century, even before Palestine became a British Mandate and before the beginnings of Jewish mass immigration, that shaped the strategic choices and experiments in institution building which have lent the labor movement in Israel its enduring specificity. This period set the stage for an alliance between organized Zionism, a settlement movement without settlers, and the self-styled pioneers, a workers' movement without work.

In the pre–World War I period, the worker-pioneers sought to establish

8. For introductory material on Zionism, see Walter Laqueur, *A History of Zionism* (New York: Schocken, 1972), and Arthur Hertzberg, ed., *The Zionist Idea: A Historical Analysis and Reader* (New York: Harper & Row, 1966).

9. See Gershon Shafir, *Land, Labour and the Origins of the Israeli-Palestinian Conflict, 1882–1914* (Cambridge: Cambridge University Press, 1989). The present discussion of the labor market context also draws heavily on Anita Shapira's seminal volume on the "Hebrew Labor" struggle, *Futile Struggle: Hebrew Labor, 1929–1930* (in Hebrew) (Tel Aviv: Tel Aviv University and Kibbutz Meuhad, 1977). Other sources on the formative years of the Zionist labor movement in Palestine include Shapiro, *Formative Years*, and Zvi Sussman, "From a National to a Branch-Level Wage Policy" (in Hebrew), *Rivon Lekalkala* 16 (1969): 331–41. For more extended discussion and documentation, see Shalev, *Labour and the Political Economy in Israel.*

themselves in the Jewish villages or "colonies" based mainly on plantation agriculture. But the planter-capitalists faced powerful incentives to employ cheaper, more productive, and more compliant Arab laborers. The Jewish workers' initial response to their competitive disadvantage was to demand the displacement of Arab labor, but confrontational tactics failed to move the farmers. In time, Jewish labor responded to its labor market problem[10] by adopting what may be called an economic-collectivist strategy. One of its concrete forms was the self-employed contracting gang. Another was the producer cooperative, which sought to transfer Jewish-Arab competition from the labor market to product markets. Fully socialized communes (the forerunners of the kibbutzim) went a step further, striving for total autarky. But collectivism in all its forms was simply not feasible without the participation of "national capital" (the funds of organized world Zionism), both to provide the initial infrastructure and to subsidize the workers' losses. The collectivist strategy thus went hand in hand with partnership between organized workers and the Zionist movement.

The worker-pioneers possessed compelling attractions to organized Zionism. Unlike most of its other sympathizers, the workers were willing to move to Palestine. Once there, in contrast to the farmers, they sought to develop economic frameworks that would enhance Jewish autonomy and provide the basis for absorbing new immigrants. They were ready actively to compete with or help circumscribe Arab labor, rather than reinforcing the Arabs' presence by giving them jobs. And they were more amenable to taking on arduous and financially unrewarding roles in the settlement process than immigrants who were cushioned by personal assets.

By the time of Britain's conquest of Palestine in 1917, the workers' options were similarly confined. Most of the prewar pioneers had deserted Palestine, and the minority who remained had fled the plantations. The urban economy was as yet undeveloped and the prospects for private investment were dim, but the emergent alternative of communitarian rural settlement was unrealistic without massive outside assistance. That assistance would not be forthcoming unless labor was unified. In any case, the two workers' parties that later formed Mapai were determined to put an end to their hitherto unsuccessful attempts to woo wage laborers by operating rival labor exchanges and communal services (workers' health, housing, and kitchens). The solution was to combine these functions in a central organization for both rural and urban labor, which would be structured so as to be amenable to direction and control by the party. Late in 1920 this project

10. The problem of conflicts between "cheap" and "expensive" labor is far from unique to Palestine. See Edna Bonacich, "Advanced Capitalism and Black/White Race Relations in the United States: A Split Labor Market Interpretation," *American Sociological Review* 41 (1976): 34–51, and the important extensions to her model suggested by Yoav Peled and Gershon Shafir, "Split Labor Market and the State: The Effect of Modernization on Jewish Industrial Workers in Tsarist Russia," *American Journal of Sociology* 92 (1987): 1435–60.

came to fruition with the establishment of a central labor organization, the Histadrut.[11]

In comparison with other peak associations of labor, two of the newly born organization's most striking features were its preference for economic collectivism over trade union struggle and its deliberate confinement to the Jewish segment of Palestine's emergent working class. Economic backwardness, unemployment, and the workers' occupational and geographical instability undoubtedly constrained the growth of trade unionism. But the Histadrut was also reluctant to mobilize workers for class conflict because of its political commitment to the settlement effort. To the extent that labor militancy might succeed in pushing labor costs above the necessary "Jewish minimum," it carried the risks of deterring the creation of jobs in the private sector, protecting established labor at the expense of new immigrants, and attracting workers out of collectivistic frameworks dedicated to the service of Zionism. The Zionist connection also explains the contradiction between the encompassingness and class rhetoric of the Histadrut and its policy of barring Arabs from direct membership and forcefully opposing their employment by Jews.[12] Nevertheless, as I have already pointed out, this posture of exclusivism originated in economic conflict—the competitive threat to Jewish wages and jobs posed by Arab labor. During the interwar period the struggle for Jewish-only employment also came to be directed at political targets: mobilizing the rank and file of the Jewish labor movement and attracting the support of the nonlabor strata, which Mapai's leaders came to regard as essential political allies.

Working-class mobilization in the Yishuv thus differed strikingly from experience in Europe, which was inspired mainly by labor's demands for the right to vote and to bargain collectively with employers, as well as by workplace struggles connected with craft resistance to the dilution of skills and loss of control over production. Not only the initiative for but also the sequence of collective action was different. First came the parties, then the labor center (Histadrut), and only then—and decidedly marginally at first—the trade union function. Moreover, for the most part the development of local organizations followed rather than preceded processes of centralization. The Histadrut was born as a corporate peak organization, rather than evolving through aggregation of subunits and accretion of functions and powers. It was also born at the behest of political parties. The Histadrut never developed the capacity to lead and innovate strategically for both

---

11. Though conventionally rendered in English as the "General Federation of (Jewish) Labor," the literal meaning of the word *Histadrut*—organization—is more faithful to its character, which is anything but that of a federation of trade unions.

12. I have analyzed the evolution of the Histadrut's policies toward Arab labor in Michael Shalev, "Jewish Organized Labor and the Palestinians: A Study in State/Society Relations in Israel," in Baruch Kimmerling, ed., *The Israeli State and Society: Boundaries and Frontiers* (Albany: State University of New York Press, 1989).

wings of the labor movement. In effect, it was expected to function as the executive arm of a clientelistic party machine.

The Political Impotence of the Right

During the 1920s the parties that established the Histadrut found it necessary, if they were to secure the political exchange with Zionism on which the workers' movement as a whole was premised, to expand their electoral appeal sufficiently to become the dominant force within the domestic and international Zionist polity. This goal was achieved virtually from the moment of Mapai's creation in 1930, when the two leading Zionist workers' parties founded at the beginning of the century joined forces. At the Twelfth Zionist Congress in 1921, labor parties collectively polled a mere 8 percent of the worldwide vote. Ten years later, united Mapai's share was close to 30 percent, and thereafter it rapidly overtook the parties of the center and right. As in the analysis of class relations in general, the balance of forces between parties representing different classes is most appropriately understood *relationally*. The labor movement's political conquest of organized Zionism reflected not only the opportunities enjoyed by the left and their skillful exploitation but also the barriers that faced political mobilization of the right.

Many of the difficulties facing the right in Palestine were *structural* in character (a concrete indication of this is the pattern of domestic voting within the Yishuv, which from very early on awarded a pivotal position to the labor parties). They reflected a number of profound biases in the political economy of the Yishuv which favored the labor movement and impeded its political opponents.

1. The class structure of the Yishuv featured a broad middle layer of landlords, artisans, shopkeepers, and small-scale contractors and manufacturers. Satisfaction of key existential needs of these middle strata depended more critically on organized labor than on the bourgeoisie.
2. While it proved virtually essential for the propertyless followers of the workers' movement to mobilize politically to find solutions to problems of basic economic survival, no such impetus prevailed among business interests.
3. Both labor and capital confronted acute internal cleavages. But whereas on the workers' side the principal division—that between Jews and Arabs—contributed to organization and solidarity, divisions within the capitalist class hampered the emergence of collective action and consciousness.

The Middle Strata. At first sight it might have been expected that the same economic logic that drove the propertyless to organize would also have affected the Yishuv's sizable petit bourgeoisie. Many were vulnerable to considerable hardship during the sharp cyclical downturns of the Palestinian economy because the bulk of their (typically modest) assets were eaten up by investment in homes and businesses. But like the old middle class everywhere, they were endowed with limited inherent capacities for collective action as a result of economic dispersion and individualism and their contradictory class position between capital and labor. In good times they did not need to organize, and in bad times the labor-controlled Zionist movement could do more to relieve them from hardship than could the capitalists. They might still have become a major counterforce to labor's political dominance had they become the target for political entrepreneurship of any substance. But the "natural" leadership of the petit bourgeoisie largely stayed away from Palestine.

At the end of the 1920s, a major challenge from the right emerged with the intention of filling this vacuum. The "Revisionist" party under the leadership of Vladimir Jabotinsky (the forerunner of Menachem Begin and the Likud party) was founded in 1923 as a protest against what was perceived as a lack of militance in the Zionist movement against British restrictions on Jewish immigration to Palestine and periodic Arab attacks on Jewish life and property. The subsequent entry of a wave of nonsocialist petit bourgeois immigrants emboldened the Revisionists to embrace a program that would appeal to the substantive economic interest of the middle strata, for instance by demanding that they receive a bigger share of subsidies from the world Zionist organization.[13]

The fundamental barrier facing the Revisionists' (or any other) attempt to draw the petit bourgeoisie into an effective antilabor political movement was the indispensability of organized labor for addressing crucial existential issues. The labor movement, not the Revisionists, channeled subsidies to the financially stricken, set the outer limits of the Jews' de facto territorial presence, and organized their defense against Arab attack. None of this prevented the Revisionists from accusing the labor movement of fulfilling

13. On the character of the petit-bourgeois immigrants of the 1920s, see Shulamit Carmi and Henry Rosenfeld, "Immigration, Urbanization and Crisis: The Process of Jewish Colonization in Palestine during the 1920s," *International Journal of Comparative Sociology* 12 (1971): 41–57. The discussion here draws in part upon Yonathan Shapiro, *An Elite without Successors: Generations of Political Leaders in Israel* (in Hebrew) (Tel Aviv: Sifriat Hapoalim, 1984), pp. 28–32. The Revisionists' deliberate adoption of an economic plank targeted at the middle strata has been documented by Lilly Weissbrod, "Economic Factors and Political Strategies: The Defeat of the Revisionists in Mandatory Palestine," *Middle Eastern Studies* 19 (1983): 333–34. Scholarly work on the Revisionists' failure is thin. Yonathan Shapiro stressed Mapai's superior organizational capacities in *Formative Years* and, eventually, its powers of co-optation in *Party System*, pp. 155–56. Weissbrod, in "Economic Factors" and "The Rise and Fall of the Revisionist Party, 1928–1935," *Jerusalem Quarterly*, no. 30 (1984): 80–93, emphasizes the Revisionist movement's lack of "positive" and burden of "negative" ideological weight. Weissbrod's articles provide useful documentation of the Revisionists' rise and fall, and although I disagree with their central thrust, the present discussion borrows from several of her specific arguments.

these responsibilities with insufficient vigor—an appeal which in the early 1930s helped raise their political stock. Indeed, Revisionism became a serious threat to the left; its followers undercut Histadrut members in the labor market and its leaders began to attract organized farmers, manufacturers, and others to the idea of a united right-wing coalition.

Mapai's leaders responded to this threat by a strategic reorientation intended to emphasize its commitment to the nation as a whole and to build political bridges beyond the labor movement. Mapai's mass base was consciously widened, in part by the new legitimation of the contributions of the middle classes to the nation-building project. Indeed, during the 1930s the party's urban following became predominantly middle class. Meanwhile, in the extraparliamentary arena Mapai did its best to appease employers and their allies by reining in union militancy. Attempts to commit the Histadrut to an explicit peace treaty in industry failed, but the labor movement elite communicated is conciliatory stance in other ways—by its handling of labor relations issues at enterprise level, informal contacts with top employer representatives, and a willingness to sanction joint business ventures with private capital.[14]

Alongside its express determination to keep the peace between the classes within the Yishuv, the labor movement embraced an unwritten commitment to go to war with outsiders. Even though the 1932–36 period was one of economic prosperity and declining unemployment, a demonstrative struggle was launched against the employment of Arab labor by Jewish employers. The effect was to cement the popular identification of the labor movement as the vanguard of the Jewish national struggle, while at the same time branding the two most significant right-wing sectors (the citrus farmers and the Revisionists) as anti-Zionist because of their practical opposition to Histadrut demands. In 1936 the Arabs of Palestine launched a general strike-cum-insurrection which seemingly vindicated the labor movement's policy of promoting Jewish economic self-sufficiency and its leaders' view that the conflict between the two national movements was intractable. The Arab revolt was exploited by Mapai to reinforce its nationalist appeal to nonlabor groups. Underlying this success was a policy of national separatism that was complementary to the economic interests of the great major-

14. The trend toward crystallization of the right was noted by Shapira, *Futile Struggle,* pp. 252–57, and Weissbrod, "Economic Factors," p. 335. Shapiro, *Formative Years,* and Shapira, *Futile Struggle,* discuss, respectively, the ideological transitions summed up in the slogans "from class to nation" and "peace in the Yishuv." Yael Ishai, *Factionalism in the Labor Movement: Faction B in Mapai* (in Hebrew) (Tel Aviv: Am Oved, 1978), p. 29, characterizes Mapai as predominantly a party of the middle classes. Dedi Tsucker of Tel Aviv University reviews joint ventures between private and Histadrut capital in a dissertation in progress. There is a chapter titled "The Failure of Class Accommodation in the Mandatory Era" in my *Labour and the Political Economy in Israel,* which is devoted to the nonemergence of "peace agreements" between labor and capital together with evidence of de facto class cooperation. This chapter also contains details and sources regarding other aspects of the presovereignty period for which no references are supplied in the present essay.

ity of Jews, including those capitalists—the majority—who neither employed Arabs nor were commercially linked to them.[15]

The Bourgeoisie. Business opposition to Jewish economic separatism was limited to only a few sectors of capital, which, despite their economic strength, were obliged to pay a penalty of political isolation. A good part of the disunity among the bourgeoisie in the Yishuv derived from the differing labor market interests of the various "fractions" of capital. A handful of large industrial enterprises had the resources to develop internal personnel policies that segmented Jewish and Arab labor in different jobs, whereas medium-sized industry tended to recruit only Jews. Construction, the other major branch of the private urban economy, required a less skilled and stable work force, which it recruited from unorganized (though mostly Jewish) as well as Histadrut labor. In private agriculture the leading branch was citrus. Here again labor requirements, coupled with employers' proximity to rural Arab society, prompted many farmers not only to circumvent the Histadrut but also to defy the "Hebrew labor" norm prevailing in most urban branches. As a profit center that was the only significant exporter in Palestine, citrus might in principle have taken the political initiative on behalf of business. But precisely because they were exporters, these farmers were isolated from other sections of the bourgeoisie, whose dependence on the domestic market (and on various forms of Zionist subsidy) encouraged assent to the policies of the leadership of the labor movement and the Zionist institutions.

The leadership vacuum among the bourgeoisie was a result not only of the differing interests of its major fractions but also of a fundamental feature of the Yishuv economy—its lack of virtually any comparative advantages and consequent failure to attract big capital. The absence of major natural resources, a limited domestic market, relatively expensive labor for the region, and constricted credit facilities inevitably deterred large private investors (either immigrant or absentee). Moreover, the Jewish bourgeoisie in Palestine for the most part felt little compulsion to turn to collective action. In the field of labor relations, employers were generally favored by labor market conditions; they enjoyed the sympathy of the authorities (who were willing to employ force against strikers); and the attitude of the Histadrut in labor relations matters was basically cooperative. The other potential incentive for organization—that of extracting economic policy concessions from the state—was dulled because the Mandatory authorities deliberately adopted a low profile in economic affairs.

To sum up, in the circumstances of the Yishuv capital was weak in every

15. Shapira, *Futile Struggle,* documents the revival of "Hebrew labor" and its political (rather than economic) rationale. Simha Flapan, *Zionism and the Palestinians* (London: Croom Helm, 1979), pp. 227–29, provides fascinating documentation of the role of economic interests in the response of Jewish elites to the Arab revolt.

respect that theoretically might have provided a counterweight to the *political* standing of the labor movement: it lacked either coherent common interests or a leading sector strong enough to impose its own project, was fragmented in ownership, and faced only weak incentives to organize or engage in formal political action. Capital did, however, enjoy ascendancy over most of the working class in *market* relations. Nevertheless, the role of private investment in the political economy at large was less decisive than is normal in capitalist societies. The privileged position of the bourgeoisie under capitalism is owing essentially to the impact of profitability on investment and thus on the prosperity of the society as a whole. Although the flow of private Jewish funds into Palestine far exceeded the sums transferred by the Zionist movement, as in other settler societies much of the money was sunk into land purchases and construction rather than capital accumulation, and most productive investment was small scale. The prosperity of Palestine was dependent mainly on Jewish immigration and capital inflow and thus on factors exogenous to the Yishuv economy—the intensity of anti-Semitism in Europe, the feasibility of alternative destinations for immigrants, the wealth the newcomers brought with them, and the extent of Jewish and Zionist philanthropy emanating from the Diaspora.[16]

No less important, in the Yishuv context what were earlier termed "existential" needs extended beyond the purely economic, to the Jews' personal and collective security and their future in Palestine. In this respect, the significance of the labor movement's historic alliance with Zionism went beyond the opportunity for attracting material support for the movement and its followers. For what organized labor brought to the marriage—its commitment to Jewish nationalism, settlement, and self-defense—provided the basis for a genuine hegemony within the Yishuv.

The Failure of the Left Opposition

Mapai's simultaneously ideological and instrumental strength also helps to illuminate its success in dominating the labor movement camp internally. Not only could the party provide workers with an uplifting role in national rebirth, but it did so alongside many eminently practical activities addressed to their present and future security in Palestine and their immediate material interests. Through the Histadrut, Mapai was able to offer Jewish wage earners access to employment and vital social services. These weighty assets notwithstanding, the party was no more immune to threats from the left than it was spared the Revisionist challenge. In fact, throughout the prestate

16. A classic exposition of the "hostage" interpretation of capitalism is Charles E. Lindblom, *Politics and Markets: The World's Political-Economic Systems* (New York: Basic Books, 1977). Dan Giladi, "Private Enterprise, National Capital and the Political Formation of the Right" (in Hebrew), *Avanim* 5 (1965): 90–102, has discussed the paradox of private dominance of capital inflow and the political weakness of the right in the Yishuv.

period, the contradictions of the Histadrut-Mapai "model" of working-class mobilization gave rise to heated debate and at times also to substantial opposition movements.[17] Three such tensions (often overlapping in their effects) were particularly significant in this context:

1. the contradiction between Mapai's socialist rhetoric and a praxis that increasingly emphasized national separatism on one hand and class cooperation on the other;
2. resistance to the Histadrut's extreme centralization of authority and power in the hands of the party elite and the party machine;
3. the secondary status of the urban working class in the Labor Zionist paradigm, which bred opposition by some rank-and-file unionists to politicization of the trade union function and its subordination to the labor movement's national tasks.

The most important dissenters to the left of Mapai were kibbutz-based movements which regarded themselves as the socialist conscience of the labor movement and episodic mobilizations of urban rank-and-filers opposed to central Histadrut/Mapai authority. These two groups eventually joined forces in the 1940s to form a united opposition within the Zionist camp. There were also a number of communist or protocommunist fringe groups opposed in principle to the reigning synthesis of socialism and Zionism. Between the first and sixth Histadrut conventions (1920–44) the collective standing of the opposition labor parties grew from 7 to 38 percent of the ballot, leaving Mapai at the end of the period with only a bare majority with which to rule the labor organization.

This impressive showing should not be allowed to conceal the fact that it was only in the wake of two historic changes—the transition to a full-employment economy and the approach of sovereignty—that the left emerged as an autonomous and relatively broad-based political actor. The more characteristic conditions of the Yishuv era severely hampered the radical labor opposition. The same combination of propertyless colonists confronting cheap local labor which gave birth to the Histadrut points to the compelling attractions of the Histadrut model to its followers. A concrete symptom was the ambiguity expressed by most of the radicals toward class solidarity with Arab labor and their failure (except in periods of economic collapse) to rouse Jewish workers to the cause of joint labor organization. On the whole, it could hardly have been otherwise, given the potentially unlimited supply of Arab labor able and willing to work for lower wages than the minimum Jewish requirement.

17. Two valuable sources in English on internal conflicts within the labor movement are Amos Perlmutter, "Ideology and Organization: The Politics of Socialistic Parties in Israel, 1897–1957" (Ph.D. dissertation, University of California, Berkeley, 1957), and Shapiro, *Formative Years.* Ishai, *Factionalism in the Labor Movement,* is the only detailed study of the most far-reaching prestate split, the breakaway of the so-called Faction B from Mapai in 1944.

Under these circumstances the de facto rule of Mapai officials over the labor exchanges and other Histadrut services placed the party apparatus in a powerful position vis-à-vis the vulnerable unskilled majority of the Jewish working class. But in its relationship with more privileged sections of the working class the party sanctioned a markedly accommodative policy in the Histadrut, which was reflected in extremely wide de facto wage differentials between skilled and unskilled workers and a regressive dues structure.

Political skill played an important part in reinforcing Mapai's inherent advantages. Embarrassing inequalities within the working class were masked by what Moshe Lissak describes as the labor movement's earnest cultivation of "the status symbols of a 'socialist workers culture.'"[18] Internally, though Mapai made very effective use of the substantial material resources under its control, the radicals at times had difficulty keeping their top leaders fed, let alone supporting lower-level cadres. On occasion Mapai (and its principal ancestor, Ahdut Avoda) acted with extreme ruthlessness, denying jobs, medical care, and sometimes even food to their rivals and challengers. And the ability of the Mapai elite to set the constitutional rules of the game in internal Histadrut and party affairs (or to ignore them altogether) was exploited to the hilt.

Beyond the advantages enjoyed by Mapai as a result of both the structural position of Jewish labor and the party's political skill, a good part of the dissidents' weakness was internal. The three major oppositional elements (kibbutzim, urban workers, and left radicals) had partially conflicting interests and objectives. Kibbutz socialism was communitarian, and the kibbutzim were the elitist vanguard of the labor movement's Zionist project, whereas the urban militants were essentially trade unionists committed to a populist struggle against the labor bureaucracy. The genuine radicals, precisely because their dissidence was imported rather than home-grown, failed to inspire either the rank and file or other left activists. The Jewish worker-settlers were for the most part repelled by the radicals' internationalism, their opposition to collaboration between the labor movement and the bourgeoisie in the world Zionist movement, and their strong cultural and organizational ties with Diaspora Jewry. Each of these orientations flagrantly contradicted the premises on which the ability of the labor movement to serve both individuals' instrumental needs and more lofty national goals depended.[19]

18. Moshe Lissak, "Strategies of Class Formation: The Case of the Labor Movement in the Jewish Community of Palestine, 1918–1948," in Erik Cohen, Moshe Lissak, and Uri Almagor, eds., *Comparative Social Dynamics: Essays in Honor of S. N. Eisenstadt* (Boulder, Colo.: Westview Press, 1985), pp. 245–61.

19. Giora Goldberg, "The Struggle for Legitimacy: Herut's Road from Opposition to Power," in Stuart Cohen and Eliezer Don-Yehiya, eds., *Conflict and Consensus in Jewish Political Life* (Ramat Gan: Bar-Ilan University Press, 1975), has studied the definitive case (the labor exchanges) of Mapai control of a resource materially crucial for workers. Shapiro, *Formative Years*, esp. pp. 118–19, provides considerable detail on the implications of Mapai's

The question remains of why Mapai's success in the 1930s, predicated as it was on the party's retreat from its laborist roots, failed to spawn a more effective opposition. Part of Mapai's rightward transition was a response to the shifting class structure of the Yishuv. From the mid-1920s on, both immigration and the economy altered in ways that enlarged the middle classes and strengthened the market at the expense of labor movement—sponsored economic collectivism. Mapai moved toward the middle ground to combat the double threat immanent in this development, of strengthening both the right and the left. On joining the Zionist Executive in 1933 Ben-Gurion, Mapai's leader, advocated that as he had done, the labor movement should subordinate itself (and the class interests of the workers, if necessary) to the good of the nation. Yet as Przeworksi[20] and other students of labor movement parties insist, there is usually a price to be paid, in the alienation of core supporters and weakening of the class consciousness on which labor solidarity feeds, when leftist parties seek an electoral majority by embracing cross-class appeals.

Specific conjunctural forces, appearing against the backdrop of the more enduring handicaps of the left, explain why Mapai succeeded in overcoming the predicted reaction. After 1934 the Palestinian economy entered a prolonged recession which gravely weakened the capacity of workers to pursue their class interests independently. At the same time, party figures at the apex of the Jewish Agency successfully trimmed the power of the Histadrut by shifting a number of its public functions into the agency's domain. The net effect was to narrow the capacity of Histadrut members and officials to challenge the new strategic drift. Finally, the Arab strike/revolt that broke out in 1936 and the rise of European anti-Semitism, which heightened tensions with the British over immigration quotas, invited Mapai to shift the center of political debate to the national plane. The party capitalized on these developments by formally escalating Zionism's political demands to encompass territorial independence. Just as it had done by reviving the Hebrew labor struggle in the preceding period, Mapai was able once again to shape and exploit the politics of nationalism to defend its hegemony.[21]

---

monopoly over patronage jobs for the radical opposition. On the material basis for Jewish-Arab estrangement in the labor market, see Shafir, *Land, Labour and the Origins,* and Shalev, "Jewish Organized Labor." The Histadrut's relationship with skilled workers is described by Sussman, "From a National to a Branch-Level." Documented instances of Mapai's repression of opposition groups may be found in Zeev Tsachor, "The Histadrut—The Formative Period" (in Hebrew) (Ph.D. dissertation, Hebrew University of Jerusalem, 1979), and Aharon Yitzhaki, " 'Ahdut Avoda' . . . as a Trade Union and 'Hevrat Ovdim' (1919–1926)" (in Hebrew) (Ph.D. dissertation, Hebrew University of Jerusalem, 1974). Elkana Margalit, *Anatomy of a Left [Movement]: Left Poale Zion in Palestine (1919–1946)* (in Hebrew) (Jerusalem: Hebrew University, 1976), is the most important source on the radical left.

20. Adam Przeworski, *Capitalism and Social Democracy* (Cambridge: Cambridge University Press, 1985).

21. On Ben-Gurion's ideological turnabout, see Shapiro, *Formative Years,* pp. 239ff. The beginnings of "nationalization" of quasi-state Histadrut functions are noted by Horowitz and Lissak, *Origins of the Israeli Polity,* p. 82.

The Transition to and from Sovereignty

In spite of the cataclysmic historical transitions that occurred in the course of four decades of Mapai rule—the Jews' transformation from an unwelcome minority to the majority in a sovereign state, four major wars, mass immigration, and rapid economic development and growth—Mapai's structure, ideology, and even office holders exhibited a marked degree of continuity. Nevertheless, Israel's creation in 1948 blunted several of Mapai's traditional assets and created significant new challenges and opportunities. The party's hegemony had already required renegotiation as a result of developments during World War II. Indeed, several of the most compelling issues Mapai faced after 1948 originated in wartime, in particular, the delayed formation of a modern working class and the growth not only of a modern economy but of one in which the labor movement itself was the largest investor and employer. Mapai dominance in the first decade of Israeli sovereignty must thus be viewed in the context of developments during the preceding decade.

Wartime Transformations

In Palestine, as in many other countries, the war ushered in a number of far-reaching changes in the structure and functioning of the political economy linked to industrial advance and the shift from a depressed to a full-employment economy. The growth of a Middle Eastern market closed off from traditional sources of imports, and above all the emergence of vigorous British demand for Palestinian goods and services to meet wartime needs, had by 1941 begun to pull the economy out of a six-year period of stagnation. Industry was transformed into the leading sector, and by war's end employed close to a third of the labor force (some 10 percent more than previously).

The Struggle for Working-Class Loyalty. Not only were there more industrial workers in the Yishuv, but they were more concentrated, both geographically and by enterprise, than before. An accumulation of grievances from the Depression period, the new conflicts engendered by rapid wartime expansion and inflation, and the enhancement of worker's bargaining power by labor shortages resulted in a turbulent period of grass-roots mobilization and militancy. Both plant-level workers' committees (shop stewards) and wildcat strikes mushroomed. Employers responded with a new readiness to deepen relations with the Histadrut in the enterprise; written collective agreements including union-administered fringe benefits became the norm. But the Histadrut and its political leaders were understandably fearful of institutionalizing labor relations solely at the workplace level because this could only reinforce the damage their authority had already suffered. They responded to rank-and-file activism by beefing up the traditionally negligible involvement and authority of central Histadrut organs in the field of wage bargaining. With the help of the government—now Jewish industry's most important client—the Histadrut and the Manufacturers' Association for the first time began to engage in economywide pay negotiations.

The emergence of a substantial new proletariat, often with no prior partisan commitment but considerable self-confidence because of prosperity and full employment, seriously threatened Mapai's standing among the mass public. The factions and parties of the left were much more supportive of labor militancy than Mapai, and their following among urban trade unionists spread. The kibbutz-based opposition was also strengthened politically by its custodianship of an elite strike force (the Palmach), which during the war became the leading arm of the Yishuv's expanding paramilitary activity. Against the background of continuing friction between the left and right over long-standing issues—class cooperation, the internal governance of the labor movement, and Palestine's political future—these developments prompted the leftist Faction B to secede formally from Mapai in 1944. Four years later, it became the major partner in a short-lived experiment in left unity, the Mapam party.[22]

Since the late 1930s Mapai had been actively strengthening its capacity to exploit the Histadrut as a means of attracting the growing number of politically uncommitted workers by stepped-up social provisions (benefits dependent directly on Histadrut membership and indirectly on political loyalty), attempts to centralize Histadrut trade union activity, and vigorous political competition with the left for control of workers' committees. Beyond the labor market arena, Mapai chose openly to endorse partition as its immediate political objective in the national struggle. The party's commitment to statehood even at the cost of territorial sacrifice enjoyed far broader appeal than the argument of the left-wing kibbutzim that partition would be premature because the settlements had not yet completed their mission of establishing a territorial and socialist infrastructure for the future Jewish state. Faction B and other left-wing groups did enjoy considerable success in mobilizing those Histadrut members who had not yet been drawn into Mapai's net, but their numbers were insufficient to upset Mapai's majority in the labor organization. Outside of the Histadrut, except in the kibbutzim

22. When Faction B left Mapai in 1944 it formed a new Ahdut Avoda, reviving the name of the party that had earlier (together with the more conservative Hapoel Hatsair) formed Mapai. The new Ahdut Avoda merged with Hashomer Hatsair (a Marxist but Zionist kibbutz-based party) to form Mapam in 1948, breaking away again in 1954 and then in 1969 merging with Mapai to form the Israel Labor party. In most elections since then the residual Mapam has participated in a joint electoral slate (the Labor Alignment) with the Israel Labor party.

the left made only weak electoral headway. In any case, its gains were offset by Mapai's stepped-up efforts to attract members of the middle strata such as artisans and small merchants.[23]

The Labor Movement Economy. Another wartime innovation that proved to be a harbinger of Mapai's future success was the Histadrut's expanding role in a rapidly modernizing and growing economy. At the time of the labor organization's foundation, Ben-Gurion had envisioned it as the epicenter of a tightly centralized network of cooperative enterprises on which both economic development and the settlement program of the Yishuv would rest. Instead, what became known as the labor economy became divided between two forms of economic enterprise, both relatively independent of central direction. One of these is a congeries of frameworks for collective self-employment (such as the kibbutzim or Israel's bus and truck cooperatives), which, in both ownership and control, are only loosely tied to the Histadrut. The other consists of corporations owned by the Histadrut but managed by salaried executives, who, though subject in some respects to political selection and guidance, from the outset behaved more or less like their private sector counterparts (except that profits, if any, were plowed back in their entirety rather than being distributed to shareholders, who in this case were nominally the entire Histadrut rank and file).

Even during the interwar period, there were sections of the Labor Economy (notably in transportation and mixed farming) which dominated their respective branches; and during big construction booms the Histadrut's contracting company was by far the largest employer in the industry. But before the war, both of the Palestine economy's most consistently expanding productive branches—manufacturing and citrus farming—had been almost exclusively in private hands. As a result of the hostilities, however, citrus exports were halted while manufacturing and large-scale construction each received a tremendous boost. Solel Boneh, the Histadrut building company, expanded rapidly and began to diversify into industry. Consequently, the Histadrut for the first time controlled an enterprise that was simultaneously a large-scale employer, a big profit maker, and a leading power in the most dynamic and "modern" sector of the economy.[24]

23. The primary source for this discussion of the political history of the 1940s was Perlmutter, "Ideology and Organization," esp. chap. 7. Mapai's tilt toward the middle classes is noted by Horowitz and Lissak, *Origins of the Israeli Polity,* pp. 88–89.

24. Ephraim Kleiman, "From Cooperative to Industrial Empire: The Story of Solel Boneh," *Midstream,* March 1964, pp. 15–26, and Yitzhak Greenberg, "From Workers' Society to Workers' Economy: Evolution of the Idea of Hevrat Ovdim in the Years 1920–1929" (in Hebrew) (Ph.D. dissertation, Tel Aviv University, 1983), trace the historical development of the Labor Economy; David Horowitz, *The Palestinian Economy in Development,* 2d ed. (in Hebrew) (Tel Aviv: Dvir for Mossad Bialik, 1948), pp. 30–34, 157–60, provides indications of its relative significance in various branches of the economy. For a more recent survey, see Ephraim Kleiman, "The Histadrut Economy of Israel: In Search of Criteria," *Jerusalem Quarterly,* no. 41 (1987): 77–94.

Important new political-economic opportunities followed. First, a major bloc of wage earners directly dependent on the Histadrut for employment constituted fertile ground for the recruitment of party activists and the instilling of mass loyalty. Second, a thriving enterprise could furnish the party with a generous fund of well-paid patronage jobs, as well as direct (but covert) financial subventions. Third, ownership of a large, rapidly growing concern situated on the forefront of the country's economic development implied a significant political capacity to steer the economy in general. Of course, each of these potential advantages for Mapai depended on its capacity to exert political control over the managers of Solel Boneh. Not surprisingly, the latter, although party appointees, were able to exploit the very potency of the resources under their control as a lever for gaining autonomy. But in return for the freedom to build up their economic power, Histadrut entrepreneurs were willing to yield at least partial access to the potential political benefits.

Sovereignty and the Reconstruction of the Labor Movement

The Histadrut was always a critical component of Mapai's political hegemony, particularly in mediating the bonds between individual workers and the party. The wartime developments just reviewed indicate that the centrality of the Histadrut became even more pronounced. The labor organization was home to an important new challenge to Mapai's dominance: the rise of rank-and-file mobilization, which threatened to split the working class into autonomous fragments unattached to the party or, worse still, under the sway of the left. At the same time, part of the Histadrut elite—the managers of its economic enterprises—was presiding over the rise of a Mapai-affiliated economic sector with weighty implications for political recruitment of the mass public and political management of the economy. The dilemmas associated with control of both the workers and the labor movement entrepreneurs intensified after 1948. But in addition, the first decade of sovereignty introduced several new challenges to Mapai dominance, for which the party also sought solutions via the Histadrut.

First, after 1948 the electorate grew dramatically and, more important, altered in composition. Mass immigration of Eastern (or Sephardi) Jews from North Africa and the Middle East and the enfranchisement of those Palestinian Arabs who remained within Israel's borders generated sizable blocs of voters lacking any a priori basis for identification with Mapai and with little a priori basis for developing such identification.[25] A second and

---

25. Just how sizable were these new groups? Data from the first labor force survey, in June 1954, indicate that of the 1 million voting-age persons in the country, 22 percent were new immigrants from Eastern countries (Asia and Africa), and another 8 percent were non-Jews. Thirty years later the comparable proportions had roughly doubled for Easterners (immigrants and their children) and had risen by over half for non-Jews.

more fundamental innovation derived directly from the attainment of sovereignty. Paradoxically, Mapai's very success in state building implied that the party's unique role in colonization and self-defense, and thus its indispensability for serving the perceived long-term interests of all social strata, was at an end. The role of the Histadrut in the post-1948 political economy is the key to the persistence of Mapai's dominance under these dramatically altered conditions.

Strengthening the Histadrut. After 1948 state authority was harnessed along a broad front to remedy the Histadrut's long-standing institutional lacunae as a would-be corporate peak association. During the Yishuv era, rival minority labor organizations and competition from Arab and unorganized Jewish labor had made it impossible for the Histadrut to achieve a representational monopoly. These obstacles were definitively removed by a mix of informal and statutory interventions. The state also proved to be a potent ally of Mapai's Histadrut chiefs in competition for workers' loyalty and struggles over trade union autonomy.[26]

Not only the structure but also the functions of the Histadrut were revised following the attainment of sovereignty. The major issue at stake was the division of labor between the Histadrut and the state proper vis-à-vis public functions previously in the domain of the labor organization. The motives and maneuvering involved in this process were complex, but, as Asher Arian has shown,[27] the overriding political logic is clear. Mapai forcibly "nationalized" those Histadrut responsibilities which had become important power bases for the left opposition (the Palmach military force and the labor school system), along with resources (such as the labor exchanges) which were likely to generate no less political payoff in a state than a "movement" framework. But the labor organization's social services and its affiliated economic enterprises were permitted to remain in the movement sphere and came to enjoy substantial informal privileges, on the understanding that they would continue to serve the needs of the party. Thus the Histadrut's Sick Fund was largely shielded from competition with either public health authorities or private organizations. Its ranks were swollen by granting automatic trial memberships to new immigrants, paid for by the Jewish Agency. The Histadrut's pension and provident funds were given free rein to expand by the social policy of the state, which deliberately circumscribed

26. The legal framework is reviewed by Arie Shirom, *Introduction to Labor Relations in Israel* (in Hebrew) (Tel Aviv: Am Oved, 1983). Yoram Ben-Porath, *The Arab Labor Force in Israel* (Jerusalem: Falk Institute, 1966), documents the treatment of Arab labor. The most dramatic instance of internal conflict occurred in 1952, when police and strikebreakers were used to end a bitter struggle for trade union autonomy by merchant seamen loosely associated with the rival Mapam party (Zvi Segal, "The Seamens Union, 1935–1953: From Local to National Union" (in Hebrew) [M.A. thesis, Tel Aviv University, 1976]).

27. Asher Arian, "Political and Administrative Aspects of Welfare Policy in Israel," research report submitted to the Ford Foundation (Israel Trustees), mimeo, Tel Aviv University, 1978.

potentially competitive public income-maintenance programs. Special exemptions from standard tax and investment requirements later turned these funds into an enormous source of cheap finance for the expansion of Histadrut-owned enterprises.[28]

Complementary to these interventions by the state, the party itself played an active role in subordinating a strengthened Histadrut to political ends. At the rank-and-file level, an aggressive and successful campaign was launched to undermine the standing of the left opposition among veteran rank-and-file workers and to preempt control of workers' committees formed to represent new immigrants. At the Histadrut center, the party supported reforms extending the centralization of the trade union function that had begun during the war. Mapai also acquired a major role in mediating and in some cases arbitrating between Histadrut and state elites on matters of national wages policy. Because Histadrut leaders were appointed by the party and the state was in a position to manipulate its regulation and subsidization of the labor organization's nonunion functions (economic enterprises, health care, and the like), the Histadrut cooperated in endorsing and policing wage restraint.[29]

Politicization and "corporatization" of the Histadrut fostered some important preconditions for the perpetuation of Mapai's rule. The Histadrut was encouraged, on one hand, to perform a mobilizing function by bringing the mass public into the labor movement's sphere of influence and furnishing instrumental dependencies and a political milieu in which their loyalty could be cultivated, and on the other hand, to act in its capacity as the country's premier organized interest association to legitimate Mapai's policies in government (especially those with distributive implications) and at times actively to rein in worker militancy in accordance with government stabilization policies.

The Role of Histadrut Enterprises. The Labor Economy was also called upon to contribute to the twin objectives of mass political mobilization and political management of the economy. Its role was accentuated by the dramatic expansion of Histadrut-affiliated corporations and collectives after 1948. By the late 1950s the Solel Boneh concern alone generated 8 percent

28. For research on the Histadrut Sick Fund and the relationship between Histadrut and state social services, see respectively Yair Zalmanovitch, "Histadrut, Kupat Holim, Government" (in Hebrew) (M.A. thesis, Haifa University, 1981), and Abraham Doron, "Development of National Insurance in Israel, 1948–1965" (in Hebrew) (Ph.D. dissertation, London School of Economics, 1967). On the Histadrut pension funds, see Marshall Sarnat, *Saving and Investment through Retirement Funds in Israel* (Jerusalem: Falk Institute, 1966).

29. Sources on the postindependence politicization of workers' committees and wages policy include Medding, *Mapai in Israel,* and Zvi Sussman, "The Wage Policy of the Histadrut: Its Effect on Israel's Economy," in Isiah Avrach and Dan Giladi, eds., *Labor and Society in Israel: A Selection of Studies* (Tel Aviv: Tel Aviv University and the Histadrut, 1973). Arie Shirom, "Comment on 'Political Parties and Democracy in the Histadrut,'" *Industrial Relations* 19 (1980): 231–37, has assembled evidence of the Histadrut's oligarchic internal regime.

of Israel's national income and the Labor Economy as a whole encompassed a quarter of all economically active citizens. As a result, fully half of all economically active Histadrut members were to some extent dependent on the labor organization for their livelihood. The Histadrut's economic activity had also experienced a number of quiet but far-reaching internal changes which further concentrated economic power in the large enterprises and their managers. The result was a bitter struggle, which climaxed in 1959, when the party decreed that Solel Boneh be split up into three subunits and removed its chief executive from office.

Within the shifting limits of party control over the Histadrut-owned business sector, it became enormously important to the postindependence regime of Mapai dominance.[30] The political loyalties of thousands of newcomers, mostly Easterners, were tied to their jobs (initially at a time of high unemployment) in Histadrut construction and industrial firms. As in the past, these enterprises also enriched the party with jobs and money. But the Labor Economy served deeper purposes as well; 1. by providing a realistic mechanism for politically managed economic development: 2. by simultaneously dividing and compensating the bourgeoisie proper: and 3. by easing the management of class conflict.

1. The role as a growth mechanism of the economic arm of the Histadrut was almost inevitable given the continued paucity of private entrepreneurial capital at home and the unattractiveness of Israel to foreign investors. The alternative possibility, to concentrate public economic initiative in state-owned enterprises, was barely considered. It would have entailed serious political risks, perhaps alienating American politicians and Jewish sympathizers abroad and upsetting the tradition of cordial relations between Mapai and the bourgeoisie at home. The Labor Economy constituted an attractive alternative to nationalized industries. Both aesthetic considerations (public corporations were inevitably subject to public scrutiny) and Mapai's commanding position in the Histadrut (which it controlled outright, being spared the power-sharing imperatives which the party faced in the parliamentary sphere) meant that it was easier to steer this form of public sector by political criteria and for partisan gain.

2. Mapai's implicit strategy vis-à-vis capital was one of divide and rule. Shimshon Bichler has shown that Histadrut enterprises and the larger private business interests both benefited from a political shareout of the principal means of accumulation (imported capital, "abandoned" Arab lands and property, official permits and concessions), all of which were under state control.[31] Mapai's key economic policy makers apparently recognized that exclusive nur-

30. This thesis was argued by a prominent Israeli journalist in the early 1960s in Yeshayahu Ben-Porat, "Control of the Labor Economy—the Key to Control of the State" (in Hebrew), *Yediot Aharonot*, a series of six articles published December 1963–January 1964. Data cited earlier on the growing scope of the labor economy were drawn from A. V. Sherman, "Power Politics in Israel's Economy," *New Leader*, September 22, 1958, pp. 14–16, and Margaret L. Plunkett, "The Histadrut: The General Federation of Jewish Labor in Israel," *Industrial and Labor Relations Review* 11 (1958): 155–82.

31. Shimshon Bichler, "Insights into the Tsena [Austerity] Period" (in Hebrew), unpublished seminar paper, Hebrew University of Jerusalem, 1985.

turing of the Histadrut sector would have upset the internal distribution of power within the party, while on the other hand, undue favoritism toward private capitalists would have hampered political control of the economy and provided the potential for an upsurge of the political right. The Labor Economy's very existence scotched any possibility of capital mobilizing solidaristically behind a single political movement. At the same time, the more significant private entrepreneurs were silenced politically by economic concessions, some of them distributed by the Labor Economy itself.

3. For many workers the Histadrut simultaneously wears the hats of union and boss, and this relationship has at times generated severe problems of internal coordination and external credibility. But another consequence of this unorthodox arrangement is that the labor organization has internalized the capitalist logic that profitability is the essential precondition for workers' gains. With this innate taste for labor restraint, as well as its excellent contacts (through the labor economy) with big business in other sectors, a two-headed Histadrut— though it can by no means ignore rank-and-file sentiment—makes an attractive partner for the state when public policy goes in search of wage moderation.[32]

The Mobilization of New Publics

The growth of the Labor Economy, and the various state and party interventions designed to strengthen external and internal political direction of the labor organization bore tangible (and measurable) fruit for Mapai at the polls. As late as the 1969 elections (the first for which appropriate published data are available), the vast majority of Histadrut members voted for the Labor Alignment, and they also contributed the vast majority of all Alignment votes. Voters' personal indebtedness for distributional advantages like housing and employment was evidently integral to the Histadrut's success in instilling political loyalty.[33]

32. Stephen Schecter, "Israeli Political and Economic Elites and Some Aspects of Their Relations" (Ph.D. dissertation, London School of Economics, 1972), has discussed the non-emergence of a debate over nationalization after 1948. The postsovereignty shareout and Mapai's role in the formation of Israel's capitalist class are the subject of Bichler's "Insights into the Tsena." Lev Grinberg, "The Jewish-Arab Drivers' Association Strike of 1931" (in Hebrew), unpublished paper, Department of Sociology, Tel Aviv University, 1986, has analyzed the role of Histadrut enterprises in the field of wage restraint.

33. Data compiled by Alan Arian, *The Choosing People: Voting Behavior in Israel* (Cleveland: Case Western Reserve University Press, 1973), Tables 5.1 and 5.2, suggested that just short of 80 percent of Histadrut members voted for the Labor Alignment and that the same proportion of alignment voters were Histadrut members. Paul Burstein, "Social Structure and Politics in Israel: Voting in the 1969 Israeli Elections" (Ph.D. dissertation, Harvard University, 1973), Tables 5.10 and 4.8, found that receipt of Histadrut aid in obtaining jobs or housing raised individuals' probability of voting for the Alignment by about one-third and that employment in Histadrut enterprises raised this probability by nearly half in comparison with private sector employees. Ecological data also support these inferences. See Airam Gonen and Shlomo Hasson, "The Use of Housing as a Spatio-political Measure: The Israeli Case," *Geoform* 14 (1983): 103–9, and Amiram Gonen, "A Geographical Analysis of the Elections in Jewish Urban Communities," in Dan Caspi, Abraham Diskin, and Emanuel Gutmann, eds., *The Roots of Begin's Success: The 1981 Israeli Elections* (New York: St. Martin's, 1984).

The Histadrut's activities in mobilizing the mass public were complementary to those of the party machine at the neighborhood level. In both cases Mapai's pull was greatest among newcomers of Eastern origin. There was a glaring discrepancy between Israel's official ideology of welcoming the Jews of North Africa and the Middle East after their centuries of "exile" from the Holy Land and a harsh reality of cultural prejudice and economic discrimination against Eastern Jews and their subjection to crude political manipulation for partisan gain. Despite these disappointments, most of the immigrants who poured into Israel from Morocco, Yemen, and other countries of the region during the first decade of statehood were relatively easily drawn into Mapai's sphere of influence. Sentiments of messianism associated with Israel's establishment and the Easterners' admiration for Ben-Gurion, the party's charismatic leader, played a part in forging this unlikely alliance. But even more important was the extreme vulnerability of most Eastern-origin newcomers, who arrived in Israel without independent means and had great difficulty in using either personal connections or collective action to influence the terms of their entry into Israel's economy and society.[34]

The Easterners formed the largest but not the only bloc of new voters on which Mapai's continuing electoral plurality depended after 1948; Arabs and the new Jewish middle classes also provided Mapai with badly needed support. In each of these cases, the party's pull—both its instrumental attractions and the mediating role played by the Histadrut—was different.

The post-1948 Arab minority had experienced a trauma of vast proportions. The combined effects of panic, expulsion, and new boundary lines rendered the non-Jewish population of the new state of Israel little more than one-tenth the size of the Arab community in all of Mandatory Palestine at the time of British withdrawal. Moreover, the losses included the Palestinian Arabs' most prominent strata and leadership figures in both the political and economic spheres. At the material level, the disaster was compounded by Israel's large-scale confiscation of land and water resources, combined with initially strict regulation of Arabs' entry to the Jewish economy as wage laborers. A political regime was established for the Arab sector which combined local administration and supervision by a military government with the freedom to vote in national elections. In the latter sphere, the Arabs were of some significance, constituting close to a tenth of all voters.

---

34. The evolution of local party bosses is traced by Yael Azmon, "Urban Patronage in Israel," in Cohen, Lissak, and Almagor, eds., *Comparative Social Dynamics*, pp. 284–94. The absorption of the Eastern newcomers is the subject of a large literature. For a vivid historian's reconstruction, see Tom Segev, *1949: The First Israelis* (New York: Free Press, 1986). Important theoretical and empirical work in a critical vein has been carried out by Deborah Bernstein, "Immigrants and Society—A Critical View of the Dominant School of Israeli Sociology," *British Journal of Sociology* 31 (1980): 246–64, and Deborah Bernstein and Shlomo Swirski, "The Rapid Economic Development of Israel and the Emergence of the Ethnic Division of Labor," *British Journal of Sociology* 33 (1982): 64–85.

Until the late 1950s, when economic and political pressures combined to undermine the viability of military rule, Mapai was well placed to capture the lion's share of these ballots. In the 1955 elections, for example, the party received only one-third of the Jewish vote. But in conjunction with nominally independent but actually subsidiary Arab slates, it garnered two-thirds of the votes cast in Arab localities.

In the 1960s, the Israel Labor party retained its Arab majority by a combination of co-optation, repression, and barter. But the policy of all Israeli governments has been to deny either a Palestinian or a pan-Arab national identity to the Arab minority and to impose restrictive, particularistic criteria on the distribution of public goods and services to Arab citizens and communities to sustain their political and economic subordination. The major vehicle for (largely symbolic) Arab opposition to these policies, aside from the option of nonvoting, has been the Communist party in its various incarnations. Beginning in 1961, both the Communist share of the Arab vote and the proportion of abstainers rose for five elections in a row. Nevertheless, until the 1970s Mapai/Labor and its associated Arab lists clung to their majority.

Typically, Arab loyalty to Mapai rested on the co-optation of local leaders, who were given effective powers to allocate privileges controlled by the military government. The system was most effective in small villages and other traditional and hierarchical communities but was supplemented by more "modern" forms of co-optation and exchange administered by the Arab departments of the Histadrut and central government ministries. In the background there were and still are powerful constraints on Arab-sector politics. By and large Arabs are dependent on Jews (or Jewish-controlled public institutions) to make a living. And Israel's security forces are responsible for extensive vetting, surveillance, and at times outright repression of Arab political activity.[35]

Mapai's success among Jewish voters in the middle strata and the bourgeoisie rested partly on positive incentives and partly on the political vacuum on the right caused by the party's co-optation of major producer groups. From the first systematic political opinion polls, it was evident that members of the higher strata were no different from all others in awarding Mapai a plurality of their vote. In fact, support for Mapai seemingly tended to rise with one's position in the class hierarchy. One reason was the success of rival parties in capturing elements of the working class: veteran Ashkenazim (Westerners) who supported the labor left, traditional-minded

---

35. The changed position of the Arab minority after 1948 has been documented by Charles S. Kayman, "After the Catastrophe I: The Arabs in Israel, 1948–1951," *Middle Eastern Studies* 23 (1987): 453–95, and 24 (1988): 68–109. Sabri Jiryis, *The Arabs in Israel* (New York: Monthly Review Press, 1976), and Ian Lustick, *Arabs in the Jewish State: Israel's Control of a National Minority* (Austin: University of Texas Press, 1980), provide comprehensive treatments of the politics of the Arabs in Israel. On the Histadrut's role, see Shalev, "Jewish Organized Labor."

workers among the new immigrants who favored religious parties, or Easterners who voted for the right-wing Herut party in protest against their
treatment by the Mapai establishment. Nevertheless, Mapai's relative success among the middle and upper strata was not only an artifact of its
incomplete capture of lower-class voters. The willingness of many professionals, managers, and businessmen to vote Mapai was striking, especially
in light of their antipathy toward the labor movement's economic ideology.

To some extent this paradox is attributable to the ruling party's generosity toward what Henry Rosenfeld and Shulamit Carmi have aptly described as the "state-made middle class"—entrepreneurs and middlemen
who made their fortunes through government concessions and subsidies, as
well as the vast salariat of clerical and professional workers in public employ.[36] Most of this upward mobility affected veterans of the prestate era,
many of whom retained an emotional attachment to the labor movement
and expressed appreciation for their good fortune by remaining loyal to
Mapai. The traditional middle class and notably the self-employed, however, tended to favor the General Zionists (later, Liberals) or Herut, the two
parties that began running together in the 1965 elections and later formed
the Likud alliance.[37]

The Constraints on Opposition Parties

The inability of Mapai's opponents (on both left and right) seriously to
challenge its hegemony persisted after 1948, and for essentially the same
reasons.

On the left, Mapai's major challengers (Mapam and Ahdut Avoda) typically gained only one-third as many Knesset seats as Mapai, and always less
than half. They were thus unable to participate in government except on
terms acceptable to Mapai. The opposition was stronger in the Histadrut,
but it played an ambiguous role there, organizing rank-and-file militancy
yet at the same time participating as junior partners in the Histadrut "cabinet." Both the strength of Mapai and the Zionist left's internal weaknesses
stymied its potential to take over the labor movement and thus the state,
rather than (its ultimate fate) to be marginalized within both.

36. Henry Rosenfeld and Shulamit Carmi, "The Privatization of Public Means, the State-
Made Middle Class, and the Realization of Family Value in Israel," in J. G. Peristiany, ed.,
Kinship and Modernization in Mediterranean Society (Rome: Center for Mediterranean Stud-
ies, 1976), pp. 131–59.

37. For the first scholarly survey to demonstrate the upside-down class basis of Mapai's
mass support, see Aron Antonovsky, "Classification of Forms, Political Ideologies, and the
Man in the Street," *Public Opinion Quarterly* 30 (1966): 109–19. A series of surveys carried
out under labor movement auspices by Michael Lotan, "Public Opinion Studies prior to the
Histadrut and Knesset Elections of 1965" (in Hebrew), *Avanim*, no. 6 (1966): 141–60, demonstrated that Mapai was perceived by the electorate as relatively neutral toward all of the
major strata (except state employees). The continued attachment of upwardly mobile veterans
to Mapai was studied by Avraham Zloczower, "Occupation, Mobility and Social Class,"
Social Science Information 11 (1972): 329–58.

The opposition faced a formidable opponent. Mapai, and specifically its longtime leader Ben-Gurion, did not hesitate to exercise the prerogatives of the state to undermine the power bases of the left. The nationalization of former Histadrut functions and Mapai's successful struggle to regain control of renegade national unions and workplace shop committees have already been noted. In the same vein, during a period of intense ideological dispute in the kibbutz movement during the early poststate years, Mapai encouraged a formal split that followed party lines. In national politics the retreat of the left was signaled when intense struggle and cooperation with Mapai gave way to participation in government, electoral collaboration, and ultimately actual or virtual mergers.

Certainly the left suffered from its own liabilities as well. The perennial tension between moderates and radicals was brought to almost unbearable heights by the Cold War and growing ambiguities in the Soviet Union's stance toward Israel and the treatment of Jews in the Eastern bloc. In addition, the contradictions of the marriage between the urban and kibbutz components of Mapam and Ahdut Avoda continued to haunt these parties. Important sections of the kibbutzim brought to the marriage hawkish instincts inherited from the heroic era of settlement and statemaking which conflicted with the left's commitment to external and internal Arab-Jewish coexistence. Dovishness suffered not only from contradictory ideologies but also from the status of the kibbutzim as major recipients of abandoned or confiscated Arab land. At times urban and kibbutz activists took conflicting positions which reflected their differing material objectives—high wages and high agricultural subsidies, respectively.

After a promising start, the Communists fared even worse than Mapai's immediate rivals within the Labor Zionist camp. In Israel's first three Knesset elections Maki (the Communist party of Israel), with two-thirds Jewish voters and the other third Arab, enjoyed an expanding share of the vote, approaching 5 percent in 1955. Subsequently, however, Jewish support fell off, and by 1965 separate Jewish and Arab parties were officially constituted. Research in progress by Stanford historian Joel Beinin has uncovered new evidence for the early postsovereignty years of Maki's significant appeal among Jewish voters and the readiness of the Arab party leadership to come to terms with the state of Israel. Nevertheless, the nationalist sentiment aroused (to some extent deliberately, by Mapai leaders) before and following the 1956 Sinai campaign tarred Maki with a rabidly anti-Zionist appearance in the eyes of the Jewish public and provoked disenchantment among many of the party's Jewish activists. Growing disparity between Jewish and Arab feeling toward the Soviet Union further reinforced this divide. Disappointment in the early 1960s with the failure of the new and increasingly militant Jewish working class (the Eastern immigrants) to respond to Communist appeals put an end to the remaining Arab interest in binational activity. Since the mid-1970s radical politics (radical in relation to both national and class questions) have been the preserve only of fringe groups in the Jewish sector.

Meanwhile, the Communist party (in various incarnations) has continued to function primarily as an expression of protest against feelings of discrimination and frustrated national identity which are widespread among Arab citizens. Its appeal is greatest in Israeli-Arab communities relatively free from either the bonds of traditional clan-based politics or dependence on Jewish-controlled political and bureaucratic apparatuses.[38] Supported by the Jewish consensus that despite its legality and Knesset representation the Communist party is by definition anti-Zionist and bordering on treasonous, the authorities and the Zionist parties actively oppose its influence. An important consequence of this delegitimation is that the Communists are unable to offer their supporters access to the state-controlled budgets, permits, and public services vital to the well-being of Arab communities, which have thus far been mediated exclusively by Mapai and other governing parties.[39]

It is clear, then, that sovereignty and its aftermath failed to eliminate— and indeed actually reinforced—the suffusion of left politics by the logic of the national conflict. Mapai's immediate rivals on the left were gradually absorbed into today's Labor Alignment, while the radicals fractured into an insignificant Jewish and a large but isolated Arab wing. In contrast, since 1948 the political right has experienced growing unity and strength. Nevertheless, the right suffered from profound disabilities during the first two decades of Israeli sovereignty. In part, these difficulties were no more than the mirror image of the labor movement's success in claiming ideological provenance over the transition to statehood. The new Herut (Freedom) party, a synthesis of older Revisionist political elements and one of the terrorist undergrounds of the presovereignty period, was portrayed by Mapai as a radical movement which had jeopardized the struggle for independence and now endangered Israeli democracy. Indeed, some observers regard Mapai's delegitimation of Herut and its leader, Menachem Begin, as the exclusive determinant of right-wing defeat. This is an exaggerated view and cannot account for an equally significant cause of right-wing weakness, namely the failure of the more respectable (and electorally more significant)

---

38. Tellingly, the establishment of local labor councils (mini-Histadruts) in Arab localities provides a particularly favorable basis for the growth of Communist political influence, a correlation which, once it became noticed by the Labor party, resulted in a policy reversal in favor of annexing Arab localities to existing councils in Jewish areas. See Shalev, "Jewish Organized Labor."

39. As Nadim Rouhana, "Collective Identity and Arab Voting Patterns," in Ashner Arian and Michal Shamir, eds., *The Elections in Israel—1984* (Tel Aviv: Ramot, 1986), pp. 121–49, surmises, this was an important reason for the emergence in the 1984 elections of a new Arab-oriented party which tried unsuccessfully to build bridges to Jewish-controlled resources while adopting a radical (in Jewish eyes) position on the national conflict.

"liberal" parties of the right to challenge Mapai's political hegemony.[40]

Developments in the political economy appear to be of greater relevance in this connection. Before 1948 private capital, however internally divided in its interests, had provided most of the output and employment in the Yishuv economy. But after Israel's creation capitalist immigration dried up, and almost the whole of the inflow of foreign capital, which continued to be indispensable both for bridging the trade deficit and financing economic development, acquired the form of gifts to the Israeli government from foreign states and Jewish communities. Finally, private agriculture—a pivotal branch of the economy for most of the interwar period—was now dwarfed by state-supported collective and cooperative farming. Theoretically, private industrialists and the not insignificant petit bourgeoisie might nevertheless have mobilized as a serious counterforce to Mapai in either pressure-group or party politics. In practice, however, the Manufacturers' Association remained organizationally weak and tangential to public policy making. The association and major individual businessmen were content to advance their economic interests informally within the political status quo, working in cooperation with Mapai politicians, bureaucrats, and labor economy executives. In the party arena, both the voters and leaders of the Liberals and (to a lesser extent) Herut were indeed closely identified with business interests and the petit bourgeoisie. But here again, just as with the left opposition, Mapai used its assets to great advantage. It helped divide Herut and the Liberals by pursuing opposite strategies toward them, of exclusion and inclusion, respectively. The Liberals were offered cabinet portfolios, and major businessmen active in the party or close to it were granted generous state aid.

On a related front, Mapai successfully combined its proven talent for political organization with its unique capacity to direct distributional flows through the state so as to co-opt each of the interest groups that might have turned into economic bases of right-wing political mobilization: farmers, the self-employed, and the new middle class. In a classic case, Mapai captured the national organization of self-employed artisans by granting them favorable access to the politicians and officials whose decisions determined

---

40. On the thesis of Herut's "delegitimation," see the divergent views of Ariel Levite and Sidney Tarrow, "The Legitimation of Excluded Parties in Dominant Party Systems: The Cases of Israel and Italy," *Comparative Politics* 15 (1983): 295–327, and Peter Y. Medding, "The Founding of Israeli Democracy: Parties, Politics and Government," unpublished manuscript, Department of Political Science, Hebrew University of Jerusalem. As for the "liberal" right, in the first five Knesset elections (1949–61) the probusiness General Zionist (later Liberal) party gained an average of 13 seats (out of a total of 120) compared with 14 for Herut, 17 for Mapam (including Ahdut Avoda), and 17 for the religious parties. The Progressive (later Independent Liberal) party, which was ideologically and politically closer than the Liberals to Mapai, contested four of these same five elections, gaining from 4 to 6 seats. Had there been a combined liberal bloc, it would thus have been larger than any of the three other opposition groupings.

the artisans' economic fate. The party's strength in agriculture did not necessitate the takeover of an existing organization. The very creation of the rapidly proliferating collective sector was presided over by party officials (usually from Mapai), and it was heavily dependent on party-regulated access to land, water, credit, and marketing.

Both the mediation of vital economic interests and exposure to an intensely partisan milieu were more difficult to achieve in relation to a third potential constituency of the right, the rapidly growing salaried managerial and professional class. The professionals—most of them state employees—were particularly troublesome to Mapai because their jobs were less politicized and their labor market position was stronger than any other section of the work force. Nevertheless, despite a series of celebrated revolts against Histadrut wage policies, the university-educated workers failed to erect an independent associational structure on which political opposition to Mapai might have rested. With the support of the government, following independence the Histadrut waged a successful campaign to stymie autonomous professional organization, and to this day nearly all of the relevant associations remain within the Histadrut fold.[41]

The Renegotiated Hegemony

The new regime of dominance that Mapai constructed in the postsovereignty era rested above all on the Histadrut's role as handmaiden to the party/government in managing the political economy, attracting new constituencies, and denying footholds to the opposition. The success of each one of these strategies, it must be stressed, was in large part contingent upon Mapai's remarkable ability to exert political direction of economic processes. This is equally true of the party's capacity to harvest the political fruits of the labor economy, its success in co-opting middle-class organizations, and the effective use of instrumental incentives to attract individual voters to Mapai. Although the literature on Israeli politics in the era of labor movement dominance has widely recognized the importance of, in effect, vote-buying among citizens who had few alternatives, there has been less appreciation of the political significance of Mapai's ability to structure economic development and thus also social stratification.

Political control of the economy in this sense was the precondition for

---

41. For evidence of the direct role of the right-wing parties in representing the business sector, see Moshe M. Czudnowski, "Legislative Recruitment under Proportional Representation in Israel: A Model and a Case Study," *Midwest Journal of Political Science* 14 (1970): 21–248, and Czudnowski, "Sociocultural Variables and Legislative Recruitment: Some Theoretical Observations and a Case Study," *Comparative Politics* 4 (1972): 561–87. Mapai's relationship with the three nonworker strata mentioned in the text, as of the 1960s, is well documented by Medding, *Mapai in Israel*. Joseph Ben-David, "Professionals and Unions in Israel," *Industrial Relations* 5 (1965): 48–66, reviewed the Histadrut's incorporation of professional unions after sovereignty.

forming instrumental ties between the ruling party and voters from many different strata. The capacity of the state as an employer and its effective command over profitability in the business sector (through control over land, credit, and exchange rates, as well as direct capital subsidy) laid the foundations for Mapai's success among the new middle strata, as well as for the support it enjoyed among privately owned big business. With respect to the new immigrants, Mapai's capacity to build up relations of dependency going far beyond the mere purchase of votes was very clear. Party-directed public bureaucracies kept newcomers out of the labor market at the initial stages, directed them into employment in party-controlled public and Histadrut enterprises, and created agricultural and urban settlements of immigrants from the ground up with built-in party mediation of life chances.

The emergence of an enormously interventionist state in the postsovereignty period has usually been attributed to the necessities of the hour (mass immigration and defense), the relative wealth of the state as a result of gifts from abroad, and the limited scale of private investment. But political control over the economy must in addition be recognized as a strategy for maintaining one-party dominance. It follows that, as I will argue at the close of this essay, the erosion of political control provides a powerful explanation for Mapai/Labor's eventual fall from power.

The Unraveling of One-Party Dominance

In the course of three elections—in 1969, 1973, and 1977—the number of seats in the 120-member Knesset held by the Labor Alignment (including its Arab satellites) plummeted from 60 to 54 to 33. Concurrently, the number gained by the Likud (or its predecessor, Gahal) rose from 26 to 39 to 45. Evidently, by 1977, when Labor was forced to leave office, the right had already made its major gains. Labor's fate was sealed by the ephemeral appearance of the Democratic Movement for Change (DMC), a new party that succeeded in winning 15 Knesset seats in 1977.

These remarkable electoral swings of the 1970s serve as a dramatic reminder that a dominant party—to borrow Maurice Duverger's widely quoted dictum—"bears within itself the seeds of its own destruction."[42] Such seeds of destruction can be identified in the Israeli setting. First, mass publics recruited to Mapai as indifferent or reluctant supporters ceased to vote Labor once they acquired personal and political choices. Second, the viability of the Histadrut as a mobilizer, legitimator, and political-economic instrument was undermined by rank-and-file alienation, friction between party leaders in the Histadrut and government arenas, and the growing independence of labor economy managers. And third, in the business sector

42. Duverger, *Political Parties*, p. 312.

at large, in no small measure because of the effects of public policy, big business grew and solidified and the government's capacity to control the economy according to political criteria was impaired. In other words, the very bulwarks of Mapai's strength in an earlier epoch—its capacity to form dependency ties with economically less advantaged voters, its reliance on the Histadrut, and its nurturing of the statemade middle class—ceased to be effective or even became counterproductive.

This interpretation of Israel's political upheaval is not offered as a self-sufficient alternative to the innumerable hypotheses in the voluminous literature on the subject of Mapai/Labor's fall from power.[43] Rather, the purpose is to draw attention to explanations that are marginal to or absent from this literature yet have powerful theoretical and historical resonance. Specifically, just as the nexus between politics/the state and markets/the economy has been largely foreign to scholarly analysis of Mapai's climb to hegemony, so it is that the triumph of right over left in Israel has been understood almost exclusively in terms of three explanatory domains: the dynamics of parties and party elites, the political culture of voters, or the interface between domestic politics and the Arab-Israeli conflict. A brief review of this work will place my interpretation in context and sketch the broader context of Mapai's decline.

Party Dynamics. This is the story of Mapai's internal decomposition and, conversely, the creation (or in Herut's case, rehabilitation) of a credible alternative to Mapai rule. Party figures in the government lost their sensitivity to public opinion and grass-roots political trends and as a result were taken by surprise by protest movements that created a new extraparliamentary political arena free of party control. At the same time, the party's oligarchic mode of self-governance became intolerable even to its own functionaries and activists, and prominent leaders became publicly tainted with corruption.[44]

These processes reflect what is commonly called the arrogance of power, a thesis which in essence lays the blame on the party leadership. Other commentators have suggested that Mapai/Labor suffered from structural strains which sooner or later were bound to take their toll.[45] Among such strains were the succession crisis and failures of leadership resulting from the contrasting objectives and abilities of the labor movement's founding fathers and their sons; the declining ideological and organizational coherence which resulted from the alliances Mapai had to endure to remain in power (including, during the late 1960s, a "unity" government with the right); and long-standing contradictions between the party's four great

43. For representative illustrations of the literature on the upheaval, see the series of *Elections in Israel* volumes edited by Asher Arian.

44. Myron J. Aronoff, *Power and Ritual in the Israeli Labor Party: A Study in Political Anthropology* (Amsterdam: van Gorcum, 1977).

45. Shapiro, *Elite without Successors.*

power bases—the agricultural collectives, the military, the Histadrut, and the urban machine.

Concurrent with Mapai's degeneration from within, the right-wing opposition engineered a successful course of regeneration.[46] Beginning in the mid-1950s, Menachem Begin and his allies in the Herut party gradually and systematically set about forging political alliances and repairing Herut's public image as an extremist single-issue party. The result was a successful electoral alliance with the probusiness Liberal party and recognition from Mapai itself of the right as worthy of a legitimate role in government. Later, following the nearly disastrous Yom Kippur War, a coalition of figures on the periphery of the political elite joined forces to create the DMC, the centrist party that proved so costly to Labor in the critical 1977 elections.[47]

Political Culture. Opinion poll analysts in particular are prone to argue that changes in the composition and orientation of the electorate shifted Israel's dominant political culture to the right without any corresponding adjustment by the dominant party.[48] From this perspective Labor's decline was at root the result of demographic shifts that increased the numbers of voters who tend to be sympathetic toward the right and antagonistic to the left—young and Eastern-origin Jews. Ethnic polarization of the vote has been culturally explained in diverse ways—Easterners are more traditional and religious than Western Jews, they hold more hawkish positions on issues relating to security and the national conflict, and they are allegedly less committed to liberal democracy and more vulnerable to demagogy. The Sabra (Israeli-born) generation lacks the memories that still bind their parents to Mapai, instead perceiving the labor movement as corrupt, oppressive, and outdated. In particular, Sabras have a tendency to reject the labor movement's collectivist values in favor of market individualism and to prefer a hard line to compromise on defense matters.

The National Conflict. A third and more novel approach to explaining partisan realignment in Israel starts from the assumption that the "external" conflict decisively structures the parameters of "internal" politics.[49]

46. Goldberg, "Struggle for Legitimacy."
47. Nachman Orieli and Amnon Barzilai, *The Rise and Fall of the DMC* (in Hebrew) (Tel Aviv: Reshafim, 1982).
48. As Seymour Martin Lipset, "Review of *Political Change in Israel*," *Contemporary Sociology* 8 (1979): 381–84, points out, Eva Etzioni-Halevy and Rina Shapira, in *Political Culture in Israel: Cleavage and Integration among Israeli Jews* (New York: Praeger, 1977), enjoy the unusual distinction of having in effect predicted the change of government in 1977 before the event. Michal Shamir, "Realignment in the Israeli Party System," in Arian and Shamir, eds., *The Elections in Israel—1984*, pp. 267–96, is a definitive contribution in this genre which has updated and refined their analysis.
49. Gershon Shafir, "Changing Nationalism and Israel's 'Open Frontier' on the West Bank," *Theory and Society* 13 (1984): 803–27; Baruch Kimmerling, *Zionism and Territory: The Socio-Territorial Dimensions of Zionist Politics* (Berkeley: Institute of International Studies, University of California, 1983).

Concretely, the conquest of new and symbolically highly charged territory in the June 1967 Israeli-Arab war reopened divisive issues concerning the fundamental character of Zionism and the concrete problem of security. Both the agenda and the center of gravity of political debate shifted. The right easily fell heir to the very elements which in the prestate context had succored Mapai's ideological dominance—nationalism, militarism, messianism, and settlement. Moreover, because the identity of the Sabra generation, which now led the labor movement, was so bound up in the presovereignty project of territorial and political conquest, it lent de facto support to the project of the right. Consequently, whereas in the past Mapai had been notably successful in shaping and exploiting Jewish nationalism for its own political benefit, after 1967 Labor reacted ambiguously to the occupation and as a result lost support from both the war-weary middle class and nationalists pressing for annexation.

My purpose is not to adjudicate between these differing explanations of the decomposition of Mapai hegemony but to complement them with two different directions of analysis. As well as being on top of key political issues and operating with internal coherence and effectiveness, dominant parties also need to be able to attract large blocs of voters. The insight that dominance rests on the micromobilization of the citizens is incomplete if it fails to recognize the role of economic interests in voters' behavior and that, particularly in the Israeli context, such interests may be masked by political-cultural differences. From a macro perspective, the dominant party must manage the economy effectively; ideally, it must satisfy capital, the mass public, and the party's own interests. The conventional wisdom regarding Mapai's rise and fall has largely ignored this requirement. There are several grounds for arguing that the party's eroding political control over the economy was at the heart of its diminishing capacity to rule.

Who Stopped Voting for Mapai and Why?

By examining studies of voters' behavior carried out at the very peak of Mapai's hegemony, it is possible in retrospect to discover clear pointers to the future erosion of the party's mass support. Inquiries carried out in the 1960s support the hypothesis that substantial numbers of voters chose Mapai reluctantly, under personal pressure or because no existing party embodied their aspirations, or they preferred not to vote at all. Aaron Antonovsky's pioneering study of mass political attitudes among Jewish Israelis showed that a sizable minority of Mapai's own voters (particularly the younger generation and those of Eastern origin) were more hawkish than Mapai on security issues.[50] An even wider gap separated the party

---

50. Aaron Antonovsky, "Socio-Political Attitudes in Israel" (in Hebrew), *Amot* 6 (1963): 11–22; Antonovsky, "Ideology and Class in Israel" (in Hebrew), *Amot* 7 (1963): 21–28.

from its supporters on the question of Histadrut's involvement in the economy, particularly among managers and professionals. On the other side of the socioeconomic divide, many of those in the overlapping categories of Eastern ethnicity and lower class position shunned the existing parties and the prevailing ideological discourse altogether (although some may have cast votes for Mapai anyway). Research repeatedly pointed to the above-average proclivity of Eastern voters toward Herut. The decline of personal dependency on Mapai's bounties and the emergence of credible vehicles for frustrated constituencies were preconditions for the mobilization of disaffected groups behind opposition parties. Thus in 1977 large numbers of former Labor voters of Eastern origin voted for Likud, and masses of young and/or middle-class Jews of European origin deserted to the DMC.[51] A further, less remarked-upon source of Mapai's electoral decline occurred among Arab citizens, who in both 1973 and 1977 decreased their support of Labor and its associated "Arab lists," mostly in favor of the Communist party.

Of the three readily identifiable blocs of voters whose abandonment of Labor had such disastrous consequences for the party in 1977 (cutting its share of the popular vote to only one-fifth), the loss of Eastern Jewish supporters merits the greatest attention because it made the most critical and durable contribution to Mapai's disqualification as a dominant party. As the 1988 elections made explicit, the non-Labor Arab vote is largely divided among parties willing to throw their parliamentary support behind Labor providing only that the latter can muster sufficient strength to block a nationalist-clerical coalition. Ashkenazim largely returned to the Labor party after the speedy demise of the DMC, which began the moment the party had to decide whether to join a Likud government.

On the basis of the number of voters the Labor Alignment would have netted in 1977 if it had maintained its 1969 share of the electorate, it may be estimated that close to one-fifth of the party's losses were Arabs. The Arab vote swing appears to have resulted in part from the expression at the polls of a rising Palestinian consciousness, especially after the Land Day protest in 1976. But it also reflects inroads into traditional party patronage which resulted from Arab citizens' increasing affluence and education and the political experience and self-confidence acquired in Arab communities in the course of the transition from military rule to a measure of local self-government. The result was the breakdown of clan-based patronage politics

---

51. These swings are evident in both survey and ecological data. See respectively, Shamir, "Realignment in the Israeli Party System," and Avraham Diskin, "The 1977 Interparty Distances: A Three-Level Analysis," in Asher Arian, ed., *The Elections in Israel—1977* (Jerusalem: Jerusalem Academic Press, 1980), pp. 213–29. Evidence for an "ethnic vote" before the 1977 elections was not confined to Antonovsky's work. See also Judah Matras, *Social Change in Israel* (Chicago: Aldine, 1965), and Moshe Lissak, *Social Mobility in Israel Society* (Jerusalem: Israel Universities Press, 1969).

and rising Arab demands for more tangible and widely distributed rewards and benefits in return for their votes.[52]

The Democratic Movement for Change gave voice to a variety of political frustrations among its almost exclusively middle-class and Ashkenazi constituency. It also captured displeasure at sharp tax increases coupled with government resistance to pay increases in the public sector in the first few years after the oil crisis. In more strategic terms, the emergence of the DMC represented the continuation of a debate that had been going on since at least 1948 over the status of the Histadrut. Most DMC supporters rejected the Mapai tradition of mobilizing voters through the Histadrut and relying on Histadrut enterprises for political management of the economy. Instead, they favored a self-serving program of economic liberalization: not necessarily a smaller public sector, but more freedom for Histadrut and public managers to behave like capitalists and more independence for professional workers and their unions coupled with greater reliance on market criteria in determining occupational rewards.[53]

The Sephardi Vote Swing. Jews of Eastern origin were the most critically endangered Labor constituency in 1977. The Likud's share of the two big parties' Eastern voters doubled, and the Eastern vote has remained heavily pro-Likud in the 1980s. Signs of this dramatic switch first appeared in the 1965 elections and at the beginning were confined mainly to the more established cities and members of the Israeli-born generation. But by 1977 there was no longer a single "Oriental" locality in which Labor voters outnumbered Likud supporters, and opinion polls showed that only one-third of those Eastern voters (whether immigrants or their children) who voted for the two major parties continued to support the Labor Alignment. The corresponding figure had been close to 80 percent before the 1969 elections.

A diverse set of competing hypotheses purport to explain the Easterners' estrangement from Labor. The Likud's growing attraction has most often been attributed either to the relative hawkishness and other supposed features of the Easterners' mentality or to anger at cultural and economic blows suffered at the time of their arrival in Israel.[54] Both of these explana-

52. Published empirical research on the Arab vote is much less extensive than for Israel's Jewish electorate (for instance, they are routinely left out of opinion polls). Moreover, much of what passes for research on this subject is self-serving and ideologically biased. The interpretation suggested here is consistent with recent work by Rouhana, "Collective Identity."

53. Basic information on the DMC and its supporters is found in Asher Arian, "The Israeli Electorate, 1977," in Arian, *The Election in Israel, 1977* (Jerusalem: Jerusalem Academic Press, 1980), pp. 253–76. The role of government wage and tax policies in galvanizing the DMC electorate is explored in a research paper cited by Asher Arian, *Politics in Israel: The Second Generation* (Chatham, N.J.: Chatham House, 1985), p. 44n.

54. For data on the vote swing among Eastern Jews, see Gonen, "Geographical Analysis," Table 3, and Shamir, "Realignment in the Israeli Party System," Table 1. Michal Shamir and Asher Arian, "The Ethnic Vote in Israel's 1981 Elections," *Electoral Studies* 1 (1982): 315–31, and Shamir "Realignment in the Israel Party System," review and attempt to assess (within the limits of opinion poll data) various interpretations of the phenomenon.

tions play down the possible role of persistent economic inequalities and conflicts of interest in Israeli society. Partly as a result of continued East-West gaps in educational opportunity, ethnic occupational differences and Ashkenazi advantage in the labor market have remained robust, possibly even sharpening among the younger generation. And the economic disadvantages of Easterners in production are often reinforced by their position in consumption, particularly housing. The ethnic grievances of the Easterners are thus, in part, class grievances in disguise. Yet two questions remain open: why the Likud and why in 1977?

Easterners' attraction to the Likud is partly the mirror image of their revulsion toward Labor—the party that (with the Histadrut) presided over the creation and reproduction of an ethnic division of labor. But employment-related interests also help explain the Likud's positive attraction to Eastern voters. First, the party openly supports the interests of the class of small businessmen and the self-employed to which many Easterners have aspired to rise. Second, the Likud's hawkish insistence on retaining the occupied territories and its commitment to the continued marginality of Israel's Arab citizens are of considerable economic significance for many Easterners. Though ethnic relativities among Jews persist, since the Six-Day War the Sephardim have nevertheless experienced several forms of absolute upward mobility: movement into cleaner and more secure jobs as wage earners or into self-employment. An important factor facilitating this mobility was the availability of cheap and relatively powerless Palestinian labor from the occupied territories, for these workers often took over jobs formerly assigned to Eastern Jews or went to work for those who entered self-employment.[55]

The question of timing—why the Easterners' flight from Labor did not become serious until the late 1960s and peaked in 1977—also cannot be

---

55. On the persistence of ethnic inequality among Jews, see the research on trends in the socioeconomic "ethnic gap" carried out by Yaakov Nahon, "Ethnic Gaps—A Longitudinal Portrait," in Naama Cohen and Ora Ahimeir, eds., *New Directions in the Study of the Ethnic Problem* (in Hebrew) (Jerusalem: Jerusalem Institute for Israel Studies, 1984), pp. 23–43. On the role of consumption cleavages, note that housing density (inhabitants per room) has been found to correlate more strongly with the ethnic vote than occupation, income, or education. See Gadi Yatziv, "The Class Basis of Party Affiliation" (in Hebrew) (Ph.D. dissertation, Hebrew University of Jerusalem, 1974); Shamir and Arian, "Ethnic Vote." See also Shlomo Hasson, "Social Differentiation among Public Housing Projects in Israel," *Geografiska Annaler* 65 (1983): pp. 95–103, for a penetrating analysis of "housing classes" among Sephardim. The thesis that ethnic gaps reflect class inequalities is most closely associated with the work of Shlomo Swirski. See his article "The Oriental Jews in Israel," *Dissent* 77 (Winter 1984): 99. On the significance of self-employment for Easterners' class position, see Emmanuel Farjoun, "Class Divisions in Israeli Society," *Khamsin* (London), no. 10 (1983): 29–39, and Ephraim Yaar (Yuchtman), "Economic Entrepreneurship as a Socioeconomic Mobility Route: Another Aspect of Ethnic Stratification in Israel" (in Hebrew), *Megamot* 29 (1986): 393–412. The implications of the entry of noncitizen Palestinians into the Israeli labor market have been discussed by Avishai Ehrlich, "The Oriental Support for Begin—A Critique of Farjoun," *Khamsin* (London), no. 10 (1983): 42–46, and Moshe Semyonov and Noah Lewin-Epstein, *Hewers of Wood and Drawers of Water: Noncitizen Arabs in the Israeli Labor Market* (Ithaca: ILR Press, 1987).

fully answered without reference to voters' material interests. Growing access to alternatives to Histadrut or government-provided employment and the widening scope for individual advancement in a rapidly growing economy gradually liberated formerly helpless immigrants from dependence on party-mediated jobs, housing, and social services. The shifting economic conjuncture also played a role. The 1969 elections followed a traumatic experience for the new working class forged when Eastern immigrants were absorbed into construction and industry in the late 1950s and early 1960s. These workers had just begun to experience the material benefits and enhanced self-confidence of a period of sustained prosperity and full employment when the economy entered a state-backed slowdown which threw large numbers of Eastern Jews (and also Arabs) out of work.[56] After the 1973 elections the government once again attempted to combat economic crisis with deflationary measures, further breaking down the instrumental barriers to realignment among Eastern voters.[57]

Managing the Political Economy

Political-economic analysis of one-party dominance must assess not only the impact of economic stratification and interests on election outcomes but also the capacity of governing parties to manage the political economy—to develop a workable and politically effective formula for economic growth; to find solutions to problems of industrial peace and political legitimation with respect to the organized working class; and to establish a supportive relationship with the international environment. In Israel, from roughly the Six-Day War onward Labor party governments suffered from a marked deterioration in these capacities. Two trends were especially prominent: the declining usefulness of the Histadrut as a mechanism of political-economic governance and the state's diminishing ability to steer capital rather than be steered by it.[58]

56. Michael Shalev, "Labor, State and Crisis: An Israeli Case Study," *Industrial Relations* 23 (1984): 362–86.

57. On the slowdown of the mid-1960s, see ibid. Nothing like the mass unemployment of the mid-1960s was permitted after the oil crisis, but the government's highly restrictive wage policy (an irritant to the middle-class salariat) was particularly damaging to weaker groups of workers. Zvi Sussman and Dan Zakai, *Changes in the Wage Structure of the Civil Service and Rising Inflation—Israel: 1974–81* (Jerusalem: Bank of Israel Research Department, 1985), based on the Hebrew version published in April 1983. Moreover, subsidies on basic goods and services with particular significance for lower-income Easterners were cut, and private consumption grew sluggishly compared with the period between the 1967 and 1973 wars, making only a modest preelection comeback (Bank of Israel annual reports and Uriel Ben-Hanan and Benny Temkin, "The 'Overloaded Juggler': The Electoral-Economic Cycle in Israel, 1951–1984," in Arian and Shamir, eds., *The Elections in Israel—1984*, pp. 15–35).

58. These are virtually uncharted issues in Israeli scholarship, and their elaboration in any detail cannot be entertained here. See my "Israel's Domestic Policy Regime: Zionism, Dualism, and the Rise of Capital," in Francis G. Castles, ed., *The Comparative History of Public Policy* (Cambridge: Polity Press, 1989), for more extensive discussion and sources.

The Histadrut's influence over its mass membership was seriously weakened by the rapid economic growth and relatively full employment that prevailed for most of the period between the late 1950s and the Yom Kippur War. Its leaders were obliged to pay more attention to rank-and-file sentiment, and they became correspondingly less susceptible to party direction. The ability of Labor governments to rely on receiving mass assent to their domestic policies via the Histadrut suffered accordingly. Histadrut leaders also became less effective at restraining public employees in order to protect the state from inflationary deficit spending and politically embarrassing strikes. By the 1970s labor strife had become concentrated in the public sector, among workers able to defy Histadrut wage policy by virtue of their strong labor market position or the damaging secondary consequences of their militancy.[59]

In the Histadrut's economic enterprises, meanwhile, a new generation of business school–trained executives drew strength from the growing ties of joint ownership and joint ventures among large concerns affiliated with different ownership sectors. These developments reduced the Labor Economy's usefulness to both the party and the government. The party was hurt by heightened resistance to treatment of the posts and profits of Histadrut enterprises as political spoils. Exemplifying their conflicts with the Mapai old guard, some Histadrut magnates were prime movers behind the DMC's challenge to Labor in the 1977 elections. In addition, the government's capacity to steer the economy suffered from the long-term effects of its policy of splitting state subsidies between the biggest enterprises in each ownership sector. For in the process it helped to crystallize a dual economic structure topped by an increasingly powerful tier of big business united by overlapping interests and outlooks.[60]

Another striking trend in the political economy originated in the arena of interstate relations. Beginning in 1971, U.S. aid to Israel grew to major proportions to finance a new escalation of Israel's military might. During the decade following the October 1973 war, Israel typically received roughly $1 billion worth of free American-made war matériel each year, together with substantial dollar loans which helped it to manage the country's chronic current account deficit.[61] Arie Arnon has persuasively argued that this

59. See Grinberg, "The Jewish-Arab Drivers' Association," for elaboration of this rank-and-file challenge and the significance of the sectoral split.

60. These processes were identified by Yair Aharoni, *Structure and Performance in the Israeli Economy* (in Hebrew) (Tel Aviv: Cherikover, 1976), and elaborated and updated by Shimshon Bichler, "The Political Economy of National Security in Israel: Some Aspects of the Activities of the Dominant Blocs of Capital" (in Hebrew) (M.A. thesis, Hebrew University of Jerusalem, 1986).

61. Israel's total military imports from the United States were considerably larger than this $1 billion annual figure, amounting to more than 10 percent of the national product. See Leora Meridor (Rubin), "The Financing of Government Expenditures in Israel, 1960 to 1983" (in Hebrew), *Seker Bank Yisrael* 64 (1987): 3–31. Aggregate U.S. aid, including loans as well as grants and ignoring the distinction between economic and military aid, was also much larger.

dramatic enlargement of U.S. generosity reflected a "change toward a U.S. strategy based on a 'strong Israel' " and a desire to exploit America's potential as a broker of peace agreements in order "to attract more and more Arab regimes and forces into the sphere of U.S. influence."[62] Unlike the German reparations and Jewish philanthropy which fed Israel's economic-growth machine in the late 1950s and early 1960s, the inflow of foreign capital in the form of American arms contributes little to the microeconomic reach of the state. It has on the contrary encouraged a far-reaching militarization of the economy, in the framework of which defense-related production has been lavishly subsidized. This has done a great deal indirectly to stimulate the profitability of the large manufacturing concerns. But the state has received in return only a fragile solution to Israel's economic problems and a limited prerogative to direct the military-industrial complex for political gain.[63]

Its inability to channel U.S. aid in the most economically and politically rewarding directions was one important constraint on policy responses to massive rises in Israel's energy costs and military expenditures in 1973–74. These dual shocks occurred at a time when the government was unable to combat the crisis by traditional stabilization measures except at enormous political risk. Its vulnerability was the result of the already changing balance of electoral forces between Labor and Likud and the weakened condition of the Histadrut's restraining and legitimizing powers. This was the context in which a shift in the relations between the business sector and the state became evident: in spite of the state's fiscal crisis, capital subsidy increased dramatically. The large banks and corporations, once so dependent on the goodwill of the authorities, had over time been bolstered by Mapai's economic policy elite. The coddling of major private investors, along with the state's commitment to Histadrut and state enterprise, had stimulated both concentration and cohesion among capital and raised its political stock. The state had also undermined its own powers by delegating key economic tasks

The calculation in the text reflects only genuine gifts (including foregone loan repayments) after deducting the cost to Israel of servicing past U.S. military loans. For a review of U.S. aid policy, see Leopold Y. Laufer, "U.S. Aid to Israel: Problems and Perspectives," unpublished paper, Leonard David Institute for International Relations, Hebrew University of Jerusalem, May 1983.

62. Arie Arnon, "Israel-U.S. Relations, 1967–1985: The Economic Aspect and Beyond" (unpublished paper, Ben Gurion University of the Negev, Israel, 1986), specifies the following three developments as having precipitated these shifts in American strategy: Israel's emergence from the 1967 war as the region's strongest military power; growing Soviet influence in the Middle East, which the United States could not counter militarily; and the possibility (in 1970–71) of an Israeli-Egyptian peace agreement, which threatened to diminish rather than enlarge U.S. influence.

63. On the growth of military-related production and its subsidization by the state, see Bichler, "Political Economy," Shmuel Hadar, "Blurring of the Boundaries between Public and Private in Relations between State and Industry" (in Hebrew) (Ph.D. dissertation, Hebrew University of Jerusalem, 1988), and Alex Mintz, "The Military-Industrial Complex: The Israeli Case," *Journal of Strategic Studies* 6 (1983): 103–28.

(especially in banking) to the business sector and by throwing its weight behind more effective associational action by business interests.[64]

The effect of these trends toward increasing the autonomy of big business was a threatening symmetry in the state's relationship to the strong sectors of labor and capital—neither could be subjected to sufficient political discipline to help the government resolve the economic crisis. By the mid-1970s Labor had not only exhausted its success with the politics of nationalism and other sources of popular legitimacy, it also no longer possessed the capacity to manage the political economy effectively. It was in this double sense that Israel had arrived at the end of the era of Mapai hegemony.

Mapai in Comparative Perspective

Nearly thirty years ago, Amitai Etzioni pointed out that the Israeli experience of one-party dominance defies straightforward comparison to the Western nations (those that constitute the frame of reference for the dominant-party paradigm). Etzioni argued that

> Mapai can be fruitfully compared to other state founding parties which have become highly institutionalized in young nations [like India and Ghana] . . . . All seem to have in common a leader and a party with the charismatic role of gaining independence and establishing a state; left of center ideologies and control over the labor organizations; state-regulated economies; [and] a high degree of economic dependence on external sources.[65]

The obvious relevance of a "young nation" (or Third World) model of democratic dominance is the result of three distinctive features of the Israeli context which sharply distinguish it from other democratic capitalist societies, despite its resemblance to them in political structure and culture, economic system and level of development, and geopolitical orientation. These three features are (1) the political urgency of issues of national identity, security, and drawing of boundaries; (2) the labor movement's emergence before either the formation of a democratic regime or the growth of an industrial capitalist economy and the primacy afforded to national re-

64. Data showing the rise in capital subsidy during the crisis period are presented in Shalev, "Israel's Domestic Policy Regime." The range and importance of the state's levers over private investment decisions and business sector profitability in the era of Mapai dominance is detailed by Aharoni, "Structure and Performance." But as Aharoni pointed out, writing in the midst of the post-1973 crisis, "The big companies and ownership groups have a great deal of influence on economic policy and the manner in which the resources of the state are allocated, and the state apparatus is often turned into being dependent on them to implement some action or another" (p. 117). Shirom, *Introduction to Labor Relations,* p. 176, stressed the paradox that Labor governments had "fostered and strengthened the private economic sector and brought about the formation of strong employers organizations."

65. Amitai Etzioni, "Alternative Ways to Democracy: The Example of Israel," *Political Science Quarterly* 74 (1959): 214.

vival and state-building goals in working-class mobilization; and (3) the singular contribution to Israel's (and formerly Jewish Palestine's) economy, which has always been made by capital accumulated beyond the country's borders, whether the assets of immigrants, donations from sympathetic foreign governments and Jewish communities, or the more recent American-financed military buildup.

As I pointed out at the opening of this chapter, when discussing the gap between the real and apparent similarities between social democracy in Israel and Sweden, it is by no means obvious to what family of one-party dominant Western regimes the Israeli case belongs. In Etzioni's day Mapai seemed to be programmatically closest to the moderate left in Britain and Europe, but interpretively could best be compared to successful parties of the right in France and Germany, which were similarly reliant on the aggregation of diverse interests under the sway of an influential leader. More recently both Asher Arian and Samuel Barnes, who sought to rationalize Labor's success,[66] and Ariel Levite and Sidney Tarrow, who proposed an explanation for its fall from power, chose Christian Democratic Italy as their referent.[67] Mapai's affinity to these contemporary examples of right-wing hegemony is indeed striking. For unlike the successful labor movement parties of Sweden and Austria, dominant parties of the right like those in Italy or Japan combine the support of a variety of publics, including farmers, the old and new middle classes, and "traditional" workers. Similarly, while successful left parties draw their primary strength from a distinctively working-class organizational and ideological milieu, popular support for the hegemonic right is more dependent on particularistic and calculative incentives, whether the vote-buying and patronage of political machines, "pork barrel" alliances, or preelectoral pump-priming.[68]

Nearly all of the abundant literature on Israeli politics confirms that nominally social democratic Mapai encapsulates each one of these hallmarks of right-wing dominance. Scholars continue to disagree about the extent to which the Mapai of the Yishuv era took its socialist pretensions seriously; but they are virtually unanimous concerning two central features of the party's dominance during the post-1948 period. One is that Mapai managed to mobilize a plurality of voters within all classes and exercised a determinate influence over all of the major organized economic interests (farmers and the self-employed as well as blue-collar workers). The other was the all-important role played by Mapai's judicious use of material

66. Arian and Barnes, "Dominant Party."
67. Levite and Tarrow, "Legitimation of Excluded Parties."
68. Several of the essays in the present volume illustrate both the role of the labor movement in social democratic success and the heterogeneous and opportunistic character of the social sectors linked to the most successful parties of the right in Japan and Italy. For an empirical demonstration that recourse to "electoral business cycles" varies systematically between social democratic and other regimes, see Lorenzo Bordogna, "The Political Business Cycle and the Crisis of Keynesian Politics," paper presented at the Annual Meetings of the American Sociological Association, Toronto, August 1981.

incentives to individuals and communities through such mechanisms as the urban party machine and the electoral business cycle.[69]

Mapai has been at one and the same time a settler cum national-liberation movement and an opportunistic catchall party, and yet like other leftist parties it relies on organized labor as its principal power base. This situation is confusing although fundamental to the complexity and peculiarity of the Israeli case. For those who seek an understanding of one-party dominance in the abstract, this interpretation of Israel clearly suggests that no one model of the phenomenon will suffice. Recourse to a typology of alternative paths to dominance would equally misunderstand the Israeli case were the typology to rely solely on the oversimplified categories of left and right dominance. For Israel at least, the analysis of hegemonic parties cannot proceed independently of historical and contextual specificities.

The more universal message of this essay from an analytical standpoint is its claim in favor of the fruitfulness of a political economy approach to dominant-party systems. Applied to the Israeli case, this approach has highlighted the unduly narrow orientation of more conventional treatments of dominance, especially those that view the dominant-party system, in Arian and Barnes's words, as "one in which politics is king, in which dominance results from strategic political decisions made by the party elite."[70] The present analysis has instead been premised on the view that neither the acquisition of a parliamentary majority nor successful governance can be understood in the realm of the "purely political" alone. For they are also heavily embedded in intersections between politics and the economy, among them, the impact of economic stratification and interests on voter alignments and the role of the state in defining and addressing problems of capital accumulation and class conflict and in linking the domestic political economy with the international environment. From this perspective this study of Israel may be treated as an illustration, and perhaps even a paradigm case, of the possibility and indispensability of political-economic analysis. But we must never lose sight of the distinctiveness of the Israeli case, which ultimately goes back to Israel's ongoing dialectic with external forces—the inflow of population and capital and the national conflict with the Palestinians and the Arab states, both of which act upon, and are acted upon by, domestic politics and economics.

69. For diverse views concerning the role of Mapai's socialist ideology in the Yishuv period, consult the authorities cited earlier and also Gadi Yatziv, *The Class Basis of Party Affiliation— The Israeli Case* (in Hebrew) (Jerusalem: Hebrew University, Papers in Sociology, 1979). The party machine and the party's control of economic interest groups during the epoch of Mapai's postindependence dominance are well documented. See Medding, *Mapai in Israel,* and Aronoff, *Power and Ritual in the Israeli Labor Party.* The multiclass character of the Mapai constituency has already been noted. Yoram Ben-Porath, "The Years of Plenty and the Years of Famine—A Political Business Cycle?" *Kyklos* 28 (1975): 400–403, and more recently Ben-Hanan and Temkin, "The 'Overloaded Juggler,' " are among those who have discerned a pronounced electoral business cycle in Israel.

70. Arian and Barnes, "Dominant Party," p. 599.

4. Defense Controversies and One-Party Dominance: The Opposition in Japan and West Germany

HIDEO OTAKE

In an abrupt departure from the party's ninety-year tradition, the West German Social Democratic party (SPD) adopted a new program at an extraordinary conference in Bad Godesberg in late 1959. In economic policy, the new program rejected socialization (nationalization) and state control of production, espousing instead essentially Keynesian economics in the form of indirect state intervention based on market competition. In politics, it replaced the notion of irreconcilable class war by adapting political pluralism, with each social group representing a particular interest and opinion. The SPD regarded itself as an aggregating agent, a *Volkspartei* (people's party). In essence, the party abandoned its traditional, doctrinaire, Marxist outlook. The following year, vice-chairman of the SPD Herbert Wehner made a speech in the parliament indicating that the party was ready for a bipartisan foreign policy with the Adenauer government on the basis of German defense efforts in the context of the Western alliance. His statement not only meant an abrupt end to the party's uncompromising opposition to Adenauer's security policy but also an explicit denial of pacifism and neutralism, permeated by the middle-class radicalism which up to that time had significantly influenced the party's security policy. Then, in 1961, the SPD adopted a new, American style in the general election campaign, emphasizing the personality of Willy Brandt rather than any ideological and programmatic appeal.

These reappraisals of previous policies and tactics were paralleled by many other European socialist parties, including those of Austria, Switzerland, the Netherlands, Belgium, and Denmark.[1] The French and the Italian

1. Harold Kent Schellenger, *The SPD in the Bonn Republic* (The Hague: Martinus Nijhoff, 1988), p. 3. See also William E. Paterson and Alastair H. Thomas, eds., *Social Democratic Parties in Western Europe* (London: Croom Helm, 1977).

socialist parties, which remained exceptions at that time, recently returned to power following lingering reexaminations and adaptations. These transformations have been characterized by political scientists as "the end of ideology," "the waning of opposition," "modernization," or the "transformation from working-class movement to catchall party." Such characterizations imply that the changes are inevitable and congruent with the stable, democratic political order presumed to be inherent in postindustrial society.

Until very recent years, the Japan Socialist party (JSP) failed to follow the examples of European socialist parties and ran counter to the expectations of many political scientists. In the midst of an affluent, middle-class society, it remained a fundamentalist opposition party with respect to program, if not practice. Although to a decreasing degree, the party still relied on Marxist terminology and analysis and was sympathetic to the concept of a united front with communists against what it called the "reactionary, fascist LDP government, whose power rests essentially in the hands of big capitalists."

At long last in January 1986, the JSP, having overcome the strenuous opposition of leftist groups within the party, adopted a program entitled "The New Declaration of the Japan Socialist Party." Although the new program is vague and abstract and lacks concrete policy measures, it unmistakenly replaces a Marxist-Leninist outlook with an essentially social democratic ideal. In politics, it emphasizes parliamentary, pluralist democracy and demands for the decentralization of power to local communities. In economics, it appreciates the achievements of postwar Japan, implicitly accepting Liberal Democratic party (LDP) claims. At the same time, it explicitly rejects the Soviet model of centralized planning and advocates the modification of market economics through government intervention. On social issues, it approves ongoing trends toward the diversification of values among the people. In addition, it rejects Marxian class concepts and expresses a desire to represent the entire nation rather than any particular class. And the JSP now declares itself ready to enter coalitions with any party on the common ground of maintaining and promoting the ideals of the existing constitution.

The party seems finally to have begun to follow the path that the SPD and other European socialist parties took a quarter-century before. But it remains to be seen whether the present leadership will be able to consolidate this line and complete the reappraisals of the previous policies in the face of intraparty opposition from the left. This opposition showed its strength by delaying the adoption of the new program for a month, although top leaders had the power to reject any revision of the proposed program. Moreover, discussions over military policies were carefully avoided by the top leadership. (This is particularly interesting because the Nakasone cabinet had provoked the leftist opposition by hawkish policies such as the Yasukuni Shrine Policy and the Anti-Espionage Bill as well as by its defense policies.) It seems unlikely that the JSP could reappraise its policy of unarmed neutrality without provoking fierce protests, although this may be changing as we enter the 1990s. In this regard, the present reformists in the JSP are in a much more difficult position than their counterparts in the SPD in 1960 because pacifism in Japan, unlike West Germany, is not mitigated by anti-communism or by a tangible Russian threat. It will be a much harder process for the JSP to complete its reappraisals and adaptations.

Following the SPD's programmatic revisions, the electoral fortunes of the party took a turn upward, and in 1966 the party entered the Grand Coalition with the Christian Democrats and gained power in 1969, with Brandt as chancellor. In Japan, the JSP, adhering to its original class orientation, watched its electoral support slide continually downward so that by the mid-1980s is held barely one-quarter of the total seats in parliament. To ask why a single party enjoys long-term dominance over a nation's government is to ask why no opposition party or coalition was able to defeat it. It is tautological to note that no party remains dominant in the face of a more powerful opposition. But why and how an opposition musters an appropriate challenge is a vital part of understanding long-term single-party dominance. The German and Japanese cases provide an insightful comparison of two countries in which the potential for long-term dominance seemed historically comparable in the 1950s but different strategies by the major opposition parties in each country led to drastically different outcomes.

In the German case, the Christian Democratic party (CDU/CSU) had been in power from the first postwar election. In 1957, under a strong and popular Chancellor Konrad Adenauer it defeated the SPD by 50 to 32 percent. Economic recovery was well under way under the guidance of Ludwig Ehrhard. If ever a party looked poised for long-term rule it was the CDU/CSU.

On the other side of the globe, the newly formed Liberal Democratic party in Japan had none of the compelling leadership once provided for the conservatives by Shigeru Yoshida. Internal factionism threatened the party. Major left-right confrontations occurred on several fronts, the most notable of which was the so-called Security Treaty Crisis of 1960, which ultimately forced the conservative Kishi government to resign in the face of massive public protests led by the left. Such problems, combined with rapidly changing demographics in Japanese society, were widely interpreted to suggest the conservatives' vulnerability. Projections of the LDP defeat and a JSP government were widespread during the late 1950s and early 1960s.[2]

The realities proved otherwise: the CDU/CSU lost power in 1969, but the LDP has continued to govern without interruption since its formation. A central thesis of this chapter is that the fortunes of the two parties were affected to a critical degree by the strategies of their major opponents, the

2. Probably the most famous of these was the article by Ishida Hirohide, "Hoshu Seito no Bijion [The Conservative party's vision]," *Chūō Kōron* (January 1963): 88–97.

SPD and the JSP. More specifically, I argue that internal conditions in each opposition party gave the two organizations very different scope for flexibility in determining long-term party strategies. It was the relative freedom of the SPD leaders to adjust to the changing circumstances, and most particularly their freedom to adopt new military and defense policies, as well as economic policies, that allowed them eventually to make increasingly popular appeals and to prevent continued conservative rule. In contrast, Japan's Socialist party, flush with what it perceived to be the popular victory on the security treaty issue and loath to isolate its militant trade union membership by rejecting the party's initial commitment to socialism and the ideology of class conflict, failed to make major policy adjustments, even though the electorate continually showed itself more and more hostile to JSP proposals and the party's electoral fortunes dropped steadily.

Controversy over military policy seems to play a critical role in JSP's continuous adherence to traditional leftist ideology. Although the JSP's economic policies did not and do not differ much from those of the ruling party, it has adhered to a radically different view concerning security. In particular, it has advocated unarmed neutrality. And the analyses and statements on the "reactionary" nature of the conservative government have referred mostly to the party's opposition to the defense policies of the government. The JSP's long adherence to fundamental opposition seems to have been motivated, or at least justified, mostly by its deep concern with what it claimed was the "reactionary tendency toward imperialism and prewar-type militarism" on the part of the governing elites. Many socialists conceded long ago that all other Marxist analyses and predictions are subject to severe critical reexaminations in the context of economic growth and stability, but the traditional Marxist argument on the military policies of capitalist states still seems to them to offer a valid and convincing diagnosis. Needless to say, Marxist diagnosis is based on the unchanging nature of the capitalist regime and hence emphasizes essential identities between trends in the 1930s and those at the present time. Thus the socialists not only fear the imperialist expansionism of Japanese capitalism, supported temporarily by U.S. capital, but they also are frightened by a rightward shift toward ultranationalism and emperor worship and the tightening of domestic control. They believe these trends are easily detected in government policies on education and religion but are most clearly manifested in its military policies.[3]

In this context, it is no wonder that the JSP considers unarmed neutrality the last stronghold of resistance against those overwhelming trends. Although most JSP supporters and members long ago lost interest in a socialist economy and a collectivist social order and stand ready to abandon socialist

---

3. See, for example, former chairman of the JSP Masashi Ishibashi's book, *Hibuso Chūritsu Ron* [On unarmed neutrality] (1980; rev. ed. Tokyo: JSP, 1983).

programs in these areas, any suggestion to reject unarmed neutrality is vehemently resisted.[4] In fact, all intraparty efforts by "revisionists" to adapt the party's program to the preferences of average Japanese voters foundered until 1986 on the resistance by leftists able to mobilize widespread neutralist and pacifist support. Concerns with the revival of militarism have been, rightly or wrongly, widely shared by a certain segment of the population beyond the JSP membership, particularly among politically conscious and active minorities, including intellectuals and young industrial workers. The major mass media share those concerns to a lesser degree, reinforcing the position of leftist groups within the party. So long as this apprehension of "Japanese militarism" is not expelled, the reexamination of security policy by the JSP is impossible, and the reappraisal of the entire party program is unlikely. For these reasons, the JSP remained isolated, and the LDP continued one-party dominance.

This chapter examines, in comparison with the West German case, the historical background of the JSP's apprehension over the revival of militarism as one of the determining factors for one-party dominance. More concretely, it focuses on Japanese and West German defense controversies in their formative years and examines how the militarist aspect was raised or avoided by the governing parties and how it was perceived and interpreted by the respective opposition parties.

Rearmament Controversies

The most striking feature in a comparison of West German and Japanese rearmament policies is how readily West German policies were accepted as legitimate by the major political parties whereas Japanese policies, as they were carried out by the ruling conservatives, engendered genuine fears and concerns about a revival of Japanese militarism. Although many aspects of West German rearmament were controversial, rearmament was always seen as necessary in the face of a perceived Soviet threat on the country's eastern border. It thus seemed more legitimate, and the issues of defense and security did less to polarize debate between the parties than was the case in Japan. Consequently, the agenda of the conservative government was gradually accommodated by the socialist opposition.

In Japan, by contrast, rearmament was carried out in ways that smacked of secrecy, hidden agendas, and, most important, clear-cut constitutional violations. In addition, facing a far less menacing Soviet presence, most Japanese were dubious about the likelihood of a serious military threat to Japan. The right wove the issues of defense and security together with other ideologically charged issues such as constitutional revision and educational

4. This position was again manifested at the party congress of 1984.

reforms, using the package as ideological weapons against their political opponents. The left and the right never agreed on security and defense issues, with the former firmly convinced that the government was moving to reintroduce fascism, militarism, thought control, and overseas expansion. From the very first, therefore, issues of defense and security had a polarizing effect on party and electoral competition. The ideological lines drawn over security in the years immediately following the end of the war were to remain largely uncrossable by the two major parties and their supporters for the next forty years. Rearmament thus remained an issue that, in Japan, had a profoundly different impact on partisan fortunes than in West Germany.

West German Rearmament

The outbreak of the Korean War forced the United States government to reexamine its policies for the defense of Europe. Intimidated by the prospect that aggression in the Far East signaled similar communist moves against a militarily feeble Western Europe, U.S. policy makers believed it was essential to strengthen North Atlantic Treaty Organization (NATO) forces by adding West German troops. This American call for immediate West German rearmament frightened the French, who were more concerned about the West German than the Soviet threat. Pressed by the U.S. ultimatum, France made a bold counterproposal, partly as a delaying tactic.[5] The Pleven Plan was designed to create a European army attached to the political institutions of Europe and was intended not only to strengthen European defense but also to contain West German armament in the European framework and prevent the revival of German militarism. It was also conceived as a step toward French-German reconciliation. This controversy started a frustrating four-year international negotiation on West German rearmament.

Adenauer, who did not necessarily share with American policy makers the fear of immediate and direct Soviet aggression, saw a West German defense contribution as important diplomatic leverage to achieve two wider political goals, the regaining of sovereignty and the political integration of West Germany into Western Europe. The political recovery of West Germany was expected to be more difficult than that of Japan not only because of Soviet but also of French obstruction.[6] Unlike Japan, the Federal Republic could not simply wait for the initiative of the occupation powers. Adenauer was therefore determined to use West German rearmament as a lever to regain sovereignty, even at the risk of alienating certain domestic

5. Robert McGeehan, *The German Rearmament Question* (Urbana: University of Illinois Press, 1971).

6. Gerhard Wettig, "Entmilitarisierung und Wiederbewaffnung Japans und der Bundesrepublik nach dem Zweiten Weltkriek," in Arnulf Baring and Masamori Sase, eds., *Zwei zaghafte Riesen?* (Stuttgart: Belser, 1977).

supporters. Relying on the argument that sovereignty would be achieved only through a West German defense contribution, he engaged, through the CDU/CSU, in active campaigns to "educate" West Germans, the majority of whom were reluctant, if not openly antagonistic, toward rearmament.

At the same time, he saw in the French proposal an effective way to achieve his lifelong aspiration: integration with the West, particularly with France. On one hand, he rejected a neutralist position on the ground that neutrality would lead to West Germany's becoming a Russian satellite. On the other hand, he feared that neutralism might lead West Germany to become an "autonomous," nationalist state. In other words, he shared much of the French apprehension of Germany's militaristic tradition and considered political integration with Western liberal democratic regimes indispensable to protect Germans against themselves. Economic integration had already started with the Schuman Plan. Adenauer saw this integration of coal and steel production primarily as a political endeavor, making war between West Germany and France impossible and leading to wider political integration. He considered the European Defense Community (EDC) another effort at integrating West Germany into Western democracy. His concept of democracy and his plan for "*Westintegration*" were thus based no less on anti-Nazism than on anticommunism.[7]

Adenauer repeated those arguments, often simplistically, over and over again, making it difficult to criticize his rearmament policies as a revival of German militarism. As a consequence, the opposition SPD, which was not hostile to West German rearmament in principle, resorted primarily to criticism of the proposals in terms of German inequality in the European framework and the repercussions of rearmament vis-à-vis reunification with the Eastern Zone. Although the danger of the revival of militarism in the newly born republic was a warning theme in some debates, few, except communists, accused the Adenauer government of intending to move the Federal Republic of Germany (FRG) toward imperialism and fascism.[8]

The EDC was rejected by the French parliament after long, heated debate and never materialized. The concept of an integrated army, however, which was originally intended to allay French fears of the revival of German militarism, played a crucial and similar role in West Germany as well during the critical few years of defense controversies.

Immediately after the defeat of the EDC, a German military contribution was achieved under British initiative by means of direct German participation in NATO. The Federal Republic initiated concrete measures for rearmament only after the NATO solution was finally secured in early 1955[9]

7. Arnulf Baring, *Außenpolitik in Adenauers Kanzelerdemokratie* (Munich: Oldenbourg, 1969); Hans-Peter Schwarz, *Vom Reich zur Bundesrepublik* (Neuwied and Berlin: Hermann Luchterhand, 1966).
8. For a comprehensive examination of the rearmament debate see Klaus von Schubert, *Wiederbewaffung und Westintegration* (Stuttgart: Deutsche Verlag Australt, 1970).
9. Norbert Tönnies, *Der Weg zu den Waffen* (Cologne: Markus, 1957).

because Adenauer wanted to avoid giving any impression that West Germany was enthusiastic about rearmament, an impression that might endanger French ratification of NATO. Adenauer also feared that a détente atmosphere in the mid-1950s might lead the superpowers to reach an agreement on a neutralistic unification of Germany. Consequently, he planned that once ratification was accomplished, rearmament would be achieved at top speed. He wanted to create a fait accompli by immediate rearmament before any such agreement could be initiated. On this issue, however, he encountered bipartisan opposition in the parliament.[10]

The defense specialists in the SPD, under the leadership of Fritz Erler, overcame the pacifist opposition within the party and secured its participation in preparing a legal framework for rearmament. This included the revision of the constitution (*Grundgesetz*). In this way they effectively contributed to the establishment of tight parliamentary control over the armed forces. They defended themselves against intraparty criticism by referring to experiences under the Weimar Constitution, pointing out the danger of remaking the German army as "a state within the state." Many conservative politicians shared this bitter memory of Weimar. Such parliamentary cooperation, which was exceptional in the history of the FRG, broke down only when compulsory conscription was introduced, with the SPD strongly opposed to this highly unpopular move. Adenauer was thus forced to delay conscription until the basic legal framework was hammered out through bipartisan cooperation. In sharp contrast to Japanese rearmament, a solid legal foundation was established before the first soldier was recruited into the Bundeswehr. Through those processes, the SPD committed itself to the establishment of a West German army and felt assured that through institutional channels the party would be able to prevent any revival of militarism. Subsequently, the defense specialists in the SPD increasingly treated rearmament problems primarily from a strategic military perspective, belittling its domestic implications.[11]

In the mid-1950s, when West Germany began concrete measures for rearmament, Western defense was undergoing revolutionary changes in military technology, particularly in the field of tactical nuclear weapons.[12] These trends were manifested in the plan for the reduction of American and British forces stationed in West Germany. Their withdrawal was to be compensated by the introduction of tactical nuclear weapons, as well as by British and French efforts to develop their own nuclear capabilities. Adapting to this transformation in strategic thinking, the Federal Republic was

10. Hans-Peter Schwarz, *Die Ära Adenauer: Gründerjahre der Republik, 1949–1957* (Stuttgart: Deutsche Verlag Australt, 1980), pp. 287–302.

11. Lother Wilker, *Die Sicherheitspolitik der SPD, 1956–1966* (Bonn: Neue Gesellschaft, 1977).

12. James L. Richardson, *Germany and the Atlantic Alliance* (Cambridge, Mass.: Harvard University Press, 1966); Catherine McArdle Kelleher, *Germany and the Politics of Nuclear Weapons* (New York: Columbia University Press, 1975).

required to reexamine its plans for a military buildup. The revision of previous goals was undertaken by an energetic new defense minister, Franz Josef Strauss. In the new policy, emphasis was on high quality instead of quantitative strength. This meant strengthening air and naval forces, including the development of the West German aero industry, at the expense of ground forces. In this context, military discussion was forced to deal with the nuclearization of German forces. Thus, even in the midst of the tense atmosphere of 1956–57 that grew out of the Hungarian and Polish uprisings, the FRG began to advocate equipping its armed forces with nuclear weapons, with the nuclear warhead to remain under American control.

The most serious opposition to this German nuclear ambition came from outside the SPD. In the "Gottingen Declaration," atomic scientists took the initiative and succeeded, because of their prestige, in attracting nationwide attention. As a result, the government encountered one of the most severe protests in the history of the Federal Republic, the campaign against atomic death.[13] At that time the SPD was wavering in its reappraisal of its previous policies and stood irresolute on this issue. Only after recognizing the electoral potential of such antiatomic sentiment, however, did the party join the protest, setting its eyes on the coming general election of 1957. The SPD demanded both the unilateral renunciation of atomic weapons by the Federal Republic and the withdrawal of atomic weapons from German territory. The party also argued, as an electoral promise, for the abolition of conscription. Such orientations reflected the influence of the neutralists and pacifists within the party at the expense of "realistic" defense specialists. (Meanwhile, the SPD continued to support the European Economic Community [EEC], advocated "Security for Free Enterprise," and, more important, carefully avoided questioning the FRG's NATO membership.)

The results of the 1957 election, which was contested heavily on foreign policy issues,[14] was deeply disappointing to the SPD. A court revolution within its top leadership ensued in which two traditionalists holding the vice-chairmanship were replaced by two prominent rightists, Carlo Schmid and Fritz Erler, as well as Herbert Wehner. And the reexamination of the party's economic policies and its ideological basis was finally initiated. At the same time, the SPD continued to commit itself to its previous military policies, intensifying its participation in a renewed "campaign against atomic death" and challenging the constitutionality of nuclear weapons. The protest movements became increasingly bitter and aggressive in the spring of 1958, as the *Land* election approached in North Rhine–Westphalia, the largest *Land* in the FRG. Both the government and the opposition viewed this election as a referendum over the nuclear issue. The SPD, which had

13. Hans Karl Rupp, *Außerparlamentarische Opposition in der Ära Adenauer* (Cologne: Pahl-Rugenstein, 1970).

14. Uwe W. Kitzinger, *German Electoral Politics: A Study of the 1957 Campaign* (Oxford: Oxford University Press, 1960).

been in power in a coalition with the Free Democratic party (FDP), suffered another severe setback, as the CDU/CSU gained an absolute majority.

Shortly thereafter, the party definitively detached itself from the anti-atomic-death campaign and quietly let the issue become dormant. Because of these lukewarm attitudes on the part of the opposition party, the subsequent conflicts over foreign and military issues have pitted the government against various single-issue movements, a pattern somewhat similar to social conflicts in the United States.[15]

It is noteworthy that the mainstream of the criticism against the government was not based on a Marxist diagnosis and that the government was rarely accused of moving toward militarism and fascism. In this respect the anti-atomic-death campaign was presented as a civic movement, detached from conflicts involving the choice or defense of entire political and economic systems. The participants were motivated by the overriding fear of nuclear war, including an accidental outbreak of nuclear exchange. These, the movement held, were equally ominous, regardless of the political system.

During the initial controversy over rearmament, Kurt Schumacher, the first postwar chairman of the SPD, accused Adenauer of being a tool of big capital and criticized his policies as an attempt to restore the reactionary order. His successors, however, tended to criticize the specific outcomes of Adenauerian security policies during the antinuclear campaign. Thus by the late 1950s the domestic implications of security policies had become less and less salient in West Germany.

The protest against nuclear weapons was short-lived. After defeat in the 1958 *Land* election, the SPD resolutely began a reappraisal of its previous policies, including its military policies. The party then became more and more inclined to discuss defense issues on military and strategic grounds, and defense discussions became professionalized, highly technical concepts being introduced. In this sense they paralleled economic discussions. By the end of the process, references to the revival of militarism from defense controversies in the Federal Republic were no longer germane.

Japanese Rearmament, 1950–1954

As in West Germany, the outbreak of the Korean War stimulated Japanese rearmament. The path for rearmament in Japan, however, was quite different. Japanese rearmament was initiated on General Douglas MacArthur's initiative without any international negotiations or domestic discussions, with the creation of the seventy-five-thousand-man National Po-

15. Georg Fülberth und Jürgen Harrer, "Geschichte und Besonderheiten der demokratischen Bewegung und der Arbeiterbewegung in der Bundesrepublik," in Ulrich Albrecht, ed., *Beiträge zu einer Geschichte der Bundesrepublik Deutschland* (Cologne: Pahl-Rugenstein, 1979).

lice Reserve (NPR) in the summer of 1950. The NPR was founded during the emergency that accompanied the outbreak of the war in Korea, when the American Occupation Authority—Supreme Commander for the Allied Powers (SCAP)—was forced to dispatch almost all the U.S. forces stationed in Japan and Korea. To fill this "vacuum," General MacArthur, in a letter to the Japanese government, ordered the establishment of a Japanese paramilitary force that would be equipped with U.S. weapons. Because of the emergency, no discussion was allowed in the Japanese Diet. The opposition parties were told that any criticisms would constitute a violation of occupation decrees and would be punished as such.[16] The National Police Reserve was thus established on a very shaky legal foundation, not to mention the absence of a domestic consensus.[17]

SCAP's plan was eventually to build a regular army on the basis of this paramilitary organization. This intention, however, was carefully disguised to avoid the expected opposition of Britain and the other Allies. This secrecy was essential because Japanese rearmament would violate the Potsdam agreement and the subsequent decisions by the Far Eastern Commission as well as the Japanese constitution imposed by MacArthur himself. Even the Japanese government was puzzled and initially learned of the U.S. intention only through the specific instructions it received from SCAP concerning the organizational structure and the equipment required for the NPR.

As the concrete steps were undertaken for the defense buildup, popular suspicion grew. Hence the Japanese government, upon which the new decision of SCAP had been imposed, had no choice but to continue officially to regard the NPR as a police reserve to protect Japan against internal uprisings. The government had no time to "educate" the people and prepare them for rearmament, even if it had wanted to. In fact, Prime Minister Yoshida had no intention of leading public opinion toward full-fledged rearmament. He himself was, at least for the time being, opposed to Japanese rearmament because he felt that Japan was not ready, economically or psychologically, to rearm.[18]

Six months later, Special Ambassador John Foster Dulles visited Japan to negotiate the peace settlement. He urged Japan to reorganize its existing forces and build up full-fledged armed forces in exchange for an American guarantee of security. Yoshida refused the request for several reasons, the same reasons that have continued to be used through negotiations with the United States whenever the latter requests a larger Japanese military contribution. First, Pacific countries, particularly the Philippines, Australia, and

16. Shukan-Shincho Henshubu, *Makkasa no Nihon* [MacArthur's Japan] (Tokyo: Shinchōsha, 1983), 2:259.

17. For a more detailed account of Japanese rearmament in this period, see my *Saigunbi to Nashonarizumu* [Rearmament and nationalism] (Tokyo: Chūōkōron, 1988).

18. For English material, see Martin E. Weinstein, *Japan's Postwar Defense Policy, 1947–1962* (New York: Columbia University Press, 1971), and Michael M. Yoshitsu, *Japan and the San Francisco Peace Settlement* (New York: Columbia University Press, 1983).

New Zealand, were strongly apprehensive about Japanese rearmament. Consequently, large-scale rearmament would prevent the establishment of friendly political and economic relations with these countries. Dulles sounded out the possibility of establishing a regional defense alliance similar to NATO that would include Japan, Australia, New Zealand, and some other Asian nations, but Yoshida never considered such politico-military integration with neighboring nations possible or desirable. Yoshida claimed that Japan could contribute more effectively to the stability of East Asia through economic cooperation with neighboring countries, promoting economic, rather than politico-military, integration. (Unlike Adenauer and Japanese leftist intellectuals, Yoshida never desired cultural or political integration of Japan with the West or with neighboring Asian nations. Although he was eager for international economic integration, he wished to maintain a distinctive cultural identity for the Japanese people. His sentimental attachment to the emperor must be understood in this context. Whereas Adenauer's unreserved orientation to the West helped erase West German leftists' concerns about the revival of militarism, Yoshida's nationalism catalyzed leftist opposition against his rearmament policies.)

Second, he claimed that full-scale rearmament would strengthen domestic opposition to the conservative government and Japan's alliance with the West and hence would menace Japan's internal as well as external stability. According to Yoshida, the Japanese people were not psychologically ready to prepare for another war and would therefore be swayed by the neutralist argument if any such preparations occurred. Furthermore, any revision of the constitution, which Yoshida interpreted as prohibiting rearmament, was considered to be impossible for the near future because of domestic opposition. Presumably, pacifist sentiment among the Japanese masses was much stronger than among the West Germans, who were directly confronted with Russian armies and had experienced a series of crises in Berlin. But Yoshida did not try to lead public opinion toward rearmament, except in such very roundabout ways as the introduction of moral education.

Third, Yoshida felt that rearmament would deal a severe if not fatal blow to Japan's economic reconstruction. He repeatedly emphasized Japan's economic vulnerability. Undoubtedly, he was much more pessimistic about the developmental potential of his nation than Adenauer was of his. Yoshida also argued, as did the SPD in Germany, that economic development and stability would bring political stability and contribute to the defense of Japan much more than would a defense buildup. Japanese economic recovery was behind West Germany's by several years, with stable high economic growth starting around 1955.

Fourth, Yoshida, like Adenauer, though to a lesser degree, was apprehensive over the possible revival of militarism and opposed any large-scale rearmament on this ground. Although this point was not raised publicly as much as other reasons, this fear was deeply embedded in Yoshida's mind.

An unspoken reason for Japanese reluctance to rearm was Yoshida's conviction that the U.S. presence in Japan was sufficient to deter a Soviet attack and that there was no need for further deterrence. Dulles and some other American policy makers thought the Soviet Union might mount a direct attack on Japan, but the Japanese elite did not believe it was possible. As a result, Yoshida, like Adenauer, saw the rearmament question essentially from political and economic rather than military perspectives. Moreover, Yoshida, unlike Adenauer, found no diplomatic goals to be achieved by the leverage of defense contribution at the risk of alienating political supporters.

In contrast to West Germany, which was expected to face French as well as Russian opposition to its restored sovereignty, Japan, it was commonly assumed, would regain its sovereignty sooner or later under the protection of the United States. There was little need for a defense contribution to attain sovereignty. Moreover, Yoshida, for the time being, was not particularly interested in Japan's political recovery beyond regaining the status of a sovereign state. Adenauer, on the other hand, was very conscious of the FRG's immediate international status vis-à-vis the other major powers in Europe, especially Britain and France, primarily because the Federal Republic, unlike Japan, had many pressing goals that could best be achieved through political influence over the major powers, as well as crucial interests to be defended through international negotiations. These issues included the status of Berlin and unification with the Eastern Zone and territory beyond Oder-Neisse. Adenauer also had to fight against occasional British and French proposals for a neutralized and unified Germany. In this context, Adenauer believed, rightly or wrongly, that military power was a prerequisite for political influence. He also calculated that rearmament in the framework of NATO would preempt any neutralization proposal. It is no wonder that he placed the highest priority on achieving full-fledged rearmament and attaining military equality. His decision to equip West German forces with nuclear weapons also stemmed largely from the political consideration of attaining a status similar to that of Britain and France.

Yoshida's perspective and undertaking were quite different. During the years critical for rearmament, he was indifferent to Japan's political equality and influence in world politics; hence he did not pay much attention to the immediate positive effect that a military buildup could have on Japan's international status. Rather, he was concerned to revitalize Japan's "national spirit," and he thought that for this purpose, moral education in the elementary and high schools was much more effective than any defense buildup and, more important, it was much less costly. Presumably, he also feared that a hasty rearmament under American pressure would create the impression of a foreign mercenary among the Japanese public as well as among Japanese soldiers. Unlike Adenauer, Yoshida was old-fashioned in that he believed no nation is fully sovereign while it relies on foreign protection for its security. Without full sovereignty in this sense, the Japanese would continue to lack the spirit of independence and self-respect which the Confucian Yoshida so highly valued. Undoubtedly he believed that independent military forces were indispensable for protecting Japan from foreign aggression and intervention and thus keeping her spirit of independence. Although he desired no more military expansion, he would not be satisfied with Japan's indefinite dependence upon foreign protection. Konoe Ayamaro's (and John Dower's) statement that Yoshida was a true descendant of imperial Japan[19] was also appropriate to his long-term defense policy objective. He, however, judged this longtime objective to be a problem that would have to be undertaken by his successors. He had more pressing objectives, including the attainment of economic recovery and political stability.[20] (Later, in the 1960s, Yoshida bitterly admitted that he was responsible for the deplorable total indifference toward Japan's security among ordinary Japanese.)[21] Many other Japanese political and economic elites in the postwar era went further than Yoshida, being satisfied solely to gain economic advantages and to abstain from competition for world power. They have retained this perspective long after Japan attained economic prosperity and political stability.

Meanwhile, during negotiations for the peace settlement, Yoshida had to concede, though only partially, to Dulles's demands by secretly promising to reorganize the NPR into a full-fledged army and to increase the armed forces by fifty thousand men. This concession was kept secret because Yoshida had explicitly committed himself and his government to the rejection of future rearmament. In retrospect, he seems to have made a serious tactical mistake by judging that in the negotiations to regain sovereignty he would be able to resist American pressure for a larger defense buildup. In subsequent years, Japan was always under pressure from the U.S. government to increase its armed forces and to attain the force goals it had agreed to as soon as possible. Washington also tried to induce Japan to accept economic aid to undertake larger defense efforts. The Japanese government thus increased its armed forces gradually in response to American pressure. As a result, Yoshida was put in an awkward position. He had to defend an increase in the armed forces and in defense budgets which he did not consider necessary or desirable. It was understandable that his statements on defense buildup appeared confusing, contradictory, and tricky.

The opposition did not appreciate, or even recognize, Yoshida's re-

19. John W. Dower, *Empire and Aftermath: Yoshida Shigeru and the Japanese Experience, 1878–1958* (Cambridge, Mass.: Harvard University Press, 1979).

20. This interpretation of Yoshido's ideology is somewhat different from the common one, which regards him as solely concerned with economic rehabilitation even from a long-term perspective. My interpretation is documented in *Saigunbi to Nashonarizumu*.

21. Yoshida's letter of November 19, 1968, to his former military adviser Tatsumi Eiichi cited in Takayama Nobutaka, *Shōwa Meishoroku* [Great generals of the Showa era] (Tokyo: Fuyoshōbo, 1980), 2:225–26.

sistance to American pressure. This reaction was natural, for the negotiations were conducted in strict secrecy. Consequently, the leftist opposition tended to interpret his lingering rearmament policy as a conspiracy designed to hide a deeper intention to make Japan a great military power and reestablish it as a militarist state. The policies of his government in regard to the police, education, and labor, which were intended, subjectively at least, to counterbalance leftist trends in postwar Japan, reinforced this conviction. In fact, Yoshida intended to implant patriotism into young Japanese by introducing moral education into the elementary and secondary education systems. He expected this approach would pave the way to an acceptance of a defense buildup in the long run. But his educational policy proved counterproductive, aggravating domestic conflict and further strengthening the leftist opposition among Japan's teachers.

The left fully cultivated pacifist sentiments among the population. When Hatoyama Ichiro and other conservative politicians returned to the political scene in the early 1950s advocating immediate and bold rearmament policies to rouse nationalist aspirations, they made Yoshida's rearmament policy appear even less convincing to the public. Although Yoshida's policy contributed to rapid economic recovery by minimizing national security costs and at the same time keeping the alliance tolerable for Washington, it frustrated the rightists and increased the suspicion of the leftists, eventually leading to wider party cleavages on defense controversies.

Japanese Rearmament, 1955–1980

When Yoshida was forced to retire in late 1954, his rearmament policy was under severe criticism from the right as well as the left.[22] The right advocated an autonomous, independent foreign policy, meaning bolder rearmament policies and a more equal security arrangement with the United States. To achieve this, they said, Japan would have to make a more positive contribution to the Western defense effort. More concretely, they proposed revising both the constitution to give unambiguous legitimacy to the Self-Defense Forces (SDF) and the security treaty with the United States, so as to introduce mutuality and equality to the defense relationship. Such an approach by the right reflected grass-roots nationalism, which viewed the existing alliance with the United States as subordination. The Hatoyama and Kishi cabinets, which followed Yoshida's and governed in the latter half of the 1950s, tried to cultivate popular support by appealing for autonomous defense. In brief, they brought to the surface Yoshida's hidden aspiration.

22. This section is a summary of my article in Japanese. For documentation, see "Hatoyama-kishi Jidai no Boeiseisaku [Defense policies during the Hatoyama-Kishi era]," in Miyake Masaki, ed., *Shōwashi no Gunbu to Seiji* [Military and politics in the history of Showa], Vol. 5 (Tokyo: Daiichi Hoki, 1983).

Encouraged by these rightist slogans, the Defense Agency advocated a number of innovative measures during the Hatoyama and Kishi years. The agency, established five months before the Hatoyama cabinet was formed, wanted to reexamine the policies that had grown out of Yoshida's reluctant submission and adaptation to American pressures. There were, among others, at least three measures with rightist implications.

First, the Defense Agency wanted to put more emphasis on strengthening naval and air forces. Successive Defense Agency director generals particularly urged strengthening the air force. This argument reflected the position of defense-related committees in the conservative party. Although these demands for the modernization of the armed forces showed a striking parallel to the West German debates during the late 1950s, the Japanese arguments were more strongly influenced by nationalist sentiments and less by strategic thinking than were those in Germany. The Japanese officials and the conservatives argued that Japan should have balanced armed forces and should not remain an auxiliary of the U.S. military. Up to that time, the United States had mostly demanded increases in ground forces to create a strategic division of labor between itself and its Asian allies. Representing nationalist sentiments within the SDF and among the general public, the Defense Agency advocated larger budgets for the navy and air force to erase the image of Japanese soldiers serving as mercenaries in an American force.

Second, from 1955 to 1962 the Defense Agency repeatedly proposed that it be reorganized and upgraded into a ministry of national defense with the authority to coordinate national security policies. This was also intended to appeal to nationalist aspirations. The term *national defense* (*kokubo*) evoked nostalgia among rightists of the old generation and hence caused negative reactions from the left.

Third, the Defense Agency directors advocated the establishment of a militia, in part to cope with feared domestic communist uprisings but also to give spiritual training to Japan's youth, whom they thought vulnerable to communist propaganda.

The Defense Agency, however, encountered serious opposition within the government as well as from the opposition parties and was unable to secure the support of top government leaders in conflicts with other ministries. Above all, the Finance Ministry opposed the costly program of strengthening naval and air forces and developing defense industries. Successive finance ministers, as well as ministry officials, were firmly committed to the idea of a balanced budget and refused to finance economically risky and unproductive projects. In the face of this powerful opposition, the newly established Defense Agency was in a weak position. The party in power was more concerned with satisfying the electorate by means of domestic programs and did not want to cut the welfare and public works budgets to increase defense spending.

Although the defense budget was gradually increased, it was done in accordance with the plan constructed during the Yoshida cabinet. These increases were largely the result of continued American pressure, rather than Defense Agency efforts. Thus there was no drastic reorientation of Japan's budgetary allocations. The ratio of the defense budget to GNP as well as to total budget expenditures actually decreased during the latter half of the 1950s.

Meanwhile, socialist opposition to defense-related issues that bore implications of domestic security measures and rightist ideology was particularly strong. The concept of a national militia encountered particularly fierce protests from the JSP, the mass media, and intellectuals and failed as a result. The top leaders of the conservative party did not wish to confront the opposition over these defense proposals.

In spite of its slogan of autonomous defense, top conservative leaders did not actively support the Defense Agency in its attempted policy innovations. Why? In part political opportunism suggested that the party avoid open direct confrontation with the socialist opposition over such a delicate matter. Party leaders were also preoccupied with constitutional and U.S.-Japan Security Treaty revision proposals, the normalization of relations with the Soviet Union, and the intraparty struggles these issues engendered. But there were other important reasons as well.

First, the thaw in Cold War tensions which occurred after the Eisenhower-Krushchev Geneva Conference in 1955 and Nikita Krushchev's criticism of Stalin in 1956 led many Japanese to believe that the Soviet threat, if it ever existed, was rapidly decreasing. The Hatoyama cabinet's reestablishment of diplomatic relations with the Soviet Union was possible only in this political climate. The normalization agreement was seen as further proof that it was unnecessary to strengthen the SDF to prevent Soviet aggression. The argument for autonomous defense was also based on an assured easing of tensions, allowing Japan to become less dependent on American military protection. In fact, both right and left in Japan acclaimed the large reduction of American forces in Japan. The Japanese government repeatedly expressed its desire for such reductions. In sharp contrast to West Germany, few, if any, protested that these reductions would impair the credibility of American deterrence. Meanwhile, the government, pressured by popular protests, officially rejected the American request to deploy nuclear weapons on Japanese territory. American bases and nuclear weapons were regarded as symbols of American domination over Japan rather than as a necessary deterrence against a possible Soviet attack. In this context, autonomous defense did not necessarily mean the expansion of Japanese military power.

A second reason why Defense Agency proposals were not more warmly received by LDP leaders concerned their fears of Japan's opposition. Hawkish statements by Hatoyama, Kishi Nobusuke, and their close followers were primarily motivated by their anxiety over domestic leftist movements, not Soviet aggression. They felt that Japanese communists, supported by misguided socialists, could very well come to power, and they considered it unlikely that the Soviet Union would launch a direct attack. These conservative leaders were particularly concerned that Japanese youth were influenced and softened not only by Japan's unwillingness to defend itself by being dependent on U.S. military protection, but also by American materialism and hedonism. Consequently, they felt that Japan's youth were particularly vulnerable to communist propaganda. As a result, they advocated the strengthening of defense primarily to cultivate nationalist consciousness and traditional Japanese values. In other words, they were more interested in the ideological function of defense than in defense capabilities as such. It is therefore understandable that these leaders did not pay serious attention to proposals for costly defense buildups.

This attitude, in turn, exacerbated the growing domestic political polarization. It created a much more serious domestic confrontation than would have been the case had the government prepared only for an external threat. Thus the domestic implications of defense policies became the focal issue, while strategic arguments were given only secondary attention. The defense issue was regarded basically as an internal security and educational issue by both right and left. This situation has continued through the present and has contributed to the unique character of defense controversies in Japan.

Furthermore, it was not recognized or appreciated by the groups opposing rearmament that any ambitious defense buildup plan was always slowed down by the top LDP leadership or through interministerial negotiation. Ambitious proposals and recommendations by the Defense Agency, the defense-related LDP committees, and armament industries were extensively and sensationally reported by the mass media, but the subsequent setbacks and rejections of these plans were rarely covered. Intentionally or not, the public gained an exaggerated image of Japan's defense buildup, and the opposition was reinforced in its conviction that the government intended to move Japan toward becoming a great military power.

More important than these developments, however, were the attempts by the conservative government to revise the constitution. Before coming to power in 1954, Hatoyama Ichiro had repeatedly said that the constitution should be revised because the status of the Self-Defense Forces was questionable under Article 9, the so-called peace clause. He also referred in this context to the need to reexamine the clauses related to education and the family. These statements reflected his traditional value system. He and his followers considered the outcome of the occupation reforms, including the constitution, excessively foreign and a threat to good Japanese traditions. The opposition viewed such expressions of traditionalism, which were essentially Confucian, as fascist. Thus insensitive provocation by conservatives further intermingled the defense issue with rightist domestic policies.

As soon as Hatoyama became prime minister, he proposed a law that would establish a Diet committee on the revision of the constitution and pushed forward preparations for such a revision. The results of the February 1955 general election were disappointing. Although his Democratic party, mostly at the expense of Yoshida's Liberal party, won more seats than in the previous election, the two socialist parties, particularly the more leftist one, also increased their number of seats and secured one-third of the votes in the lower house, enabling them to prevent the passage of any constitutional revision. The increase in popular support for the socialists was the result primarily of their campaign that the revision of the "peace constitution" would pave the way to a revival of prewar militarism and fascism.

Other election results also showed that popular support for the socialists was increasing. Japanese voters at that time were polarizing along lines of left versus right; the influence of the "realistic" defense position was fading. To break through the deadlock in the Diet, Hatoyama attempted to introduce a reform of the electoral law. This proposal created fierce opposition not only from the socialists but also within the Liberal Democratic party (which was established through the merger of the two conservative parties in late 1955). Hatoyama's new election law was, as many had suspected, based on factional considerations. Some conservative leaders also feared that single-minded attempts to revise the constitution would further polarize Japanese politics and give credibility to socialist charges that the LDP was moving toward becoming a prewar-style regime. Election reform was thus blocked, as was constitutional revision, at least for the time being.

This failure to revise the constitution had serious implications for the legal and political status of the Self-Defense Forces. The constitutionality of the SDF remained unresolved, as it does to this day. Its constitutionality has been repeatedly debated, especially when there is an attempt to introduce innovations or to rationalize the Japanese defense system. More important in the context of this discussion were the misgivings and suspicions of the JSP, which intensified with the conservative government's revision attempts. Since then, any reference to the revision of Article 9, even if it aims only at legitimizing the status quo of the SDF, raises the suspicion that the conservative party is attempting to revise the entire structure of the constitution and return to fascism and militarism.

Having failed to revise the constitution, the conservative government, now led by Prime Minister Kishi Nobusuke, embarked on revising the U.S.-Japan Security Treaty, which the Japanese elite regarded as "subordinative." Although Japanese elites were convinced that the treaty provided Japan with sufficient military guarantees, they shared the opinion of the left that the "unequal" treaty symbolized continued occupation. The constitution, which the government failed to revise, unambiguously prohibits overseas operations, as well as any Japanese contribution to regional defense beyond her own territories. Full-fledged mutuality and equality with the United States were therefore unattainable. The primary objectives of the Japanese government were a revised treaty that would provide an explicit guarantee of American military protection in the case of a direct attack, would give them a decisive voice in the equipping and deployment of the U.S. forces in Japan, would set a fixed term for the treaty, and would eliminate the so-called insurrection clause, which allowed the United States to intervene in domestic conflicts in the case of "internal riot and disturbances." All of these concessions had been withheld by the U.S. government in its negotiations of the peace settlement and accepted by Yoshida as the price to be paid for the rejection of full-fledged rearmament. The Japanese government now claimed that with such revisions the U.S.-Japanese partnership would be built on a closer and more stable basis. After long and sometimes tense negotiations, the United States accepted most of the Japanese demands. The new treaty was signed in early 1960.

The socialist opposition, espousing a neutralist line and demanding the complete abolition of the treaty, argued that the new security treaty would increase, rather than decrease, Japanese subordination to the United States by dragging Japan more deeply into America's global "imperialist" designs. Encountering repeated obstruction in the Diet, the governing party excluded the socialists from the final vote that ratified the treaty. Fierce protests mushroomed in response to the government's high-handed measure, which was considered a serious challenge to the still weak and immature democratic system. The previous year's attempt to reinforce the police enforcement authority, by which Kishi had intended to preempt the anticipated socialist opposition to the revised treaty, only served to confirm popular apprehension over his government. It was widely believed that Prime Minister Kishi, who had been a minister in the Tojo government during World War II and who was imprisoned as a war criminal, was attempting to turn Japan into a militaristic state. As a result, the opposition parties were backed not only by left-leaning trade unions and student organizations but by moderate citizen groups, organizations of housewives, and most of the mass media. The prime issue, then, was not the revision of the treaty but protection of democracy against fascism and militarism. The entanglement of the security issue with such wider political conflicts reached a peak during the crisis over the security treaty in the spring of 1960. Confronted with this unprecedented massive protest, Kishi was forced to resign, although the revision of the security agreement remained intact.

The "struggle of 1960" was taken very seriously by Japanese conservatives. Many believed Japan was on the brink of revolution. Thereafter, discussion of the security issue became taboo, and the government avoided or delayed as long as possible decisions and discussions on military questions, at least until the late 1970s. The U.S. government also became sensitive to Japanese reactions and refrained, throughout the 1960s, from pressuring Japan for a larger military commitment.[23] In spite of these cautions and self-restraints, however, deep cleavages on the defense issue remain

23. I. M. Destler et al., *Managing an Alliance: The Politics of U.S.-Japanese Relations* (Washington, D.C.: Brookings Institution, 1976), chap. 2.

imprinted on Japanese politics to this day. The acrimonious controversies over defense during the 1950s, exacerbated by their fusion with conflicts over education, public safety, and religion (Shintoism), were entrenched and institutionalized in interparty conflicts and influenced intraparty conflict over policy reappraisals within the JSP.

I have argued that Japanese defense policies, in contrast to West Germany's, have always contained rightist elements that perform the ideological function of strengthening traditional values. Unlike its West German counterpart, the Japanese elite does not take seriously the Soviet military threat and is more concerned with domestic ideological confrontation with the Japanese left. As a result, defense issues are always intermingled with domestic issues such as education and internal security.

The Japanese conservative party thus provoked the opposition parties by its rightist policies and unintentionally strengthened the influence of the left wing in the socialist parties. This has, in turn, isolated the JSP in wider political situations and created a condition for one-party dominance by the conservative party. It is true that the LDP learned a lesson from the crisis of 1960 and since then has taken a conciliatory attitude toward the opposition. But the LDP has never explicitly denied its attempt to revise the constitution or prevented its right wing from advocating extreme policies on religion, education, or police reform. Although the mainstream LDP has never allowed such rightist propaganda to dominate in the party's program, the right wing has remained vocal and provocative. Although many voters are satisfied with the realistic policy outcomes of the LDP, active minorities are, from time to time, provoked and irritated by the occasional outbreaks of rightist rhetoric. The JSP in particular has concentrated on its fight against this "shadow," while it remains isolated among the wider electorate as a result of the successful economic policies of the LDP government. In this way, the LDP, ironically, has strengthened its political dominance by an intensification of partisan controversies over ideological issues. Although Adenauer consciously used similar tactics on some occasions and succeeded in isolating the SPD, his policy tended in general to remove the SPD's concerns over the revival of militarism and fascism in West Germany and to facilitate party reform on the part of the opposition. This contrast seems to be one of the prime factors contributing to the contrasting responses of the opposition parties in the two respective nations.

Intraparty Conflicts within the Opposition Parties

The defeat in the 1957 general election gave a specific stimulus to the SPD's reappraisal of previous policies, although the defeats in the elections of 1949 and 1953 had culminating effects on their reappraisal. Since the SPD had succeeded in mobilizing massive protests against rearmament, conscription, and nuclear weapons and winning successive local elections, the electoral defeat was felt all the more severely and gave momentum to intra-party opposition to the party leadership. By 1960, it became apparent that the right had won the intra-SPD battle, achieving a reform of the party program and consolidating its new leadership position.

A similar attempt was initiated by Eda Saburo, the new secretary general of the JSP, after the party's disappointing defeat in the 1960 general election. The JSP had also expected a great victory on the basis of its successful mobilization of massive protests against the security treaty half a year before. Like the SPD reformers, Eda, after the election, criticized the party's traditional Marxist outlook and advocated instead a new, realistic program to attract popular support beyond organized labor and leftist intellectuals. Although carefully disguised, his approach represented democratic socialist ideals similar to those of the Scandinavian countries. He avoided security issues, focusing exclusively on domestic issues. His failure became apparent, however, when he was forced by leftist criticism to resign from his position as secretary general in late 1962.

The timing and contents of these intraparty debates in the two parties showed striking similarities. Above all, the socialists in both countries were confronted with the unprecedented success of the economic policies carried out by the two conservative governments. The Marxist diagnosis of the inevitable crisis and downfall of capitalist economies became increasingly unconvincing in the face of the West German and Japanese "economic miracles." Both the SPD and the JSP had tried to rely on foreign policy issues in attacking the governments, but both failed to come any closer to power. These "objective" conditions seemed to lead the two socialist parties in similar directions. Nevertheless, the two parties ultimately responded quite differently to internal reform initiatives.

The SPD and Reform

The reform was initiated essentially by two groups. First, Social Democratic mayors, including Willy Brandt (West Berlin), Max Brauer (Hamburg), and Wilhelm Kaisen (Bremen), had long advocated moderate and practical economic policies as well as cooperation with the United States on military issues, partly because of the tactical necessity of coalition with the conservative parties in local politics but also because of their actual governing experience.[24] Second, the parliamentary group, particularly its younger members, who were directly exposed to the changing opinions of the electorate, began to revolt against the control of the central party organ. These "rightists" included specialists on defense (Fritz Erler and Helmut Schmidt),

24. The background of a reformist mayor in West Berlin is extensively analyzed in Abraham Ashkenasi's *Reformpartei und Außenpolitik. Die Außenpolitik der SPD Berlin-Bonn* (Cologne: Westdeutscher Verlag, 1968).

on economics (Heinrich Deist and Karl Schiller), and on electoral campaign tactics (Klaus Schütz).

The opposition to reform involved an ironic alliance between conservative party functionaries and radical leftists. Party functionaries were opposed to the abandonment of Marxist rhetoric because of their psychological attachment to the traditional value system of socialism as well as their concern with protecting their own established status within the party. For ideological reasons, radical socialists, mostly young, vehemently rejected any proposed reexamination. In addition, active participants in peace movements, who were not necessarily Marxists or socialists, were antagonistic to any reforms that would lead to the explicit denial of pacifism and neutralism. As this alignment took shape, the competition developed around which side would gain more support from less committed party members and "opportunistic" top leaders.

During the immediate postwar period, a basic consensus emerged over foreign policy between the major parties in West Germany; in the Cold War confrontation and in general support for European integration both parties were pro-West. Kurt Schumacher was no less anticommunist than Adenauer. Both leaders rejected pacifism and neutralism and were ready to defend the Federal Republic against Soviet "imperialism," with arms if necessary. Their differences on rearmament and foreign policy were essentially tactical in nature.[25] Consequently, the first general election of 1949 was fought primarily over the economic issues of a free market economy versus socialization and planning.

Despite its uncompromising battle against communists on many issues, the SPD shared with the communists a common Marxist diagnosis and prescription concerning economic issues. (The principal difference lay in their beliefs concerning democracy, that is, their different evaluations of parliamentary democracy. Schumacher, who was a true believer in parliamentarism, his conviction being reinforced by his experience with Hitler's rise to power, rejected extraparliamentary activities as dangerous to democracy.[26] Schumacher and Adenauer shared a common apprehension of the German masses.) Schumacher saw proof of the Marxian analysis in the catastrophic conditions of the postwar period; he concluded that the time was ripe for building a truly democratic, that is, socialist, state. After the currency reform of 1948, however, the spectacular success of Erhard's free-market economy eroded the foundation of his political strategy.

As a result, the SPD was forced to focus its criticism of the government on foreign policy issues, the most prominent of which was the rearmament

25. Ulrich Buczylowski, *Kurt Schumacher und die deutsche Frage. Sicherheitpolitik und strategische Offensivkonzeption vom August 1950 bis September 1951* (Stuttgart: Seewold, 1973).

26. Waldemar Ritter, *Kurt Schumacher. Eine Untersuchung seiner politischen Konzeption und seiner Gesellschafts- und Staatsauffassung* (Hannover: J. H. W. Dietz, 1964); Lewis J. Edinger, *Kurt Schumacher: A Study in Personality and Political Behavior* (Stanford: Stanford University Press, 1965).

question.[27] But the basic consensus between Adenauer and Schumacher over military policy hindered the latter in presenting any clear-cut alternative such as a neutralist or pacifist line. When Schumacher, the overwhelmingly dominant figure in the SPD, died in 1952, he left the party in a very confused and ambivalent position on rearmament and European integration. During the subsequent several years, the party leadership, under a typical party functionary, Erich Ollenhauer, intensified its criticism of Adenauer's security policy. While the leadership's alternative remained ambiguous, pacifists increased their influence within the party. In 1954, such pro-U.S. local leaders as Brandt or Kaisen as well as a rightist defense specialist, Erler, were further isolated and were blocked from joining the executive committee, though three pacifists were newly elected. The pacifist position was reinforced by the SPD's participation in extraparliamentary movements against rearmament, against West German entry into NATO, against conscription (1955–56), and against nuclear weapons (1957–58). Understandably, the rightists tended to avoid confrontation over sensitive security issues and to concentrate their reform proposals on economic issues.

While pacifist and neutralist orientations gained strength within the SPD, the traditional socialist ideology began to fade. The decline of socialist ideology was detected in the long, lingering process of discussions over reformulating a basic party program. During the immediate postwar period, Schumacher turned down rank-and-file proposals to formulate a new comprehensive party program on the ground that the party had to be flexible in such a rapidly changing situation. In preparation for the 1953 election, the party leadership issued an *Aktionsprogram,* listing the relatively specific demands that formed the basic policies of the party. Although it was nothing but the sum of old policies, including planning and socialization, the socialist elements were given less prominence, partly as an electoral tactic designed to woo the farmers and the urban middle class.

After the party's electoral defeat, both the left and the right claimed that lack of clarity in the party's position had been responsible. This time, the reformists were more vocal than the radicals in their criticism of the party leadership. Pressured by these criticisms, a committee was set up to formulate a new program. In the 1954 party congress in Berlin, the committee presented a new preamble containing certain reformist ideas to be added to the *Aktionsprogram* of 1952. After accepting this preamble as a provisional program, the party congress decided to establish another committee to formulate a fundamental program. In this party congress, most debates were devoted to the discussion of defense issues. This was contrary to the reformers' intention and represented a tactical success by the radicals.

27. The following analysis is based mostly on Wilker, *Sicherheitspolitik;* Udo F. Löwke, *Die SPD und die Wehrfrage 1949 bis 1955* (Bonn: Neue Gesellschaft, 1976); Klaus-Peter Schulz, *Opposition als politisches Schicksal?* (Cologne: Verlag für Politik und Wirtschaft, 1958); and Hartmut Soell, *Fritz Erler. Eine politische Biographie* (Bonn and Bad Godesberg: Dietz, 1976), vols. 1 and 2.

The new committee failed to produce a program by the time of the 1957 election, partly because of the lack of enthusiasm on the part of the traditional leadership. As the election approached, conflicting statements were issued by different SPD leaders. Ollenhauer talked of the need for a modest form of public control. Eichler upheld the traditional idea of socialization, and Deist rejected socialization as out of date.[28] Yet during the electoral campaign, the party leaders responded to the changing public atmosphere by deemphasizing socialist concepts. In fact, the SPD made it clear that it accepted a free-market economy in principle. Without a dramatic reorientation, however, the party could not convince the electorate that its conversion was sincere and not simply an electoral tactic. In addition, the SPD suffered throughout the campaign from the conservatives' attempt to identify the socialists with the communists. A dramatic change was thus required if the party wanted to gain power in the foreseeable future.

Meanwhile, a subtle but important development could be detected in the SPD's intensified opposition to Adenauer's foreign policy; reference to Marxian analysis became less and less salient. This change was most clearly manifested in the party's discussion of the Schuman Plan and European economic integration,[29] but it was also shown in its opposition to Adenauer's rearmament policies. The basic political, social, and economic structures of the existing regime were increasingly accepted, at least implicitly, even as specific military policies were vehemently criticized.

Then came the defeat in the 1957 election. Immediately after the election, such SPD mayors as Brauer, Kaisen, and Brandt demanded drastic reforms of the party program. The parliamentary group also revolted against the party leadership and elected as its vice-chairman two prominent reformists, Erler and Carlo Schmid, as well as Herbert Wehner, who joined the reform group. The previous vice-chairmen, Wilhelm Mellies and Erwin Schoettle, were replaced against Ollenhauer's will. Ollenhauer remained as chairman, but his position in the parliamentary group became mostly symbolic. From their newly acquired parliamentary leadership, the reformists eventually gained the leadership of the party itself.

The *Apparat* further lost power through the election for the executive committee in the 1958 Stuttgart party congress. Debates and resolutions over economic issues in this congress also showed an increasing acceptance of reformist ideas. From then on, discussions continued on various levels of the SPD organization. Finally, the Bad Godesberg congress in November 1959 adopted by an overwhelming majority a new program embodying reformist ideas. A resolution against the reform proposed by the left was severely defeated.

28. Kitzinger, *German Electoral Politics.*
29. Rudolf Hrbek, *Die SPD, Deutschland und Europa. Die Haltung der Sozialdemocratie zum Verhaltnis von Deutschlandpolitik und Westintegration 1945–1957* (Bonn: Europa Union, 1972).

The victory of the reformists on economic policies was thus virtually complete. In the process of drafting a new program, little attention was paid to foreign and military affairs. The SPD had attacked Adenauer's security policy primarily on the ground that it would endanger reunification. To make reunification acceptable to the Soviet Union, the party presented as an alternative a collective security system that would include the United States, USSR, and a unified Germany. Although the SPD never explicitly rejected the principle of a national defense with armed forces or its existing alliance with the West, the concepts of collective security satisfied pacifists and neutralists. Furthermore, the plan for a nuclear-free zone or arms reduction was often connected with the argument for the collective security system.

In March 1959, the SPD presented the *Deutschlandplan,* in which concrete steps toward reunification in a collective security system were elaborated for the first time. A similar prescription was included in the Godesberg Program eight months later. In addition, the resolution against nuclear weapons presented by the executive committee was revised in the party congress to satisfy the delegates' strong antinuclear sentiment. The SPD leadership, however, succeeded, after heated discussions, in avoiding explicit commitment to the abolition of conscription. The Godesberg Program thus contained no reference to conscription, and the leadership reaffirmed its opposition to conscription on the ground that it would hinder reunification. Furthermore, the party leadership, against the objections of some delegates, secured inclusion in the program of the affirmation of national defense.

In spite of these changes, the basic foreign policy orientation of the SPD remained intact; the party gave top priority to unification and evaluated every military policy from the viewpoint of whether it would have a positive or negative effect on reunification. Although the reasoning was different, the SPD leadership shared policy goals with pacifists and neutralists.

A split soon emerged. In March 1960, Wehner abruptly rejected the *Deutschlandplan* as out of date. This was all the more surprising because he himself was the chairman of the committee that had drafted the plan. The SPD leaders thus abandoned their hope for reunification through negotiation with the Soviet Union and hence the concept of collective security. Since the SPD had not had any interest in disengagement or neutralism per se, its abandonment of reunification efforts led to the drastic reorientation of military policy. Three months later, in parliament, Wehner proposed a bipartisan foreign policy with the Adenauer government on the basis of West German participation in NATO. (Wehner was silent on nuclear and conscription questions because there was no intraparty consensus on these controversial questions even within the executive committee.) The rank-and-file members were thus presented with a fait accompli by the party leadership.

Because of the tight centralization of the party organization, the absence of clear-cut factional groupings, and traditional loyalty to the party leadership, the reformists were able to secure their position once they succeeded in penetrating and controlling the top leadership of the party. The role of Wehner, a vice-chairman who had converted to the reformist group, seemed critical in this context. Dissenting leftists lacked an institutional base from which to block the change. Consequently, the Hannover party congress in November 1960 approved a new foreign policy orientation. Meanwhile, the SPD severed relations with the student affiliate, the Socialist German Student Federation (SDS) in July 1960. The SDS had moved to the left as the party moved to the right. Thus the party's conversion was completed.

The development of the party's foreign policy has been described as "relatively unaffected by the evolutionary process which produced the Bad Godesberg Program."[30] Certainly, if we focus on the crucial period 1957–60, we cannot avoid such an impression. As the socialist economic ideology faded, the SPD's search for foreign policy alternatives was intensified. And it was precisely the reformists, Erler, Carlo Schmid, and Helmut Schmidt, who proposed disengagement and collective security and contributed to the drafting of the *Deutschlandplan*. And it was also these reformists who subsequently initiated and secured the abandonment of these "traditional" SPD foreign policy alternatives. In this sense, one scholar rightly denies the classification of party leaders as traditionalists and reformists regarding foreign and military policies.[31]

A closer look, however, reveals an underlying linkage between reforms in economic policy and those in foreign policy and the enduring, although sometimes hidden, ideological conflicts between the pragmatic right and the moralist/traditionalist left. And as the idealistic influence of mass movements faded, the strategic thinking of defense specialists became increasingly stronger. The specialization of decision making and the technocratization of thinking within the SPD leadership[32] were thus parallel to those on economic issues. The foreign policy reformists, who lingered over disengagement and collective security and shared these concepts with the pacifists, had a common orientation with the economic policy reformists.

The JSP and the Failure of Reform

In the immediate postwar period, the Japan Socialist party was founded at the initiative of Nishio Suehiro and his close colleagues and remained under their leadership during the first socialist cabinet (May 1947–February 1948).[33] Like Schumacher, Nishio was a stern anticommunist as well as

---

30. Schellenger, *The SPD in the Bonn Republic*, p. 36.
31. Stephan J. Artner, *A Change of Course: The West German Social Democrats and NATO, 1957–1961* (Westport, Conn.: Greenwood Press, 1985), p. xvii.
32. Wilker, *Sicherheitspolitik.*
33. On the JSP's right wing, see my *Saigunbi to Nashonarizumu*, chap. 4.

a faithful parliamentarian, a defender of parliamentary democracy against the undue influence of extraparliamentary activities. Moreover, unlike Schumacher, he was ready to cooperate with conservatives. In fact, the socialists gained power in 1947 through a coalition with the conservative parties, the Democratic party and the National Cooperative party.

Meanwhile, the leftists increased their influence within the party through the support of radicalized labor unions and intensified intraparty conflicts, and as a result, the socialist cabinet fell. After a severe electoral defeat for the JSP in 1949, the right wing lost its control of the party, and the left became increasingly predominant in deciding party programs and leaders. At the same time the peace settlement was put on the agenda, foreign policy issues became dominant in both intra- and interparty controversies. Idealistic neutralism gained wide popular support and strengthened leftist influence within the party. Furthermore, the outbreak of the Korean War and Japan's sudden rearmament gave the leftists an opportunity to mobilize popular pacifist sentiments by uncompromising opposition to rearmament. Its active participation in massive "nonpartisan" peace movements enabled the JSP to recover its electoral support.

Nishio and other rightists, however, opposed this strategy. In late 1951, the Socialist party split into the Right-Wing Socialist party (RWSP) and the Left-Wing Socialist party (LWSP). The campaign for the 1952 general election focused on the rearmament issue, and the LWSP made great gains, while the RWSP gained only modestly. Thus when the two parties merged in 1955, the left socialists outnumbered the right socialists in the Diet.

A classical Marxist doctrine, derived from a prewar Marxist school called *Rono-ha,* became dominant within the LWSP and was adopted as official party doctrine in the 1954 party congress. The Japan Communist party (JCP) inherited a competing prewar Marxist tradition, *Koza-ha.* Although the LWSP and the JCP engaged in a fierce "theoretical struggle" with each other, both parties believed that socialist revolution was inevitable and indispensable to hinder the conservatives' attempt to move Japan toward becoming a militarist state. Popular support for the LWSP, however, was derived mostly from its uncompromisingly antimilitarist attitude. It is doubtful that most LWSP supporters desired a socialist revolution.

Throughout the mid-1950s, "nonpartisan" peace movements were further activated by one death and several serious injuries to Japanese fishermen as a result of American nuclear tests in the Pacific as well as by residents' protests against American military bases in Japan. In addition, the defense policies, the constitutional revision, and the security treaty revision all intensified antigovernment movements in the latter half of the 1950s. Needless to say, within the reunified socialist party these massive protest movements weakened the influence of the right, which adhered to parliamentarism. The Nishio faction in particular, which supported the U.S.-Japan Security Treaty and accepted the constitutionality of the Self-Defense Forces, was isolated within the party. In the 1958 party congress, Nishio tried to reverse the left-wing trend, arguing for the transformation of the party from a class party into a "national party." This attempt, however, further weakened his position within the party. The Youth Division of the JSP, which opposed revision of the security treaty, proposed that Nishio be expelled for expressing opinions contrary to the official party line. Isolated within the party, Nishio and his followers left the JSP and founded the Democratic Socialist party (DSP) in January 1960, several months before the security treaty crisis.

When the crisis was over and the next general election approached, the government under the new prime minister, Ikeda Hayato, took a conciliatory "low posture" toward the opposition and the electorate. To meet this new challenge from the LDP government, the newly elected JSP secretary general, Eda, announced a new policy proposal called "structural reform." In part to counter the DSP's challenge, Eda criticized traditional Marxist doctrine, particularly the *Rono-ha* argument; he rejected its all-or-nothing attitude and advocated instead gradual, pragmatic reforms.[34]

Until he was elected secretary general, Eda had been known as a leftist. Indeed, he belonged to the leftist Suzuki faction and had strongly opposed Nishio and vigorously supported his expulsion. He had been an agricultural specialist, however, which put him in a minority group within the party, whose mainstream consisted of former labor leaders. It is no wonder that from the beginning his policy orientation differed from orthodox Marxism and its secondary treatment of farmers. Eda and other Diet members whose constituencies were in agricultural areas could not rely on the support of labor unions for election and were forced to cultivate electoral support through concrete, realistic policy proposals. Hence they were more inclined toward party reform. Most leftist Diet members, on the other hand, had to depend heavily on young activists within labor unions for their electoral campaign because the JSP lacked mass party membership. Regardless of whether they sincerely believed in Marxist doctrines, these parliamentarians had to pay lip service to traditional Marxist rhetoric to acquire the indispensable votes of young radicals.[35]

Eda concentrated his reform proposal on domestic issues. Immediately before the 1960 election, the JSP executive committee decided to take a more neutralist position, meaning a less prosocialist line, and to send a party delegation to Washington the following autumn. It also declared that the JSP welcomed closer economic and cultural relations with the United States even as it rejected any military alliance. Meanwhile, the committee, presumably under Eda's initiative, emphasized the importance of cultivating farm-

34. *Eda Saburo: Sono Roman to Tsuisō* [Eda Saburo: His romanticism and our recollections] (Tokyo: Eda Saburo Kankokai, 1980), p. 80; Eda Saburo, *Atarashii Seiji wo Mesashite* [Aiming at new politics] (Tokyo: Nihonhyoronsha, 1977).

35. Asahishinbun Nagano-shikyoku, *Shinshu no Shakaitō* [The JSP in Shinshu] (Tokyo: Asahi Sonorama, 1981).

ers' support and also of consolidating the party's organizations in residential areas so as to reduce its heavy dependence on labor unions.

After the 1960 general election, even though the DSP experienced a severe electoral defeat, Eda intensified his reform efforts, encouraged by favorable attention from the mass media. On foreign policy, he dared to say that the Soviet Union, as well as the United States, was responsible for the Cold War and that the JSP, unlike the JCP, could not regard the Soviet Union as a "peaceful power" (*Heiwa-Seiryoku*). Eda was, naturally, confronted by severe criticism from the leftists. When the January 1962 party congress approached, in which the post of secretary general was at stake, he became more cautious and more leftist so as to consolidate his position within the party. Once he was reelected, however, he advocated his reform program more openly. In July 1962, he publicized "The Eda Vision," which was intended to adapt the party program to Japan's new prosperity and stability. He thought the JSP should have three goals: to equal the standard of living of the United States, to obtain social security comparable to that in the USSR, and parliamentary democracy similar to Great Britain's, all built around the peace constitution (unarmed neutrality) in Japan. The lack of a Marxist outlook astonished the JSP's leftists. And the intraparty conflict was intensified.

Although he was popular among the general public, Eda lacked a solid factional basis in his party. Nor did he enjoy close ties with labor unions. Meanwhile, Nishio and his followers had left the party. Antagonism toward Nishio and his DSP was still overwhelming, even among the reformers within the JSP. As a result, Eda and Nishio were hindered in forming a coalition against the leftists in spite of their ideological similarities. On the contrary, Eda had to be extremely cautious to avoid being identified with Nishio. This caused confusion in reform controversies. Factional rivalry and envy of Eda also helped isolate him within the party, and after heated debates he was unseated as secretary general in November 1962.

Controversies over "structural reform" continued within the party, but thereafter the leftists took the offensive. From the mid-1960s on, the leftists increased their influence by gaining the support of the anti–Vietnam War movement, which enjoyed fairly widespread popularity. Eda himself further moved to the right, accepting social democratic ideals and rejecting Marxist ideology. As his position became clearer, he lost more influence within the party. When he finally left the JSP in 1977 after a long, frustrating intraparty struggle, he had few followers within the party, despite his many supporters outside party ranks.

It would be appropriate to examine here the basic alignment within the JSP in comparison with that in the SPD and to point out some structural variables leading to different policy outcomes. As was pointed out previously, the reformists within the SPD represented an alliance between parliamentary members, who, unlike party functionaries, were directly subject

to the changing atmosphere among voters, and local leaders with administrative experience as mayors and *Land*-level leaders. The opposition to
reform came from traditional party functionaries and young radicals. This
basic conflict alignment was detected in the JSP as well, although the balance of power was quite different, as was the attitude of the top leadership,
presumably reflecting differences in the power balance. (In the JSP, Diet
members with technical expertise, such as Wada Hiroo and Ueda Tetsu,
were generally sympathetic to the reform attempts.)

Above all, the parliamentary groups in the JSP have been heavily dependent on the support of trade unions, in part because the JSP lacks the mass
organization of the SPD. The other side of the coin is that once a parliamentary member secures the support of a particular trade union such as the
Japan Teachers' Union or the Federation of Steel Industry Unions (which
are organized in a peak association called Sohyo, the General Council of
Trade Union Federations), his electoral victory is almost certain. Even if he
fails in the election, the union will take responsibility for his subsequent
career. The trade unions under Sohyo provide JSP politicians with political
financing, campaign workers, and even candidates. The political activities
of Sohyo have been, in turn, dominated by a top leadership with leftist
orientation by young radical trade union members.[36]

There are complicated historical reasons why Sohyo, unlike most peak
labor unions in the advanced nations, came to be dominated by the left.
Sohyo, which was originally organized with the encouragement of the occupation authorities in opposition to communist efforts to dominate and
manipulate the labor movement, turned to the left as the rearmament issue
came to the fore in the early 1950s. And through their constant struggles
against the "reactionary," "militarist" tendencies within the conservative
government, union leaders became progressive, less inclined to achieve interest representation through bread-and-butter unionism and more interested in defending the constitution and their interpretation of its antimili-
tary implications. This radicalism of the unions was directly reflected in the
JSP because of the party's dependence on the unions.

It is true that there were and are socialist Diet members who are not so
dependent on union support. But they are minorities. The advocates of
reforms within the JSP were mostly recruited from these groups. It is no
accident that Eda was a former agrarian movement leader. These party
members usually have their own supporting electoral organizations in their
home districts and are therefore less dependent on the unions. Most of the
democratic socialists, who split with the JSP in 1960 over security issues,
have similarly independent electoral organizations. Such politicians have no
need to pay lip service to radical rhetoric, but they are also subject to the

36. Nakamura Kenji, *Shakaishugi kyōkai wo kiru* [Analysis of the Socialist League] (Tokyo:
Nisshin Hodo, 1977); Sugimori Koji and Yamaguchi Asao, *Rōsō Giin ga Shakaito wo
koroshita* [Union Diet members killed the JSP] (Tokyo: Nisshin Hodo, 1980).

changing opinions of the electorate. In contrast, union-dependent politicians have to be very careful not to offend the young leftist union members who are indispensable in their electoral campaigns, but they are relatively free from the need to adapt to changing public opinion. These trade-union-dependent politicians behaved more and more similarly to the "traditional" party functionaries in the SPD, concerned only with defending their party positions, and conservative and antagonistic toward any reform proposals.

In Japan, as the political apathy of postindustrialism emerged, trade unions became more and more dependent on ideologically motivated young activists willing to engage in time-consuming electoral campaigns. A paradoxical situation resulted. As Marxist diagnosis lost its persuasive power among the general electorate, the JSP clung more tightly to Marxist terminology to maintain its declining power base. In this somewhat desperate situation, the last stronghold from which the JSP hoped to broaden, or at least maintain, its support beyond union members was among citizens concerned with the "reactionary" tendencies of the LDP government toward "fascism and militarism." There has been no shortage of rightist statements or policy proposals from LDP politicians, which could be interpreted as reflecting a desire to restore the prewar regime; these opinions have been most saliently manifested on defense issues.

The JSP thus continued to concentrate on defense issues, presenting itself as a defender of liberal democracy (instead of as an advocate of socialist order). The party tried both to mobilize status quo–oriented citizens around a commitment to postwar democracy and to cultivate the deep-rooted pacifist sentiment among the Japanese masses. An irony is that moderate conservatives tolerated the outbursts of rightist rhetoric among LDP members primarily as an ideological counterweight against the dangers of communism. Subjectively, their "reactionary" statements stem more from defensiveness than from an offensive position. In any case, the JSP has come to regard itself, and is regarded by its supporters, as a single-issue veto group, whose prime concern is to defend the existing constitutional framework, rather than as an alternative governing party. Article 9 of the constitution, the war renunciation clause, was thus given a symbolic meaning; its defense, and hence the maintenance of unarmed neutrality, has become the last line of defense for the liberal democratic constitutional regime.

The JSP has achieved the task assigned it by the trade unions and citizen groups fairly well. Only in this context can one appreciate the irony that the JSP has wielded much stronger influence than the SPD over national defense policies. This influence prevailed in spite of, or rather because of, the one-party dominance of the conservatives. Whereas the SPD failed to prevent Adenauer's rearmament policy and played only a marginal role in defense policy making, the JSP succeeded in imprinting its preferences on Japanese defense policies, as can be seen, for example, in Japan's "three non-nuclear principles," the magical 1 percent of GNP limit and defense spending, and the difficulties the Japanese defense establishment has faced in its efforts to engage in strategic planning. Although the LDP maintained an unprecedented one-party dominance, its concrete policies strongly reflect the preferences of the opposition. In contrast, the SPD broke the seventeen-year one-party dominance by CDU/CSU only at the price of abandoning its original policy goals.

Conclusion

Faced with the Cold War confrontation, the socialist parties in the West in general, and in West Germany and Japan in particular, were put in a difficult position; they could not easily abandon one of their traditional ideals, pacifism, yet they, or at least their leaders, had to face the reality of the Cold War, which demanded or at least justified military protection by the United States. The acceptance of this military alliance had another serious domestic implication: it also meant acceptance of the American, that is, capitalist, economic order. The lure of American foreign aid posed one more dilemma. The conservatives, on the other hand, were in an advantageous position. Although they might sense an identity crisis in attempting to replace (at least partially) traditional nationalism with cosmopolitan liberalism, it was easier for them to accept American military protection and the capitalist economic order because the traditional conservatives and the Americans shared the rejection of socialism, not to mention communist imperialism. Both in the FRG and in Japan, these advantages were exploited by the conservatives and resulted in stable conservative dominance; a seventeen-year one-party dominance (*Der CDU-Staat*[37]) and a forty-year one-party dominance by the LDP.

In addition to this international factor favorable to the conservatives, there was and is another, probably more serious, factor inherent to the socialist parties, which further weakens their chances to gain and maintain power—internal conflicts within socialism. Socialism traditionally had three components: first, a principle of governance including nationalization and planning; second, the interest representation of organized labor (trade unionism); and third, an idealistic social movement. The conflicts among these three elements often hindered, or at least postponed, the gaining of power by the socialists. It also made, and still makes, stable governance by the socialists difficult.[38] In advanced industrial societies, the first two components have been gradually institutionalized in party politics and collective bargaining (and political representation of labor in the government).[39] The

37. Gert Schäfer und Carl Nedelmann, eds., *Der CDU-Staat. Studien zur Verfassungswirklichkeit der Bundesrepublik* (Munich: Szozeny, 1967).
38. See developments in the SPD during the early 1980s as well as those in the Labour party in Britain.
39. Ralf Dahrendorf, *Class and Class Conflict in Industrial Society* (Stanford: Stanford University Press, 1959).

third element was thus excluded from both party competition and collective bargaining—from the mainstream of political processes—and survived only as a radical third-party movement, often in a coalition with communists, or as a single-issue movement. This is what happened in most European socialist movements, including West Germany's.

Meanwhile, Japanese socialism retained or even strengthened the idealist social movement. Radical idealism survived and consolidated itself within a major socialist party as well as within major trade unions. The conflict over defense contributed to this survival and consolidation. What is this radical idealism in socialism? I cannot explore the point in depth but must satisfy myself by making a couple of comments on the radicalism of Japanese labor.

In spite of its Marxist-Leninist terminology, Sohyo's actual behavior and political culture unmistakably reflect syndicalist tendencies. This is most clearly manifested in the federation's "resistance spirit" against any authority. It not only rejects government intervention but also refuses party dominance, particularly attempts by communists to influence the labor movement. (This was the organizing principle at the time of the foundation of Sohyo.) Sohyo seeks autonomy and independence against employers as well. It inherited the radical tradition of workers' control of production, which was widely practiced during the immediate postwar period in Japan. From this tradition came also its adherence to the ideal of direct democracy and direct action. In essence, it seeks "workers' power."[40]

These "spirits" are difficult to maintain in the normality of the postindustrial society. They can survive among the masses only in crisis situations. The rightist rhetoric of the LDP, particularly statements on defense, played an important role in providing this indispensable element, helping the leadership of Sohyo maintain a crisis atmosphere among the federation's mass followers. In other words, Sohyo leaders, unlike most socialists in the West, have succeeded in defending their tradition of a radical democratic ideal against the danger of erosion by the prosaic atmosphere of an affluent postindustrial society. The cost, however, is the semipermanent one-party dominance by the conservatives because such romanticism sharply contradicts the affluence and stability which the average voter prefers.

40. See my analysis of Nisson Trade Union in "Kigyonai Kenryoku kenkei to Ideorogi [Power structures and ideologies within a corporation]," *Leviathan,* no. 2 (1988): 103–17.

5. Establishing Party Dominance: It Ain't Easy

GIUSEPPE DI PALMA

How significant are transitions from authoritarianism to democracy in building one-party dominance?[1]

One one side, it seems reasonable to expect that the exceptional circumstances, especially in the aftermath of a war, that surround the establishment of a democratic regime should favor the electoral and political dominance of one party over the others. To paraphrase T. J. Pempel's theoretical contribution to this volume, dominance should be favored because a transition to democracy represents a moment of crisis, in the pristine sense of the word, that is, a culminating moment of judgment, choice, and decision. This condition makes the politics of transition nonroutine and offers the parties capable of seizing leadership a lasting opportunity to hegemonize the political game, political culture, and political economy, while possibly isolating and delegitimizing—in Pempel's analysis—contending parties and social formations.

On the other side, a head count of democratic transitions in Western or industrial countries since World War II invites caution. Of the five democracies reconstituted as a consequence of World War II—Japan, Italy, Austria, West Germany, and France—the former two developed party systems and governments that have remained dominated by one party; the latter three did not. In West Germany, the Christian Democratic Union's (CDU) hold on postwar governments was interrupted in 1966. In France, nothing resembling party dominance appeared until the advent of the Fifth Republic. And in Austria, the two major parties—the Socialists and the Catholics—worked in government coalition to avoid dominance. Since World

---

This chapter is a revision of a paper presented at the conference on one-party dominance, Oxford University, Nissan Institute, April 2–4, 1986.

1. I am using dominance as defined for this volume by T. J. Pempel.

War II, none of the three European democracies inaugurated in the 1970s has developed one-party dominance: neither Greece, nor Portugal, nor Spain. If we add that Japan's dominant liberal democratic forces did not unify into a party until 1955, past the first phase of reconstruction, it could be strictly asserted that Italy is the only country in which democratic reconstruction has arguably helped the development of one-party dominance.

I shall examine the eight cases to show by what means dominance succeeds, or why it fails. I shall also examine them to emphasize that, in assessing the impact of democratic transition on one-party dominance, one should not exaggerate its favorableness. Occasional appearances notwithstanding, it is usually difficult for a party to monopolize support by democratic means. Its acquisition of dominance must be constantly renewed through strategies that are often changing, often unclear in their consequences to those who practice them, rarely preordained, and both contingent and aleatory. Analysts looking back at cases in which such strategies have nevertheless succeeded time after time, giving a party a string of victories, may believe that every victory, beginning with the first, prepared in close order the next one, so that every additional victory needs less explanation. In effect, a prospective reconstruction of events, with an eye to contingencies and risks at the time, may well show that such retrospective collapsing of how dominance is built are so many optical illusions.

Let me offer two considerations in support of caution. The first is that, even assuming that unique historical conditions such as war or democratic reconstruction favor dominance, political parties must work hard to benefit from those conditions. They must still overcome competition and achieve dominance in a context of freshly renewed competitive rules. Hence dominance may not be achieved after all, or it may be achieved by parties other than those that seemed to have the best chances at the time. The second consideration is that party strategies for dominance may change not only from democracy to democracy but also over time within the same democracy and for the same parties. More precisely, staying dominant after the transition may be predicated on reshuffling party strategies. I suggest in particular that the range of strategies available to a party in the first period of democratic transition, when it has yet to consolidate power and state resources, is ideally different from the range after consolidation. On this point, I refer the reader to Tarrow's chapter on Italy in this volume. Thus the endurance of dominance is not foregone, and the ability or willingness to adapt strategies and resources when required is rare indeed. Both considerations begin to suggest why, though the initial conditions surrounding their democratic transitions seemed favorable to single-party dominance, our eight countries went their separate ways.

I shall return briefly to the theme of changing strategies for dominance only at the very end of the essay. My contribution, otherwise, is almost exclusively devoted to dominance within democratic transition. I confess that I am as intrigued by the dynamic of transitions, of which dominance is one outcome, as I am by dominance per se, of which transitions are one suitable context. The gist of my argument will be that, within transitions, the establishment of dominance is a matter of delegitimizing the opposition, removing its governing credibility, and asserting instead one's own politicocultural hegemony. But it is also a matter (crucial to a democratic transition) of reconciling dominance with a new competitive order. Success is therefore more a matter of strategies, alliances, and coalitions than it is of objective qualities—either of parties or of context. These strategies are available in principle to all parties. But it is what I call the moderate parties that can usually put them to most effective use. For different reasons, the extreme right and, especially, the extreme left are not as ready to combine dominance with competitiveness. Either one or the other may have to give way. I will illustrate these claims by means of the eight case studies.[2]

Dominance and Competitiveness

To reword what I just said, transitions to democracy can be at one and the same time the context for two quite different sets of impulses and motivations. On one side, we may detect an impulse toward dominance; on the other, the new democracy must also guarantee the competitiveness of democratic rules and the openness of the democratic game. Guaranteeing competitiveness is a minimal requirement for the acquisition of loyalty by disparate groups and parties. Though one-party dominance is by itself insufficient to cause the disloyalty of other parties (or more precisely their refusal to play the democratic game), one cannot fail to appreciate how the prospect of one party monopolizing government by the delegitimation of the opposition can be the source of unacceptable strains for the new democracy.

Ironically, these strains can be strong, especially in countries in which the acquisition of democratic loyalties is tested by the presence of constituencies

2. The cases are used to illustrate, not to demonstrate. Demonstration would require reliance on a fairly parsimonious paradigm. But working with paradigms does not come naturally to me for two reasons. First, despite slippage into the language (and the evidence) of probability, my interest in one-party dominance is a normative one. I am interested in the normative outer limits, as it were, of dominance: those limits beyond which dominance violates basic democratic tenets. My eight cases serve well to illustrate those limits; but analyses by means of paradigms lend themselves poorly to the task. In the second place, paradigms—because they deal with probabilities—are difficult to develop for rapidly changing contexts such as regime transitions. During transitions, the structural and behavioral parameters that usually guide political outcomes under normal circumstances hardly operate. Given the special weight of conjunctures, explanations for the same outcomes (especially the failure of dominance) tend to become idiosyncratic. In support of these points see Guillermo O'Donnell and Philippe C. Schmitter, *Transitions from Authoritarian Rule: Tentative Conclusions about Uncertain Democracies* (Baltimore: Johns Hopkins University Press, 1982), pp. 3–5; Albert O. Hirschman, "The Search for Paradigms as a Hindrance to Understanding," *World Politics* 22 (1970): 329–43.

located at the extremes of the political spectrum. I am speaking of sectors of the political right implicated or identified with the fallen dictatorship, as well as sectors of the left that may have fought the dictatorship in the name of something other than a conventional democratic order. Although the outright delegitimation of these sectors may be somehow justifiable and at times unavoidable for democracy's sake, it may also be a risky and less than optimal choice. I have discussed elsewhere how transferring the loyalties of what I will call henceforth the extremes from dictatorship to democracy, though difficult, is also crucial and not necessarily impossible.[3] It is crucial because rare is the case in which a new democracy comes into being because support for—and supporters of—antidemocratic solutions on the left and right have withered away of their own accord. It is also not impossible because support for dictatorship is more often a matter of relative calculus than one of set values and because democracy is a game open to all who wish to play it—provided that specific guarantees of participation in the game are supplied. The task of attracting loyalties to democracy by no means ends with the collapse of dictatorship, and abandoning the task because of challenges from the political extremes raises some fundamental dilemmas.

This explains why democratic transitions marked by the presence of significant political extremes often appeal to interpartisan cooperation. And whatever the specific interpartisan arrangements, all such forms of cooperation are noncompetitive, yet in a sense that seems almost exactly the opposite of dominance.[4] This is not to say, despite what common sense may suggest, that interpartisan cooperation is incompatible with the development of party dominance. Nevertheless, I will show that it takes considerable virtue, or perhaps unwitting fortune, for a party to emerge as dominant in a context of cooperation, and maybe exactly because of it. Indeed, Italy's Christian Democracy seems to be just about the only fitting case.

In sum, the mere existence of a transition to democracy does not favor processes of delegitimation, *even of the extremes,* unless special additional circumstances (to be examined later) are present. Hence the achievement of one-party dominance by means of delegitimation is exceptional in more than one way. It is exceptional in the sense that it requires those exceptional circumstances (raising the question of its survival past them), in the sense that it requires exceptional management to balance it with the acquisition of interpartisan democratic loyalties, and in sum in the sense that it should be a relatively uncommon occurrence.

3. Giuseppe Di Palma, "Government Performance: An Issue and Three Cases in Search of Theory," *West European Politics* 7 (April 1984): 172–87.
4. Among the arrangements are the politics of accommodation, *proporz, pactismo,* governments of national unity, *política de consenso.* The first two refer basically to formulas for allocating resources and offices on an equal or proportional basis among political forces. The others refer to methods and procedures for making political actors work together.

We can reach a better understanding of why dominance is exceptional if we conceive of democratic transitions as featuring in all cases a fairly standard progression of stages, each distinguished by its own set of relevant actors and tasks.[5] As the transition progresses, it takes more and more the following features. First, there is an increase in the number of actors entering the political arena.[6] Second, center stage, which at first tends to be occupied by selected institutions and elites exploiting positional, legal, charismatic, or military advantage, is subsequently shared with social and political formations that rely on electoral or mass appeal. Third, the emergency tasks and issues of the first stage (the removal of the dictatorship and its institutional residues, the reestablishment of law and order, the definition of relations with occupying powers) are progressively overshadowed by identity issues (the definition of the constitutional order and of one's place in the international system) and by more distributive ones (the definition of the electoral games, the parties' search for electoral space, the restructuring of labor-industrial relations and the political economy, the articulation of societal interests' access to political institutions). Thus, finally, the overloaded and cramped agenda that accompanies the deflation of power of the first stages gives way to a decisional process that is better timed, more normal, more informed, and more attentive to the inputs of recognizable groups and institutions.

All of this means that, even if a party were to be the prime mover in the transition,[7] that party will be joined sooner or later by other parties and social formations, all concerned as latecomers with what place they shall occupy in what polity. How will the first party respond to their concerns? However it responds, I assume that the party will see its response as bearing directly on the acquisition of legitimacy for the new polity. One sure consequence is that the party is now compelled to reflect more seriously on whether and how to extend its dominant status. In short, the task of legitimation now encases and informs that of hegemony.

Dominance and the Extreme Left

Let me then turn to the type of party that may dominate the early stages of the transition.[8] It is implicit in the previous section, with its emphasis on

5. For an analysis of democratic transitions as a sequence of stages see O'Donnell and Schmitter, *Transitions from Authoritarian Rule.*

6. Such a trend possibly reverses itself in part, however, as a result of constitutional and electoral developments, when transition proper ends and the new democracy enters a phase of consolidation. During this phase sociopolitical relations are collapsed and encased within newly established sociopolitical institutions.

7. This is not unlikely because at the outset a number of actors stay or are left out of what is in the first stages an undefined and improvised game.

8. Before I proceed further, I should remind the reader that one-party dominance in the early stages of transition is simply one and by no means the most likely way in which the transition

preserving competitiveness and attracting loyalties, that some parties are more likely than others to combine legitimately the democratic path with a continuation of their own dominance. The parties that have the greatest difficulty in this regard are orthodox Marxist parties and more in general parties fitting my definition of the extreme left. The undoing of the extreme left is exactly in its unique propensity to see its hegemony and system legitimation as one and the same thing—to fuse them in one ideological bloc and one strategic project. The puzzle of how a tightly woven strategy can fail (or fail to produce democracy) unravels as I unfold the scenario. The closest illustration comes from the Portuguese transition.

The initial political strength of the left, by making it unduly confident, may mark its undoing. As I have discussed elsewhere, a left cast by circumstances and its own actions in the role of the driving force in the demise of a dictatorship is almost bound to draw from this unique combination a surplus of meaning about the scope of its political mission and the depth of its ethical moorings.[9] After all, and this is only one reason, the dictatorships whose replacement we are discussing are "right-wing": they came into being—we are often instructed—for the explicit purpose of suppressing the popular left. Be that as it may, once in power, they invested considerable energy attending to and claiming credit for that task. Thus it is the left, more than any other political force, that will feel vindicated by their demise. And if the left has played the crucial role in that demise, it must also feel that not just the extreme right but a whole spectrum of political forces that acquiesced in the past, or were less than forthcoming in the final fray, are morally and politically bankrupt, possibly beyond recovery. In turn, the very fact that the demise of the dictatorship has not occurred in the ambiguous and compromising ways of other demises—often dominated by more "opportunistic" forces—must make the left confident that purity of goals will follow purity of struggle. This explains why the left should nourish few doubts that its hegemony and the legitimation of the new system are integral parts of the same design: legitimation requires that the leadership of the left be extended to the competitive stage of the transition.[10]

This means that the left will try to combine strict guidance of the constitutional process—especially in those aspects that concern the role of parties and representative institutions—with an ambitious series of substantive policy reforms designed to remove those features of the economy, society, and the state which in the opinion of the left undermined its opportunities for class-based leadership and made the dictatorship possible. Thus legitima-

opens. I have chosen it because it may appear to be an especially favorable stepping-stone to what, I think, is difficult to achieve: lasting party hegemony.

9. Giuseppe Di Palma, "Party Government and Democratic Reproducibility: The Dilemma of New Democracies," in Francis G. Castles and Rudolf Wildenmann, eds., *Visions and Realities of Party Government* (Berlin: De Gruyter, 1986), chap. 6.

10. It is implicit here that no such confidence in one's exclusive mission should characterize other parties, even when they are placed in an original position of control.

tion as seen by the extreme left should stress the certainty of substantive achievements and underplay institutional guarantees for competitiveness, as well as alliances on an equal footing with more moderate political parties. It all sounds like dominance, with a vengeance, but does it work, can it work in a democratic context?

The behavior of the extreme left in post-Salazar Portugal is nearly a textbook application of this scenario. Though the Portuguese Communist party and the other radical Marxist groups that soon appeared around the party were not the leaders in the military coup that put an end to the Portuguese dictatorship in April 1974, nevertheless by the end of the summer a narrow coalition of radical military groups and the extreme left was in charge. Whatever the reasons why this coalition emerged victorious after weeks of jockeying, the essential point is that, upon victory, the Portuguese transition took a radically new direction, quite different from that taken by the almost contemporaneous Spanish transition.

Victory, and the general disorganization of the moderate political sector following the sudden coup, convinced the leftist military-civilian coalition that the country was ripe for and indeed demanded a revolution of sorts, shunning the conventions of competitive politics. They also convinced the coalition that the political forces to its right could easily be marginalized. Targets of the left were not only center-right parties like the Popular Democratic party (PPD) and the Social Democratic Center (CDS), which the left linked with the defunct dictatorship, but the Popular Socialist party (PSP) as well. In effect, during this period political pluralism was nearly wiped out before it could reemerge. Consistent harassment of the opposition in all walks of life, the banning of some parties, and the takeover of crucial civil and official organizations by revolutionary committees of various sorts seemed at the time to bury the prospects for democracy. The Socialists' effort, with the cooperation of the other moderate parties, to build a conventional democracy legitimized by procedures (i.e., by a freely elected Constitutional Assembly) appeared to be losing when challenged by the extreme left's tangible program of legitimation of a new order through immediate reforms (land distribution, nationalizations, decolonization, "defascistization").

Yet it is exactly when the nature of the new order must be decided that the hegemonic plans of the extreme left can go awry. Again, Portugal in a case in point. It may be relatively easy for the left to use its initial moral and political advantage to carry along other political forces in a negative coalition against dictatorship. It is more difficult to maintain that advantage when called to build consent coalitions for a new order. Once the moment of righteous unity against dictatorship is past, and once they are faced with the more mundane task of securing their place in the new order, the other emerging parties, even parties whose democratic attachments are initially shaky, are likely to counter the left's design for continuing hegemony by making their consent minimally contingent on a set of rules guaranteeing instead open and competitive access to political office.[11] And if such democratic guarantees find no or an ambiguous answer in the left's design, the other parties—whether by conviction or by calculus of survival—will be more adamant about them, forcing the left into a dilemma: the choice between going repressive (and taking risks) or renouncing its hegemony.

In Portugal, naked repression and risk-taking were plentiful. Yet, contrary to prevailing expectations, neither paid off, and the revolutionary wind died down in a confrontation between military factions by the end of 1975. That confrontation could have gone otherwise, but this is not the point. Nor is my point that the extreme left is invariably committed to strategies of dominance in the Portuguese manner,[12] but rather that it may be more tempted than other types of parties that come onto the political scene after the toppling of a right-wing dictatorship. Above all, I have used Portugal as an instructive case to illustrate how a strategy of dominance and, reciprocally, of delegitimation of the opposition may founder if, to achieve those two objectives, it tampers with the requisites for democratic consent. What is specifically problematic with the strategy is that it may lead to unilateral and exclusionary use of constitutional and policy instruments, such as to curb beyond tolerable limits the oppositions' access to politically relevant resources. The strategy, by its directness, may backfire. Thus a transition that began with pure purposes and undaunted leadership may beget—and this is not the worst scenario—a democracy long on bickering and short on identity. Why this is in fact what happened in Portugal— why in particular the Socialists' victory over the extreme left did not establish them as the dominant party—is a question that better belongs to separate analysis.

Dominance and the Extreme Right

The case of the extreme left may be compared with that of the extreme right. The comparison will serve to move the analysis toward the demonstration that only moderate parties and the strategies they more typically embody have a chance at hegemony, at least over the span of democratic

11. Contingent consent is minimally required to allow the advent and continuous existence of a democracy. It is, in other words, the operational basis of legitimacy. See Adam Przeworski, "Some Problems in the Study of the Transition to Democracy," in Guillermo O'Donnell, Philippe Schmitter, and Laurence Whitehead, eds., *Transitions from Authoritarian Rule in Latin America and Southern Europe* (Baltimore: Johns Hopkins University Press, 1987), chap. 2.

12. Neither the Italian nor the French Communist parties pursued any such strategy after the war. Yet they had played if not an exclusive at least a decisive role in the struggle against dictatorship and in the first phases of reconstruction. The important point is that the temptation was there and was set aside after considerable, if suppressed, disagreement within each party.

transition and consolidation. Assuming that the extreme right is the initiator of the transition—in that, for example, the crisis of the dictatorship is precipitated by a secession of liberalizing factions within the regime—the question is whether that right is capable of maintaining hegemony in a democratic context when the left fails. The answer is a guarded yes. Similarly to the case of the left, the ambiguity as to the direction in which the right will move occurs because the right has undefined and provisional attitudes on whether the transition should move in a competitive democratic direction.[13] More than being wedded to democracy, this right is tempted by the prospect of its own hegemonic survival in a soft, liberalized dictatorship. But that prospect can be marred by the popular discredit surrounding a seceding right, since secession is likely to be seen as an act of betrayal or of self-serving calculus at best. Thus, though a victorious left does not feel called to prove its moral and political claim to leadership,[14] a seceding right must work against its questionable credentials. In one scenario, discredit may soon induce the right to push beyond liberalization, thus in effect favoring a democratic outcome in ways that the scenario of a victorious and self-righteous left may not. In so doing, it may even give a thus reformed right a second chance (but only a chance) at hegemony, *within that democratic outcome*. It is this scenario that I will follow here, and the Spanish case—the case of a regime that reformed and finally abolished itself—is its best illustration.

The initial skepticism with which the seceding right will be greeted by other opponents of the regime, coupled with the initial resistance to liberalization by the regime hard core and straddlers, means that the secession cannot proceed past its first moves without addressing the problem of coalitional support. There is, however, no real dilemma as to where to turn first. The seceding right cannot build support further to its right without in effect renouncing liberalization, and there is no safe journey back either.[15] The seceding right will instead be able to stay in the game only if it turns first toward the emerging democratic forces. In other words, even if not in the cards originally, this should be the most likely scenario. And this is the scenario that unfolded in Spain, after a few months of stalling by the

13. This is, in fact, part of the constitutive definition of the extreme right. Like the left, the right is classed as extreme if it holds those undefined and provisional attitudes. This is the way I will use the term *extreme* throughout my analysis, whereas *moderate* will qualify any party (left or right, it is irrelevant) once it accepts the democratic game. For the sake of brevity, I have and will at times refer to the left or right without further qualifications. Whether or not they are extremes should appear from the context.

14. Even if its role in the demise of the old regime is secondary or nonexistent—as it was in Japan, Germany, Greece, and Spain—the left will rely on an opinion climate of general disenchantment with that regime to build special legitimacy for itself.

15. For a detailed analysis of why this is so and how the coalitional options of the right are played out, see Guillermo O'Donnell, "Notas para el Estudio de Procesos de Democratizacion a Partir del Estado Burocratico-Autoritario," *Desarrollo Economico* 22 (July–September 1982): 231–48.

continuista government of Arias Navarro, once the government of Adolfo Suárez took over in the summer of 1976. If on one side the death of Francisco Franco had left his successors still in charge, with no obvious crisis of the regime in sight, on the other side the gathering mobilization of regime oppositions and civil society in response to his death and to the indecisiveness of the new government, coupled with the resistance of the regime hard core to even stilted liberalization, suggested that firmer choices should be made. As long as they were positionally advantaged with respect both to the regime oppositions and to its hard core, Suarez and the king who appointed him chose the democratic path.[16]

A seceding right that moves in a democratic direction, however, may very well have to take two steps (as it did in Spain) to make its move credible; and they are steps with consequences for dominance. First, given the skepticism of the opposition forces toward the right's motives and their fears of being trapped in a vicious circle of stalling and blackmailing, they will exact from the right a price perhaps previously unthinkable. They will demand nothing short of explicit deeds to prove that the process is moving past liberalization toward full democratization. Most explicit among these deeds are institutional measures to open the political market to all forces ready to play by its rules, including possible electoral arrangements to prevent a stacking of market outcomes in favor of the right. In Spain, the Suarez government actually anticipated the demands of the opposition by consciously speeding up the democratic election of a constituent assembly and by opening the political arena to all parties, while at the same time quickly disbanding the most central of the regime's institutions. In effect, by abolishing its own institutions (the self-abolition of the Cortes was exemplary in this regard) and by seizing control of the democratic process, the Spanish secession beat the democratic opposition at its own game.

The second step is a consequence of the first: if the right intends to form or support a party and exploit electorally its contribution to democratization, it has no choice but to embrace the democratic game unreservedly.[17] In Spain, Suarez's final decision openly to support the Union of the Democratic Center (UCD)—originally a loose federation of ideologically diverse moderate groups—was in effect the key to its victory and to the decisive entry of the reformed right into democratic politics.

16. To try instead to keep control of a partially liberalized regime, by mobilizing the state and institutional resources it may still control, is for the right to curtail its chances of survival. A good case in point is that of the Italian monarchy after the war. Though it was the chief agent in the sudden dismissal of Mussolini and the fascist government (July 1943), the monarchy resisted devolution of all power to the antifascist parties and its armed resistance wing during the rest of the war. This alienated monarchist sectors of the moderate right and led to the adoption of a republican form of government in the national referendum of 1946.

17. I am putting the statement in the hypothetical form because the right is likely to consist initially of factions and institutional cliques. Though the left has no problems resurrecting and standing on its party and ideological image, a seceding right has obvious problems of identity and organization, which may induce it to throw its support to parties other than its own.

In sum, the contrast between the scenarios of the two extremes restates one central point of this study: the challenge to democratic dominance begins only when political parties begin competing for support, and the ultimate test is popular vote. We have just seen how the right may face the challenge with greater chances of success than the left. It can do so because, in synthesis, it has a greater incentive to transform itself into a moderate party—moderation being here the code for acceptance of the norms of competition and alternance in government, with no substantive policy implications attached. The sudden demise of UCD and Suarez by the early 1980s clearly demonstrates, however, that this is not a sufficient condition for dominance. It is only a necessary one. To understand why, I turn to the prospects of dominance by moderate parties.

Dominance and the Moderate Parties

Parties that enter the transition with established democratic credentials may ordinarily do so with some delay and not in a dominant position.[18] But there are transitions of a type that instead accelerates the reorganization of democratic parties and may place them in a position of legal privilege with respect to the political extremes. These are transitions supervised or heavily influenced by occupying powers; the significant example is the postwar transitions in Austria, Germany, Italy, France, and Japan.[19] Moderate parties that take an early start (and by extension all moderate parties) can count for purposes of dominance on a special quality of theirs—that same quality that sets democracy apart from dictatorship and makes it a relatively more attractive option to some of its opponents as the crisis of the latter passes the point of easy return.

To go back to one of the introductory themes of my analysis, moderate parties are, by definition, normatively committed to establish a game the entry into which is open to loyal and converted players alike and whose outcomes are open-ended—a game with no fixed players, winners, or losers, and yet a game that, uncertain in its unfolding, is certain in its rules. The notion that parties committed to openness are in a better position to achieve dominant status sounds surprising. Yet that commitment is the

18. One reason is prudence and risk-aversion; another is lack of the apparatus ready to resurface that the extreme left is capable of keeping underground during the dictatorship; a third is persisting legal bans that moderate leaders are not willing to defy openly.

19. Another transition that can lead to an early reorganization of moderate parties is one preceded by a long and undecisive crisis of the dictatorship and by timid liberalization *within* the regime. Typically, various semiclandestine interparty juntas tend to be formed, in which moderate and extreme parties sit together to prepare the transition proper. It would be interesting to pursue this scenario's implications for party dominance. Moderate parties may also be able to reorganize early if the transition follows a short and unconsolidated dictatorship such as the Vichy regime in France or the regime of the colonels in Greece. In such cases there will be no delays because of the need for party licensing.

Procrustean bed (the normative limit, if you wish) within which, but also the platform on which a particularly virtuous moderate party can defuse the challenge of its more radical opponents. In so doing it can dispel public concern with democracy's erraticism and vulnerability[20] as well as build its indispensable role as guarantor of an orderly and stable transition. Being able to say which moderate party (since each country may have a few), and by dint of which additional objective conditions, subjective qualities, or select strategies is, however, a difficult task. It does not lend itself to easy predictions, except those that border on the idiosyncratic or tautological.

The Role of Objective Factors

It appears that objective factors act largely as no more than facilitators; and even as facilitators their role should be taken with a grain of salt. Let us take, for example, one factor that I just mentioned. Though being placed early on in a position of influence, perhaps by occupying powers, may constitute an advantage (and also a risk), the advantage is not sufficient for dominance past the early stages of the transition. A party in an early position of preeminence may lose it for a variety of reasons. In four of our countries, the first free elections rewarded the key role played from the outset by a single party: the Christian Democratic Union in West Germany, Christian Democracy in Italy, Suarez's UCD in Spain, Nea Demokratia in Greece. For all these parties, the future looked very promising. But of the four, only the Italian party has kept its political and electoral preeminence; one, the German CDU, lost it in the late 1960s, and the other two lost it within one or two rounds of parliamentary elections.

This prompts me to take a more critical look at another set of heralded factors for preeminence. Much emphasis is put on the role of geopolitics (war, defeat and occupation, international alignments) in the demise of a dictatorship and in charting thereafter the path of transition. In particular, by the record of postwar transitions, occupying powers are seen as crucial in buttressing a party's dominance. One tempting reading of the difference between the postwar transitions and those of the 1970s is that occupation, a nonfactor in the latter transitions, made dominance possible in some of the former. Leaving aside for the moment the accuracy of this parsimonious interpretation, it bears emphasis that, by the interpretation itself, geopolitical factors act only as conditions—at times favoring, at times confining. It may be true that the impact of occupying powers "can be very great in shaping political choices at critical junctures in a country's history. Not every election is the same, and in a period of vulnerability and volatility such as occurs after a war, such a foreign force can reshape coalitions and set a

20. That concern may be much greater if traditional images are buttressed by very recent memories of democratic failure, as experienced by the same generations who are now witnessing a return to democracy. France after Vichy is a case in point.

political trajectory that is continued even after the initial pressure is removed—very much like bending a young tree will affect its subsequent shape."[21] But this line of analysis does not rule out the likelihood that parties buttressed by foreign support either have much more to offer to begin with (hence, usually, the support) or else decline once foreign powers withdraw. That is, the political trajectory just cited is not kept by inertia alone. To put it somewhat differently, foreign influence is more successful—even determining—in narrowing options, thus excluding some for the foreseeable future, than in making the residual ones victorious. The final isolation of the extremes in postwar transitions is a case in point, to which I will return later.

As to the victorious options, both German and Italian Christian Democracy—and more so Japan's conservatives—had much more going for themselves, which brought them to the attention of the Allies. Also, we cannot overlook the well-known fact that external support did not arrive unsolicited: it was intelligently elicited and won by these parties, as part of their strategies. In the case of West Germany, Allied attitudes toward Christian Democracy were at first very guarded, and support went to the Social Democratic party as well. Nor should the failure of the Popular Republican Movement (MRP), the French equivalent of Christian Democracy, to maintain its momentum, despite its emergence as the first party in the crucial elections of June 1946, be attributed to the fact that the Allied forces (which, after all, included France) had no direct voice on French domestic politics and lent no special support to any specific party. The resurrection of party politics after an interlude of only four years and, partly because of this, the inability of the MRP to hegemonize the electorate that typically should rally to a Catholic popular movement are (we shall see) better explanations.

One last objective factor to consider, before moving to the analysis of strategies, has to do with a moderate party's social bases. Some analyses have placed emphasis on the leadership exercised by Christian or Catholic parties on postwar democratic reconstructions, owing especially to their ingrained subcultural appeal. The unquestionable advantage of religious appeals addressed to a moderate public opinion and to middling classes is that, in view of the weak class bonds of these strata, the appeals can cut across them (and reach the popular hunting grounds of the left). Also, postwar religious parties had the advantages of being closely connected with an organized church, of offering a popular alternative to Marxism (not just anticommunism), and of being at the same time untainted by the old regimes in ways that other moderate parties of secular-bourgeois origins were not.

Yet a party's subcultural rooting as a factor for dominance presents limits similar to the other objective factors mentioned above. True, religious par-

21. Personal communication by T. J. Pempel.

ties in Germany and Italy successfully exploited their vast subcultural appeal, though in France, Spain, and Portugal they did not.[22] But the real question is how much those successful appeals can explain about dominance. Indeed, the crucial point about the social bases of party support and other factors (a position of early advantage and foreign support) is that they are not different in kind from any objective factor generally associated with single electoral victories. They are not able to look at political parties as more than electoral machines and at dominance as more than a string of electoral victories reflecting underlying group behavior. But dominance is more than a string of victories, more than the political projection of group behavior. Dominance, at least in these case studies, begins to be built in the nonroutine context of democratic transitions, when issues and electorates are not frozen, and when holding the new democracy together is often an item of utter priority. In this context, partisan appeals to one's own social bases, to undecided voters, and to changing issue opinions—in sum, the stuff of normal voting behavior—seem to me not decisive in explaining how a party establishes from scratch a renewable basis of credibility, how it sets itself on the probable path to electoral and government preeminence for years to come. In the open and uncertain context of a transition, where normal social science explanations do not hold, explanations having to do with strategies and choices should then be of greater help.

The Role of Strategy

The importance of strategy stems from our basic assumption: the path of dominance is initially entered in response to a compelling problem of democratic legitimation or identity. It is in answer to this, and not to a generic bid for votes, that a moderate party may be able to blend what we know as difficult: the assertion of its own indispensable role as a guarantor of an open yet orderly political game, with a readiness to withhold credibility from the other parties—those "naturally" relegated to the opposition and possibly those to be held as minor government partners. But more than a strategy, this is a marching order, an uncharted path still to be traveled. True, depending on such factors as the party's social bases, its early role in the transition, and international alignments, dominance can be pursued with various degrees of control, intent, and resolve. But it strikes me that, however inventive and driven a moderate party may be, the strategy to follow is rather confined and the path narrow. Not even the presence of intent and consciousness (per se not necessary) is sufficient to bring dominance within reasonable reach.

22. The French MRP's success lasted only a short season. Spanish Christian Democracy never got off the ground, despite the predictions of most analysts before Franco's death. Portugal's CDS, the closest thing to Christian Democracy, is today the weakest of the five national parties sitting in parliament.

The strategy is set in the context of the second stage of the transition, dominated by jockeying for electoral and constitutional space. Parties will attribute to constitutional and electoral developments during this stage an inordinate importance in shaping their and the country's future. In this context, a moderate party's path to dominance should thus be mapped by the claims of its competitors in regard to the new order. There may be disagreement between moderate and extreme parties on democratic legitimacy and—almost as significant—disagreement between moderate parties on democracy's exact identity. I shall first treat the former.

Dealing with Legitimacy. I have stressed the importance of the extremes because their presence touches directly upon who shall govern and who instead lacks credibility. On one side, the more the "nostalgic" right and the radical left are significant, and the more they exhibit mental reservations toward democratic evolutions, the more the field of parties with governing credibility shrinks. All of this is by now abundantly clear. On the other side, the outright delegitimation of significant parties is not a sufficient governing strategy: it has costs for the new democracy and for the moderate parties that employ it. This too should be abundantly clear. One observation in this regard is that, for all the questions about their loyalty, the position of the political extremes is rarely one of clear disloyalty and more one of suspended, provisional, or contingent compliance. This is the more so if, being numerically or politically significant, the extremes are preoccupied with preserving their own advantage and with the tangible prospect of governing; and the more so if they have played a role in the liberalization of the dictatorship (as in the case of the seceding right) or in its demise. Indeed, with the exception of the Portuguese communists, who were offered a risky but attractive alternative by the alliance with the radical military, the other extremes that achieved at least some visibility in the transition either showed, in different degrees, muted attitudes toward the democratic game (the communists in France and Italy, the monarchists in Italy), or quickly converted to and controlled that game (the seceding right in Spain).

The situation I am addressing is one in which, at the resumption of electoral politics, moderate and extreme parties are unable to discount each other. They are interdependent in that they cannot do without each other and cannot unilaterally impose their solutions.[23] Thus a moderate party cannot maintain its governing credibility, except in the short run, by appealing only to anticommunism, antifascism, international alignments, the defense of the republic, and the like. Though these levers of mass loyalty have importance, the competitive context within which they must operate points away from any unilateral, exclusionary, go-it-alone strategy as unfeasible (i.e., fraught with great systemic and subjective risks).

23. O'Donnell and Schmitter, *Transitions from Authoritarian Rule.*

Rather, strategies of concerted interpartisan cooperation appear structurally more cogent and, if initiated by a moderate party already advantaged on objective grounds, capable of eventually confirming that party's leadership. Exactly which strategies? I mentioned in the opening pages a number of these strategies. At one extreme we find what Guillermo O'Donnell and Philippe Schmitter call *pactismo* in constitutional, governance, and possibly socioeconomic matters. The emphasis is on engineering coexistence by expressly negotiating that selected political forces shall take a rather fixed share in the political process and its outcomes. Formal agreements tend to replace the uncertain and therefore dangerous political market. But *pactismo* seems appropriate when two fairly equal political forces with uncertain loyalties confront each other, or when authoritarian incumbents lead the transition. An example of the former is postwar Austria. In Austria, the coexistence of two parties, the Socialist party and the People's party (Catholic), whose conflict had led to the demise of democracy in the 1930s, was handled by the adoption of a strict system of *proporz* in the allocation of political and parapolitical positions and resources and by the formation of a grand coalition of the two parties. It was an arrangement expressly against hegemony so that neither party emerged as dominant when the coalition ended in 1966.[24]

A strategy located in some ways at the other extreme from *pactismo* in the spectrum of interpartisan cooperation, and one that is exemplary in grasping the nuances of democratic dominance, is what I have called *garantismo*.[25] The strategy is appropriate when a moderate center is confronted with political extremes. It should come as no surprise to the reader that the party that comes closest to the strategy is Italy's Christian Democracy (DC). The purpose of *garantismo* is not only cooperation in the constitutional process but cooperation for the express intent of creating an open political market.[26] Maximal access to the process and to the constitutional setup that emerges from it—by means of arrangements such as accentuated parliamentarism, proportional representation, or procedural guarantees

24. As to *pactismo* guided by authoritarian incumbents, its minimal components are a narrowing of political participation to the more "reasonable" democratic forces and the protection and preservation of some of the old regime's corporate institutional bases (the armed forces). Though I cannot pursue the analysis, some Latin American cases suggest that authoritarian incumbents fail sooner or later to control competition and that their resistance to an open game undermines their ability to hegemonize that game.

25. Di Palma, "Party Government."

26. Hence Spain's UCD is also a good illustration. Though Spain contains some elements of *pactismo*, the fundamental fact is that electoral competition was completely open. The difference between Italy and Spain is rather that the reformed right that converged within UCD had to establish its democratic credibility. It is this need, more than the inability of UCD to discount the extreme left and those sectors of the right that remained more ambiguous toward democracy, which explains UCD's *garantismo*. At the same time, *pactismo* (especially in constitutional and military matters) combined with *garantismo* as an extra measure to secure the credibility and political clout of the reformed right while avoiding the most painful *rupturas* with the past.

protecting the oppositions—provides a measure of mutual survival that has the virtue of possibly achieving two further objectives.

It can constitutionalize the extremes. Confronted with a hypothetical choice between a managed political market, which they may be unable to control, and an open one, the extremes may have little hesitation—or little choice. Indeed, *garantismo* may impose itself not so much at their sufferance but as a second-best, which the extremes soon come to defend because they are incapable of exclusionary solutions. At the same time, a moderate party that pushes *garantismo* is not condemned to an equal role with the extremes. On the contrary, its ability to hold together a delicate strategy of cooperation and constitutional accommodations may help it emerge from the stage of democratic reconstruction as the clear dominant party, by shedding some of the shackles that interpartisan cooperation had initially placed on its preeminence in government.

There is no doubt that Italy's Christian Democracy is the party that most consistently followed, beginning with the provisional governments before the end of the war (1944–45), a strategy of cooperation and participation in government with the extreme left (the Communist party and its then allied Socialist party). The strategy culminated in 1947 with the collective formulation and nearly unanimous adoption by the democratically elected Constituent Assembly of the most strongly *garantista* charter issued after the war. More important, *garantismo,* which the extreme left had soft-pedaled when its political and governmental prospects looked rosier, became the constitutional capstone—as well as the cherished tenet of the left—when its political prospects were undercut by the growing East-West split in 1947. At the same time, the DC's ability to avoid, through *garantismo,* both a confrontation with and a surrender to the extreme left, although in the Constituent Assembly elections of 1946 the left controlled somewhat more votes than the DC, must be understood as crucial in its emergence as the party holding the absolute majority in the 1948 parliament elected under the new constitution.

Though the last outcome was not foregone, consider the following. A party's ability to lend legitimacy to policies of reconciliation, and to stay as well equally distant from both excessively advanced and niggardly forms of democratization, its ability in sum to hold the center, may give it an image of democratic sturdiness that sits well with the new electorate. And sturdiness is a very apt depiction of the DC in the first postwar years. Indeed, that a moderate party emphasizes cooperation in government and constitution making does not mean that the party will not use or even impose cooperation as a vehicle for its hegemony. In some cases, consent and cooperation by other parties may be sought, but only one party will sit in government (the case of UCD in Spain); in other cases, co-opting and even compelling potential oppositions to join a government of national reconstruction may be a way for a party to sanction and build upon its original advantage. True, co-opting the extremes may reduce their disloyalty, in image and in fact. But it may also allow the moderate party, once the stage of democratic reconstruction comes to a close, to soft-pedal the cooperative elements of that stage, to terminate national reconstruction governments if they existed, and to give instead freer rein to those fundamental issues (international alliances, domestic and international identities of the extremes, economic reconstruction) which are likely to relegate the extremes to a minority role for the foreseeable future. Needless to say, this is precisely what happened in Italy as the constitutional process came to a close.

The same, however, did not happen in France. Yet the interpartisan arrangements of the French transition very much resembled Italy's. A tripartite alliance of Communists, Socialists, and members of the MRP, practically identical to the Communist-Socialist–Christian Democratic coalition in Italy, governed France during the constitution-making period. As well, the final charter, with its strong elements of *garantismo,* resulted from a compromise of the three parties. And the MRP was not dissimilar from Italy's DC in playing a linchpin role in interpartisan transactions. But by the end of the 1940s its electoral strength was cut in half. To argue that the MRP never had the electoral strength of its Italian counterpart, even at its peak, is to beg the question. That the MRP never conveyed that image of sturdiness so typical of the DC was at least as much a cause as a reflection of its electoral limits.

Does the failure of MRP therefore refute our analysis of dominance? Not at all; rather, it confirms, perhaps all too easily, that building democratic dominance, even under very favorable strategic conditions, is not easy. In fact, strategic conditions seem very favorable only under our simplified, ideal rendition. And that is where the answer to the fate of MRP ultimately lies. To be sure, a number of objective factors, some of which I have mentioned, worked against the MRP. They are the lack of a tradition of Catholic political organization before the war, French anticlericalism, weak ties between the party and the church, and an ideology to the left of the traditional Catholic electorate. Nor did France, one the Allied powers, experience the foreign supervision of party reconstruction that might have compensated for those shortcomings. But the key point is that the French case was not so much a transition from dictatorship to democracy as one from democracy to democracy. The brief Vichy interlude served only to highlight—in more vivid ways than the experience of dictatorship did in the other transitions—the defects of a recently defunct democracy. Pursuing the matter further would take us far afield. Suffice it to say that what was at issue in France was not democracy versus dictatorship—left or right. More directly at issue was how the new democracy should avoid the instability, ineffectiveness, and divisiveness of the Third Republic, defects all so tragically embodied in its capitulation at the beginning of the war. The proponent of a radically different and sturdier democracy—an alternative hegemonic project in its own right—was Charles de Gaulle, the symbol of new

France and a man who, as the ups and downs of the Gaullist movement during the Fourth Republic show, was particularly insensitive to practical partisan accommodations. But when de Gaulle resigned from office and solemnly withdrew from active politics in January 1946, the MRP, left alone to check what became now the most immediate challenge, that of the extreme left, failed to heed at the same time the Gaullist project, a failure spelling doom for a party that had started with a program of "fidelity" to the general. Failing to heed Gaullism, the MRP's decision to continue governing instead with the extreme left seemed defensive more than anything else. Thus the decision finally to drop the communists in the spring of 1947 (at the same time as the DC dropped Italy's communists) did not add sturdiness to the governing center. French constitutional *garantismo* was lame and reactive. The fate of the MRP became the fate of the Fourth Republic. Or, as the saying goes, the Fourth Republic was born dead; it had given way to the Third.

I have started the treatment of strategies for dominance by moderate parties by considering first the case of a moderate party that confronts sizable extremes holding reservations toward the democratic compromise. I treated it first because in such a case, for all its strategic complexities, dominance is structurally more cogent and culturally more justifiable. By comparison, other patterns of opposition make dominance less cogent and justifiable, except perhaps in the short range. This is so because the ingredient the absence of which best justifies dominance—democratic loyalties—is not centrally at issue. One example is when the extremes are politically insignificant, competition is between moderate parties, and the parties are not too far apart on constitutional and substantive issues. In this case, dominance would have no space. Indeed, the system would enjoy interparty legitimation and a widely shared identity, making rotation in government possible. Dominance, insofar as it differs from a simple string of victories, starts instead with an inability of the oppositions to govern, for credibility more than for numerical reasons. But between the well-marked path to dominance, when the extremes are significant and difficult to reform, and the fading path just described there exist intermediate possibilities. I will treat them next. Japan, West Germany, Greece come to mind.

Dealing with Identity. Parties equally committed to a democratic compromise may substantially disagree on constitutional solutions, as well as domestic and international issues, in ways that go to the core of a new democracy's identity. These disagreements, without impeaching democratic credentials, may undermine the governing credibility of some parties while giving others control of the debate around those disagreements. A combination of substantial disagreement with a collective commitment to a democratic outcome may encourage a moderate party in a position of initial advantage to eschew interpartisan cooperation as less needed and cogent.

Instead, that party may well be attracted by the prospect of consolidating its advantage through a straightforward strategy that puts the accent on unilateral constitution making, strong executive features, majoritarian laws, governing alone, the exploitation of divisive issues, or any prudent combination thereof. But how successful is this path to dominance?

In all three countries just mentioned the extremes had limited or no significance in the transition. In all three, however, there existed basic disagreement between the democratic parties on constitutional, domestic, or foreign issues. In all three, but most clearly in Greece, we find little or no emphasis on interpartisan cooperation, no special accommodation of the opposition beyond what is expected of any competitive system, no political culture of *garantismo*. We find instead great emphasis, especially in West Germany and Greece, on measures to rationalize party and parliamentary politics and to strengthen the government.

The Greek transition of 1974 shares some elements with the French, in that the seven-year military rule that came to a close that summer was a *régime d'exception,* not yet institutionalized at its fall, and—like Vichy—with limited claims to legitimacy. Therefore, what was at issue when the colonels, following the Cyprus debacle, devolved power to the self-exiled Constantine Karamanlis and the civilian conservatives was not authoritarianism versus democracy but the adoption of a democratic system that would end the manipulations and distortions so typical of Greek competitive or pseudo-competitive politics. The weakness of the colonels and their supporters, plus the insignificance and divisions of the communist left, which played no role in the devolution, allowed Karamanlis to follow immediately a "Gaullist" strategy (de Gaulle, instead, waited fourteen years after his return to liberated Paris). That strategy met with and was fed by the resistance of the Socialist party (PASOK), which objected to Karamanlis's penchant for presidential democracy. In addition, because of its national-populist Third-World image, PASOK was also seeking a cleaner break with the past and a new international identity for Greece. Thus the party strongly objected to Karamanlis's socioeconomic and foreign as well as constitutional policies. Socialist resistance did not prevent the overwhelming electoral victory of Karamanlis's Nea Demokratia party, the formation of a one-party cabinet, and the adoption of a semipresidential constitution with strong Gaullist components.

In Japan and West Germany, the extremes, both right and left, were of little significance in the transition because of partially overlapping combinations of domestic and geopolitical factors: the persecution or (Nazi Germany) elimination of the left by the dictatorship; the opprobrium attached to right-wing dictatorships at the end of the war; the partition of Germany, leaving in East Germany traditional pockets of social support for both extremisms; hatred toward the Soviet Union in Japan and, more so, in Germany; and active Allied policies directed at purging, or impeding the reorganization of, the extreme right (especially in Germany) and the extreme left (especially in Japan after 1947). Whatever the reasons for the weakness of the extremes, the significant oppositions in both countries were represented instead, from the very beginning, by the two Socialist parties—JSP in Japan and SPD in West Germany. As in Greece, though both parties proclaimed themselves Marxist, little or no doubt surrounded their acceptance of democracy, especially in the case of SPD. But though they did not challenge democracy as such, they did challenge in a direct and (JSP) doctrinaire fashion a conservative and Western vision of the new democracies. As in Greece, an important component of their challenge reflected a search for a different and less aligned international identity. As in Greece, the answer to these fundamental challenges was less than accommodating and brought instead the Socialist parties into direct competition for enduring dominance with their conservative counterparts, the CDU in Germany and the closely allied Liberals and Democrats in Japan.

Seen in prospect, it seemed at the time that the conservative parties of the three countries would keep their lead and emerge victorious from the respective confrontations, remaining dominant at least through the phases of transition and consolidation. And so it was in the German and Japanese cases, but not in Greece, where Nea Demokratia was soundly defeated by PASOK in the parliamentary elections of 1981 and still remains the smaller of the two parties. These are mixed results that need interpretation. As I will argue in the next section with an eye to Greece, partisan confrontation on issues that deeply touch on the identity of a new democracy does not produce clear and lasting victors as easily as we may think. In its very simplicity and more overt accent on the objective of dominance, confrontation coupled with the constitutional pursuit of strong party government has drawbacks that may negatively affect that objective. Additional and special circumstances may be needed—and they may still be insufficient.

Let me illustrate with reference to the German and Japanese cases. True, their conservative parties remained largely unchallenged through transition and consolidation; but is this a tribute to their strategy of confrontation? Only in a way: only if we pay as much tribute to the weight of international factors. They froze domestic options in such a way as to constrain and retard the ability of the Socialist parties to win in a confrontation unless they reformed themselves. The virtue of the conservative parties was to understand and ride with that contextual advantage which was absent in Greece. There lies their contribution. In Greece constitutional and foreign policy developments reflected largely the choices and actions of the conservative party based on a calculus of substantially internal partisan balances, but in Germany and Japan they reflected more heavily choices made in behalf or to the advantage of their conservative parties by the occupying forces.

Japan shows this pattern of interaction at its clearest. Japan's disarmament and active renunciation of war were firmly dictated by the American occupation forces. But they proved immensely popular with the Japanese, as did the American shield of that disarmament. This, perhaps more than the Americans' less than sympathetic behavior toward the Socialist party, made it difficult for the party to turn the foreign policy debate into an issue about neutrality. Similarly, it is well known that Japan's democratic constitution was drafted in two weeks by the Americans (February 1946), delivered to the Japanese government for adoption, and promulgated with very few changes in November of the same year. It could thus be said that by acting as its guardians and freezing certain options early on, the Americans made it easier for the Japanese government to dispense with the interpartisan accommodations that were required in France and Italy. But there is more at work here than American forthcomingness. What is often overlooked is that the American actions did not take place, nor were they received, in a void. Contrary to hackneyed views of the matter, and despite extensive purges of past politicians and bureaucrats, the Americans explicitly and heavily relied on the closest collaboration with an imperial government that survived the war intact. This collaboration and the emphasis on conservative continuity under an imperial institution above the parties are the secrets to the success of a foreign-guided democratization and of the Liberal Democrats as its main interpreters. Thus Japan, even more than Spain, is the one new democracy among those we are considering whose identity—let alone legitimacy—should have least divided its supporters. Challenging it would no longer pay off. What seems therefore surprising (but see the remarks that will close my treatment of Germany) is the "stubbornness" of Japan's Socialists. They proved unable or unwilling to remove what was at the time and still is a decisively losing response to conservative dominance, a dominance based on a model of growth whose recognized success, both cultural and socioeconomic, is tenaciously rooted, still today, on a sort of small-power aligned neutrality.

Allied impact on West German political development was, by comparison, more complex, and relations between the Allies and the Germans were less smoothly predictable. Four occupying powers, not one, met on German soil; the issue of West Germany's international place and identity was much more vexing, both because of Soviet proximity and because of Western European concerns and fears; for the same reasons greater concern surrounded West Germany's ability to develop a sturdy democracy as a factor of peace; and, further to cloud the future, no German government had survived the war to implement reconstruction. Much of this explains the deliberately slow process of party licensing by the Allies, the initially more guarded attitude toward CDU as a prospective governing party, the lack of national elections and a truly national government until the country's Basic Law was adopted in 1949 (by which time Japan had already had three national elections). It also explains why the CDU under Adenauer's leadership behaved as more of an initiator and stimulus, even when dealing with the Allies, in constitutional reconstruction and in foreign policy, and why the Socialists were more actively challenged to make a new and better case for themselves domestically and internationally. Adenauer and the CDU faced a difficult task of persuading the Allies and the Germans that West Germany's democratic revival needed a foundation of German rearmament only a few years after German aggression and defeat. It was certainly more difficult than the task Prime Minister Yoshida faced at the same time in Japan, as he first embraced an essentially opposite foreign policy formula and then tried to preserve it against American pressures at the start of the Korean War. Similarly, the lack of conservative continuity in government did not make the new conservative leadership of Germany more dependent or more attuned to the Allies. On the contrary, the long-drawn-out process of political reconstruction, in its very enormity, gave the CDU and Adenauer a central, more visible, and more debated role in fostering constitutional development toward strong party government and a "chancellor democracy."

But these circumstances—the controversial saliency of West German domestic and international identity in the eyes of the Allies and Europe; the lack of a sealed continuity in government; in sum, the fact that the German political environment, domestic and international, did not reach the overdetermination and complementarity of Japan—offered the German Socialists an opportunity that escaped their Japanese counterpart (hence the latter's "stubbornness"). It was the opportunity to seek by the 1950s and 1960s a rebounding of the party, tied to a rethinking of its positions and well timed by a change in domestic and international contexts. Bad Godesberg and the SPD's basic acceptance of rearmament within a context of firm European integration were the essential steps in that rebounding. Thus, whereas in Japan the conservatives were way ahead of the Socialists already by 1948 and have stayed that way ever since, in Germany the CDU's significant lead over the SPD lasted twelve years (from the elections of 1953 to those of 1965).[27] By 1966 the SPD was in government.

Comparing Strategies. Whatever the differences between the two, both Japan and Germany point in turn to a major difference between the 1940s to 1950s and the 1970s: the presence in the former years, but not in the latter, of a frozen geopolitical environment favoring the dominance of conservative parties not only over the extremes but also over equally democratic socialist parties. Thus I can now move to the treatment of a point introduced earlier. I have characterized the strategy adopted by the conservative parties of Japan and Germany as one with emphasis on open disagreement with the democratic opposition and on a strong executive. The point I made

27. In the elections of 1949 CDU's lead was less than 1 percent.

is that, if such a strategy is unprotected by a frozen geopolitical environment—as in the case of Nea Demokratia in Greece—limits to its effectiveness in achieving dominance become more apparent. Essentially, it is a winner-take-all strategy, less protected from reversals in the conditions that make its success possible, less adaptable and resourceful in the presence of change, than the strategy of *garantismo*.

For one thing, since the extremes, as a near necessity for the strategy, will be insignificant, the strategy is most likely to occur at the same time as the emerging party system acquires the features of a numerically limited one. Therefore, and as part of the strategy, the party with prospects of dominance is likely to govern alone or with minor partners, and in sum to count on electoral victories, rather than coalitional games, to keep other parties at bay. Hence the strategy cannot cope with electoral reversals and cannot prevent them. Minimally, the use of electoral laws with majoritarian features, typical of the strategy, may prove a mixed blessing. It may retard defeat, but it may also magnify it. Thus a party that, like Nea Demokratia, attributes decisive importance to its initial control of the transition and to initial electoral victories as capable of freezing the electorate for years to come may still be confounded in its expectations. For another thing, a winner-take-all strategy that threatens to remove credibility from the opposition for years to come while leaving it little space for accommodation—either through coalitional opportunities, or through channels of co-optation, or by an especially open and *garantista* setup—gives that opposition no incentives to acquiesce but good reasons to resist sectarian isolation.

Breaking out of isolation may be helped by the fact that, despite other disagreements, the opposition enjoys, as stipulated, democratic credentials. What is at issue is not its democratic legitimation but those other disagreements. Basic as these are, insofar as they touch upon the constitutional or international identity of the new democracy, questions can be raised about their endurance as factors in the isolation of the opposition, especially since, as I just stated, the opposition should have an interest in breaking out of that isolation. None of this says that the opposition will in fact break out, or how it will. But the point of my analysis is not to make predictions about specific cases, or to show by what concrete appeals PASOK, for instance, managed to overturn its previous defeats. The point is to identify the strategic confines within which dominance operates.

Bearing further on this, and as Ariel Levite and Sidney Tarrow put it, delegitimation of the opposition as the logical corollary to political hegemony is not a natural property as much as a construction of periods of crisis and transformation. As privileged a role as a dominant party plays in defining the political debate on fundamental issues bearing on delegitimation, that role is not irreversible. Delegitimized parties, for one, may have a range of responses at their disposal, the two authors write, that go beyond simple sectarian isolation and the consolidation of subcultural solidarity. Levite and Tarrow's insights are especially appropriate if, as here, the problem with the opposition is not its democratic legitimacy but its view of democratic identity.[28]

Aside from the fact that some of the objective issues and the political agenda that place the opposition at a disadvantage, or the way public opinion looks at them, may change of their own accord as time passes, the opposition itself may also be induced to intervene to speed up those changes; or it may come around to embrace more popular views. One would have to look for some combination of these factors to trace the immediate causes of PASOK's victory, or for that matter the causes of the SPD victory in Germany, once the international environment began to thaw. To give one concrete example, disagreement on some basic constitutional feature of a new democracy (for example, presidentialism versus parliamentarism) can be turned around in two ways. The opposition may finally embrace the actual constitutional setup (and hope to take institutional advantage of it) as its prospects of electoral victory improve or as a way to improve those prospects. Or the opposition may make capital of those events and developments that, by undermining the working of the new democracy, can prove the superiority of its own constitutional design. An example of the former is again PASOK, which, as it moved toward power, came to soft-pedal its resistance to the electoral and governing features introduced by its adversary. An example of the latter comes from the French Fourth Republic, when the Algerian crisis finally allowed Gaullism to enact that constitutional design for democracy over which it had diverged from the governing center.

Conclusions

In conclusion, the comparison between the strategies of dominance followed more typically when democratic identity or loyalty are respectively at issue suggests that, of the two, the latter is especially compelling and promising for the prospects of dominance by a moderate party. Though this is what I wanted to convey, Levite and Tarrow's observations and the general thrust of my analysis, with its insistence on the obstacles in the path to dominance, recommend adding caution to this conclusion. To be sure, the fact that under the latter strategy, that is, under *garantismo*, delegitimation is based on a more fundamental question of democratic disloyalties makes delegitimation more difficult to dispel. The passage of time, intervening events, and changing opinion climates may not be as decisive. In addition,

28. Ariel Levite and Sidney Tarrow, "The Legitimation of Excluded Parties in Dominant Party Systems: A Comparison of Israel and Italy," *Comparative Politics* 15 (April 1983): 295–328.

the very ability of the dominant party to combine dominance with attraction and coalition makes its replacement in government a less compelling and more complex affair.

Italy is a good illustration of all these points. At the same time as the neofascist Italian Social Movement (MSI) has kept its electoral strength practically intact through forty years of democracy (hovering between 5 and 9 percent of the vote), and as the Communist party has surpassed 30 percent of the vote, the process of legitimation of the latter, let alone the former, has proved very slow. Communist responses to changing international environments and opinion climates, though not lacking, have been guarded and deliberate, leaving the party still some distance from a complete turnaround and from government. At the same time—a proverbial trait of postwar Italian politics—Christian Democracy has kept itself in power and defused political tensions by combining constitutional *garantismo* with the selective co-optation of the opposition in the systematic practice of what Sidney Tarrow calls political exchange.

Yet, I would like to close my analysis of dominance with two cautionary notes in keeping with its subtitle: it ain't easy. As to the first note, it may be a measure of its success that under certain conditions *garantismo* may not simply alleviate but remove and resolve the question of loyalty. The very fact of having taken the extremes into *garantismo* may belie in part the ultimateness of their illegitimate status, especially since the position of the extremes is more often one of suspended loyalty than one of clear disloyalty. Thus, if other factors, such as a gathering discredit for the international ideologies and forces to which the extremes appeal, further weaken their blackmailing power in the transition, *garantismo* may achieve a more successful and speedier conversion of those extremes. A governing party that has developed a taste for dominance may then have to resort to, but may not be able to rally, other strategies and other resources to stay in power past the transition.

In Spain, for example, both the Communist left and the most sizable sector of the potentially "nostalgic" right (the one that rallied around Fraga Iribarne's Alianza Popular) achieved an early level of democratic conversion unparalleled by similar force in the 1940s. The reason can be found in the combination of the particularly successful *política de consenso* followed by the transition government, with the lesser international appeal enjoyed by communism in the 1970s—when compared with the 1940s—and with the permanent discredit of right-wing authoritarianism. The greater conversion of the extremes, however, made it so that the real antagonist of the governing UDC became the Socialist party, which, furthermore, quickly reabsorbed any significant disagreement it may have nurtured with the government on the domestic and international identity of the new Spain. Although this pattern of opposition may not have much to do with why UCD disintegrated by 1982, it goes a long way in explaining why dominance had little reason to exist past democratic reconstruction.[29]

This takes me to the second cautionary note. None of the strategies considered here, not even *garantismo,* applies as is beyond that phase of the transition which is concerned with electoral and constitutional reconstruction. Once that stage comes to a close, and even more as a new democracy enters and proceeds beyond the phase of institutional consolidation, party dominance can and sometimes must be reinvented in response to new issues tied to the new phases (and to exogenous changes). It can and sometimes must rely on partially new resources and on revamped and newly blended strategies. One central set of new resources, not available before, has to do with the reconstructed state apparatus and the ways in which, from country to country, it is linked to corporate-economic and partisan interests. I have mentioned Italy's practice of political exchange. As it developed, beginning in full force in the 1960s, it blended in its own special way state and partisan resources—a way which appears substantially different, for instance, from Japan. But these comparisons are the object of other contributions to this volume.

29. One interesting and thoroughly documented essay on the demise of UCD is Richard Gunther, "El Hundimiento de UCD," in Juan J. Linz and José R. Montero, eds., *Crisis y cambio: Electores y partidos en la España de los años ochenta* (Madrid: Centro de Estudios Constitutionales, 1986), chap. 10. In an interesting way, the evolution of the Portuguese transition after the adoption of the 1976 constitution is the opposite of the Spanish, though its outcome (no dominance) is the same. The original discord between Portugal's moderate parties and the extreme left did not disappear following the defeat of the Communist-military hegemonic project. Though its intensity diminished dramatically, it was compounded by a new discord: between the Socialists, now in control of the government, and the other moderate parties. It is a discord on a question that borders on constitutional identity, that is, how fast and how deeply to excise those radical institutional and social features that the new democracy was compelled to incorporate during the period of military guidance. This compounding of discord made it extremely hard for the Socialists to preserve, by any strategy they could devise, the broad support they had conquered when they inspired the resistance against Communist-military hegemony. Their fate resembles in some ways that of France's MRP, caught as the latter was between Gaullism and the extreme left. So, whereas Spanish developments made dominance obsolete, Portuguese developments made it well-nigh unreachable.

6. The Political Economy of Conservative Resurgence under Recession: Public Policies and Political Support in Japan, 1977–1983

TAKASHI INOGUCHI

Following the first oil crisis of 1973, ruling parties in the industrial democracies increasingly saw their power bases eroded, and many were forced to surrender their control of government. During the period 1973 to 1985, Australia (1975), New Zealand (1975), Sweden (1976), Israel (1977), the United Kingdom (1979), the United States (1981), West Germany (1982), Canada (1984), and France (1985) experienced what can be taken as a power shift from the left to the right very loosely defined whereas countries like the United Kingdom (1974), the United States (1977), France (1981), Italy (1983), Australia (1983), and New Zealand (1984) registered what can be taken as a power shift from the right to the left, again very loosely defined. In the industrialized world only Japan has seen the ruling party remain continuously in power during the fifteen years following the oil crisis.[1]

More important, various opinion polls indicate that the LDP has been

This chapter is a revised version of a paper presented at the conference on one-party dominance, Oxford University, Nissan Institute, April 2–4, 1986. Earlier versions were presented at the Center for International Studies Seminar, Massachusetts Institute of Technology, and at the Political Behavior Seminar, Harvard University, both on November 4, 1981, at the Annual Meeting of the Japanese Political Science Association, Osaka, October 16–17, 1982, and at the workshop on comparative public policy, Kona, Hawaii, January 9–12, 1983. This essay has built further on my work in the Japanese language. I gratefully acknowledge helpful comments received on these and other occasions on earlier versions of this paper. Those of Douglas A. Hibbs, Jr., Takehiko Mutoh, and T. J. Pempel are especially worthy of note.

1. This admittedly selective summary of government changes is based on John Sallnow and Ann John, *The Electoral Atlas of Europe, 1968–1981* (London: Butterworth Scientific, 1982), and Kyōdō tsūshinsha, *Sekai nenkan 1986* [World annual 1986] (Tokyo: Kyōdō tsūshinsha, 1986).

enjoying increasingly higher public support since mid-1977.[2] Although the LDP's public support started to pick up slowly, it did not appear at that time as though the LDP would be able to turn this support into an electoral revival.[3]

This impression was reinforced by the outcome of the 1979 general election, which was unfavorable to the LDP. But the steady increase in the level of public support resumed after a brief drop that followed the second oil crisis of 1979. Then in the two-house election of June 1980, the LDP recorded a landslide victory, returning to the number of parliamentary seats it held in the late 1960s. Even after June 1980 various opinion polls consistently recorded generally high levels of support for the LDP. The electoral setback in the December 1983 general election did not seem to indicate any fundamental erosion of basically high support for the LDP. The percentages of the LDP's votes in the 1976, 1979, 1980, and 1983 general elections were 41.8, 44.6, 47.9, and 45.8, respectively.[4] Then in the 1986 election the party won another handsome victory with 49.4 percent of the vote and nearly 59 percent of the seats in parliament.

What explains the LDP's resurgence after 1977? It is a rare phenomenon among the troubled economies of the industrial democracies. This chapter gives three partial and mutually complementary explanations for this increase in LDP support.[5]

2. The Jiji monthly survey since June 1960 and the Yomiuri monthly survey since August 1978 are notable examples. I rely heavily on the former for the period 1977–81 and on the latter for the period thereafter. The data of the former after July 1981 were not public at the time of writing. The turning point toward the conservative resurgence came around mid-1977, when LDP support in opinion polls started to pick up, although at the time it was not noticed as the prelude to a trend that would reverse the earlier pattern of diminishing LDP support. LDP support increased to around 30 percent in the Jiji survey in mid-1977 from the nadir of 25 percent in 1974–77, and from mid-1980 on it went up to the level of around 30–35 percent in the Jiji survey and 40–50 percent in the Yomiuri survey. The Jiji survey and the Yomiuri survey ask the same question about party support. But their response categories are slightly different. The former allows respondents to choose not only parties but also the following two somewhat ambiguous categories, "the Conservatives rather than the Progressives" and "the Progressives rather than the Conservatives," but the latter survey does not. In examining LDP support in the Jiji results, I look only at the percentage of those who choose "the LDP." I do not include the percentage of those who choose "Conservatives rather than Progressives." That is why there is a discrepancy of 10–15 percent between these two monthly survey results with respect to the LDP support level.

3. Takashi Inoguchi, "Explaining and Predicting Japanese General Elections, 1960–1980," *Journal of Japanese Studies* 7 (Summer, 1981): 285–318.

4. Both the 1979 and 1983 general elections yielded somewhat unexpected outcomes in that most preelection opinion polls indicated far higher levels of support for the LDP. Even the percentages of votes cast for the LDP basically reflect these high levels of support. The LDP's electoral setbacks in 1979 and in 1983 are still topics of controversy. But an emerging consensus seems to be that the antitax issue played an important role in the 1979 election and that the general decline in turnout of conservatively inclined voters in the 1983 general election in light of the sufficiently "safe" parliamentary majority of the LDP established by the 1980 general election were the major factors. For the former see Araki Toshio et al., *Tōhyo kōdō niokeru renzoku to henka* [Continuities and change in voting behavior] (Toyko: Bokutakusha, 1983), and for the latter see Inoguchi, "Explaining and Predicting Japanese General Elections."

5. The dependent variable is *not* higher LDP popular votes or seats in certain elections *but* improved ratings in popularity polls. Although I refer to opinion polls at general election times

Figure 6.1. Public support for the LDP, 1960–80 (annual average)

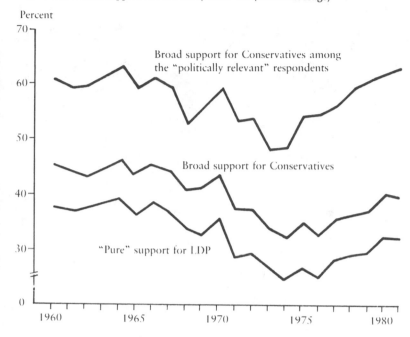

Source: The Jiji monthly survey 1960–81.

The Jiji survey has the following characteristics:
(a) population: Japanese over 20 years old;
     sample size: 1,250 (June 1960 to March 1966) and 2,000 (April 1966 onward)
     random sample: two-way stratification by (i) administrative size and (ii) industrial charac-
     teristics; three-step sampling by (i) census emulation districts, (ii) administrative units, and
     (iii) individual respondents (June 1960 to March 1966); two-step sampling by (i) census
     emulation districts and (ii) individual respondents (April 1966 onward).
(b) response rate: 72.9–90.3 percent (June 1960 to March 1966) and 71.8–85.6 percent
     (April 1966 onward).
(c) question wording: "Which political party do you support?" Response categories are the
     Liberal Democratic party (LDP), the Japan Socialist party (JSP), the Democratic Socialist
     party (DSP), the New Liberal Club (NLC), the Clean Government party (CGP), the United
     Socialist Democratic party (USDP), other parties, the Conservatives rather than the Pro-
     gressives, the Progressives rather than the Conservatives, do not support any political
     party, and do not know.

The eighth and ninth categories are tailored to those respondents who do not like to
specify any explicit political party support but do have a clear inclination either to the
Right or to the Left. These two party-non-specific categories register 5–9 percent almost
constantly. If the LDP and "the Conservatives rather than the Progressives" are combined,
the support level goes up by 5–9 percent. The last two categories of "do not support any
political party" and "do not know" amount to roughly 25–40 percent almost constantly.

The unbroken line corresponds to "the LDP" response; the dotted line corresponds to
"the LDP" and "the Conservatives rather than the Progressives" combined; and the
uppermost line corresponds to "the LDP" plus "the Conservatives rather than the Progressives" over the total responses minus the "do not support any political party" and "do
not know" responses.

Figure 6.2. Public support for the LDP, 1978–83 (six-month average)

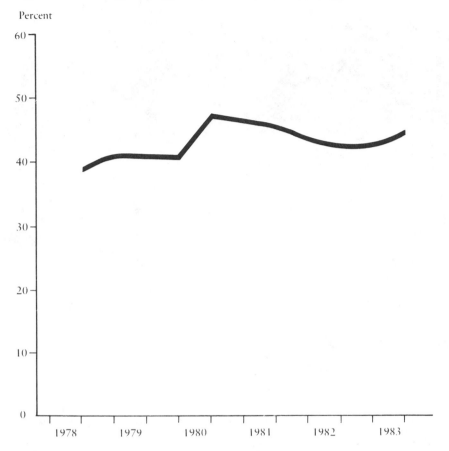

Percent

Source: The Yomiuri monthly survey 1978–83.

The basic characteristics of the Yomiuri monthly survey are as follows: The population is Japanese citizens over 20 years old and the sample size is 3,000. The response rates vary but on the average are 70–80 percent. The sampling method is a stratified three-step random sampling. Taking into account administrative units, city size, and industrialization rate of districts, 250 districts are chosen. Then 12 persons are selected in each of 250 districts. Interviewing is made by semiprofessional persons contracted with the Yomiuri newspaper.

The three explanations involve economic performance, political clientelism, and policy adaptation. Each will be examined in relation to three socio-occupational groups that appear most strongly influenced: the population at large, especially residents in smaller urban settings; farmers and

or general election results, this is because that is when there is the greatest concentration of academically inspired polls, which provide the strongest evidence related to causality.

small business holders; and interest groups concerned with social welfare and the environment.

An explanation based on economic performance is the most fundamental and important of the three possibilities: it explains a large bulk of the conservative revival via the public's comparative evaluation of the parties' competence, particularly given the general economic difficulties and the widely shared expectation that dire consequences would follow from a change in government. Furthermore, this economic explanation underlies the other two. The explanation based on political clientelism deals specifically with the two main groups, which represent the traditional middle strata. It is concerned with the LDP's attentiveness to these clients in moderating and mitigating economic difficulties which a large majority of the public feels only the LDP can handle. Thus the first explanation underlies the second, at least partially. The policy adaptation explanation deals with those voters who were aroused to oppose the conservatives because of the "new" issues of the high growth period, such as environment and welfare, but who returned to support the LDP by the late 1970s and early 1980s. The LDP successfully dissipated such issues by adopting the same policy line as the opposition parties at the national level and by implementing it at the local level. Then, as economic difficulties mounted, the LDP reversed its policy again in response to popular demand and thus attracted more fully those "returnees" into its camp. Such people constitute the bulk of what is called the new middle strata, principally in large urban settings. This explanation also assumes that there were general economic difficulties, which a vast majority feel can be handled well only by the LDP. In that sense, the first explanation also at least partially underlies the third explanation.

First, I will construct a regression model by occupational groups along the line of the first explanation. Second, to the first explanation I will add the second explanation concerning farmers and small business holders and the third explanation for those social groups that were seriously concerned about welfare and environment. The second and the third explanations are added specifically to analyze what seems to be left largely unexplained by the first explanation with regard to some groups. In this way I will attempt to identify the multidimensional socioeconomic underpinnings of the conservative resurgence and provide new insights into the politicoeconomic dynamics underlying the conservative revival in the industrial democracies during recessions.

My approach basically follows the line rigorously formulated by Gerald Kramer.[6] It focuses on the incumbent party's allocation of benefits to various socioeconomic groups. Instead of focusing on issues and underlying ideologies in electoral politics, this approach examines how the incumbent and opposition parties attempt to use different strategies to attract various

6. Gerald Kramer, "Electoral Politics in the Zero-Sum Society," paper presented at the Annual Meeting of the American Political Science Association, Denver, September 1–5, 1982.

socioeconomic groups into their camp. In the Kramer formulation, the incumbent party attempts to woo all groups evenhandedly and catch them all, whereas the opposition parties attempt to attract particular groups into their camp by raising controversial issues and discrediting benefits either to the electorate at large (e.g., benefits accrued to macroeconomic management) or to specific targeted groups (e.g., agricultural subsidies for farmers and pension programs for the aged). In this framework, a voter's main interest, according to Samuel Popkin et al.,[7] is "What have you done for me lately?" instead of "Where do my affections lie?" or "What promises are closest to me?" In other words, the voters try to assess how much benefit they have gained from a given candidate or party.[8]

In assessing the impacts or effects of public policies on the level of support for the incumbent party, we must be cautious on two general points: the structural conditions that the incumbent party has inherited from the recent past and factors not related to the incumbent party's public policies. With these points in mind, this chapter will examine how the conservative resurgence in Japan from 1977 to 1983 is related to three public policy fields of major importance. In doing so, it will also show that public policies often have very important differentiated bearings on the political support patterns of various socio-occupational groups.

Although my primary task is to explain the Japanese conservative resurgence, broader questions related to one-party dominance and its maintenance and consequences will also be addressed.

Economic Performance

Economic performance is here examined in relation to economic expectations held by the public. I argue that a noticeable decrease in public expectations toward economic performance served to reinforce the public image of the LDP's economic plans as basically inevitable. This in turn contributed to the increase in political conservatism through a comparative assessment of the government's and opposition parties' abilities to govern. First, however, it is necessary to summarize the basic thrusts of macroeconomic policy to show that actual economic performance was an indirect but important basis for the high LDP support.

The most basic point is that the Japanese economy did well under the LDP's rule. GNP grew, albeit more slowly than before; inflation was curtailed; and unemployment never reached the heights of many of the OECD (Organization for Economic Cooperation and Development) countries. The

7. Samuel Popkin et al., "Comment: What Have You Done for Me Lately? Toward an Investment Theory of Voting," *American Political Science Review* 70 (September 1976): 779–805.
8. Nobutaka Ike, *A Theory of Japanese Democracy* (Boulder, Colo.: Westview Press, 1978).

LDP's economic policy thus was a positive factor in its electoral fortunes. What was that policy? First, macroeconomic policy generally conformed to the market in a positive direction and did not create major disturbances to the economic forces working in Japan.[9] Three characteristics of post-1974 monetary policy were an emphasis on anti-inflation policy by a stable and tight money supply with the $(M_2 + CD)$ growth rate registering about 11 to 12 percent between 1974 and 1980;[10] avoidance of interest rate manipulation in favor of constant expansion of the money supply and the liberalization of interest rates especially after the mid-1970s;[11] and avoidance of intervention in the exchange rate system.[12]

Fiscal policy was not used in any vigorous way to stimulate private demand (or for fine-tuning). Controlling inflation was given higher priority than stimulating and reflating of the economy, especially in 1977–78 and 1981–82.[13] Growth in tax revenues stagnated because the taxation system is very sensitive to business conditions. Thus to keep up with steadily expanding public expenditures for welfare, education, and transfers to localities, government bonds became a major means to manage national finance. Fiscal policy thus seems to have been used largely for resource allocation and income redistribution rather than for Keynesian-type demand management.[14] On these five points both monetary and fiscal policies largely conformed to the market in the sense that they did not attempt to stimulate private demand countercyclically if that would disturb and disrupt the stable working of the economy. Such market conformity and strong consistency in macroeconomic management distinguished Japan from some other major OECD countries during this period.

As a partial consequence of macroeconomic management, economic conditions were conducive to political-economic attitudes favoring financial frugality, political conservatism, the political status quo, and support for the LDP. The public perception of its standard of living was always, first, very stable and, second, resiliently affirmative. From the mid-1960s those who

9. Yoshitomi Masaru, *Nihon keizai* [The Japanese economy] (Tokyo: Toyokeizai, 1981); Shinkai Yoichi, *Gendai makuro keizaigaku no kaimei* [Anatomy of contemporary macroeconomics] (Tokyo: Tōyō keizai shimposha, 1982); Jeffrey Sachs, "Wages, Profits, and Macroeconomic Adjustment: A Comparative Study," *Brookings Papers on Economic Activity* 2 (1979): 269–319.

10. Suzuki Yukio, *Nihon keizai to kinyū* [Japanese economy and finance] (Tokyo: Tōyō keizai shimposha, 1981).

11. Suzuki, *Nihon keizai to kinyū*; Kuroda Akio, *Kinri no kōzō* [Interest rate structure] (Tokyo: Tōyō keizai shimposha, 1982); Goto Shinichi et al., *Nihon no kinyū kakumei* [Japan's financial revolution] (Tokyo: Yūhikaku, 1982).

12. Komiya Ryutaro, "Shōwa 48–9 nen infureishon no genin [The causes of inflation in 1973–74]," *Keizaigaku kenkyū* [Economic studies] 42 (April 1976): 2–40.

13. Shimpo Seiji, *Gendai Nihon keizai no kaimei: sutagufureishon no kenkyū* [Anatomy of contemporary Japanese economy: A study of stagflation] (Tokyo: Tōyō keizai shimposha, 1979); Yoshitomi, *Nihon keizai;* Shinkai, *Gendai makuro.*

14. Noguchi Yukio, "Nihon de Keinzu seisaku wa okonawaretaka? [Was Keynesian economic policy ever implemented in Japan?]," *Kikan gendai keizaigaku* [Quarterly contemporary economics] 52 (1983): 163–83; Shinkai, *Gendai makuro.*

rated their standard of living as "middle class" continuously hovered around the 90 percent level.[15] Clearly, a large majority of the public perceived their living standard as basically acceptable;[16] following 1974, however, people became very modest about their expectations of economic improvement. A large majority (about 90 percent) came to think that their economic standard of living had not improved in the recent past, and since 1974, 75 to 89 percent of the people expect no improvement in their economic life in the near future.[17] In light of the high standard of living already achieved, the curtailment of inflation so it does not eat away so easily what the public has already achieved, and the lowered real economic growth rate which is likely to remain for the foreseeable future, it makes sense that people have acquired a very realistic but contented outlook toward their economic life. The proportion who responded that they were satisfied with their present economic life increased from the lowest level of 51 percent in November 1974 to 66 percent in May 1982. The proportion who found psychological satisfaction, spiritual fulfillment (*jujitsukan*), or both in their present life increased from the lowest level of 52 percent in November 1974 to 72 percent in May 1978.[18] Despite a widely held hope for a fuller recovery after the mid-1970s, global recession continued, yet people's quasi-resignation was reinforced as this gray picture became increasingly evident. The second oil crisis further strengthened such convictions.

This process of increasing economic conservatism seems to have preceded the revitalization of political conservatism. The disparity between those who perceive their living standards as having recently improved versus those who expect their living standards to improve in the near future is measured against the LDP support levels in Figures 6.3 through 6.8. It becomes fairly clear that support for the LDP increases as the disparity decreases. In other words, as public expectations about economic improvement become more realistic, the LDP gains more support.

This point becomes clearer when the relationship between LDP support

15. The OPM survey of economic attitudes has the following characteristics:
(a) Population, Japanese over twenty years old; sample size, 20,000 (1958–74) and 10,000 (1975 onward); random sample; two-way stratification by (i) administrative size and (ii) industrial characteristics; two-step sampling by (i) census emulation districts and (ii) individual respondents.
(b) Response rate: 79.3–86.5 percent (1957–82).
(c) Question wording: "When looking at your present standard of living, do you think that it has improved, deteriorated, or remained the same, compared to a year ago?" and "Do you think that your standard of living will improve, deteriorate, or remain the same from now?"
16. Yasusuke Murakami, "The Age of New Middle Mass Politics: The Case of Japan," *Journal of Japanese Studies* 8 (Winter 1982): 29–72; Tominaga Kenichi, ed., *Nihon no kaisō kōzō* [The structure of Japanese stratification] (Tokyo: University of Tokyo Press, 1979).
17. Murakami, "The Age of New Middle Mass Politics." See also Office of Prime Minister, *Kokumin seikatsu nikansuru yoronchōsa* [Opinion polls concerning people's living] (Tokyo: Office of Prime Minister, 1953–82).
18. Murakami, "The Age of New Middle Mass Politics." See also Office of Prime Minister, *Konshū no Nihon* [Japan today] (Tokyo: Office of Prime Minister, 1982).

Figures 6.3.–6.8. Economic attitude and LDP support (or economic realism and political conservatism)

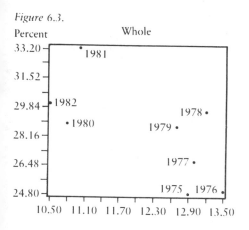

Figure 6.3.

Whole

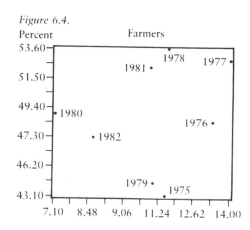

Figure 6.4.

Farmers

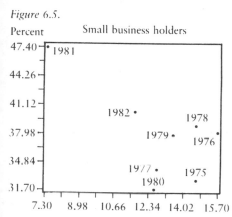

Figure 6.5.

Small business holders

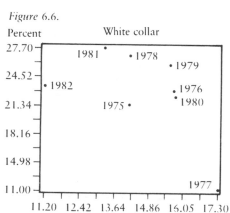

Figure 6.6.

White collar

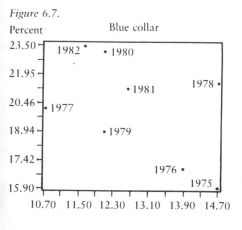

Figure 6.7.

Blue collar

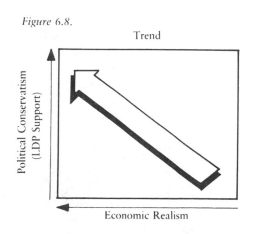

Figure 6.8.

Trend

Table 6.1. Economic attitude and support for the LDP (or economic realism and political conservatism)

Independent variable and summary statistic	Whole	Farmers	Small business holders	White collar	Blue collar
R²	0.63	0.05	0.52	0.68	0.40
R²	0.49	−0.33	0.33	0.55	0.16
D.W.	2.28	1.79	2.69	2.64	2.56
Constant	45.44	46.07	52.33	32.58	33.44
Share of LDP seats					
regression coefficients	0.0036	−0.0011	0.0044	0.0097	0.0035
standard deviation	0.0024	0.0058	0.0049	0.0042	0.0032
t statistics	1.50*	−0.19	0.90	2.31*	1.09
Economic attitude					
regression coefficients	−1.5494	0.2967	−1.3206	−1.0030	−1.1697
standard deviation	0.6204	0.8044	0.6018	0.6994	0.6769
t statistics	−2.50*	0.37	−2.19*	−1.43	−1.73*

*Significant at 10 percent level.

and economic attitudes is examined through regression equations. In this model, the dependent variable is the LDP support (as revealed in opinion polls), and the two independent variables are the percentage of LDP seats in the House of Representatives and of Councillors, and the disparity between public expectations about economic improvement in the near future versus public perceptions of economic improvement in the recent past. Since the basis of the LDP support is the percentage of LDP seats in the Diet and the representatives' level of activities in home districts and the Diet, it is impossible to weigh the importance of the economic attitudinal variable without taking this variable into account.[19]

Since respondents' attributes are organized differently in the two polls, it is impossible to construct a model including a variety of social groups. Thus my model is confined to the following five groups: the whole, agriculture, self-employed, white collar, and blue collar. The results are shown in Table 6.1.

Since the number of observations is very small (N = 8), estimates of regression coefficients are not always highly significant and conclusions drawn from this exercise are suggestive. On the whole, however, the signs of coefficient estimates and R²s show reasonably satisfactory figures.

19. The LDP support variable is drawn from the Jiji monthly opinion polls, and the percentage of LDP seats in the Diet is based on the data obtained from the secretariat of both houses. The data on economic attitudes is drawn from *Kokumin seikatsu nikansuru yoronchosa* conducted almost annually (mostly in May) by the Public Relations Department of the Cabinet Secretariat, Office of Prime Minister. (Although opinion polls were conducted twice, in May and November, during each of the two years immediately after the first oil crisis, I have excluded the two November polls so as to make a uniform number of observations per year. The percentage of LDP seats is measured for the month when *Kokumin seikatsu nikansuru yōronchōsa* are conducted.)

Viewed by occupational categories, it is apparent that the economic attitudinal variable is less important for farmers than for some other groups. This suggests that farmers are most indirectly affected by macroeconomic conditions and that great importance must also be given to more direct, more specific economic variables such as subsidies as well as political activities such as LDP politicians lobbying specifically for agricultural interests (see the section on political clientelism). The model fits most perfectly for the white-collar sector. Yet the portions directly affected by the economic attitudinal variables are slightly smaller than those for the self-employed or blue-collar sectors. This suggests the importance of postindustrial values and issues in determining the party support pattern of white-collar employees (see the section on policy adaptation). The economic attitudinal variable is clearly important to blue-collar workers. At the same time, the smaller R^2 for blue-collar workers may suggest the presence of other important variables.

For blue-collar workers, expectations of economic improvement—rather than the disparity between expectation of economic improvement in the near future and perception of economic improvement in the recent past—may play a more important role. If one explores, as independent variables, the percentage of LDP Diet seats and expectation of economic improvement, then the estimate of regression coefficients of the economic expectation variable and R^2 increase only for the blue-collar sector. Also, if as independent variables, one compares the perception of economic improvement and the percentage of LDP Diet seats, then most t values and R^2s become smaller (see the survey of economic attitudes referred to in note 15 for further explanation of the rise in blue-collar workers' support for the LDP). All this seems to suggest that the decrease in economic performance is followed by lowered perceptions of economic improvement, and this increased economic realism leads to increased support for the LDP or growing political conservatism (see Table 6.2).

To give more evidence of the link between economic realism and political conservatism, it is helpful to consider the public's comparative evaluation of competing parties' competence and ability to manage the country. The public rated the LDP better able to govern than the other parties, especially the JSP. As evidence, two examples are cited.

First, in Kyoto in 1980 the LDP enjoyed the rating of 52.6 percent compared to the JSP's 3.7 percent in perceived ability to govern.[20] Considering that 32.7 percent of the respondents answered that no party was reliable or

20. The question is, "Which party do you think is most reliable in handling the following problem—to manage the government in this difficult time?" The Kyoto survey was conducted in June 1980 after the 1980 general election by the Kyoto Municipal Election Management Committee. The population was Kyoto citizens and the sample size was 1,020. The response rate was 69 percent (N = 705). The sampling method was a stratified two-step sampling. First, sampling was made out of electoral districts, taking into account the industrial-commercial-residential characters and average turnout rates of each district. Interviewing was done by undergraduate students in political science of Kyoto and Kyoto Sangyo universities.

Table 6.2. Economic expectation and support for the LDP

Independent variable and summary statistic	Whole	Farmers	Small business holders	White collar	Blue collar
R^2	0.69	0.02	0.34	0.65	0.70
R^2	0.57	-0.37	0.07	0.51	0.58
D.W.	2.38	1.77	3.03	2.83	2.01
Constant	42.69	48.85	50.58	30.40	44.89
Share of LDP seats					
regression coefficients	0.0039	-0.0016	0.0044	0.0106	0.0033
standard deviation	0.0022	0.0059	0.0058	0.0043	0.0022
t statistics	1.77*	0.27	-0.76	2.47*	1.50*
Economic expectation					
regression coefficients	-1.7339	0.3950	-0.6438	-0.4807	-1.2000
standard deviation	0.2543	0.4521	0.4473	0.4010	0.3610
t statistics	-2.89*	0.87	-1.44	-1.20	-3.32*

*Significant at 10 percent level.

else "did not know," the LDP's figure of 52.6 percent shows the party's virtual monopoly of general public confidence. More specifically, on the ability to contain inflation and stabilize the economy, the LDP enjoyed a rating of 31.1 percent, far surpassing the others, with the JCP getting only 12.5 percent, the Clean Government party (CGP) 6.1 percent, and the JSP 6.0 percent.[21] On ability to overcome the oil crisis, the LDP enjoyed a rating of 42.6 percent, with the JCP, the CGP, and the JSP following with the percentages of 4.1, 3.1, and 2.0, respectively.[22] When the LDP was walking a tightrope in the Diet, the bulk of a basically conservative public became apprehensive about the likelihood that the LDP might succumb to a coalition government, dominated by a JSP viewed as far less competent. Public criticism of the LDP turned into support as this eventuality became more conceivable, especially in 1979 and 1980.

A second bit of parallel evidence can be cited. Among voters in Sapporo who switched from non-LDP support or abstention to support for the LDP between the two general elections of 1979 and 1980, those who rated the LDP's ability to govern increased from 37.6 to 66.7 percent.[23] In contrast,

21. The question is, "Which party do you think is most reliable in handling the following problem—to control the rise in commodities prices and to stabilize the economy?"
22. The question is, "Which party do you think is most reliable in handling the following problem—to overcome the oil crisis?"
23. Araki Toshio et al., Tōhyō kōdo niokeru renzoku to henka [Continuities and changes in voting behavior] (Tokyo: Bokutakusha, 1983). The question is, "Among the following characteristics, check those you think are most pertinent to the LDP. You can check as many as you think pertinent.
(a) the LDP thinks seriously about the working people.
(b) the LDP does not have international perspectives.
(c) the LDP is not cohesive.

the JSP's rating on the question of its ability to govern decreased from 9.2 to 7.8 percent. Furthermore, the Sapporo surveys showed that the issues that discriminated most clearly those "returnees" to the LDP from non-LDP supporters were those that had been tackled head-on, namely, defense, administrative reform, energy, and recession. Issues that had aroused protest against the government's alleged ineptness such as political corruption (a 1976 election issue), environmental pollution (a 1972 election issue), and tax increase (a 1979 election issue) seem to have been largely set aside in 1980. In other words, for returnees to the LDP the party's perceived competence in handling those mundane but essential issues seems to have loomed large, causing their return.

Thus the major intervening variable between perceived economic conditions and public support, including voting choices, seems to be the public's assessment of the competence of the LDP and the opposition parties. Put differently, these returnees seem to have been prompted by the economic and other difficulties which they believed only the LDP could handle. They seemed to cling to the known quantity, in much the same way as the Sicilian saying, "Better a known evil than an unknown good."[24] Yet this is passive approval of the government's economic performance. It seems that unless pushed further to answer the question of the likely macroeconomic consequences of a change in government, the public normally expresses a fairly high rate of dissatisfaction with the government.[25] But once the problem becomes the likely economic consequences of a change in government, the public seems to show much stronger support for the government.

Any particular social-occupational group is unlikely to be affected disproportionately by economic performance over the short term. No group is exempt from the pervasive influence of macroeconomic conditions. Yet in a longer perspective, the picture differs slightly. Some particular social-occupational groups have recently benefited economically, belatedly enjoying the fruits of high growth in the 1960s. They are residents in small urban

---

(d) the LDP is clear.
(e) the LDP is reliable in managing the economy.
(f) the LDP is vulnerable to pressure from particular groups.
(g) the LDP is outmoded.
(h) the LDP is thinking of Japan's future in the world.
(i) the LDP is competent in managing the government."
The Sapporo survey was conducted twice, once in October 1979 immediately after the 1979 general election and again in June 1980 immediately after the 1980 general election. The population was Sapporo citizens. The sample size was 2,241, and the response rate was 67.4 percent in 1979 (N = 1,509). The 1980 survey was conducted among these 1,509 persons. The response rate was 77.9 percent (N = 1,175). The sampling method was as follows. First, a random sample was drawn choosing 90 persons from each of 25 of the 199 districts in the city. Out of 2,250 sampled, nine policemen were excluded because it was known that they always refuse to answer questionnaires. Interviewing was done by undergraduates taking political science courses at Hokkaido University.
24. Judith Chubb, *Patronage, Power and Poverty in Southern Italy* (Cambridge: Cambridge University Press, 1983), p. 210.
25. *Asahi* (Tokyo), May 25, 1983.

settings, small business holders, farmers, and wage earners in smaller business. The general large-scale rise in real wages in the first half of the 1970s had effectively raised the wages of such groups, but after 1976 this income-equalization process had slowed down.[26] The lower growth rate of the latter half of the 1970s and early 1980s effectively protected the existing income levels of these groups, especially in smaller urban settings. Also, the enormous investments in the socially, economically, and regionally "weaker" sectors continued.[27] By 1982, in real income, residents in smaller urban districts and rural localities were better off than those in metropolitan areas.[28] It is no wonder that the LDP found its strongest support among these groups. Between 1976 and 1980 the LDP's support level changed most in cities other than the ten largest (34.1 percent increase) and in other, less urban units (28.8 percent increase). It changed least in Japan's ten largest cities (19.2 percent increase). Yet it must be stressed that one of the important factors that distinguishes Japan from some of the major OECD countries is that differences in economic improvement are not so large as to make class-based cleavages very salient politically.[29]

Political Clientelism

In this section I will analyze behavior by traditional conservatives, farmers, and small business holders by means of the politicoeconomic variable called political clientelism.

Looking at the twenty years of enormous economic and demographic changes from the vantage point of the incumbent party, the most important question was how to prevent depreciation of the party's traditional power bases while promoting the economic well-being of the nation as a whole.[30]

26. Ishizaki Tadao, *Nihon no shotoku to tomi no bunpai* [Distribution of income and wealth in Japan] (Tokyo: Tōyō keizai shimposha, 1983).

27. Ministry of Construction, *Kensetsu hakusho* [The white paper on construction] (Tokyo: Ministry of Construction, 1982).

28. Economic Planning Agency, *Kokumin seikatsu hakusho* [The white paper on people's living] (Tokyo: Economic Planning Agency, 1982).

29. Malcolm Sawyer, *Income Distribution in OECD Countries* (Paris: OECD, 1976); Ishizaki, *Nihon no shotoku;* Alan A. Blinder, "The Level and Distribution of Economic Well-Being," in Martin Feldstein, ed., *The American Economy in Transition* (Chicago: University of Chicago Press, 1980), pp. 415–79; Lester Thurow, "The Disappearance of the Middle Class," *New York Times,* February 5, 1984.

30. The following works on French and Italian politics were very instructive in writing this section: Suzanne Berger, ed., *Organizing Interests in Western Europe: Pluralism, Corporatism and the Transformation of Politics* (Cambridge: Cambridge University Press, 1982); Berger, "The Traditional Sector in France and Italy," in Suzanne Berger and Michael Piore, *Dualism and Discontinuity in Industrial Societies* (Cambridge: Cambridge University Press, 1981); Berger, "Politics and Antipolitics in Western Europe in the Seventies," *Daedalus* 108 (Winter 1979): 27–50; Pierre Birnbaum, *The Heights of Power: An Essay on the Power Elite in France* (Chicago: University of Chicago Press, 1982); and Chubb, *Patronage, Power and Poverty in Southern Italy.*

One of the pillars of the LDP's power since its inception has been traditional conservative forces such as farmers and small business holders, but these two groups were subject to the expansionary threat from more competitive sectors of manufacturing and service run by big business. The LDP also had to accommodate the demands and interests of urban wage earners whose numbers increased as industrialization and urbanization progressed. Needless to say, other, more specific occupational groups such as construction companies and medical doctors receive special treatment.[31] I chose to focus on farmers and small business holders because in examining these two groups, it is possible to reveal how the LDP handled the usual dilemma of incumbent right-wing parties by a clever combination of political protection and economic competition vis-à-vis these two basically conservative groups.

Demographic statistics show a rapid decline in the number of those engaged in agriculture: 45 percent in 1948, dropping to 10.9 percent by 1978.[32] Furthermore, the percentage of agricultural households dependent solely on agriculture had become a mere 1.9 percent.[33] The figure for those small business holders engaged in commerce and manufacturing remained relatively stable, registering 11.1 percent in 1948 and 12.6 percent in 1978.[34] During 1974 the support level for the LDP among those engaged in agriculture was around 46.5 percent. By 1980 the figure had risen to 57.3 percent. The comparable figures for those engaged in small shopkeeping and manufacturing were 35.2 percent in 1974 and 46.2 percent in 1980.[35] The increase of over 10 percent in the support level from these two occupational groups was made possible by two major factors. First, the economic growth rate was reasonably favorable. Second, the LDP recognized the importance of regaining and/or holding on to its most loyal clients by using its time-tested policies of providing material benefits through public policies. Some specifics about such benefits can be gleaned from a discussion of policies related to taxation, public subsidies, and political representation.

Agriculture

Tax policies have been especially favorable to farmers. In 1949 there was a fundamental change in the taxation method designed to emphasize direct taxation and creating a tax payment formula that differentiated between wage earners and nonwage earners. This system became cause for serious

31. Hirose Michisada, *Hojokin to seikentō* [Subsidies and the ruling party] (Tokyo: Asahi Newspaper, 1981).

32. Tōyō keizai, *Shōwa taisei sōran* [Encyclopedia of the Showa era] (Tokyo: Tōyō keizai shimposha, 1980).

33. Ministry of Agriculture, Forestry, and Fishery, *Nōka chōsa hōkokusho: 1980 nen nōringyo sensasu kekka* [Report on the agricultural households] (Tokyo: MAFF, 1982).

34. Tōyō keizai, *Shōwa taisei sōran.*

35. Jiji tsushinsha [Jiji News Agency], ed., *Sengo Nihon no seitō to naikaku* [Postwar Japanese parties and cabinets] (Tokyo: Jiji tsushinsha, 1981).

concern. The imbalance in tax burdens has been increasing between wage earners, whose tax is automatically withheld before wage payment, and nonwage earners, who pay according to tax forms they file themselves.[36] The ratio between taxes due and taxes actually paid among wage earners, self-employed merchants and industrialists, and farmers is widely thought to be 9 : 6 : 4 or even 10 : 5 : 3. Farmers obviously benefit from this system.[37] Also, taxation on arable land is extremely low. A large piece of land in the Tokyo suburbs, for example, is often registered as arable land. For land in this category the tax remains low until the value goes up high enough for the land to be put up for sale. An attempt was made to revise the taxation system for arable land in cities, but the revised tax law was made "toothless" in response to the strong pressure exerted by agricultural lobbies.[38]

The LDP is also generous with public subsidies.[39] The immediate postwar reconstruction policies included a large-scale subsidy system that set up a national priority list for industrial rejuvenation. Extreme inflation resulted in part from this subsidy system; harsh economic policies were adopted in response in 1949. The sacrifice by farmers for economic reconstruction was to be compensated when the economy went up soon after the outbreak of the Korean War in 1950. The farmers' backlash started in 1951, when a private member bill on agricultural subsidies for heavy-snow, low-temperature areas passed the Diet. After this bill, various other subsidy bills were passed in the Diet to cover diverse categories of the agricultural sector. Although agricultural subsidy policies to promote "structural adaptation" or positive adjustment were propounded in the Basic Agricultural Law of 1961, in reality these tended to degenerate into a negative adjustment policy. Two major factors are important: farmers' search for a rationale for subsidies even after food had become abundant and their response to a call from big business for rationalization in view of competing demands between a needed stable supply and anticipated trade liberalization.

Agricultural subsidies were subject to increasing criticism as the government's budget deficits became enormous and as international criticisms became vehement, but the basic structure did not change for various reasons. Among them are the bureaucratic interests of the Ministry of Agriculture, Forestry and Fisheries (MAFF); the vigorous network of agricultural cooperatives (Nokyo) and their successful co-optation of consumer cooperatives by allowing them to buy certain agricultural products, including im-

36. Sato Hiroshi and Miyajima Hiroshi, *Sengo zeisei shi* [A history of postwar taxation system] (Tokyo: Zeimukeiri kyōkai, 1979).
37. Ishi Hiromitsu, *Zaisei kaikaku no ronri* [The logic of financial reform] (Tokyo: Nihon keizai, 1982).
38. Official Gazette, "Sōzei tokubetsu sochi no ichibu kaiseisuru hōritsu [Law partially revising special tax measures]," *Kampō*, March 31, 1982.
39. Imamura Naomi, *Hojokin to nōgyō-nōson* [Subsidies, agriculture, and agricultural villages] (Tokyo: Ieno Hikari kyokai, 1978).

ported ones, more cheaply;[40] the inability of the government, for electoral as well as national security reasons, to proceed with structural adaptation policies (both of the latter considerations argue against trade liberalization of certain agricultural products); and the more narrowly profarmers' lobbying by the opposition parties. (The LDP has two major, diametrically opposed clients in its camp with regard to agricultural liberalization, namely, farmers and big business. Opposition parties do not pay much attention to the preferences of big business on liberalization.)

Agricultural representation in the LDP has always been very strong.[41] The agricultural work force decreased by 43.6 percent between 1965 and 1978, but those residing in farm households declined in number by only 26 percent during the same period. However, "the disequilibrium within the House of Representatives' electorate in 1978 was such that eligible voters in rural and semirural constituencies (who constituted a little over 20 percent of total voters) decided 30 percent of the total number of seats."[42] Various social and economic interests of farmers enjoy semiexclusive representation within various subbodies of the LDP Policy Affairs Research Council (PARC), which in recent years served as a major key to interest representation, diluting to a significant degree the hitherto dominant influence of bureaucrats in policy formation.[43] Membership in these divisions is determined by individual preference with each Dietman belonging to a maximum of three divisions (although one of them is determined in contingency with the House of Representatives' or House of Councillors' committee membership which is decided by the party headquarters). The PARC's Division on Agriculture, Forestry and Fishery consists of 170 members, along with those on Commerce and Industry (152), Transport (117), and Communica-

40. Even among consumers, opinion against liberalization of agricultural products is strong. As many as 68.7 percent of the respondents to the question on agricultural trade liberalization in a recent survey of agriculture were opposed (*Nihon keizai*, October 7, 1982). Also the Japan Cooperatives' Association recently issued a resolution against liberalization of agricultural products (*Nihon keizai*, August 24, 1982). The only vigorous force supporting agricultural liberalization is big business peak associations such as the Federation of Economic Organizations. See Hosen Mitsuo, "Nōsanbutsu jiyuka ni hantaisuru shōhisha dantai [Consumer groups against agricultural liberalization]," *EPS* (Economy, Polity, Society), 127: 56–60.

41. Aurelia George, "The Japanese Farm Lobby and Agricultural Policy Making," *Pacific Affairs* 54 (Fall 1981): 409–30; Hirose, *Hojokin to seikento*, 1981.

42. George, "Japanese Farm Lobby," pp. 409–30.

43. Muramatsu Michio, *Sengo Nihon no kanryōsei* [Postwar Japanese bureaucracy] (Tokyo: Tōyō keizai shimposha, 1981); Far Eastern Economic Review, *Asia 1983 Yearbook* (Hong Kong: Far Eastern Economic Review, 1983); Takashi Inoguchi, "Politicians, Bureaucrats and Interest Groups in the Legislative Process," paper presented at the Workshop on One-Party Dominance, Ithaca, New York, April 7–9, 1984. A revised version will be included in Haruhiro Fukui, ed., *Public Policies and Policymaking in Post–Oil Crisis Japan* (forthcoming); Takashi Inoguchi and Tomoaki Iwai, "The Growth of *Zoku*: LDP Politicians in Committees," paper presented at the Annual Meeting of the Association for Asian Studies, March 23–25, 1984, Washington, D.C.; Inoguchi Takashi and Tomoaki Iwai, *Zoku giin no kenkyū: Jimintō seiken o gyūjiru shuyakutachi* [A study of policy tribes: Major actors of the LDP government] (Tokyo: Nihon keizai shimbunsha, 1987).

tion (113).[44] More indicative of their strength is the number of members on research commissions and special committees under the LDP's PARC. Membership in these subbodies is totally discretionary. The Research Commission on Comprehensive Agricultural Policy has the largest number of members, 247. That means that 58.8 percent of the LDP Dietmen are members of the LDP PARC Research Commission on Comprehensive Agricultural Policy.[45] Another dramatic indication of the solid agricultural representation can be seen from the number of votes cast in 1980 for a former MAFF bureaucrat candidate for the House of Councillors' nationwide district. When that vote is correlated with agricultural subsidies for land improvement, the correlation coefficient is 0.78. In other words, the candidate earned his votes in almost direct proportion to the amount of money poured into districts for land improvement projects when he was vice-director of MAFF Bureau of Land Structural Reform.[46]

Small-Scale Business

The LDP's protection of small-scale commerce and industry is also very well known. One result is the presence of a large number of small-scale wholesalers and retailers in Japan.[47] Despite a total population half that of the United States, Japan has about the same number of small-scale enterprises. Even France, a country of artisans and merchants, pales next to Japan in this respect.[48] "[In] 1977 60 percent of the Japanese retail outlets still employed no more than two people and 45 percent of the wholesalers employed four people or less. . . . The number of wholesale and retail outlets increased by 44 percent and by 15 percent respectively during the 1970's. In absolute numbers, wholesale outlets increased by 50,000 since 1975. Eighty percent of them have a capital of less than U.S. $40,000."[49] The flourishing wholesale and retail business is explained by three major factors: consumers prefer service tailored to the various needs in the local neighborhoods; such businesses serve as an unofficial social welfare system for some retired or semiretired citizens, an important element because of the fairly early retirement age in Japan (around fifty-five); and their political muscle is strong. The first two factors are outside my primary interest, hence more attention is given to the political aspects, taxation, regulation of competition, public subsidies, and political representation.

44. LDP, *Jiyuminshūtō yakuin meibo* [Directory of the LDP officers] (Tokyo: LDP Headquarters, 1982).
45. Ibid.
46. Hirose Michisada, *Hojokin to seikentō*, pp. 19–28.
47. "Japan: A Nation of Wholesalers," *Economist,* September 9, 1981, pp. 88–89; Nikkei ryutsu shimbun, ed., *Ogataten shinkisei jidai no kōrigyō* [Retailing at the time of the new regulation of large-scale stores] (Tokyo: Nihon keizai, 1982).
48. *Nihon keizai,* February 13, 1983.
49. "Japan: A Nation of Wholesalers."

The LDP's lenient taxation policy toward such enterprises has been noted earlier. Regulation of competition also favors small-scale business. In 1974 legislation was passed to regulate the establishment of supermarkets.[50] Approval from local authorities was required to open stores with floor space larger than fifteen hundred square meters. In 1978 and 1979, this regulation was strengthened to allow local Chambers of Commerce and Industry (CCI) to approve or disapprove the opening of any store with a floor space larger than five hundred square meters. As a consequence, opening new stores was made subject to the approval of the association that represented the existing small local retailers most affected by the new competition. Likewise, the CCI's approval became necessary to open a store that rented small plots to retailers. As a consequence, the rate at which new stores were opened declined steadily after 1976 and the growth of supermarket chains stalled by 1980.

A question may be raised as to whether the LDP's lenient policy toward small business holders may not be able to offset the formidable problems that they face in a prolonged economic recession. The point here, however, is that the LDP did try to moderate and mitigate the negative repercussions of economic difficulties unlike, say, the French economic management under Raymond Barre, which tightened the economy with little mixing in of sweeteners.[51]

The LDP also gave subsidies to small-scale shopkeepers and factory owners. When the LDP suffered a great setback in many of its urban districts in the 1972 general election, Prime Minister Tanaka Kakuei was persuaded to take measures to try to stem the desertion by urban voters. To mobilize the votes of small shopkeepers and factory owners, a law was passed in 1973 which stipulates that shops with two or fewer employees and factories with five or fewer employees may have access to unguaranteed 7 percent loans for up to 1 million yen for facilities and half a million yen for operation. The CCI must approve the loans. In 1974 the annual budget for this policy increased from 30 billion yen to 120 billion yen. The figure was 240 billion yen for 1975, 350 billion yen for 1976, 470 billion yen for 1977, and 510 billion yen for 1978, 1979, and 1980. In 1977 another kind of loan was introduced to help shops with five or fewer employees and factories with twenty or fewer employees for up to 3 million yen. Furthermore, in view of the stagnant economic conditions in anticipation of the 1983 national legislative elections, a September 1982 law gave further privileges to small industrialists.[52]

50. Ibid.
51. Pierre Birnbaum, *The Heights of Power: An Essay on the Power Elite in France* (Chicago: University of Chicago Press, 1982); Peter A. Hall, "Socialism in One Country: Mitterrand and the Struggle to Define a New Economic Policy for France," in Philip Cerny and Martin Schain, eds., *Socialism, the State and Public Policy in France* (London: Frances Pinter, 1984).
52. The 1973 law resembles the Royer Law of 1973 in France (Birnbaum, *Heights of Power,*

Political representation of these interests is very strong in the LDP. The percentage of former businessmen entering the House of Representatives was 19.2 percent in 1972, 18.6 percent in 1976, 26.7 percent in 1979, and 17.1 percent in 1980.[53] These figures are somewhat misleading because a large number of those who represent small-scale business interests centering around the CCI enter the world of politics first as local politicians and secretaries of Dietmen before they actually run for the Diet. The point is that their interests are well represented. The LDP PARC's Divisions on Commerce and Industry, on Construction and on Transportation, and its Research Commissions on Taxation (with 202 members), on Small Scale Industry (181), on Roads (202), and on National Land Development and its regional subcommissions (total, 509) are all related to the interests of small-scale shopkeepers and company owners. Party bureaucrats with their power based on these LDP organizations often dominate a significant portion of major policy decisions in contrast to the hitherto prevalent picture of bureaucratic dominance over policy making.[54]

These policies plus certain economic conditions favorable to such merchants, such as higher unemployment rates which pose less of a problem to them than to blue- and white-collar workers, translated into increasing support for the LDP. If the contribution index of Robert Axelrod[55] is used, as of June 1980 farmers' contribution to the LDP was 22.0 percent, that of commerce and manufacturing was 24.2 percent, that of housewives, 23.2 percent, that of the white-collar sector, 12.0 percent, and that of blue-collar workers, 16.7 percent. Since the Axelrod index is determined by size, loyalty, and turnout of a group in relation to the total support for a party, the figures for the farmers and the commerce and manufacturing sector are significantly higher than their proportion of the total electorate (5.5 percent and 16.5 percent respectively). Their high loyalty and turnout rate in voting enable them to remain very visible and loyal groups despite the adverse demographic and occupational trends. The only nationwide survey of LDP party members ever conducted by the LDP (in May 1981) reveals the very high representation of farmers and small business holders. As percentages of

pp. 93–98). The difference between the French RI and the Japanese LDP is that the latter was able to retain small business holders within its camp throughout whereas the former was not able to capture a sizable portion of their support in 1981 (ibid., pp. 128–37, and David B. Godley and Andrew F. Knapp, "Time for a Change: The French Elections of 1981, I. The Presidency," *Electoral Studies* 1 [April 1983]: 3–42, esp. Table 2; "Japan: A Nation of Wholesalers," pp. 88–89). Nikkei ryutsu shimbun, *Ogataten shinkisei jidai.*

53. Naka Hisao, ed., *Kokkai giin no kōsei to henka* [The sociological composition of Dietmen and its change] (Tokyo: Seiji kōhō senta, 1980).

54. "Jimintō seichōsakai [LDP Policy Affairs Research Council]," *Sentaku*, May, June, and July, 1982, pp. 44–47; Utsumi Kenji, "Riken ni muragaru 'atsuryoku giin' no jittai ["Pressure Dietmen" seeking after perks]," *Gendai*, August 1982, pp. 14–59; FEER, *Asia 1983 Yearbook.*

55. Robert Axelrod, "Where the Votes Come From: An Analysis of Electoral Coalitions, 1952–1968," *American Political Science Review* 66 (March 1972): 11–20.

the total electorate, farmers represented 6.9 percent and small-scale business holders 12.4 percent, but they make up 27.1 percent and 28.4 percent respectively of the LDP membership.[56] Thus the LDP's vigorous client-oriented tactics are matched by the resilience of these traditional groups, which in turn gives enormous strength to the Japanese conservatives (see Table 6.3).[57]

Do the politics of special treatment that date back to the period before 1977 have relevance in explaining events of the 1977–82 period? Without policy continuity the public cannot trust the government, and these two clients are no exception. Only with policy continuity do the cumulative effects of policy become tangible, normally with a certain period of time lag.

The political clientelism explanation focuses on the two traditional categories of conservatives who are most vigorous in LDP interest representation, farmers and small business holders. The LDP was largely successful in continuously reincorporating traditional conservatives and in channeling their vigorous participation into the "normal" political process of benefit allocation. The LDP managed to tone down the two major cleavages among its clients, that between the traditional conservatives and big business and that between the traditional conservatives and urban wage earners. Although the rate of government revenue growth slowed down substantially after 1974, the government managed to provide for its traditional clients with the help of government bonds, though by the early 1980s this posed an alarming problem. (The government extraordinary, or so-called deficit, bond issue started to accelerate after 1975. By 1979 government bonds occupied a 39.6 percent share of the general account budget. The cumulative balance of government bonds was more than one-third of the GNP by 1981.[58])

Although the LDP continued to be about as attentive to its traditional

56. LDP, *Tōin ishiki chōsa* [Opinion poll of party members] (Tokyo: LDP National Organization Committee, 1981); *Nihon keizai,* November 18, 1982.

57. A comment is warranted on the rise in the support for the LDP among blue-collar workers in Table 6.3. Although more survey data are needed to clarify the statistics, it seems that two factors are most important. First, a large bulk of blue-collar workers came to enjoy higher income and to constitute an important part of what is often called the new middle mass (Murakami, "The Age of New Middle Mass Politics," pp. 29–72). Second, despite slowly rising rates of unemployment, which more strongly affect the 30 percent of blue-collar workers who are unskilled, and falling real income, which was not too serious for most of them during the 1977–83 period, blue-collar workers in relatively higher income brackets did not suffer very much from tax increases. By contrast, white-collar workers tended to belong to relatively higher income brackets and were harder hit by the fixed income tax rate. Thus unskilled workers decreased their support for the LDP from 31.1 percent to 20.5 percent between 1973 and 1978 and skilled workers increased their support from 26.3 percent to 32.5 percent in the same period: Nihon hōsō kyōkai hōsō yōron chōsasho, *Daini-Nihonjin no ishiki* [Japanese consciousness, second version] (Tokyo: Shiseido, 1980). Because of the numerical domination of skilled blue-collar workers, a rise in their support for the LDP is observed, as in Table 6.4.

58. Yatsushiro Naohiro, ed., *Gyōzaisei kaikaku no keizaigaku* [The economics of administrative and financial reform] (Tokyo: Tōyō keizai shimposha, 1982).

Table 6.3. Contribution of various racial groups to the LDP's support

Month	Year	Total number	LDP support(%) (total LDP support(%))	Turnout(%)		10 largest cities	Other cities	Other units	Farmers	Commerce & industry	White collar	Blue collar	Housewives
Dec.	1976	1,545	26.1 (34.8)	86.4	Size(%)*	20.5	55.1	22.4	6.5	12.9	14.5	19.4	33.3
					Loyalty(%)*	24.9	25.0	29.7	52.5	38.7	20.1	17.4	21.6
					Turnout(%)*	78.5	87.0	91.2	93.0	90.1	87.9	83.9	84.7
					Contribution(%)	17.8	53.2	29.3	14.1	19.9	11.4	12.5	27.0
Oct.	1979	1,560	29.3 (37.9)	82.9	Size(%)*	19.2	55.3	25.7	9.7	12.6	15.3	19.3	31.5
					Loyalty(%)*	21.5	27.4	39.2	53.9	35.2	18.4	22.9	26.5
					Turnout(%)†	73.0	84.4	87.3	92.5	88.1	82.4	81.7	80.0
					Contribution(%)	12.3	52.6	36.2	20.0	16.0	9.6	14.9	27.5
June	1980	1,551	30.0 (40.5)	87.0	Size(%)*	20.4	55.1	24.5	5.5	16.4	13.4	18.5	31.1
					Loyalty(%)*	19.3	29.6	39.7	62.8	44.9	25.0	25.1	25.5
					Turnout(%)†	85.1	87.0	88.6	95.1	92.1	86.5	85.2	85.7
					Contribution(%)	12.6	54.4	33.0	22.0	24.2	12.0	16.7	23.2

The totals of contributions by occupational groups do not add up to 100% because contribution figures of such occupational groups as the jobless and managerial and professional position holders are not calculated owing to the incongruence between the Jiji survey's categories and the APFE survey's categories.

*The Jiji monthly survey in Jijitsushinsha, ed., Sengo Nihon no seito to naikaku [Postwar Japanese parties and cabinets] (Tokyo: Jiji Tsushinsha, 1981).

†The APFE general election survey in Association for the Promotion of Fair Elections, ed., Shugiin giin sosenkyo no jittai [Outcomes of House of Representatives elections] (Tokyo: Association for the Promotion of Fair Elections, 1977, 1979, and 1980). The APFE survey has the following characteristics:

(a) population: Japanese over 20 years old;
   sample size: 3,000 (1972–80)
   random sample: two-way stratification by (i) administrative size and (ii) industrial characteristics; two step sampling by (i) census emulation districts and (ii) individual respondents;
(b) response rate; 79.0–82.9 percent (1972–80);
(c) question wording: "Would you mind telling me which party the candidate you voted at the House of Representatives election belonged to?"
(d) Interviewers visit each respondent at home to get his or her verbal responses.

clients in agriculture and small business as it had before, that same level of attentiveness, combined with the prolonged economic difficulties of 1977 and 1978 and the worsening situation faced by wage earners, seems to have led farmers and small business holders to increase their loyalty to the LDP. The amount of tax paid by wage earners, self-employed business holders, and farmers in 1978 and 1982 shows that farmers and self-employed business holders were better off than wage earners: wage earners paid 148,000 yen per capita in 1978 and 234,000 yen per capita in 1982; self-employed business holders, 151,000 yen per capita in 1978 and 172,000 yen per capita in 1982; farmers, 97,000 yen per capita in 1978 and 79,000 yen per capita in 1982.[59] Around 1973 for the first time in modern Japanese history, the per capita disposable income of farmers surpassed that of wage earners, and from 1975 until 1982 it registered about 113 percent of the latter.[60] Furthermore, income disparities among regions (ten large cities, medium-sized cities, large small cities, smaller small cities, towns, and villages) show a clear reversal. In 1965 the ranking was by degree of urbanization. But since 1975 towns and villages have ranked first, the ten largest cities last, and the other cities in the middle.[61] Since the percentage of wage earners is higher in the ten large cities than in other localities, this evidence, when combined with other information, suggests that not only farmers but also small business holders became, on the whole, better off than wage earners.[62]

The problem became that extreme political courting of the traditional conservatives could further encourage and accelerate political cartelization, allowing key groups to continue as politically "sacred" segmented territories. This in turn could reduce the capability of the LDP as a whole in effectively performing the role of interest aggregation. When evenhandedness should be the incumbent's strategy, especially with increasing financial difficulties, the LDP's adherence to its rather unbalanced strategy could have resulted in difficulties in holding together all the groups in its grand conservative coalition. More recently, however, the LDP seems to have become more balanced and evenhanded by accommodating the demands of various "nonprivileged" strata such as wage earners and large city dwellers, especially following the electoral setback of the 1983 general election.

One can even say that the LDP is slowly trying to pull the rug out from under these groups without their realizing it. Indeed, a new tax policy will be harsher on farmers and small-scale business holders;[63] a new import policy is hurting the farmers;[64] and a new antimonopoly regulation practice

59. *Yomiuri shimbun,* January 25, 1983.
60. Economic Planning Agency, *Kokumin seikatsu hakusho,* p. 77.
61. Ibid., pp. 78–79.
62. Kato Eiichi, "Toshi no fukushu: Echigo daimyo 'Mejiro' dono no kōzai [Revenge of cities: Good and bad legacies of Mr. 'Mejiro' (Kakuei Tanaka)]," *Chūō kōron,* June 1983, pp. 72–89.
63. *Asahi shimbun,* February 22, 1983, January 11–16, 1984.
64. *Asahi shimbun,* April 22, 1983.

is becoming looser in favor of rationalization and bigness in industry.[65]

But the strength of the LDP lies in being a blend of liberals and conservatives and maintaining an alliance among the party's traditional clients, big business, and wage earners. Perhaps the weight is now shifting toward wage earners, big business, and market forces and away from the traditional clients. But during the period 1977–83 no such decisive one-sided tilt took place. Even the fiscal year 1984 budget is best described by the title of a newspaper article, "Japan Budget: Give a Little, Take a Little."[66]

One can point out that traditional conservative groups receive similar preferential treatment in other countries without responding with such strong loyalty to their incumbent conservative parties as do their Japanese counterparts. There seem to be two major differences. First, the LDP has been in power long enough to build strong clientelist networks. Second, the LDP is a reasonably balanced union of liberals and conservatives and of modernizers and traditionalists, thereby differentiating it from liberals like Giscard d'Estaing, who are more oriented to reform and economic modernization and who lost power in part by not being able to attract sufficient support from these groups.[67] It is also different from conservatives like the Gaullists, who are interested in preserving traditional ways of life, the state, and nationalism even at the expense of economic liberalization. This is why the LDP has more of the characteristics of a broadly based catchall party, solidly holding the Downsian center than some of the other right-wing parties such as those in France. In fact, some would argue that in Western Europe, disillusion with political parties for interest articulation and aggregation and with the state for providing public goods often brings about antipolitical protest movements and thus defections from government support among the traditional conservatives.[68] In a similar vein it is argued that in the United States these two groups, like many other interest groups, are regionally segmented and do not present themselves as political forces rallying behind either of the two major national parties.[69]

Policy Adaptation

This section analyzes the factors that are largely unexplained by the first explanation, specifically for a fraction of those once-aroused groups in the

65. *Nihon keizai shimbun*, December 21–22, 1982.
66. *New York Times*, February 5, 1984.
67. Birnbaum, *Heights of Power;* Godley and Knapp, "Time for a Change."
68. Berger, ed., *Organizing Interests in Western Europe;* Jack Hayward, "Dissentient France: The Counter Political Culture," *West European Politics* 1 (October 1978): 53–67.
69. Anthony King, "The New American Polity in the Late 1970's: Building Coalition in the Sand," in King, ed., *The American Political System* (Washington, D.C.: American Enterprise Institute, 1978), pp. 371–95; Graham K. Wilson, *Interest Groups in the United States* (Oxford: Oxford University Press, 1981).

welfare and environmental policy areas who, as general economic difficulties mounted, returned to support the LDP.

The LDP incorporated a large number of somewhat disgruntled groups through its capacity to wield influence in the mainstream policy process in which programmatic resource allocation is conducted in the name of public policy.[70] The social groups thus incorporated are largely associated with two controversial issues salient in the late 1960s and throughout the 1970s: social welfare and environment.

Throughout the 1960s, the government's first priority was economic growth; welfare, environment, and all other issues were relegated to secondary importance.[71] The opposition called for a rectification of the "growth at any cost" policy, but this was only partially done by the government. The steady erosion of conservative power bases from the late 1960s throughout the 1970s and the rise of "progressive" administrations in many Japanese localities *faute de mieux* forced the LDP to adopt at the national level many of the same policy measures called for by the opposition and which these progressive administrations were implementing at the local level.[72] The LDP strategy resembled that of the incumbents as characterized by Kramer's model of electoral strategy in which candidates appeal directly to particular groups by offering them specific targeted benefits or services. To a remarkable extent in the late 1960s and most of the 1970s the opposition was able to generate controversial issues out of social welfare and the environment. The LDP steadily softened the electoral impact of these controversial issues, however, by offering specific targeted benefits in these policy areas, gradually bringing into its camp a large portion of voters dissatisfied with the party's previous policy performance in these areas. By the mid-1970s Japan had the world's strictest standards on auto emission, a high standard of social welfare programs comparable to Western Europe and North America, and a rate of house ownership, 60.4 percent, superior to that of Western Europe.[73] Japan's life expectancy became the highest in the world alongside that of Iceland, with both public health information and inexpensive medical services generously available.[74]

70. T. J. Pempel, *Policy and Politics in Japan: Creative Conservatism* (Philadelphia: Temple University Press, 1981).

71. Kozo Yamamura, *Economic Policy in Postwar Japan* (Berkeley and Los Angeles: University of California Press, 1967); Nakamura Takafusa, *Senzenki Nihon keizai seicho no bunseki* [An analysis of prewar Japanese economic growth] (Tokyo: University of Tokyo Press, 1971); Kosai Yutaka, *Kōdo seicho no jidai* [The age of high economic growth] (Tokyo: Nihon hyoron, 1981).

72. Kurt Steiner et al., *Political Oppositions and Local Politics in Contemporary Japan* (Princeton: Princeton University Press, 1980); Margaret McKean, *Environmental Protest and Citizen Politics in Japan* (Berkeley and Los Angeles: University of California Press, 1981).

73. *Nihon keizai shimbun*, February 13, 1983.

74. Furukawa Toshiyuki, "Shakai shihyō karamita bunmei to jumyo" [Civilization and life expectancy as seen by social indicators], in Abe Hiroshi et al., eds. *Kōreika shakai no kōzō* [The structure of aging societies] (Tokyo: Saiensusha, 1981), pp. 36–55.

Carbon monoxide and sulfur dioxide levels fell sharply.[75] Furthermore, the sewage index improved from 6 percent in 1960, to 16 percent in 1970, 23 percent in 1975, and 30 percent in 1980,[76] and garbage processing went from 75.6 percent in 1970 to 88.5 percent in 1980.[77] This rapid improvement came about for three major reasons. First, the extremity and ubiquity of environmental destruction forced the government to tackle the problem head-on. By the late 1960s the combination of limited space, a large population, vigorous industrial production, the intensive use of chemical fertilizers, and the voluminous use of insecticides in agriculture all made Japan "an environmentalist's nightmare."[78] Second, domestic and international criticisms of the government for its neglect of this environmental destruction and for the resulting human miseries touched the nerve of Japanese citizens, who were very conscious of being somewhat backward in adoption of environmental regulations. The most dramatic example concerned the regulation of auto emissions. The drastic nature of the Muskie Bill in the United States in the early 1970s was sufficient to prompt Japanese car producers and other industrialists to accommodate the legislation of no less drastic measures against pollution.[79] Whereas in the United States the bill foundered, in Japan it became law. Third, local progressive administrations in many major industrial cities initiated and implemented radical policies of environmental control which convinced the LDP government of the political necessity of adopting similar policy lines. The LDP's environmental policy could best be characterized as unabashed policy adaptation.

Provisions of free medical care to those over seventy years old and from 1972 onward a substantial increase in social welfare expenditure and pensions were implemented. The Basic Socio-Economic Program approved by the cabinet in 1973 called for the creation of a welfare society, thus redirecting the priorities of the higher growth years. Despite lower growth rates, various insurance programs improved steadily during the latter half of the 1970s. Social security transfers increased rapidly as a percent of national income: 3.2 percent in 1960, 4.3 percent in 1970, 7.5 percent in 1975, and 12.7 percent in 1980.[80] Thus, within ten years the figure tripled. The post-1972 acceleration of expenditures on social welfare programs had by

75. The level of carbon monoxide in the air measured in front of the Tokyo Metropolitan Government building registered 6.33 ppm in 1965, 10.0 in 1969, 3.5 in 1973, 2.6 in 1977, and 2.1 in 1979; sulfur dioxide was recorded at 7.9 pphm in 1965, 5.5 in 1969, 2.9 in 1973, 2.1 in 1977, and 1.8 in 1979; meanwhile, nitrogen dioxide was recorded at 1.7 pphm in 1965, 3.5 in 1969, 3.6 in 1973, 3.8 in 1977, and 4.9 in 1979 (Tokyo Metropolitan Government, *Taiki osen joji sokutei jissokutei kekka hōkokusho* [Report of the continuous measurement of air pollution] [Tokyo: Tokyo Metropolitan Government, 1978, 1979]).
76. Minister of Construction, *Kensetsu hakusho*, p. 12.
77. Economic Planning Agency, *Kokumin seikatsu hakusho*, p. 134.
78. Pempel, *Policy and Politics in Japan*, pp. 218–54.
79. Steven R. Reed, "Environmental Politics: Some Reflections Based on the Japanese Case," *Comparative Politics* 13 (April 1981): 253–70.
80. Association of Local Financial Affairs, *Chihō jichi handobukku* [Handbook on local self-government] (Tokyo: Association of Local Financial Affairs, 1980).

1982 placed the Japanese pension program on a rough par with other major industrial democracies both in absolute terms and in the ratio of monthly pension to average monthly wage.[81] By 1983 Japan surpassed West Germany, one of the countries long considered extremely advanced in the ratio of monthly pension to average monthly wage.[82]

The dramatic improvement of social welfare programs under troubled economic conditions was made possible by four major factors.[83] First, since pension programs are a long-term project, the government did not need to worry so much about expenditures during the initial years of program implementation. Second, despite declining economic growth rates, the government continued to issue government bonds to sustain expanding programs such as welfare. (The catches to such a strategy are apparent: economic growth is likely to remain low while government bonds accumulate alarmingly; pensions steadily reach maturity; new public policy priorities are set to cope with new policy agendas. Partly in anticipation of such a dilemma, the administrative-financial reform policy package was begun in an effort to stall the expansion of social welfare programs.) Third, the demographic structure was very favorable. The aged population did not occupy a large portion of the whole population, especially the working population, around 1970. (But as Japanese life expectancy improved steadily to reach the number one status in the world, the aged population reached an alarming proportion of the total population by the early 1980s, bringing in its wake a jump in the demand for pensions, health benefits, and other transfers.) Fourth, the LDP government was eager to accommodate the opposition's criticism of its poor social welfare programs and to catch up with other industrial democracies in this field since by the early 1970s Japan had basically caught up with the West in industrialization.

The steady expansion of social welfare programs during the early 1970s and the establishment of the Environment Agency in 1971 were two major keystones in the government's policy adaptation. By this adaptation, in-

81. Office of Prime Minister, *Konshu no Nihon.*
82. It is often overlooked that when comparing the percentage of social security transfer over national income by country, it is necessary to control for demography. Otherwise, those countries with higher percentages of the elderly tend to have higher figures than those with higher percentages of youth. Therefore, it is important to make comparisons not only of the percentage of social security transfer over national income but also of the ratio of monthly pension to monthly average wages. One such example is Edward S. Mason et al., *The Economic and Social Modernization of the Republic of Korea* (Cambridge, Mass.: Harvard University Press, 1980), a comparison of South Korea, Taiwan, Malaysia, and Japan, all relatively young countries in 1973, with some OECD countries, all older countries in 1973. See also Bruce Cumings, "The Origins and Development of the Northeast Asian Political Economy: Industrial Sectors, Product Cycles, and Political Consequences," *International Organization* 38 (Winter 1984): 1–40, who relies on Mason et al. to characterize what he calls the Northeast Asian political economy.
83. Yatsushiro, *Gyōzaisei kaikaku no keizaigaku;* Hayashi Hideki et al., "Choki shakai-hosho moderu no keisoku to bunseki" [Measurement and analysis of a long-term model of social security], *Shakaihōsho kenkyū* [Social security studies] 16 (September 1980): 59–93; Noguchi, *Shiron gyōzaisei kaikaku.*

terest groups tied to social welfare programs were given the same treatment as agriculture and small business.[84] This new category of interest group is characterized by the near consensus about policy between the government and the opposition;[85] considerable influence on public policy formation by the opposition through such interest groups; primarily divisible benefits, at least from the recipient's viewpoint; and the redistributive character of government public policy, giving protection and strength to the "socially weak" actors.[86]

It is necessary to establish the relationship between issue salience, party support, and social groups. The Office of Prime Minister's annual survey on economic attitudes consistently indicates that the unemployed, the elderly, and holders of managerial and professional positions want the government to put its first priority on social welfare whereas white-collar workers, urban residents, and youth believe first priority should go to the environment. (The question was, To which [policy area] do you think the government should give its first priority?)[87] The Jiji monthly survey indicates a significant increase in the support level for the LDP between the general elections of 1976 and 1980 by these social groups, especially the unemployed, the elderly (those in their fifties, sixties, and thereabouts), white-collar workers, urban residents (especially in smaller cities), and youth (those in their twenties and thirties). Furthermore, all these groups (except holders of managerial and professional positions) are known for lower electoral participation, being apathetic, disgruntled, and the like.[88] The post-1980 general election survey by the Association for the Promotion of Fair Elections gives interesting indirect evidence for my argument.[89] It indicates that in a sample of 2,427, those who, by a ratio of 64 to 17, did not choose any one of the party-specific categories about their party support in the 1979 general election but who voted for the LDP in the 1980 general election outnumbered those who voted for the LDP in the 1979 general election but whose voting pattern was not party-specific in the 1980 general election. Since crossovers between support for the LDP and the opposition parties almost cancel one another out (47 changed from the opposition in 1979 to the LDP in 1980, and 45 changed in the opposite way), this ratio seems to strengthen, if not fully validate, my argument (see Table 6.4).

84. Kosaka Masataka, ed., *Kōdō sangyō kokka no reike seiji katei to seisaku: Nihon* [Interest group politics and public policy in industrialized states: Japan] (Tokyo: Toyota Foundation, 1982), pp. 84–132.

85. Iwai Tomoaki, "Kokkai niokeru seitō no rippo kōdō no keiryo bunseki [A quantitative analysis of parties' legislative behavior in the national diet, 1965–1981]," in Keio University, ed., *Keio gijuku 125 shunen kinen ronbunshu* [Volume published in commemoration of the 125th anniversary of Keio University] (Tokyo: Keio tsushin, 1983), Table 5.

86. Noguchi, *Shiron gyōzaisei kaikaku.*

87. Office of Prime Minister, *Kokumin seikatsu nikansuru yōronchōsa.*

88. Association for the Promotion of Fair Elections, *Shūgiin senkyō no jittai, 1972–80.*

89. Ibid., 1980.

Table 6.4. Support for the LDP by social groups, 1976 and 1980 (annual average)

Various social groups	1976	1980	Percent growth
Total	25.1	32.7	130.3
Ten largest cities	21.3	25.4	119.2
Other cities	23.2	31.1	134.1
Other units	32.3	41.6	128.8
Farmers	49.3	57.3	116.2
Commerce and industry	35.9	48.2	128.7
White collar	18.2	24.6	135.2
Blue collar	17.7	23.8	134.5
Managerials and professionals	37.6	45.5	121.0
Housewives	20.2	26.9	133.2
Others	27.1	35.2	130.0
Male	29.6	38.5	130.1
Female	21.8	28.2	129.4
Twenties	15.0	18.8	125.3
Thirties	20.6	26.2	127.2
Forties	26.2	33.3	127.1
Fifties	31.4	39.7	126.4
Sixties and above	37.0	48.7	126.2
Junior high school graduates	27.4	38.3	132.5
High school graduates	23.4	31.2	133.3
University graduates	23.0	28.3	123.0

Source: Jiji monthly survey in Jiji tsushinsha, ed., *Sengo Nihon no seito to naikaku* [Postwar Japanese parties and cabinets] (Tokyo: Jiji tsushinsha, 1981).

More direct evidence as to issue salience is provided by the Sapporo panel surveys of 1972, 1976, 1979, and 1980. The issue salience of environmental and social welfare issues for those years were 40.9 percent, 6.2 percent, 4.3 percent, and 3.6 percent for the former and 61.8 percent, 33.2 percent, 30.6 percent, and 31.9 percent for the latter.[90] These issues clearly ceased to be major concerns after 1972 and were not taken advantage of by the opposition parties at least at the national level. The LDP's policy actions taken on these issues in 1971 and 1972 brought about two phenomena until about 1978. First, government expenditure for these two items, especially social welfare, rose each year, thus denying the opposition parties the opportunity to take advantage of them at the national level. Second, at the local level, non-LDP governments began to give way to broad coalition governments that included the LDP. From the late 1970s on, the LDP gradually established a hegemonic position within such coalitions as economic difficulties

90. Araki Toshio et al., *Tōhyō kōdō niokeru renzoku to henka*, pp. 187–202.

and fiscal crisis became severe, even though doing so meant in effect back-tracking on these two policy issues.

This explanation focuses on those social groups concerned about social welfare and the environment which developed in the late 1960s and early 1970s and thus were largely outside the "normal" public policy process of benefit allocation; the number of interest groups in these areas was small and their interest representation both in the bureaucracy and the LDP was limited. Needless to say, this argument explains only part of these groups' increased support for the LDP. A large proportion of their increased support for the LDP seems already accounted for by the particular interactions between macroeconomic conditions and public assessment of the parties' comparative competence.

The successful co-optation of these groups by the LDP is different from certain West European cases in which demands in ecology and welfare as well as others such as pacifism developed into an antipolitics with its basis mainly outside the parliamentary and bureaucratic political processes.[91] Meanwhile, policy adaptation in the United States seems to aim more directly at quickly attracting voters who perceive themselves alienated by and antagonistic to the incumbent president than by the adoption and incorporation into the longer-term government program of the basic policy tenets of opposition parties.[92] "The disappearance of the middle class"[93] seems to exacerbate, not resolve, social antagonisms.

Conclusions and Conjectures

My examination suggests that the conservative resurgence in Japan during the 1977–83 period resulted from a number of policy-related factors. Economic performance was among the most important preconditions for public acceptance of conservative dominance. Client-oriented politics targeted at revitalizing the support from traditionally conservative socioeconomic groups worked better during economically difficult times than it had under rapid economic growth. A friend in need is a friend indeed. Finally, policy adaptation aimed at socioeconomic groups in the environment and welfare fields, which had been working outside "established" public policy processes, allowed the LDP to outflank its opposition. Originally the opposition had been most vocal and insistent in calling for vigorous policy action in these two fields, but the LDP's co-optation of these issues reduced their thunder. Although precise figures are not available for the percentage of variance explained by each of these factors, some important evidence is

91. Berger, ed., *Organizing Interests in Western Europe.*
92. Edward R. Tufte, *Political Control of the Economy* (Princeton: Princeton University Press, 1978).
93. Thurow, "Disappearance of the Middle Class."

apparent about their impact on the conservative resurgence. It seems that three major conditions underlie the apparent success of the LDP's very short-term incremental public policies: the resilience and robustness of the Japanese economy; bureaucratic consistency and effectiveness, especially in economic management; and the continuation of one-party dominance.

Before moving on to conjectures about the LDP's fate, it is necessary to comment on the popular argument that the major causes for the LDP's resurgence rest with semi-institutionalized givens, such as the electoral system and the inability of the opposition to topple the government.[94] These givens are insufficient, if necessary, conditions for the post-1977 conservative revival because these forces have been invariably at work both before and after 1977. Some may also argue that a more fundamental cause can be found in the nation's historical experiences, relating conservative dominance to the pattern of economic and political development in Japan.[95] In the sense that no social phenomenon is free from historical constraints and legacies, this argument carries considerable weight, supplementing or even underlying the three explanations concerned about the more immediate and contemporary factors. But this argument alone cannot explain the steady conservative revival since mid-1977. Common national experiences do not discriminate between the pre-1977 period of conservative stagnation and the post-1977 period of conservative revival. The government's public policy must have had some more than insignificant impacts on certain portions of the electorate, as has been argued above.

What can be said, then, about the future of the Japanese conservatives in

94. See, for example, Yukio Hori, "Gisei no ueni naritatsu hoshu fukucho [Conservative revival based on institutionalized tricks]," *Ekonomisuto*, July 27–31, 1980; and Masanori Takahashi et al., *Gendai Nihon no seiji kōzō* [The structure of contemporary Japanese politics] (Tokyo: Seri shōbo, 1982).

95. Comparable insights may be obtained from reading the following works: Alexander Gershenkron, *Economic Backwardness in Historical Perspective* (Cambridge, Mass.: Harvard University Press, 1962); Barrington Moore, *Social Origins of Dictatorship and Democracy: Lord and Peasant in the Making of the Modern World* (Boston: Beacon Press, 1966); Robert A. Dahl, *Polyarchy: Participation and Opposition* (New Haven: Yale University Press, 1971); James Kurth, "The Political Consequences of the Product Cycle: Industrial History and Political Outcomes," *International Organization* 33 (Winter 1979): 1–34; and Kurth, "Industrial Change and Political Change: A European Perspective," in David Collier, ed., *The New Authoritarianism in Latin America* (Princeton: Princeton University Press, 1979), pp. 319–62; Francis G. Castles, ed., *The Impact of Parties: Politics and Policies in Democratic Capitalist States* (London: Sage, 1982); Martin Shefter, *Patronage and Its Opponents: A Study and Some Empirical Cases*, Western Studies Program Occasional Papers No. 8 (Ithaca: Cornell University, 1977); William W. Lockwood, *The Economic Development of Japan* (Princeton: Princeton University Press, 1965); Nakamura Takafusa, *Senzenki Nihon keizai seicho no bunseki* [An analysis of prewar Japanese economic growth] (Tokyo: University of Tokyo Press, 1971); Masumi Junnosuke, *Nihon seito shiron* [Treatise on Japanese political parties], 8 vols. (Tokyo: University of Tokyo Press, 1965–81); Stephen Large, *Organized Workers and Socialist Politics in Prewar Japan* (Cambridge: Cambridge University Press, 1982); and Bernard S. Silbermann, "The Bureaucratic State in Japan: The Politics of Authority and Legitimacy," in Tetsuo Najita and J. Victor Koschmann, eds., *Conflict in Modern Japanese History: The Neglected Tradition* (Princeton: Princeton University Press, 1982).

light of the above analysis? To answer that question, it may be useful to look at the two major issues of the period receiving top newspaper coverage: the dominance of the Tanaka faction and the administrative-financial reform efforts. These two issues are indicative of the problems surfacing during conservative dominance. The dominance of the Tanaka faction in membership size and influence on LDP politics reveals the vastly expanded and consolidated nationwide network of clientelistic politics.[96] Assertion of social interests is most successfully made through the network of professional politicians with their increasing dominance in public policy formation and implementation.

Tanaka Kakuei formally left the LDP shortly before he was indicted for his part in the Lockheed scandal, but he was consistently very powerful in LDP politics with his followers steadily increasing to 114 out of 396 LDP Dietmen in the early 1980s. The Tanaka faction's expansion owes much to its resourceful network, created largely during the period when it managed LDP politics as the indispensable core of any LDP government, in acting as intermediaries linking his faction men, "his" bureaucrats (bureaucrats over whom he believes—correctly most of the time—he can wield considerable influence), and his clients (district people and interest groups). Besides including the largest number of Dietmen, his faction consisted of an especially large reservoir of former bureaucrats (whom he attracted during his service as minister of posts and telecommunication, of international trade and industry, and of finance, as secretary general of the LDP, and, most important, as prime minister). Of all the factions his had the highest ability to raise political funds if the amounts collected by his lieutenants are also included.[97] His faction controlled the largest number of ministerial and party executive posts. Six ministerial posts were assigned to the Tanaka faction in the Nakasone cabinet of January 1983 compared with four in the Suzuki cabinet, six portfolios were retained in the second Nakasone cabinet of January 1984. Thus it is not difficult to imagine Dietmen being attracted to join his faction so as to take advantage of the network in conducting constituent services and advancing their own power and careers. The factions tend to monopolize the role of intermediaries.

Another major factor is concerned with the supply side of political money. The serious financial difficulties in post–oil crisis Japan have placed big business in a dilemma regarding its allocation of political money. To be effective without exceedingly increasing its donations, big business has become more "target-specific." And good targets include a strong all-round faction like Tanaka's as well as the recently much-commented-upon LDP *zoku* (literally tribes). These latter refer to LDP members who base their power on policy specialization organized around the LDP PARC's divisions, research commissions, and special committees on specific policy fields, such

96. *Asahi shimbun*, May 9, 1982.
97. Ibid.

as agriculture, transport, commerce and industry, and taxation.[98] These somewhat cartelized groups representing special interests have become very vigorous. The political experience of these groups is up while lower economic growth has become "normal." Of course, the LDP headquarters makes efforts to prevent donors from being too target-specific, preferring instead that donations be channeled to the National Political Association (NPA), an organization for big business contributions. A recent example is the banking peak association, which tries to be exclusively target-specific, refusing to donate to the NPA. This group was forced to yield under LDP pressure and resume its contributions to the NPA. In addition, however, the banking peak association continued the target-specific allocation of its political money as well.[99]

One of the limits of such politics is, however, to be found in the increasingly alarming problem of government deficits accumulated during the latter half of the 1970s and into the 1980s because of stalled tax revenue, inflated budgetary demands, and newly added public policy agendas. The tax system being somewhat oversensitive to economic fluctuations, especially to corporate profits, contributed to this problem of government deficits. Furthermore, incumbent politicians have increasingly entrenched themselves in their districts and social-bureaucratic interests have steadily consolidated their spheres of influence.[100] These phenomena worked against effective interest aggregation at the top and allowed for slightly inflated expenditure outlays because of lateral competition among budget units. That is, if so much is given to one, the same should be given to another. To aggravate the deficit problem, new and costly public policy agendas emerged in the fields of trade, finance, and defense.

The steady increase in tax burdens, accentuated by the widening intergroup disparity in burden sharing, continues to be a serious problem but is not likely to disturb the structure of conservative-dominated political economy in the foreseeable future. Urban wage earners are not well organized politically to make effective demands for tax relief, and intergroup disparity is yet to have an impact on public policy process. Instead, the tension has become one between the private sector (both big business and small-scale business), which coped with the extraordinary difficulties following the oil crisis, and the public sector, which is criticized as rife with organizational slack and lack of financial responsibility. Under the corporate tax system, profits to corporations were stripped to a meager sum. This led the private sector to take an even harsher posture toward the public sector. One answer, albeit admittedly less than comprehensive, has been the administrative-financial reform package.

98. Inoguchi and Iwai, "The Growth of *Zoku*"; Inoguchi and Iwai, *Zoku giin no kenkyū*.
99. "Jimintō seichōsakai," *Sentaku*, pp. 44–47.
100. Inoguchi, "Politicians, Bureaucrats and Interest Groups"; Inoguchi and Iwai, "The Growth of *Zoku*"; Inoguchi and Iwai, *Zoku giin no kenkyū*.

These reforms—hinted at during Ohira Masayoshi's tenure (1978–80) with disastrous consequences in the 1979 general election but accentuated in 1980 upon Suzuki Zenko's ascension to power—represent a cumulatively molded policy package that aimed at two goals: fundamentally transforming policy priorities to liberate them from inertia-ridden public expenditure patterns thus allowing them to cope with new public policy agendas growing out of rapidly changing demographic patterns, lowered economic performance, and the need to increase industrial competitiveness and to respond to increasing international frictions and responsibilities; and to maintain the conservative-dominated grand coalition of 1955 without alienating specific elements that might opt out from general conservative policies for such specific reasons as taxes, corruption, pacifism, ecology, and welfare.[101]

To what extent the administrative-financial reform package will be successful in achieving the first goal is a moot question at best. That aim is not easy for the LDP or for any party in similar situations to achieve at once. A plausible scenario may be for a cumulative change in the annual budgetary expenditure patterns over the subsequent five to ten years to result in more de facto changes in state revenue and expenditure patterns than are often thought possible. The direction of change in such major expenditure items as social welfare, education, public works, defense, and science and technology seems already firmly set. Meanwhile, the LDP will tinker piecemeal with its policy package in reaction to events and issues, while considerably reshaping policy priorities. In other words, the LDP will muddle through with its time-honored, down-to-earth pragmatic politics. That the economy is steadily picking up will undoubtedly help mitigate the problem of financial deficits. Three factors moderate the seriousness of Japan's deficits. First, the saving ratio is still higher than in most other OECD countries and does not invite inflation despite deficit spending. Second, private demand is still sagging. This prevents the crowding out of capital. Third, the progressive tax system enables the government to gain a large amount of tax revenue when business improves.[102]

So far, the LDP has put considerable energy into stabilizing its rule through changes in the electoral system for its president and for the House of Councillors' nationwide district and by relying on zoku-dominated, somewhat segmented policy making. It has relied far less on mobilization and activation of potential and actual LDP supporters. Thus the prospect for its longer-term popularity cannot be as bright as it appeared in the early

101. Secretariat of the Provisional Council on Administrative and Financial Reform, *Rinchō kinkyū tiegen; Rinchō kyoninka teigen; Rinchō kihon teigen* [Trio of proposals by the SPCAFR] (Tokyo: Secretariat of the Provisional Council on Administrative and Financial Reform, 1981–82); Economic Planning Agency, *Kokumin seikatsu hakusho* [White paper on national life], 1982.

102. Far Eastern Economic Review, *Asia 1983 Yearbook*, pp. 44–45.

1980s.[103] Other factors are also turning unfavorable: the economy does not show clear evidence of a full recovery; public expectations are sagging; and yet, if the public expectation of economic recovery overshoots itself, LDP support is likely to go down. Entrenched clientelistic politics could also work against a longer-term LDP rule in the 1980s. New policy adaptations such as the administrative-financial reform package do not seem to have a bright future.[104] In other words, the conservative resurgence of 1977–83 does not seem to have been based on a long-lasting consolidation but is heavily dependent on volatile support from what are sometimes called the new middle mass, voters who tend to be critical of distributing divisible material benefits to interest groups and regions.[105]

The salience of two issues, anticorruption (a 1976 and 1983 election issue) and antitax (a 1979 and 1983 election issue) and their significantly negative impact on the LDP may presage an erosion in LDP support during the remainder of the 1980s. In the December 1983 general election, both issues loomed large and worked against the LDP. More important, a bulk of LDP supporters seems to have abstained en masse in light of the large majority the LDP now enjoys: the larger the buffer against losing its majority, the larger the number of abstainers.[106] Potential conservative voters can afford to abstain if there is only a remote possibility that the "dreadfully incompetent" opposition will come to power. Floating or postindustrial voters are a large proportion of such abstainers. Hence unexpected swings often take place as was the case in 1979 and 1983.[107] Nevertheless, the LDP will not lose enough seats to topple its foundation for the very reasons enumerated earlier. The conservative-dominant political-economic system is hard to erode in a short time, and various institutionalized safeguards prevent such erosion from taking place quickly. A critical test will come somewhat later. The nature of the conservative resurgence of 1977–83 will be more precisely comprehended at that time.[108]

In assessing some implications of the Japanese case for the maintenance and consequence of one-party dominance, the first question is, Was this period somehow particularly critical to the LDP's shifting it support base? Or was the process just a good but serendipitous mix of luck and tactics? The second question is, Is the success likely to ensure a longer future of the

103. Mancur Olson, *The Rise and Decline of Nations: Economic Growth, Stagflation and Social Rigidities* (New Haven: Yale University Press, 1982).

104. Samuel Beer, *Britain against Itself: The Political Contradictions of Collectivism* (London: Faber & Faber, 1982).

105. Murakami, "The Age of New Middle Mass Politics."

106. The 1983 general election results show that the turnout rate registered 67.94 percent, the lowest in the entire postwar period and that the LDP lost a seat in most of the districts recording a substantial decline in turnout (*Asahi*, December 20, 1983).

107. Murakami, "The Age of New Middle Mass Politics"; Ishikawa Masumi, *Nihon seiji no toshizu* [An opened-up view of Japanese politics] (Tokyo: Gendai no riron sha, 1980).

108. Kevin P. Phillips, *Post-Conservative America: People, Politics and Ideology in a Time of Crisis* (New York: Random House, 1982).

LDP as a ruling party? Or can it be reversed with bad luck and bad tactics tomorrow?

My answer to the first question leans toward the former and that to the second question toward the latter. The two oil crises and the task of economic adjustments could have toppled the LDP government. But the LDP, taking care of its traditional supporters and yet not swimming against demographic and economic tides, has been very successful in reorganizing its support blocs steadily and cumulatively. It has not alienated many of its traditional yet demographically shrinking support bases such as agriculture, and it has attracted more newly emerging demographically larger groups such as wage earners and women.

But my conjecture about the future is not the direct extrapolation of the recent success. Three conditions underlying the LDP's success based on short-term incremental public policies seem to reveal a slow metamorphosis. First, the Japanese economy faces major problems of lower growth, rapid industrial adjustment, and direct exposure to international fluctuations far more severe than many in Japan would like to admit.[109] Second, the much-vaunted bureaucracy seems to manifest increasingly its sense of irritation and impotence in public policy management, especially in its relationship with more self-assertive politicians and less docile public opinion.[110] Third, despite the high popularity ratings of the LDP in the 1980s, the increased electoral volatility attributed primarily to the intermittent salience of largely urban, middle-class, conservative-leaning, floating voters caused the LDP's electoral setbacks in two of the three recent general elections, those of 1979 and 1983.[111]

Furthermore, the LDP's occasional insensitivity to concerns on political norms (1976, 1983, and 1986 election issues) and the near inevitability of

109. A well-balanced and comprehensive assessment of the Japanese economy and its political, social, cultural, and international foundations is provided in the three-volume Japan Political Economy Research Conference studies under the general editorship of Yasusuke Murakami and Hugh Patrick: Yamamura Kozo and Yasukichi Yasuba, eds., *The Political Economy of Japan*, vol. 1, *The Domestic Transformation* (Stanford: Stanford University Press, 1987); Takashi Inoguchi and Daniel I. Okimoto, eds., *The Political Economy of Japan*, vol. 2, *The Changing International Context* (Stanford: Stanford University Press, 1988); and Shumpei Kumon and Henry Rosovsky, *The Political Economy of Japan*, vol. 3, *Cultural and Social Dynamics* (Stanford: Stanford University Press, forthcoming.)

110. Inoguchi, *Gendai Nihon seiji keizai no kōzu*; Masahiko Aoki, "The Japanese Bureaucracy in Economic Administration: A Rational Regulator or Pluralistic Agent?" in John B. Shoven, ed., *Government Policy towards Industry in the United States and Japan* (New York: Cambridge University Press, 1988), pp. 265–300; Inoguchi and Tomoaki, "The Growth of Zoku"; Inoguchi and Tomoaki, *Zoku giin no kenkyū*.

111. A similar speculation in a different scheme was made in Inoguchi, "The Sources of Stability in the Japanese Political Process," in Ronald A. Morse and Shigenobu Yoshida, eds., *Blind Partners: American and Japanese Responses to an Unknown Future* (Lanham, Md.: University Press of America, 1985), pp. 43–50. On new dimensions of political cleavages, see, e.g., protection of domestic industries versus policy alignment with the United States and the inseparability of politics (defense) and economics (trade and finance); see Inoguchi and Iwai, *Zoku giin no kenkyū*.

politically explosive tax issues (1979, 1983, and 1986 election issues) do not seem to augur well for the continuation of semipermanent one-party rule by the LDP.

Turning to the question of the consequence of one-party dominance, a set of questions is asked. Did their being in office for so long make it easier to reverse their decline, retain public confidence on economic issues, and recreate their support base? Or does long-term officeholding make it easier to continue in office because the opposition loses public credibility as an alternative governing force? Did having long-term control of the tools of public policy make it easier to respond to changing issues, including subsidization of client groups, social welfare, and environmental policy than would have been the case if their hold over the bureaucracy had been closer to that of an alternating party or a coalition government?

I can say with confidence that the LDP often made timely, client-targeted, and thus, on the whole, effective use of its public policy tools, aided by its hold over the bureaucracy. These helped reverse the party's gradual decline and reduce the opposition's public credibility as an alternate governing party. The LDP's strategy of evenhandedness in its public posture rather than in policy outcomes seems to have played an especially important role.

Why, then, did other one-party dominant parties, especially those in Israel and Sweden, undergo radical reversals during the same period? It is not an easy question to answer without undertaking a full-fledged, context-sensitive, comparative analysis, which is not the task of this essay. But it seems to me that the other two conditions underlying the maintenance of one-party dominance, that is, less problematic economic performance and more effective bureaucracy, seem to weigh more strongly in Japan than in Israel or Sweden. Although one-party dominance may have been a common denominator for these countries, it is very difficult to gauge the effect of one-party dominance independently of the other two conditions on the different fates of a party in power. It seems safe to say that its effect is not minimal but not as great as some may like to think.

On my conjecture on the future, if the three underlying conditions are less fully met, as seems likely to be the case, and some tactical blunders are made, then Japanese one-party dominance may tread a path similar to that of such parties as the Swedish Social Democrats and Israel Labor. That is, it will face far greater uncertainties when more direct competition and more frequent cooperation between parties are inevitable.[112]

112. Pempel, *Policy and Politics.*

7. The Decline of Dominant Parties: Parliamentary Politics in Sweden and Japan in the 1970s

ELLIS S. KRAUSS AND JON PIERRE

This chapter analyzes the legislative strategies of two dominant parties with different ideological orientations—the LDP in Japan and the SAP in Sweden—during periods when their dominance was in decline. Our purpose is to ascertain how such dominant parties, after holding power for over a generation, react to a period of decline and the prospect of loss of dominance, and how opposition parties in a dominant-party system, excluded from power for over a generation, react to increased strength and the prospect of gaining power.

Response to decline is one of the most neglected phenomena in the study of dominant parties. What are the parliamentary consequences of the decline in the power of the dominant party? Does greater conflict result as the dominant party attempts to reassert its ideological differences with the opposition and as opposition parties scramble to overthrow their perennial rival? Do the dominant party and its opposition become more compromising as each anticipates possibly needing the other to maintain or gain power? Or does some combination of these occur? Do different types of dominant or opposition parties react differently? We will attempt to discover the extent to which dominant parties respond flexibly or rigidly to the crisis of their eventual decline, to which opposition parties become more or

The authors thank Michael Mochizuki, Yale University, for graciously permitting us to use his data on votes in the Japanese Diet, without which this paper would not have been possible. We also thank T. J. Pempel, the Western Foundation (Western Washington University), the Ekwall Foundation, the Siamon Foundation, and the Wallenberg Foundation for financial support that enabled us to meet several times in person to discuss the findings and write various drafts of this chapter. We very much appreciate the help of T. J. Pempel, Michio Muramatsu, Jonas Pontusson, Richard J. Samuels, Andy Markovitz, and two anonymous reviewers, who provided very useful criticism and suggestions on an earlier version. We are solely responsible for the contents of the essay.

less conflictual with the dominant party, and to which the ideological orientation or pragmatic power considerations of parties in a dominant-party system determine their behavior.

Does the way dominant parties respond to decline affect their chances for staying in power? In the two cases we are studying, Japan and Sweden, the LDP managed to cling to power and eventually reassert its dominance, whereas the SAP lost power. Did the parliamentary strategies these two parties used to arrest their decline contribute to these different outcomes? We will argue that the nature of party systems and the parliamentary strategies they encourage can help explain the continuation or loss of power by a dominant party.

The Decline of Dominant Parties: Some Hypotheses

The theoretical literature on dominant parties provides only a very general, and contradictory, guide to answering questions about the decline of dominant parties. On one hand, Duverger implies that dominant parties in decline would fail to adapt their strategies pragmatically to changing times and legislative situations. In Duverger's view, "The dominant party wears itself out in office, it loses its vigor, its arteries harden. It would thus be possible to show . . . that every domination bears within itself the seeds of its own destruction."[1] This view would predict that, having set the political agenda for so long, and having become ossified in power, dominant parties, when finally faced with a challenge, would be unlikely to respond to a changing power situation and new demands from rival parties and social forces.

Arian and Barnes's analysis of the dominant-party system projects a different image of the nature and responsiveness of such parties to new situations. Although they cite Duverger's prediction that dominant parties will ossify, and they warn that there is no guarantee a dominant party will accomplish adaptation successfully, they nonetheless portray dominant parties as eminently pragmatic and opportunistic. Thus they cite one of the goals of a dominant party as keeping itself "near the center where the action is" and state that "its orientation toward power encourages it to move with long term shifts in public opinion regardless of its ideology." Further, they argue that the continuation of the party's dominance depends crucially upon "strategic political decisions made by the party elite."[2]

Finally, they recommend that the politician of the dominant party follow a strategy of "dynamic conservatism—being prepared to change in order to

1. Maurice Duverger, *Political Parties*, 2d ed. (London: Methuen, 1959), p. 312.
2. Alan Arian and Samuel H. Barnes, "The Dominant Party System: A Neglected Model of Democratic Stability," *Journal of Politics* 36, nos. 3–4 (1974): 595–99.

retain what he has."[3] Therefore, they view the dominant party, even after decades in power, as capable of pragmatic change to retain power. In contrast to Duverger's image of increasing rigidity with age, this is a view of dominant parties as perennially pragmatic, flexible, responsive, and, with proper leadership, capable of political adaptation.

Arian and Barnes do place one qualification on this flexibility by suggesting that the ideological orientation of the party may make a difference in the ease with which it can change. Comparing the DC in Italy with the Mapai in Israel, they conclude that the Christian Democrats seem to lack the flexibility of maneuver possessed by the Israeli Alignment. They suggest that in an epoch of a leftward drift in politics, common in our age, it is easier for parties of the left to shift toward the right than vice versa.[4] After the publication of their article, however, of the two parties, the Mapai soon lost power, whereas the DC continued its dominance.

The literature thus offers two somewhat contradictory hypotheses about the ability of dominant parties to respond to change after decades in power. One model views the dominant party as becoming relatively inflexible over time and probably incapable of adapting to change; the other views it as perpetually pragmatic and capable of adjustment, albeit with leftist dominant parties being more capable of changing than rightist ones.

These models of the dominant party are matched, in mirror image, by contrasting views of the behavior of opposition parties in a dominant-party system. Arian and Barnes see the flexible strength of the dominant party as its opposition's weakness. Cut off from power for so long and faced with the pragmatic hegemony of the dominant party, the opposition becomes ineffective, "reduced to a role of carping and sniping rather than that of developing immediate alternatives," rarely being in a position to take advantage of even the bad decisions of the dominant party.[5]

Such a view also implies that an opposition excluded from responsibility for governance and the exercise of power for so long may become locked into a reflexive role and incapable of adapting rapidly to new opportunities. These notions would lead us to predict that opposition parties would be incapable of responding positively to new opportunities presented by the decline of the dominant party. For example, with this perspective it is unlikely that opposition parties would move pragmatically toward the dominant party to position themselves for potential coalition government. Rather, we would expect merely the intensification of the usual politics of opposition and conflict with the dominant party.

But here too there is a contrasting hypothesis. Levite and Tarrow, in a critique of Arian and Barnes, emphasize that in periods of social change opposition parties in a dominant-party system may respond with new politi-

3. Ibid., p. 614.
4. Ibid., p. 597.
5. Ibid., pp. 599–600.

Table 7.1. Possible reactions of parties to change

Opposition party	Dominant party	
	Flexible/pragmatic	Rigid/conflictual
Flexible/pragmatic	COOPERATION [by mutual coalition]	DECLINE [by dominant party rigidity]
Rigid/conflictual	DOMINANCE [by opposition's rigidity]	POLARIZATION [by mutual confrontation]

cal strategies and effectively take advantage of that change to legitimize themselves.[6] This is an image of opposition parties under a dominant-party system as being very responsive to new situations and capable of adaptation, even in the later years of the dominant party.

We may add the distinct possibility that opposition parties deprived of alternation in government over two decades or more, when finally faced with the decline of the dominant party, would be especially anxious to cooperate with it to share power. In short, it is equally logical to argue that an opposition long deprived of power may act in a more opportunistic and pragmatic fashion when given the opportunity for power as it is to predict perpetual irresponsibility and intransigence.

We thus have two different hypotheses about dominant parties' behavior when faced with new challenges, changes in society, and decline in strength, and two different hypotheses about opposition parties' reactions in this situation. The combination of these hypotheses would predict four different possible outcomes, as shown in Table 7.1. If both dominant party and opposition react pragmatically, we would expect increased cooperation and compromise between them in this period; if both dominant party and opposition are inflexible, the outcome would be enhanced confrontation, conflict, and declining agreement. The in-between combinations of pragmatic dominant party but intransigent opposition and of rigid dominant party and flexible opposition would make unity impossible, but not to the extent of complete confrontation and polarization.

The literature cited above implies that flexibility on the part of a dominant party may be a potent asset for maintaining power. Our hypothesis, therefore, is that a flexible and compromising strategy on the part of the dominant party would be *more* likely to redound to its benefit than an inflexible and confrontational approach to the opposition during this period. If the opposition parties are rigid and the dominant party is flexible, we would predict that the dominant party might be able to reestablish the

6. Ariel Levite and Sidney Tarrow, "The Legitimation of Excluded Parties in Dominant Systems: A Comparison of Israel and Italy," *Comparative Politics* 15 (1983): 295–327.

legitimacy of its dominance; if the dominant party remained inflexible in the face of the opposition's attempt at cooperation, its ability to govern may become increasingly questionable, thereby enhancing the trend toward decline. We have thus labeled the former outcome "dominance," and the latter case "decline."

The other two possible outcomes of "cooperation" and "polarization" leave open the question of whether the dominant party or the opposition would benefit in the voters' eyes from the resulting consensus or conflict. Can dominant parties remain dominant by adopting a flexible strategy, even if the opposition responds by cooperating? Will the dominant party or the opposition benefit most from a mutually confrontational approach? These are some important, but unexamined, questions about the decline of dominant parties.

It should be recognized that each of the strategies of flexibility or rigidity has potential costs and benefits for each side. Whichever side follows a flexible, cooperative strategy is gambling on making gains with the electorate by appearing to be adaptable, pragmatic, and capable of governing. The governing party would be counting on proving its ability to govern and keep policy making running smoothly even with a decreased majority to convince the electorate to continue it in power. The opposition would be hoping to be legitimized as a potential governing party (alone or in coalition with the dominant party). This strategy also carries great risks for both sides. There is the risk of blurring the party's identity with the electorate and alienating its activists and most ardent supporters by appearing to compromise the party's ideology and identity. For the governing party, there is the further risk of legitimizing its opposition as a party capable of governing; for the opposition parties, there is the further risk of appearing to legitimate the dominant party's continuation in power and of not taking advantage of the dominant party's loss of popular mandate.

The hostile and confrontational strategy provides potentially obverse gains and risks to both sides: reasserting one's party identity and ideology at the cost of proving oneself incapable of governing; preventing the legitimation of the other side but coming to be perceived as rigid and incapable of adjusting to changing popular demands and unresponsive to the new popular mandate.

We will examine empirically how these strategies and their consequences work to produce particular outcomes of dominance or decline in one limited, but crucial, arena of relations in party systems: interparty conflict and cooperation in parliament. To discover both the level of conflict and agreement between the dominant party and its opposition, and the strategies of each side, we will use party voting data in parliament. We are assuming that the objective behavior of parties as manifested in their legislative votes can provide insights into the change or lack of change in the performance and strategies of political parties under different conditions of dominant-party power. The extent to which the parties cooperated or were hostile to each other on the votes on major policy issues in their parliaments, after all, is the ultimate test of their strategies and behavior in response to changing power situations.

Nevertheless, we are aware that a political party's parliamentary strategy and its extraparliamentary profile may not always be synonymous and that the salience of issues in the public and parliamentary arenas also may not always correspond. The salience of the coincidence of strategies and issues in the two arenas, however, is an empirical question, and one that can only be answered by exploring parliamentary as well as nonparliamentary behavior of the parties.

The data are from the Japanese Diet and the Swedish Riksdag during three different periods of dominant-party rule: a period of clear dominance, a period of decline, and a period of nearly equal strength between the dominant party and its opposition. These countries are a particularly apt test of our propositions because in both countries the dominant-party system experienced all three stages in the 1970s. Because in Japan the dominant party (LDP) is a rightist party and in Sweden (SAP) a leftist one, we are also able to test Arian and Barnes's hypothesis that the ideological nature of the dominant party may produce different capacities for adaptation. Finally, although the response of a dominant party to decline has been studied in Israel and Italy, there has yet to be a study of this phenomenon in the other two major dominant-party democracies, Sweden and Japan.

Following a brief description of the parliamentary and party systems and of the conditions of dominant-party decline in the two nations, we will operationalize and test our hypotheses.

Parties and Politics in Sweden and Japan: Dominant Parties and Their Decline in the 1970s

Both Sweden and Japan have parliamentary/cabinet systems of government,[7] although the electoral systems for selection of members differ. Sweden has a proportional representation system whereby percentage of party vote is translated into percentage of seats in the Riksdag. In Japan, an unusual medium-sized multimember district system prevails in the House of Representatives, making the translation of party popular vote percentage into seats obtained more problematic.[8]

Both Japan and Sweden have multiparty systems with five major parties.

7. In Sweden, the Riksdag was a bicameral parliament until 1971, when it became unicameral. It contained 350 seats until 1976, when this number was lowered to 349. In Japan, the Diet is a bicameral parliament, but the lower house, the House of Representatives, is the most important and influential. It had 491 or fewer members until 1976, when an additional 20 seats were added in a reapportionment effort, bringing its total to 511.

8. During the 1970s, three, four, or five representatives were elected from each district, and the LDP and the largest opposition party, the Socialists (JSP), ran more than one candidate in a number of districts, but the voter cast only one ballot.

The main parties in Sweden are the Social Democratic party (SAP), the Conservative party (M), the Liberal party (FP), the Center party (C), and the Communist party (VPK). The Social Democratic party, a socialist party in ideology, had been the party of government in Sweden since the 1930s.[9] The basic cleavage in the party system is between the socialist parties, the SAP and VPK on the left, and the nonsocialist opposition parties (FP, C, M) on the center-left, center, and right.

In Japan, the five major parties are the Liberal Democratic party (LDP), the Japan Socialist party (JSP), the Democratic Socialist party (DSP) (after 1959), the Clean Government party (CGP), and (after 1967) the Communist party (JCP). Additional minor parties also existed: the New Liberal Club (NLC) that split off from the Liberal Democrats in 1976, and the Social Democratic League (SDL) that split from the JSP in the late 1970s. The LDP held exclusive control of the government from its formation from the merger of two smaller conservative parties in 1955 until after the elections of December 1983, when, despite its majority in the Diet, it took the NLC into the cabinet so as to expand its majority and increase its control of the committee system of the lower house. The party cleavages in the Japanese case are more multidimensional than in Sweden because each opposition party is differentiated on some basic issues not only from the LDP but from one or more of the other opposition parties. There is no one cleavage that separates one group of parties from another as the socialism/nonsocialism dimension does in Sweden.

Although both the SAP and the LDP were dominant parties, they differed greatly in their governing style. The SAP provided the impetus for the very rapid emergence of the advanced welfare state for which Sweden became famous, whereas the LDP's major policy thrust was rapid economic growth, with, at least in the 1950s and 1960s, the neglect of social services to the point that Japan ranked low on most measures of the welfare state.

A second variation between the two parties related to the nature of the opposition they confronted. Whereas the LDP occupied the entire center-right portion of the ideological spectrum, and thus all opposing parties were to its left, the SAP as a moderate leftist party not only faced opposition parties to its right but also a Communist party to its left, with which it enjoyed a cooperative/competitive relationship.

A third difference between the two parties was in their relationship with labor. The SAP's dominance rested in large part on its strong support of, and close relationship to, labor. In Japan, the LDP was something of a catchall party, gaining a fair proportion of the votes of all strata but particularly dependent on farmers for consistent and overwhelming support at the polls and on big business for campaign contributions. Indeed, the one seg-

9. From 1936 to 1939 and from 1951 to 1957 and in a wartime cabinet from 1939 to 1945, SAP controlled the government in coalition with other parties. But for the rest of these four decades, including 1957 to 1976, it governed alone.

ment of society almost completely shut off from the party in power was organized labor.[10]

Finally, for most of the last thirty years, Sweden under the SAP has enjoyed a "politics of compromise"[11]—a consensus among the political elite as to what issues are crucial and a common desire to negotiate and search for "broad solutions" to those issues and problems. By contrast, politics in Japan through the 1950s and 1960s was characterized by excessive ideological polarization and severe conflict, particularly over issues of foreign policy, defense, and education. Many observers found that one of Japan's chief problems in this absence of national consensus was the lack of communication between government and opposition parties (especially the JSP) in the parliament.[12]

Despite these major differences in ideology, policies, party system, governing style, and politics, both the LDP and the SAP faced a similar challenge to their rule in the early 1970s. New issues involving the environment and the economy emerged on which long-governing parties were vulnerable. Opposition parties, the center and left in Japan and the center in Sweden, used these issues to embarrass and criticize the government. A more subtle challenge was presented by the demographic changes in the electorate that made some of the parties' support bases slightly more unstable.

In Sweden, by the 1973 election, the SAP, even if supported by the Communists, was able to manage only an even split in Riksdag seats against the combined bloc of the Conservative, Center, and Liberal parties. In the 1976 election the Social Democrats suffered an even greater "defeat." Actually, the net flow of votes was very small and the 1976 election was one of the most stable during the postwar period. Nevertheless, the nonsocialist victory was clear, with opposition parties gaining eleven more seats than the socialist bloc.

The 1976 election presented the culmination of a long-term, slow, but steady decline since the party reached its peak in 1968 with the formation of a majority government. In none of the subsequent elections following this peak was there a dramatic loss, only a gradual chipping away. This long-term tendency appears more important than the defeat in 1976, which was

10. Sweden's labor market and labor policies were distinctive enough to be characterized as a "Swedish model," involving large and centralized unions, an advanced system of collective bargaining, and relatively few industrial conflicts. In Japan, in contrast, organized labor is decentralized: most private sector unions are enterprise unions, and the national unions are merely loose federations of these company unions, lacking in militancy and bargaining power for their member unions. Public sector unions are often the most militant and politically radical. On labor's exclusion from power in Japan, see T. J. Pempel and Keiichi Tsunekawa, "Corporatism without Labor? The Japanese Anomaly," in Philippe C. Schmitter and Gerhard Lehmbruch, eds., *Trends Toward Corporatist Intermediation* (Beverly Hills: Sage, 1979), pp. 231–70.

11. Dankwart Rustow, *The Politics of Compromise* (Princeton: Princeton University Press, 1955).

12. Robert A. Scalapino and Junnosuke Masumi, *Parties and Politics in Contemporary Japan* (Berkeley and Los Angeles: University of California Press, 1962), p. 145.

Table 7.2. Popular vote and seats in elections to the Riksdag in Sweden, 1964–79 (in percentage of seats)*

	SAP	VPK	C	FP	M
1964	47 [49]	5 [3]	13 [15]	17 [18]	14 [14]
1968	50 [54]	3 [1]	16 [17]	14 [15]	13 [14]
1970	45 [47]	5 [5]	20 [20]	16 [17]	12 [12]
1973	44 [45]	5 [5]	25 [26]	9 [10]	14 [15]
1976	43 [44]	5 [5]	24 [25]	11 [11]	16 [16]
1979	43 [44]	6 [6]	18 [18]	11 [11]	20 [21]

*The first figure is percentage of the total vote; the figure in brackets is the percentage of seats the party won.

For the 1964 to 1970 elections, the vote is for the lower house (Andra Kammaren) of the Riksdag. In 1971, the two-chambered Riksdag became unicameral and thus the votes for the 1973 to 1979 elections are for this single-chambered Riksdag.

Before 1971, if the two houses disagreed, there was a combined roll-call vote to settle the fate of the bill.

but the final step of the process, as Table 7.2 shows. This long-term decline might be explained by an increasing alienation from government, the increasing joint action of the opposition parties, demographic changes, and the rise of new issues such as nuclear power on which the dominant party was vulnerable. Studies of electoral behavior in the 1976 election indicate that the SAP lost votes to all the nonsocialist parties, especially to the Liberals and the Center.[13]

In Japan, the long-dominant LDP faced similar challenges to its rule. In the late 1960s and early 1970s, a powerful reaction to the consequences of the country's "economic miracle" occurred in the form of widespread "citizens' movements" against pollution and environmental damage. Using this discontent to their advantage, by the early to mid-1970s, the opposition parties had won the mayoral or gubernatorial positions of most of Japan's largest metropolitan areas for the first time in history.[14] These challenges combined with demographic changes that worked against the LDP and the increase in urban independent voters who cast their votes on the basis of party performance in solving concrete problems,[15] to lead to a gradual decline in support for the LDP from the early 1960s to the mid-1970s as shown in Table 7.3. Its chief opposition party, the JSP, did not reap the benefits of this decline as it lost support at an even faster pace. Rather, both reaping the benefits of these declines and helping to precipitate them was the

13. Olof Petersson, Väljarna och Valet 1976 (Stockholm: SCB, 1977).
14. Kurt Steiner, Ellis S. Krauss, and Scott C. Flanagan, eds., Political Opposition and Local Politics in Japan (Princeton: Princeton University Press, 1980).
15. Gary D. Allinson, "Japan's Independent Voters: Dilemma or Opportunity?" Asian Survey 11 (Spring 1976): 36–55.

Table 7.3. Popular vote and seats in general elections to the House of Representatives in Japan, 1964–80 (in percentages)*

	LDP	DSP	CGP	JSP	JCP	IND
1963	55 [61]	7 [5]	–†	29 [31]	4 [1]	5 [3]
1967	49 [57]	7 [6]	5 [6]	28 [29]	5 [1]	6 [2]
1969	48 [59]	8 [6]	11 [10]	21 [18]	5 [3]	5 [3]
1972	47 [55]	7 [3.5]	8 [6]	22 [24]	10 [7]	5 [3]
1976	42 [49]	6 [6]	11 [11]	21 [24]	10 [3]	6 [4]
1979	44 [48.5]	7 [7]	10 [11]	20 [21]	10 [7]	5 [4]
1980	48 [56]	7 [6]	9 [7]	19 [21]	10 [6]	4 [1]

*The first figure is the percentage of the total vote; the figure in brackets is the percentage of seats the party won. The New Liberal Club (NLC), made up of a few dissident younger LDP members, split off from the LDP in 1976 and has run candidates in each election since, gathering 4 percent [3] in 1976, 3 percent [1] in 1979, and 3 percent [2] in 1980 of the votes and seats, respectively. The party is not included in the table because we do not treat it in the analysis to follow. Its origin in 1976 makes comparisons across different Diet power periods impossible.

†The Clean Government party (CGP: Komeito) did not run candidates in national elections until 1967.

challenge of a more competitive party system. One new center party, the Clean Government party, ran in its first national election in 1967 and increased its support over time; a second conservative party, the New Liberal Club, was formed by dissident younger LDP members in 1976; and a Communist party that had been a negligible electoral factor in the 1950s increased its support base with highly pragmatic policies.

The decline in the seat majorities of the dominant parties and the rise of their opposition to nearly equal power led their leaders to attempt various strategies for dealing with the new situation. During the stage of declining strength (1973–76) in Japan, Prime Minister Fukuda Takeo attempted to restore the absolute majority of the LDP but enunciated no new way of dealing with the opposition parties. With the advent of the nearly equal power situation after the 1976 election in the lower house and the fear of worse in the 1977 House of Councillors election, the then secretary general of the LDP, Masayoshi Ohira, announced that the ruling party would follow a strategy of "partial coalition" (*bubun rengō*), retaining monopoly control of the cabinet but flexibly negotiating with the opposition parties for cooperation in the passage of individual legislation.[16] When he became prime minister in 1978, Ohira reiterated his desire for relations of mutual trust with the

16. Wada Takayoshi, "Seiken-arasoi ni miru saishō no jōken [The minimum conditions for examining political rivalries]," *Asahi Jaanaru* 20 (September 1, 1978): 14–15; Uchida Kenzō, "Our New Prime Minister, Masayoshi Ohira," *Japan Echo* 6 (Spring 1979): 33; Ellis S. Krauss, "Conflict in the Diet: Toward Conflict Management in Parliamentary Politics," in Ellis S. Krauss, Thomas P. Rohlen, and Patricia G. Steinhoff, eds., *Conflict in Japan* (Honolulu: University of Hawaii Press, 1984), p. 263.

opposition parties in the Diet to ensure a smooth parliamentary process.[17] The LDP's public posture, therefore, seemed to have changed with the advent of the nearly equal power period.

In Sweden after 1973 and the advent of the balance of power period in the Riksdag, Prime Minister Olof Palme, leader of the SAP, talked about finding broad solutions to the problems confronting the nation. To implement this goal, the government sponsored three separate, informal conferences known as the Haga meetings after the building where they took place. Opposition party, labor union, and employer association leaders attended the meetings, and secret negotiations were conducted to find parliamentary and social support for labor market and tax programs. Agreements were reached with the Liberals at the first conference and with the Liberals and Center parties at the second. The Conservatives and the Communists walked out of both conferences. At the third conference, no agreement was reached with any opposition party.

Did the behavior of the dominant party toward the opposition in parliament reflect these public postures of attempted cooperation? Did the opposition parties respond in parliamentary voting as they did outside it? We turn now to parliamentary voting data to try to discover any patterns that would elucidate the strategies of these two parties, which first faced decline and then equality or near equality (which we will refer to in both cases as "balance of power") with their former minority perennial opposition.

The Data

First, we will look at the *overall patterns of voting coalitions* among the parties during the different stages. These data on the extent of voting agreement between the dominant party and the various opposition parties and among the opposition parties should give us a clear indication as to whether the parties generally responded to the changing power situations with flexibility or rigidity and with cooperative or confrontational legislative strategies.

Second, we will look at the *changes in patterns of voting coalitions on specific issues*. Increased or decreased cooperation between the dominant party and its opposition in specific issue areas should provide us with more detailed insights as to areas in which cooperation was achieved in the different stages and the strategies of each side.

Agreement by Party Coalition

One of the best indications of parties' strategy responses to dominant-party decline is whether cooperation increases or decreases as power rela-

17. Krauss, "Conflict in the Diet," p. 263.

Table 7.4. Party voting in the Japanese Diet; percentages of agreement on bills
by party combinations

Party combination	Time period		
	1970–72	1973–76	1977–80
Agreement combinations: Percent of nonunanimous decisions			
LDP + DSP	74.1	68.7	86.5
LDP + CGP	61.9	42.1	86.5
LDP + JSP	53.8	42.9	35.6
LDP + JCP	1.7	6.0	5.8
LDP + JSP + JCP	0.0	1.3	0.0
(LDP + the combined Left)			
LDP + CGP + DSP	61.8	44.2	61.5
(LDP + the combined Center)			
Agreement: Unanimous decisions as percent of total bills			
LDP + CGP + DSP + JSP + JCP	45.2	50.3	64.5
(unanimous agreement)			
Opposition combinations: Percent of nonunanimous decisions			
JSP + JCP, opposing LDP	41.1	48.9	53.8
(Leftist unity opposing)			
CGP + DSP, opposing LDP	25.8	31.3	18.2
(Center unity opposing)			
JSP + DSP + CGP + JCP, opposing LDP	23.7	27.8	18.2
(unanimous opposition against LDP)			

tions between the dominant party and its opposition change. Specifically,
we are interested in whether and to what extent specific opposition parties
and the dominant party vote more or less frequently together, and whether
and to what extent the opposition parties cooperate more or less frequently
against the dominant party. We will present data, therefore, on general level
of agreement on bills by different party combinations. The results for Japan
are shown in Table 7.4.[18]

18. The data in Tables 7.4 and 7.5 are presented in three parts, agreement combinations
(percent of nonunanimous decisions), agreement (unanimous decisions as a percent of total
bills), and opposition combinations (percent of nonunanimous decisions). This categorization
was chosen because of the Swedish Riksdag procedures in passing bills and the way the
Swedish data were collected. Bills passed unanimously are not subject to a roll-call vote; the
data collected on the Riksdag were from roll calls and thus only on bills on which there was not
unanimous agreement. We attempted to find a source of data on the exact number of bills
passed unanimously but discovered that the Riksdag secretariat does not keep such records.
Therefore, we estimated the "unanimous" bills in the Swedish case by subtracting the number
of roll calls from the total number of bills passed. Naturally, since there may be more than one
roll call on each bill, the remainder, the unanimous decisions, can only be an estimate and not
an exact number of unanimous decisions.
    The Japanese data were on bills. To make them equivalent to the Swedish data, we treated
each vote on each bill as one "roll call."
    Because of the differences in the nature of the "unanimous" data in the two countries we
separated the unanimous from the nonunanimous bills. The "nonunanimous" data, either of
agreement or opposition, are thus more equivalent in party combinations on votes than the
unanimous data. In discussion of specific issues, to have equivalent data, we use only the
nonunanimous bills from each country.

The first important point to note in Table 7.4 is that the level of cooperation between the LDP and all the opposition parties was already very high in the period of LDP dominance, higher in most cases than in the SAP's period of dominance in Sweden (see Table 7.5). Despite the overt "cultural politics" confrontation between government and opposition parties in Japan, in parliamentary voting both sides appear to have been extremely cooperative. This agreement, as several writers have pointed out, was the result of the LDP's willingness to compromise with the opposition on minor aspects of noncontroversial bills to ensure their smooth passage and on increasing behind-the-scenes communication between party leaders in the 1960s and early 1970s.[19]

Second, the data show an overall pattern of somewhat decreasing cooperation between the LDP and each of the opposition parties except the Communists once the dominant party began to decline in 1973–76. The small increase in Communist party cooperation was undoubtedly not the result of the LDP moving toward the JCP (the LDP remained anticommunist), but rather of the JCP's casting itself as a pragmatic and moderate party, concentrating on concrete issues of concern to the voters, and being willing to vote even for some government legislation, a strategy that increased the party's support base at election time.[20] Particularly striking is the moderate decline in agreement between the LDP and the centrist CGP. This was a period in which the CGP was moving somewhat leftward in its orientation, which may account for the larger decrease in agreement with the LDP in its case than in the other opposition parties.

If the JCP was becoming more pragmatic, slightly increasing its support for LDP-sponsored bills, it and the socialists also cooperated more in the second period. The "combined left" vote against the LDP, as well as with the LDP, increased in the second period. So did unity among centrist parties and among all opposition parties against the LDP. Despite a slight increase in the percentage of bills passed unanimously (probably mostly because of the JCP's increased pragmatism on some bills), during the stage of dominant-party decline there seemed to be no movement of the dominant party and opposition parties toward each other. Rather, the opposition parties appear to have cooperated somewhat more with each other against the dominant party. In other words, the threat to LDP dominance that became obvious with its declining percentage of seats in the 1972 general election does not seem to have affected the general pattern of relations between the dominant party and its center and noncommunist left opposition. The pattern remains one of overt public conflict but a surprisingly high level of cooperation on legislation in the Diet, albeit with less cooperation

19. T. J. Pempel, "The Dilemma of Parliamentary Opposition in Japan," *Polity* 8 (Fall 1975): 63–79; Krauss, "Conflict in the Diet."
20. Hong N. Kim, "The JCP's Parliamentary Road," *Problems of Communism* 26 (March–April 1977): 21–24.

with the LDP and more opposition unity against the LDP in the second stage.

During the nearly equal power stage of 1977–80, however, this pattern reversed. Cooperation between the LDP and the center opposition increased. Cooperation between the LDP and the DSP jumped by almost 20 percent, and cooperation between the LDP and the CGP doubled. Cooperation between the LDP and the JSP declined again.

Furthermore, nearly two-thirds of all bills voted on passed by unanimous agreement among all the parties. There was a sharp corresponding decline in the third period in combined centrist parties and all-opposition unity against the LDP. Clearly, the dominant party and its opposition parties, particularly those of the center, which already exhibited fairly high levels of cooperation with the LDP in the previous periods, now were in agreement a remarkable proportion of the time. The "crisis" to dominant-party hegemony of the opposition gaining almost the same number of parliamentary seats resulted in Japan in *more* legislative agreement, not less, as the LDP moved toward its center opposition and as center opposition parties moved to cooperate even more with the dominant party.

The data for Sweden in Table 7.5 show a very different pattern. First, the level of agreement in the system in the period of SAP dominance was much lower than in Japan with the exception of the Communist party, which was not an opposition party in the traditional sense. It usually sided with the SAP because its only alternative was to lose its image as a working-class party by siding with the nonsocialist parties. If we were to exclude the VPK from the average, the level of agreement in the first stage would be even lower. Thus despite the "politics of compromise" style of Swedish politics, legislative cooperation was at a much lower level than in the supposedly more confrontational Japanese case. Swedish legislative behavioral style in the dominant-party era indicates less willingness for the dominant party and the opposition parties to compromise on many issues.

After the 1970 election, when the SAP lost its single-party majority and was relegated to the status of a minority government, but one with a frequent "bloc majority" in cooperation with the Communists, we see an interesting change. Cooperation with each of the nonsocialist opposition parties increased significantly (about 14 percent in the case of the Center and Liberals, 18 percent for the Conservatives). Ironically, voting agreement with the SAP's bloc majority partner, the Communist party, declined by over 11 percent and VPK opposition to the SAP increased. Obviously, during this second stage of decline, the SAP, confident of VPK support on many issues, moved to the right to gain support from nonsocialist opposition parties on more issues and thus forced the Communists to oppose it more frequently. Even with this decline in VPK-SAP cooperation from the first to the second periods, overall cooperation in the system increased (almost 9 percent, including the VPK combination, and almost 15 percent if we ex-

Table 7.5. Party voting in the Swedish Riksdag; percentages of agreement on bills by party combination

Party combination	Time period		
	1970	1971–73	1974–76
Agreement combinations: Percent			
of nonunanimous decisions			
SAP + Conservatives (M)	24.4	42.4	47.8
SAP + Center (C)	39.7	54.0	68.8
SAP + Liberals (FP)	32.2	46.9	63.6
SAP + Communists (VPK)	83.1	71.7	64.5
SAP + C + FP	24.1	36.3	52.7
(SAP + combined center)			
SAP + C + FP + M	3.1	20.7	22.2
(SAP + combined center-right)			
Agreement: Unanimous decisions as percent of total bills			
SAP + M + C + FP + VPK	41.4	63.7	66.0
(Unanimous agreement)			
Opposition combinations: Percent of nonunanimous decisions			
M opposing SAP	73.0	59.6	53.1
(Right opposing SAP)			
C + FP opposing SAP	49.7	38.0	19.7
(Center opposing SAP)			
VPK opposing SAP	19.2	30.9	37.5
(supporting left opposing SAP)			
M + C + FP opposing SAP	37.1	26.1	12.2
(Center-right unity opposing)			
M + C + FP + VPK opposing SAP	1.3	2.1	1.1
(Unanimous opposing SAP)			

clude the combination with the Communists). Furthermore, we see a significant decline in nonsocialist opposition unity against the dominant party. Unanimous opposition against the SAP (including the VPK) was so low as to be insignificant.

After the 1973 election, which resulted in a balance of power between socialist and nonsocialist parties (even with the VPK, the SAP could not control a majority), the tendencies toward increased cooperation between SAP and its center and right opposition and decreased cooperation with the Communists continued. Although cooperation with the right, the Conservative party, increased only about 5 percent from the second stage to the third, cooperation with the Center and Liberal parties increased by around 15 percent or more, bringing the center parties to about the same level of cooperation with the SAP as the VPK, the dominant party's supposed bloc partner.

In sum, although overall cooperation in the system did not increase to the same extent as during the transition from SAP dominance to decline, most of that increase was accounted for by increasing agreement between the SAP and the center opposition parties, as shown by the large increase (14 to 16 percent) not only of the SAP individually with the center parties, but also with the combined center bloc. Meanwhile, center-right unity against the dominant party eroded by more than half between the second and third stages. Unanimous agreement did not increase nearly as much as in the transition from the first to the second periods.

The SAP met the crisis of nearly losing power with a continued movement toward the center, pulling it further away from the VPK on its left, and only marginally increased cooperation with its ideological rival, the Conservatives. The dominant party seemed to be moving toward the center, and the centrist parties toward the SAP, at least in overall voting. There was also a slowing of the increase in cooperation between the SAP and the right and in the level of unanimous agreement.

We have found different patterns of change in party voting combinations in response to the changing power situations in parliaments across the three periods. In Japan the overall level of cooperation between dominant party and opposition was much higher than in Sweden in the first period and stayed higher, belying the former's reputation for left-right confrontation and the latter's for consensus among the political elites. When the dominant party declined in the second stage, the LDP and the opposition parties seemed to respond with no more cooperation with each other, and even somewhat less, than before.

In Sweden, by contrast, cooperation increased significantly between the SAP and both the center and right opposition, bringing about a decline in agreement with its left ally, the Communists. But in the third period of nearly equal power in both countries, there was yet another pattern. The LDP and the opposition, particularly the center, now showed much more willingness to vote together on bills, whereas in Sweden the increase in cooperation was somewhat less than during the period of decline (but also was confined primarily to the SAP and the center parties).

Party Voting Agreement on Specific Issues

We have looked at general party strategies across three stages of parliamentary power by analyzing overall voting combinations of the parties. Now we turn to the specific issues on which the parties agreed or disagreed to try to discern a more detailed picture of the strategies the dominant party and opposition followed.

Figures 7.1 and 7.2[21] represent in graphic form the net change in increases in agreement between the LDP and each opposition party on specific

21. Because we do not have data on unanimous roll-call votes in the Swedish Riksdag broken down by issue, the data analyzed below are on bills passed by nonunanimous votes only.

Figure 7.1. DSP and CGP: Change in agreement with LDP by issue, first and second periods

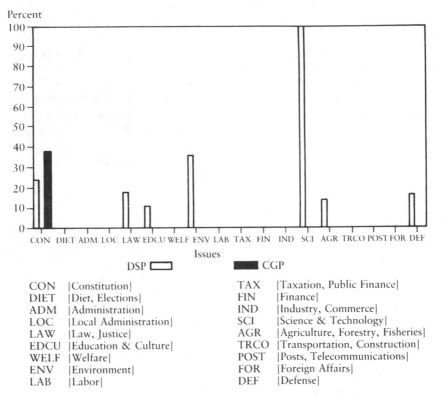

Percent

CON		Constitution		TAX		Taxation, Public Finance	
DIET		Diet, Elections		FIN		Finance	
ADM		Administration		IND		Industry, Commerce	
LOC		Local Administration		SCI		Science & Technology	
LAW		Law, Justice		AGR		Agriculture, Forestry, Fisheries	
EDCU		Education & Culture		TRCO		Transportation, Construction	
WELF		Welfare		POST		Posts, Telecommunications	
ENV		Environment		FOR		Foreign Affairs	
LAB		Labor		DEF		Defense	

issues from the first stage of LDP dominance to the second stage of decline. We considered a net change of plus or minus 10 percent to be no real change, and those issues are not represented.[22] Thus the issues listed in the figures are those on which there were substantial increases in agreement across the two periods, and the net difference between the two periods for each issue is given next to the issue. The figures are presented in the order of the opposition party's ideological proximity to the LDP, from the DSP to the JCP.

The number and nature of the issues on which agreement increased varied greatly among the parties. The DSP showed increases on the greatest number of issues (seven); the other center party, the CGP, the least (one).

22. Declines in agreement between the LDP and each opposition party from one period to the next are not represented in the figures because of the possibility that changes in the number of unanimous agreements on any particular issue could influence such results. We are dealing here only with bills passed nonunanimously. There was the possibility that declines in agreement on an issue could be caused by a significant increase in unanimous agreement on that issue from one period to the next. If that occurred, it could be reflected in a decrease in agreement on that issue in the nonunanimous votes. Therefore, we deal here only with the data for increases in agreement on the nonunanimous votes.

Figure 7.2. JSP and JCP: Change in agreement with LDP by issue, first and second periods

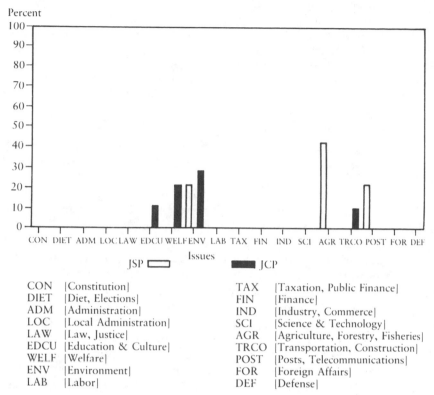

CON [Constitution]	TAX [Taxation, Public Finance]
DIET [Diet, Elections]	FIN [Finance]
ADM [Administration]	IND [Industry, Commerce]
LOC [Local Administration]	SCI [Science & Technology]
LAW [Law, Justice]	AGR [Agriculture, Forestry, Fisheries]
EDCU [Education & Culture]	TRCO [Transportation, Construction]
WELF [Welfare]	POST [Posts, Telecommunications]
ENV [Environment]	FOR [Foreign Affairs]
LAB [Labor]	DEF [Defense]

The two leftist parties were in between (JSP, three; JCP, four). Also, the issues on which these parties increased their agreement varied greatly, as did the extent of the change over the two periods. The DSP's greatest increases in agreement with the LDP were in the issue area of science and technology, which includes the controversial subject of nuclear power, and environment. The early 1970s were a period when the LDP was attempting to address environmental problems to a greater extent than previously, and it is possible that its efforts in this direction now placed it closer to the DSP's stand on this issue.

There was a smaller increase in agreement on defense issues, one of the major ideological cleavage issues between left and right in the Japanese party system. The DSP is the one opposition party that has consistently and strongly supported Japan's political and military alliance with the United States and is closest to the LDP on defense matters. It would appear that the increased agreement of the two parties on these issues does not imply a shift of the LDP to the left, as much as a possible move to the right, resulting in the DSP giving more support for its defense policies.

The CGP increased its agreement with the LDP only on the constitutional issue. This was a period in which the CGP moved somewhat leftward and thus further away from the LDP, as is shown in the lack of any major positive changes in LDP-CGP cooperation on most issues.

JSP-LDP cooperation changed substantively only on three issues, the greatest difference being in agriculture.[23] One of the other issues on which there was increased agreement was environment. The largest increases in agreement between the LDP and the JCP on nonunanimous issues also were in the areas of environment and welfare, exactly those issues on which the LDP became more responsive to grass-roots demands for attention.

Two aspects of the data stand out for the transition from the first to the second periods. The first is the movement of the DSP and the LDP toward greater cooperation on several issues and the lack of increased cooperation between the LDP and the other center party, the CGP, on hardly any issues. The second is that when increased cooperation did occur, either with the DSP or the leftist parties, it revolved around the two issues (environment and welfare) on which the LDP was substantially modifying its policies and image as a result of increased public concern.

Therefore, although we found a higher level of general parliamentary voting agreement between the dominant party and its opposition in Japan than we would expect given the polarized, confrontational history of that party system, we also found that the LDP's decline in seat strength in the 1973–76 period did *not* result in any widespread movement toward accommodation on either side. The overall level of unanimous agreement among the parties increased very little. And when there was not unanimous agreement, we found no evidence of significant increases in agreement between the LDP and the opposition on issues that define the major cleavages between the dominant party and each opposition party.

The major exception to this failure to move toward accommodation is in environmental and welfare issues. The LDP's attempt to stave off further decline by finally addressing these problems, which caused massive popular concern and protest in the late 1960s and early 1970s and contributed to its declining popularity, allowed it and the opposition parties to find more common ground. The initial reaction to dominant-party decline in Japan resulted in a pragmatic and flexible response by the LDP to grass-roots demands on two specific issues, but otherwise was greeted on both sides by a continuation of conflict and consensus as usual.

The Swedish data on issues in the period of change from SAP dominance to decline, presented in Figures 7.3 and 7.4, show a marked contrast to

---

23. During the 1970s the Socialists, in the earlier postwar years primarily an urban party, were in the process of being transformed into a party with equal support in rural areas. By 1976, when the JSP's share of the seats in the House of Representatives was categorized into five groups by percent of workers engaged in primary industries (agriculture, forestry, fisheries, and so on), the party's distribution of seats was almost equally divided among the groups. See J. A. A. Stockwin, *Japan: Divided Politics in a Growth Economy*, 2d ed. (New York: Norton, 1982).

those for Japan. Here we find a very clear and steplike movement of the SAP toward the right and of the nonsocialist opposition toward the dominant party. The SAP and its closest center-left opposition, the Liberals, showed a significant increase in agreement on the social welfare issue and marked increases on law, the constitution, and agriculture. The center-right opposition and the SAP showed strong increases in agreement on agriculture, social welfare, constitutional, and legal issues. Even with its main ideological rival the Conservatives, the SAP found common ground on agriculture and economic affairs issues.

What is fascinating about these data is, first, that there is a clear hierarchy of movement to the right in the party system. There is most agreement with the closest opposition party, a bit less with the next ideologically close nonsocialist party, and least with the ideological enemy. Second, and even more important, that agreement increased most between the dominant party and each nonsocialist opposition party on exactly those issues that have historically defined the cleavages in the party system—social welfare with the Liberals and Center and economic affairs with the Conservatives—and on major constituency issues such as agriculture (the Center's major social interest constituency).

Clearly, the SAP moved toward the right in trying to cope with its decline and tried to compromise with each opposition party in the issue area that historically most defined their differences, and the opposition responded flexibly. This interpretation is buttressed by the VPK data. By moving to the right to gain support selectively on the most salient issues dividing it from the nonsocialist parties, SAP's leftist ally, the VPK, was left behind and did not show any increase in agreement on any issue with its "bloc partner" the SAP, and is not displayed in the charts. Thus not only did both the dominant party and its opposition show a greater overall tendency toward agreement in this period, but that agreement was most salient on the most crucial issues that have traditionally divided them.

The change from single-party dominance to decline in Japan and Sweden elicited contrary responses in the two party systems. In Japan, the LDP and opposition parties reacted by making no significant moves toward accommodation on the core ideological issues that traditionally divided them, but rather by moving very selectively toward greater agreement on the environmental and welfare issues that were of vital concern to the mass public in Japan in the early 1970s. There were widespread protest movements over these issues, and the opposition parties used them to challenge the LDP successfully at the local level, undermining some of its urban support. The LDP seems to have reacted to decline by selectively responding only to those demands which it perceived to be undermining its support, and the opposition parties met the LDP primarily on these two issues.

In Sweden, the SAP and its nonsocialist opposition generally increased their accommodation particularly on the most important issues that tradi-

Figure 7.3. FP and C: Change in agreement with SAP by issue, first and second periods

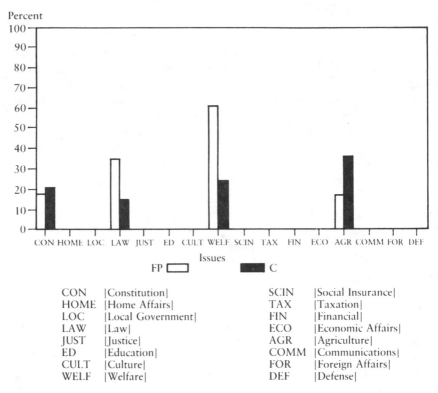

CON	|Constitution|	SCIN	|Social Insurance|
HOME	|Home Affairs|	TAX	|Taxation|
LOC	|Local Government|	FIN	|Financial|
LAW	|Law|	ECO	|Economic Affairs|
JUST	|Justice|	AGR	|Agriculture|
ED	|Education|	COMM	|Communications|
CULT	|Culture|	FOR	|Foreign Affairs|
WELF	|Welfare|	DEF	|Defense|

tionally divided them, and this rightward shift in the system somewhat divided the dominant party from its leftist ally, the Communist party. The SAP's response to decline, in other words, was both wider and more fundamental than the LDP's. It and its opposition in this period of decline agreed on more issues and more frequently on the core issues of cleavage in the party system.

Did these patterns continue in the second transition in both countries, the period from decline to balance of power? Figures 7.5 and 7.6 portray data for this period for Japan. The data on issues for the transition from the second stage (1973–76) to the third stage (1977–80) are surprising, in that they show a very different pattern from that of the first transition. The DSP showed marked increases in agreement on a few issues, as in the first transition. But there the similarities end.

First, the CGP dramatically increased its agreement with the LDP on a wide range of issues, eleven to be exact, whereas in the transition from the first to second periods the CGP increased its agreement on only one issue. Most interesting, these include the issues of foreign policy and defense,

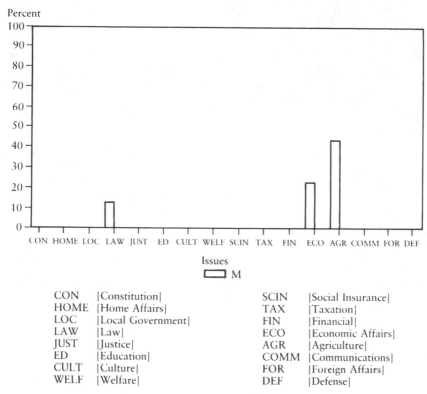

Figure 7.4. Change in agreement with SAP by issue, first and second periods

CON	[Constitution]		SCIN	[Social Insurance]
HOME	[Home Affairs]		TAX	[Taxation]
LOC	[Local Government]		FIN	[Financial]
LAW	[Law]		ECO	[Economic Affairs]
JUST	[Justice]		AGR	[Agriculture]
ED	[Education]		COMM	[Communications]
CULT	[Culture]		FOR	[Foreign Affairs]
WELF	[Welfare]		DEF	[Defense]

which in the postwar party system have been the most controversial and conflictual. In part, this movement represents a turnaround in the policy of the CGP, which had been moving leftward in the earlier 1970s, toward greater acceptance of the alliance with the United States and of the Self-Defense Forces. But because the CGP changed its program very little in other respects, its increased cooperation with the LDP must represent some movement on the part of the LDP as well.[24]

The other surprise is the pattern of LDP-JSP cooperation. Not only was there a rise in the number of issues on which agreement increased (from three to five) in the second to third periods compared to the first and second periods, but here too agreement occurred on foreign policy and defense issues. One explanation for this pattern is that with the swing of the CGP to the right, the JSP also moved toward the dominant party, fearing isolation

24. Regarding the 1970s, Stockwin, *Japan,* p. 184, writes: "The Komeito . . . had changed little over the past decade, either in its policy positions (although on matters of foreign policy it had moved slightly to the right from its formerly centre-left position) or in the profile of its Diet membership."

on the left with the Communists. Because foreign policy and defense issues constitute the major core identity issues for the JSP and because there was no fundamental shift in the party's public program on these issues, it is unlikely that this could be the only explanation. Rather, the data must also reflect a more compromising stand on these issues on the part of the LDP.

This improvement in LDP-JSP agreement, even if not to the extent of the major change in LDP-CGP agreement, isolated the JCP on the left. In the later transition period, LDP-JCP agreement occurred to a much lesser extent than in the earlier period. It is obvious that although the LDP moved toward the left on key issues after entering the nearly equal power period, and the opposition moved toward the dominant party, this change did not encompass the Communists.

We find, therefore, something of a turnabout, not only from small increases in cooperation to greater agreement in general, but from lack of agreement on issues that define the identities of the opposition parties and the dominant party and, therefore, divide the party system, to agreement on those very issues.

It seems clear from the data that the LDP, responding to the unprecedented crisis of facing an opposition with almost equal parliamentary strength, quickly moved to cooperate more with the opposition parties. It did so selectively, moving toward the left opposition on the ideological issues of foreign policy and defense and toward the center-left on a wide range of issues. The opposition parties, even though they now had an unprecedented number of seats in parliament nearly equal to that of the dominant party, did not use their new-found strength to challenge the LDP further. They too increased their cooperation with the other side, even on the most controversial issues that had previously divided them from the dominant party. This is particularly true of the CGP, but also of the JSP.

As the figures also show, the LDP moved toward the combined opposition on the one issue on which the opposition showed a united front and pushed during this period—public finance, particularly taxation and tax cuts. Thus in 1978, for the first time since the formation of the LDP, the government's draft budget bill was amended after introduction to the Diet under pressure from the opposition parties.

The continuation of divided politics as usual except for environment and welfare which we found in the first transition to decline of the LDP fundamentally changed to greater compromise, not only on the number of issues but also on the most conflictual issues dividing the two camps.

Do we find a similar dramatic change from the first transition in the case of Sweden? Figures 7.7 and 7.8 provide the answer, and it is a more complicated one than in the case of Japan. On most issues we find a continuation of the tendencies we found in the change from dominance to decline: increasing cooperation of the SAP with the nonsocialist opposition but no increasing agreement on any issue with its ally to the left, the VPK (and thus

Figure 7.5. DSP and CGP: Change in agreement with LDP by issue, second and third periods

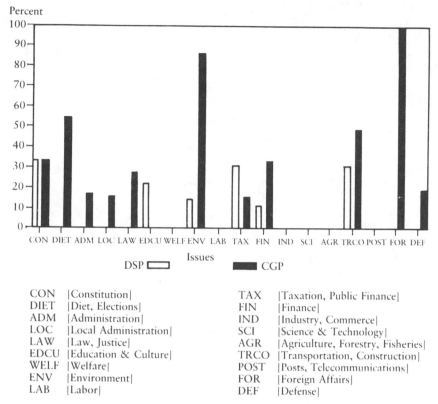

CON	|Constitution|	TAX	|Taxation, Public Finance|
DIET	|Diet, Elections|	FIN	|Finance|
ADM	|Administration|	IND	|Industry, Commerce|
LOC	|Local Administration|	SCI	|Science & Technology|
LAW	|Law, Justice|	AGR	|Agriculture, Forestry, Fisheries|
EDCU	|Education & Culture|	TRCO	|Transportation, Construction|
WELF	|Welfare|	POST	|Posts, Telecommunications|
ENV	|Environment|	FOR	|Foreign Affairs|
LAB	|Labor|	DEF	|Defense|

again the VPK does not appear in the figures). The hierarchy of agreement from center-left through center-right, to right, which appears in the figures of the transition to decline, is reproduced here, but with even more issues on which agreement occurred between the SAP and the center parties. Agreement increased with the Conservatives solely on the symbolic value issue (of importance to the Conservatives) of justice.

A closer look at the differences between the first and second transitions may disclose some important and subtle complications in these generalizations. Social welfare, the issue on which cooperation between the Liberals and SAP had increased the most, disappeared as an issue of increasing cooperation. Economic affairs, on which cooperation with the Conservatives increased, and agriculture, an issue on which there was a strong rise in agreement between the SAP and the center-right and right in the earlier transition period, showed no increase in cooperation. These very basic issues of ideology (social welfare and economic affairs) and social interest coalition (agriculture) that have traditionally divided the parties and given them much of their identity have now become issues of stagnant coopera-

Figure 7.6. JSP and JCP: Change in agreement with LDP by issue, second and third periods

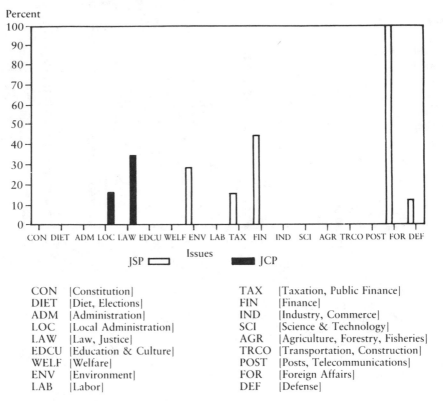

CON	[Constitution]	TAX	[Taxation, Public Finance]
DIET	[Diet, Elections]	FIN	[Finance]
ADM	[Administration]	IND	[Industry, Commerce]
LOC	[Local Administration]	SCI	[Science & Technology]
LAW	[Law, Justice]	AGR	[Agriculture, Forestry, Fisheries]
EDCU	[Education & Culture]	TRCO	[Transportation, Construction]
WELF	[Welfare]	POST	[Posts, Telecommunications]
ENV	[Environment]	FOR	[Foreign Affairs]
LAB	[Labor]	DEF	[Defense]

tion, the major exceptions to the tendency toward continued increasing agreement.

These data indicate that in the crisis of balance of power in Sweden, although cooperation continued to increase on many issues as in the period of change from SAP's dominance to decline, the dominant party and the center opposition parties now appeared to begin to draw the line of cooperation short of the one issue at the heart of their party identity and constituency mobilization (social welfare for the Liberals, economic affairs and agriculture for the Center). We see, in other words, a resistance to compromise on both sides in these vital areas.

Thus, although the "Haga spirit" of negotiated compromise between the SAP and the Liberal and Center parties seems to have borne fruit in the increasing agreement on taxation and other issues, it does not seem to have spilled over sufficiently to have stimulated a continuation of the increases in cooperation on core issues such as occurred in the earlier transition to decline.

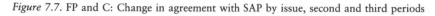

Figure 7.7. FP and C: Change in agreement with SAP by issue, second and third periods

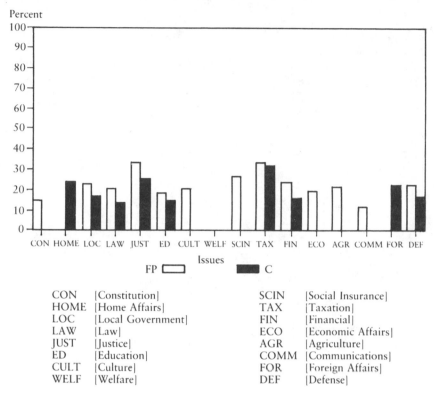

CON	[Constitution]	SCIN	[Social Insurance]
HOME	[Home Affairs]	TAX	[Taxation]
LOC	[Local Government]	FIN	[Financial]
LAW	[Law]	ECO	[Economic Affairs]
JUST	[Justice]	AGR	[Agriculture]
ED	[Education]	COMM	[Communications]
CULT	[Culture]	FOR	[Foreign Affairs]
WELF	[Welfare]	DEF	[Defense]

Whereas the LDP and the opposition parties (except the Communists) moved toward greater compromise on more issues and for the first time on core issues that represent basic cleavages in the party system during the nearly equal power period, in Sweden we find that the rise in cooperation on core issues stopped once parity of parliamentary power was realized.

There are several ironies and paradoxes of the different patterns of party behavior in parliament in Sweden and Japan in the 1970s. In Japan, a party system historically characterized as confrontational and polarized reacted to the loss of a clear majority by its dominant party with greater cooperation and less conflict than previously; in Sweden, a party system historically characterized as one of compromise and accommodation reacted by re-affirming the basic cleavages dividing the parties. What explains these paradoxes and the different responses of the parties in the different time periods? What are some of the implications of these differences for theories of dominance?

Figure 7.8. M: Change in agreement with SAP by issue, second and third periods

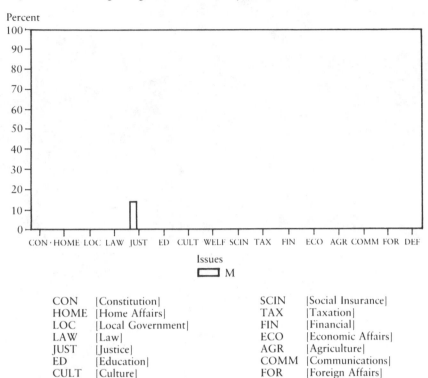

CON		Constitution		SCIN		Social Insurance	
HOME		Home Affairs		TAX		Taxation	
LOC		Local Government		FIN		Financial	
LAW		Law		ECO		Economic Affairs	
JUST		Justice		AGR		Agriculture	
ED		Education		COMM		Communications	
CULT		Culture		FOR		Foreign Affairs	
WELF		Welfare		DEF		Defense	

Explanations

The data discussed above only partially confirm the hypotheses about dominant parties and their opposition derived from the literature. First, Duverger and Arian and Barnes, despite their contrary conclusions, share the assumption that the very nature of dominant parties and perennial oppositions leads them either to rigidity or to pragmatic flexibility. In fact, the cases of Japan and Sweden show that their parties manifested each of these characteristics, but at different times, in the 1970s. Flexibility and rigidity also varied by issue. The SAP and the nonsocialist opposition were very flexible in responding to decline but, at least on the crucial cleavage issues, became more inflexible in the third stage. The LDP and the opposition parties in Japan were more inflexible than the Swedish parties in reacting to decline, except on the environmental and welfare issues, but extremely pragmatic and flexible in responding to the balance of power period. We can say that in the 1970s relations between the dominant party and the opposition in Sweden moved from cooperation to at least partial polarization (especially on core identity issues), whereas those in Japan moved from at least partial polarization to cooperation.

We also should remember that the ability of the LDP and the SAP to respond flexibly at least at some point during the 1970s was in part based on the solidification of their support base through rigid ideological confrontation in the earlier years of their time in power. Both could respond flexibly, albeit in different ways and at different times, in the 1970s, because they had been dominant for so long.

Thus our findings indicated that there is nothing in the nature of dominant parties or their opposition that inevitably leads them to be either rigid or flexible. Put another way, each of the dominant parties had been ideologically rigid while building its dominance, but once dominant and faced with decline, each also was willing pragmatically to trade ideology for legislative power; when and on what issues they were willing to make that trade, however, varied in the two countries.

We do not find any support for Arian and Barnes's assertion that leftist dominant parties are necessarily any more flexible, responsive, or likely to revive from decline. It is interesting that subsequent to Arian and Barnes's suggestion that leftist dominant parties are more responsive to changing conditions, the major leftist dominant parties in Sweden and Israel both lost power (the SAP regained it six years later), while the major rightist dominant parties in Japan and Italy continue to participate in governing. Our study uncovered no particular evidence, however, that rightist parties per se are more flexible: the conservative LDP was more flexible in the stage of balance of power, but the leftist SAP responded earlier and was more flexible on more basic issues in the stage of decline. Ideology of the dominant party does not seem a particularly good predictor of its responsiveness to change or of flexibility when in decline.

If neither dominance nor ideology explains dominant-party behavior, what does? Further, how does one explain opposition party behavior? We must look more to contextual and other variables to explain party behavior in a dominant-party system.

In each of these countries, it may be possible to find ad hoc and idiosyncratic variables to explain the behavior of the dominant party and each of the opposition parties in each period and perhaps even on each issue. We believe, however, that first an attempt must be made to ascertain whether a more parsimonious explanation involving rational strategy and party system considerations can explain the results.

We suggest that there are three major related variables that may systematically explain our findings and the behavior of parties in a dominant-party system: the nature and history of relations in the party system, the coalition strategies of the parties, and the extent of internal-external dilemma the parties face in each of the transition stages.

Party System and Coalition Strategies: The Dominant Party's Period of Decline

The party system in Japan developed in a fragmented fashion, with each opposition party arising in the postwar period around conflict on one major issue with at least one of the other opposition parties. The DSP split off from the JSP in 1959 on the issue of defense and the security treaty on which it was closer to the dominant LDP. The CGP arose in the mid- to late 1960s as a nonsocialist party pushing social welfare and dealing with the demands of formerly marginal voters not closely tied into the networks of the other parties. In other words, the lines of cleavage in the party system differentiated not only the opposition from the dominant party but also the opposition parties from each other. The opposition DSP shared the defense and security treaty orientation of the LDP as well as its anticommunism. The CGP was nonsocialist and a rival mass-based party to the Communists. The possibility of an all-opposition majority coalition has been slight because each of the party's identities revolved around a basic issue that differentiated it as much from at least one or two other opposition parties as from the LDP.

The line of cleavage in the Swedish party system was more unidimensional: nonsocialist (M, C, FP) versus socialist (SAP, VPK). Although the nonsocialist opposition parties differed with each other on some issues, they differed more with the SAP on the basic cleavage issue in the system. Therefore, the potential for coalition among the nonsocialist opposition parties has been greater in Sweden than in Japan.

Further, in Japan, the LDP monopolized the spectrum of ideology from the center to the extreme right—there are no parties to its right. In Sweden, however, the SAP had a party to its extreme left—the VPK—with which it shared a socialist ideology and which had no alternative but to cooperate somewhat with the SAP or become totally isolated on the extreme left.

Therefore, the two dominant parties' reactions to decline differed. Faced with a declining majority, the LDP was responsive to the tide of demands for a change in environmental and welfare policy. The party seemed to become flexible only on that narrow range of issues which it perceived might contribute to its further decline. Otherwise, it could afford to wait to see how the next election turned out before moving to cooperate with the opposition parties on a wider range or on more core cleavage issues because it knew that even if it lost its majority of seats in the next election, the opposition parties could not form a viable unified majority coalition. As long as the LDP held a majority and refused further compromise, the Japanese opposition parties had nothing to lose by continuing the politics of opposition.

Since its formation in 1955, the LDP always had very comfortable majorities in the Diet. It was likely that neither the LDP nor the opposition parties necessarily perceived the LDP's decline to be more than a temporary aberration from its seeming previous invulnerability. It was possible, from the LDP's perspective, that merely making adjustments in its pollution and welfare policies would be sufficient to reverse its temporarily declining fortunes. Thus it adopted a strategy of responding more to immediate public demands than to making wide and basic adjustments in its relations with the opposition parties in the Diet. Conversely, the attitude of the LDP and the possibility of its continued dominance would not necessarily induce the opposition parties to rush to compromise on the fundamental issues that had always divided them from the LDP. The SAP could not afford to wait during the period of decline for the outcome of the next election before greatly altering its parliamentary strategy. Unlike the LDP, the SAP had had comfortable majorities for only brief periods during its long tenure as a dominant party. The SAP could count on the VPK to its left for support. But confronted with the possibility of further decline and potential loss of a majority even with the support of the VPK, it faced the prospect of total loss of power should the nonsocialist opposition parties unify to form a government. Further, because of the adoption of a more perfect proportional representation system in Sweden after the 1970 election, the SAP's declining electoral strength had an immediate impact on its parliamentary power.

Therefore, it had to move quickly in the period of decline to forestall and undercut nonsocialist opposition unity. Secure in the knowledge that the VPK had no real alternative but to support it on most bills, it could compromise with each of the nonsocialist opposition parties on the issues of most concern to them. As long as the SAP and VPK had a majority, and the SAP was willing to make concessions, these opposition parties had little incentive to reject compromise with the SAP.

Thus the nature of the party system, and especially its lines of cleavage and the cohesiveness of the opposition, in part may explain the contrasting behavior of the LDP and SAP and their opposition parties in the period of decline.

Party System and Coalition Strategies: The Balance of Power Period

A corollary of the nature of the party system is the contrasting strategies of the opposition parties in the balance of power period. Once the dominant party comes close to losing its majority and the prospect of the opposition taking power materializes, the opposition parties have different incentives in the two systems. In Sweden, the possibility of nonsocialist opposition unity and coalition to form a majority government of relative equals is a more real, and tempting, alternative to each of these parties than crossing the basic ideological cleavage dividing the system to join a government with the SAP still dominant. Though they may continue to cooperate with the SAP on nonessential issues, they are more likely, as we have seen, to step back from the SAP on the core issues and reaffirm their party identities in preparation for potentially forming an alternative government. Thus the tendency in the balance of power period in Sweden is centrifugal—the opposition parties move away from the dominant party on issues of party identity.[25]

In Japan, balance of power provided incentive for the dominant and opposition parties to move closer together.[26] The LDP must cooperate with the opposition parties to get legislation passed smoothly and to prove to the electorate that it can still govern. Rather than forming a coalition government with one of these parties prematurely, it can cooperate selectively with each of them on the issues of concern to them to get individual bills passed. The partial coalition strategy of the LDP is an accurate reflection of its strategic behavior of divide and cooperate.

The only incentive for the center opposition parties, knowing that even if the LDP loses more seats they cannot form a unified opposition government, is to position themselves as potential coalition partners for the dominant party should it decline further. This involves both greater cooperation with the dominant party and proving to the party and the electorate that they are responsible enough to govern. This movement of the center creates a dilemma for the JSP, as Sato Seizaburo and Mutsuzaki Tetsuhisa have pointed out.[27] It may move toward the dominant party with the center

25. The terms *centrifugal* and *centripetal* are central to Giovanni Sartori, *Parties and Party Systems* (Cambridge: Cambridge University Press, 1976), vol. 1, and his analysis of party systems. We are using these terms somewhat differently from Sartori, however, in that we are discussing only coalitional strategies in two systems with five or more parties, whereas Sartori in discussing electoral strategies and sees systems with fewer than five parties as centripetal but those with five parties or more as centrifugal. Some of his discussions concerning inherent tendencies when there are two extreme alternatives, such as in Sweden, versus when there are not, as in Japan, might be applicable here. See especially ibid., pp. 349–51.

26. This was especially true as the LDP faced the post-1976 period in a state of crisis. The party had been badly tainted and torn by the scandals involving former Prime Minister Tanaka, and several of its younger members had split the party to form the New Liberal Club, which was enjoying great popularity in the media. For the first time since its formation, the party's electoral decline could be seen as having the very real potential for the loss of a parliamentary majority.

27. Sato Seizaburo and Matsuzaki Tetsuhisa, "Jimintō kokkai un'ei no tettei kenkyū [Thorough research on LDP Diet management]," *Chūō Kōron* (July 1985) analyze party combination voting, as well as amendments to bills and passage rates in specific committees. Although some of their results parallel ours, on one point especially there is some difference. They see the LDP-JSP leadership aspects of the Diet continuing even in the balance of power era; we have emphasized here that the movement of the center parties to the LDP is the chief characteristic of the system in this period. The difference may be primarily semantic and methodological (they emphasize initiative in proposal of bills whereas we emphasize coalition strategy considerations), rather than substantive. In any case, we agree on the dilemma faced by the JSP in this period. See ibid., pp. 408–9 and 415.

parties, or choose isolation on the left with the Communists as a perennial minority outsider but remain true to its ideology. The JSP seems to have responded with ambiguity, going along with the LDP when it becomes flexible on core issues like defense but not carrying out a programmatic or strategic about-face in other respects. In any case, the push of the center parties toward cooperation with the LDP and the threat of isolation for the JSP make the tendency in the Japanese party system in the balance of power period centripetal—toward the dominant party.

Internal-External Dilemmas of Dominant Parties

A possible third relevant variable must be considered when accounting for the different behaviors of dominant parties in Japan and Sweden during the stages of decline and balance of power. This concerns the relative abilities of different types of parties to adapt to changing circumstances owing to the nature of their power structure and organization. The literature on party organization distinguishes between parties originating in parliament, in which parliamentary leadership is dominant and which are oriented toward maximizing electoral success, versus parties originating in mass organization, with party cadres dominant and which are oriented toward internal party democracy.[28]

The former can more easily and quickly adapt their strategies toward changes in electoral preferences and other parties' strategies than the latter. Mass parties must cater to their party activists' demands, which can differ substantially from voters' and leaders' preferences.[29] In other words, mass parties face a greater internal-external dilemma[30] in adapting than parliamentary parties.

The LDP is a clear case of a parliamentary party dominated by its parliamentary leadership in which the preferences of party activists play a minor role in policy making.[31] Parliamentary leaders also have a direct incentive to respond to threats to the party's electoral success. Therefore, the LDP may have had both the incentive and the capability first to respond in its declining period to the undermining of its local support by the pollution and welfare issues and then quickly to reassess and implement a strategy of adaptation and compromise with the opposition parties in the balance of

28. For example, Duverger, *Political Parties;* and the discussion and references in William E. Wright, "Comparative Party Models: Rational-Efficient and Party Democracy," in Wright, ed., *A Comparative Study of Party Organizations* (Columbus, Ohio: Charles E. Merrill, 1971), pp. 17–54.

29. Jon Pierre, *Partikongresser Och Regeringspolitik* (Lund, Sweden: Kommunfakta Förlag, 1986).

30. Terry E. MacDougall, "Asukata Ichio and Some Dilemmas of Socialist Leadership in Japan," in MacDougall, ed., *Political Leadership in Contemporary Japan* (Ann Arbor: Center for Japanese Studies, Michigan Papers in Japanese Studies, No. 1, 1982), esp. pp. 69–84.

31. See, for example, Haruhiro Fukui, *Party in Power: The Japanese Liberal Democrats and Policymaking* (Berkeley and Los Angeles: University of California Press, 1970), esp. chap. 4.

power period. The "creative conservatism" of the LDP[32] in responding to the electorate on a few grass-roots issues in the declining period, and then more fundamentally on core identity issues during the balance of power period, in other words, was made possible in part by the nature of its party organization.

The SAP, on the other hand, is a mass party. Although in ordinary times the leadership may have a fair degree of autonomy in setting parliamentary strategy (as in the period of decline), a study of the SAP in the earlier postwar era indicates that during times of crisis, the party leadership was more likely to respond to internal demands of party cadres.[33] Thus, during the balance of power period, the party leaders may have faced greater pressure not to compromise further with the opposition parties on the core issues defining the party's identity than they had already done in the period of decline. Indeed, at a party congress in 1975 at the height of the balance of power period, the party adopted a new program emphasizing economic democracy more strongly than before.[34] Rather than ideology per se determining dominant-party behavior, party organization may be a more relevant explanatory variable.

Speculation on Dominant Parties and the Loss of Power

Can we also link the different parliamentary voting patterns in Japan and Sweden to the fate of the dominant parties following the balance of power period to explain why the LDP retained power and the SAP did not? The explanation for these outcomes is very complicated and involves the electoral system, voting behavior, social coalitions (see the chapter by Muramatsu and Krauss in this volume), and many other factors. To the extent that the parties' strategies in the previous periods may have contributed to these outcomes, however, we may speculate on the links.

In the period of decline, the SAP immediately moved to compromise widely with the opposition parties, even on core ideological issues. By inviting the opposition parties' participation in policy making at this early stage, it may have prematurely and unintentionally legitimized their policies, and thus each opposition party as a potential governing party, and blurred its own image. This process continued in the period of balance of power, but the SAP then attempted to backtrack on the core issues dividing it from the opposition parties and reassert its identity. This partial and belated turnabout could not undo the legitimation of the opposition parties as potential

32. T. J. Pempel, *Policy and Politics in Japan: Creative Conservatism* (Philadelphia: Temple University Press, 1982).
33. Pierre, *Partikongresser Och Regeringspolitik.*
34. Ibid.; also Nils Elvander, *Skandinavisk arbetarrörelse* (Stockholm: Liber Förlag, 1980).

governing parties and may have reinforced their movement toward coalition with each other.

In the period of decline, the LDP's strategy did not involve legitimation of the opposition parties' core issues against the dominant party. Faced with decline, it maintained its core profile against the opposition parties, even while responding to pressure from the mass electorate on the environment and welfare.[35] With further decline, it quickly did an about-face and compromised even the basic issues historically dividing it from the opposition. Accommodation with the opposition parties could be portrayed more as responding to necessity than as legitimation of opposition parties and also as the responsible program of a governing party concerned with continuing to operate government smoothly. The strategy of maintaining identity followed by pragmatic adjustment to changing circumstances may have been more successful vis-à-vis the voters than one of prematurely legitimizing the opposition's role in policy making and then, confusingly, attempting to reassert party identity when it lost further strength.

The routes to maintaining dominance or final decline need not only be the simple ones of dominant-party flexibility and opposition-party rigidity, or dominant-party rigidity and opposition flexibility, respectively. Continued dominance or decline may also result from a process of passing through stages of mutual cooperation and polarization, depending on the sequence of these outcomes and the context in which they occur.

The maintenance of dominance, as Tarrow argues in this volume, requires flexibility and compromise. Our study indicates that, in addition, the impact of the timing and sequence of that flexibility on voters' expectations for a dominant party's behavior must also be considered and a rational coalition strategy suited to the nature of the party system in which it operates must be devised.

---

35. These compromises on environmental and welfare issues also may have played an important role in setting the stage for compromises on a wider range and more core issues in the equal power period. The LDP's incorporation of environmental protection and more welfare into its governing program and its compromises in parliament on these issues helped pave the way for coalitions with the DSP and CGP in local executive elections. These, in turn, probably smoothed the way for the broader and deeper agreements between the LDP and these two parties in the nearly equal power period.

8. Israel under Labor and the Likud: The Role of Dominance Considered

MYRON J. ARONOFF

In this essay I explore the role that single-party dominance has played in the development of the Israeli political system from its origins in the prestate period to the present.[1] Since the term *dominant party system* was first coined by Duverger in 1951 it has received sporadic and conflicting treatment by scholars. For example, Arian and Barnes claim that "the dominant party system is *sui generis*,"[2] and Sartori argues that the concept "establishes neither a *class* nor a *type* of party system."[3]

Scholars have also differed in their assessment of whether Israel qualifies as a dominant party system. Sartori, who prefers the term *predominant party systems*, insists that the predominant party must receive an absolute majority except in countries that abide by a less than absolute majority principle. On this basis he disqualifies Israel as a predominant party system.

I am grateful to the Joint Committee on the Near and Middle East of the American Council of Learned Societies and the Social Science Research Council, which awarded me a grant from funds provided by the National Endowment for the Humanities and the Ford Foundation, and to Rutgers—the State University of New Jersey—which awarded me a Faculty Academic Study Program leave and grant that enabled me to conduct research in Israel during 1982–83. This essay is based on that and previous research in Israel over the past twenty years. I also profited greatly from the conferences on one-party dominant democracies organized by T. J. Pempel at Cornell University and Oxford University from funds provided by the Social Science Research Council. I thank T. J. Pempel for his helpful comments on an earlier draft. This essay is adapted, by permission of Transaction Publishers, from *Israeli Visions and Dimensions* by Myron J. Aronoff. Copyright © 1989 by Transaction Publishers.

1. Although a single case study, my analysis has been informed by an ongoing dialogue with colleagues working on Japanese, Swedish, and Italian politics whose work appears in this volume. Consequently this collaborative and comparative perspective has influenced my own analysis even though the comparisons are not generally made explicit.

2. Asher Arian and Samuel Barnes, "The Dominant Party System: A Neglected Model of Democratic Stability," *Journal of Politics* 36; no. 3 (1974): 592.

3. Giovanni Sartori, *Parties and Party Systems*, vol. 1 (London: Cambridge University Press, 1976), p. 199.

Blondel[4] and Arian and Barnes,[5] among others, have cited Israel under the Israel Labor party as a classic example of a dominant party system.

The case of Labor in Israel illustrates how political dominance can be established without acquiring an absolute majority in the legislature. Labor had more than twice the parliamentary representation of its nearest rival during most of the period in which it dominated the political system. Various factors precluded the formation of a viable coalition without the participation of Labor. Consequently, Labor held the key portfolios that controlled the overwhelming majority of the national budgets.[6] Almost all experts on Israeli politics agree that Labor was a dominant party during the peak of its power. But they disagree about whether the Likud succeeded in establishing dominance during its briefer rule. I shall discuss this controversy below.

Duverger posits two important aspects of domination—political and ideological (or cultural). He defines a dominant party as

> a party larger than any other, which heads the list and clearly out-distances its rivals over a certain period of time. . . . *A party is dominant when it is identified with an epoch;* when its doctrines, ideas, methods, its style . . . coincide with those of the epoch. . . . Domination is a question of influence rather than strength; it is also linked with belief. A dominant party is that which public opinion *believes* to be dominant. . . . Even the enemies of the dominant party, even citizens who refuse to give it their vote, acknowledge its superior status and its influence; they deplore it but admit it.[7]

Duverger adapted his notion from the concept of a "dominant doctrine" in the history of ideas. Ideological dominance need not be confined to situations in which an absolute majority of voters adhere to the official party ideology. If that were the case, the phenomenon would be rare indeed. Even at the peak of its power Labor would not have qualified by such a stringent definition of dominance. Duverger suggests that dominance is achieved through the identification of a party and its leaders with an epoch. One way this is accomplished, as the Israeli case vividly illustrates, is when they play a crucial role in the creation of the society and of the polity.

Duverger is vague about the nature of the relationship between the ideological and political dimensions of domination. He implies that they are covariant. To understand the process by which dominance is established, maintained, and lost, it is essential to explicate more precisely the nature of

4. Jean Blondel, *An Introduction to Comparative Government* (New York: Praeger, 1969).
5. Arian and Barnes, "Dominant Party System."
6. David Nachmias, "A Note on Coalition Payoffs in a Dominant Party System," *Political Studies* 21 (1973): 301–5.
7. Maurice Duverger, *Political Parties: Their Organization and Activity in the Modern State,* trans. Barbara North and Robert North with a foreword by D. W. Brogan (London: Methuen, 1967), pp. 308–9; emphasis added. Originally published in French as *Les partis politiques* (Paris: Armond Colin, 1951).

the relationship between the political and cultural dimensions. In so doing I employ an approach that views culture as a humanly constructed web of symbolic themes (portrayed through myths and rituals) providing the sense of common orientation and meaning essential for facilitating orderly social relations.[8] Culture is produced out of the dialectical relations between the spontaneous invention of shared meanings in significant social contexts and their reification as conventional cultural traditions. These cultural traditions "are never *absolutely* conventionalized, in the sense of being identical for all who share them; they are always loose-ended, incompletely shared, in process of change."[9]

Society is a negotiated order between groups with competing interests. The imperfect conventionalization of culture enables groups competing for status and power to engage in the continual invention and interpretation of cultural tradition in their effort to legitimate their positions. In so doing they attempt to mold wider collective perceptions to conform with their own visions by imposing their ideological interpretations on the collectivity. The relationship between the dimensions of domination need to be understood in terms of this dialectical tension.

The Origins of Labor Dominance

Identification with an Epoch

The dominance of the labor movement in Israel was established during the crisis of the early stages of nation building in the 1920s through the 1930s. Its main leaders, party,[10] and affiliated institutions (e.g., the kibbutzim and the Histadrut—Labor Federation) became identified with the

8. For a more extensive discussion of the conceptual approach I employ see Myron Aronoff, "Ideology and Interest: The Dialectics of Politics," in Myron J. Aronoff, ed., *Ideology and Interest: The Dialectics of Politics, Political Anthropology*, vol. 1 (New Brunswick, N.J.: Transaction, 1980); "Civil Religion in Israel," *Royal Anthropological Institute News* 44 (1981): 2–6; and "Conceptualizing the Role of Culture in Political Change," in Myron J. Aronoff, ed., *Culture and Political Change, Political Anthropology*, vol. 2 (New Brunswick, N.J.: Transaction, 1982).

9. Roy Wagner, *The Invention of Culture*, rev. ed. (Chicago: University of Chicago Press, 1981).

10. The main labor parties underwent several splits and mergers over the years, which resulted in name changes. Mapai was the dominant labor party from 1930 until 1968 when the Israel Labor party was formed by the merger of Mapai with Achdut Ha'avoda and Rafi. The best study of Mapai is Peter Y. Medding, *Mapai in Israel* (Cambridge: Cambridge University Press, 1972). For a detailed analysis of the Israel Labor party from its formation in 1968 to the eve of its defeat in 1977 see Myron J. Aronoff, *Power and Ritual in the Israel Labor Party* (Amsterdam: Van Gorcum, 1979). Analyses of the reasons for Labor's defeat can be found in Aronoff, "The Decline of the Israel Labor Party: Causes and Significance," in Howard R. Penniman, ed., *Israel at the Polls: The Knesset Elections—1977* (Washington, D.C.: American Enterprise Institute, 1979), and of Labor in the opposition in Aronoff, "The Labor Party in Opposition," in Robert O. Freedman, ed., *Israel in the Begin Era* (New York: Praeger, 1986), pp. 76–101.

heroic epoch of pioneering and the successful struggle for national independence. The two most important scholarly studies of the establishment of
labor dominance during this period focus primarily on one aspect of dominance and tend to underemphasize the importance of the other aspect. Yosef
Gorni emphasized the acquisition of ideological dominance by the party
through its exceptional leaders, who gained legitimacy because they were
considered to be the pioneering vanguard of Zionism.[11] They exemplified
the dominant values of the time, *chalutziut* (Zionist pioneering), voluntarism, and egalitarianism. They displayed sufficient flexibility to incorporate
a multiplicity of viewpoints as the party co-opted more groups, while projecting a coherent vision of national goals and aspirations.

Yonathan Shapiro analyzed the process through which labor gained political dominance by creating a number of original sociopolitical institutions
through which it mobilized power.[12] The most important of these was the
Histadrut, established in 1920. The Histadrut, a unique labor federation
that became a virtual state within a state in the period before independence,
played a crucial role in the creation and in shaping the character of the
present state of Israel.

It is possible to comprehend the success of labor in establishing its dominance by explicating the interactive effect of the ideological-cultural and the
political-institutional levels of dominance. They were not merely complementary. Each was essential for the success of the other. For example, the
respect which the labor leaders received from the nonsocialist middle-class
leadership of the World Zionist Organization (WZO) derived from their
perception of the labor Zionists as the most active and creative force in
settling immigrants and reclaiming (literally and figuratively) the land of
Israel. Therefore, the WZO heavily subsidized the labor movement's colonization efforts and its urban projects through the Histadrut. Through these
resources labor was able to mobilize greater political support by providing a
wide range of services to the new settlers who became clients of the party,
and at the same time labor leaders refurbished their image as the vanguard
of pioneering Zionism.

Conversely, the large and amorphous middle-class General Zionists
lacked charismatic leadership and a coherent ideology with a unifying myth,
and they failed to build their own institutions. The Revisionist movement,
which was founded in 1925, had a charismatic leader and an ideology with
a central myth, but it failed miserably to develop strong and viable institutions. The organizational failure in the early period can be largely attributed
to strategic errors of the leader, Ze'ev Vladimir Jabotinsky. As the sworn
enemies of the Histadrut, the Revisionists could not compete for a share of

11. Yoseph Gorni, *Achdut Ha'avoda, 1919–1930: The Ideological Principles and the Political System* (in Hebrew) (Ramat Gan: Hakibbutz Hameuchad Publishing House, 1973).
12. Yonathan Shapiro, *The Formative Years of the Israeli Labor Party*, Sage Studies in
Twentieth Century History, vol. 4 (Beverly Hills: Sage, 1976).

the valuable patronage of this organization. Jabotinsky focused his primary political activity on central and eastern Europe rather than Palestine so little effort was made to develop strong organizational bases in the Yishuv (the Jewish community in Palestine). His primary approach was ideological rather than organizational. His disciple and successor, Menachem Begin, made a similar strategic error in focusing almost exclusively on ideology and ignoring the building of strong institutional bases of support. Jabotinsky's decision to split away from the World Zionist Organization and to form his own New Zionist Organization in 1935 enabled Labor to gain a dominant position in the executive of the WZO and thereby to gain control of the valuable resources which accrued from this organization.

Capturing the Political Center

One of the more effective means through which labor established its dominant position was through the strategic formation of coalitions which effectively made it the indispensable partner for any viable ruling coalition. Although ostensibly a socialist party, under David Ben-Gurion's leadership labor staked its claim as the main national party in the political center. He declared his readiness to form a coalition with any legitimate Zionist party excluding the Communist party and the nationalist Herut (the political offspring of the Revisionist movement). Ben-Gurion made a historic pact with the National Religious party which brought it into every government formed by labor. By balancing coalitions with socialist parties to its left and liberal and conservative parties to its right, labor ensured its dominance and centrality. The development of a strong party machine, the bosses of which were completely loyal to Ben-Gurion, gave the prime minister the flexibility to accomplish this.

Another important tactic was the delegitimation of labor's rivals. These tactics worked with varying success at different periods with different parties. The parties of the radical left were stigmatized as anti-Zionist and/or having loyalties beyond national ones, and the rightist Herut was declared to be irresponsible and beyond the pale of legitimate Zionist politics because of its dissident activities during the war of independence and the irresponsible behavior of some of its main leaders thereafter.[13]

Loading the Dice

Seymour M. Lipset and Stein Rokkan have shown that the mobilization of power in the crucial formative period of a political system determines its development for many years thereafter.[14] James S. Coleman, reanalyzing a

13. For a more detailed discussion see Myron J. Aronoff, *Israeli Visions and Divisions* (New Brunswick, N.J.: Transaction, 1989), especially chap. 2.

14. Seymour M. Lipset and Stein Rokkan, eds., *Party System and Voters Alignment* (New York: Free Press, 1967).

large number of studies of community power, has concluded that the manner in which conflicts are resolved in the early stages of the formation of a community "loads the dice" and establishes patterns of conflict resolution which last long after the original issues have been forgotten.[15] My study of a new town illustrated such a case in an Israeli context.[16] Shapiro, following Lipset and Rokkan, argues that the leading and dominant role played by labor in the formative stages of the crystallization of the Israeli political system gave it a unique advantage which it successfully exploited to maintain a dominant position for nearly fifty years.[17]

The Maintenance of Labor Dominance

The consolidation of Labor dominance came in the period following independence in 1948 with the institutionalization of the bureaucratic agencies of the state. During the postindependence period, the character of both the ideological and the political dominance of Labor was significantly adapted to the changing social, economic, cultural, and political conditions. Many of the major services that had been provided by voluntary agencies (such as the Histadrut) before independence were transferred to the state bureaucracy after independence. The paramilitary organizations of the various political movements were abolished by the provisional government in one of its first acts, and the Israel Defense Forces (Zahal) were created. In the ensuing years the labor exchange was transferred from the Histadrut to the Ministry of Labor, and the separate school systems controlled by the political movements were abolished and a state educational system was established which provided for secular and religious options. The relinquishing by the Histadrut of the socialist-Zionist school system reflected a lengthy process whereby Labor, under Ben-Gurion's leadership, had deemphasized its socialist ideological orientation in favor of a stronger emphasis on nationalism.

David Ben-Gurion articulated a new ideology of *mamlachtiut* (statism), which asserted that the state and its agencies, for example, the army, had taken over the role of pioneering vanguard from the prestate voluntary agencies. This ideology gave legitimacy to the transfer of important functions from the Histadrut to the state. It also appealed to a large constituency of masses of new immigrants who were not particularly attracted by Labor's pragmatic socialism. Whereas the new myths and ceremonies which accompanied the advent of *mamlachtiut* appealed to larger numbers, those attracted tended to be less fervent in their support than those who had been

15. James S. Coleman, *Community Conflict* (New York: Free Press for the Bureau of Applied Social Research, Columbia University, 1957).
16. Myron J. Aronoff, *Frontiertown: The Politics of Community Building in Israel* (Manchester: Manchester University Press, 1974).
17. Shapiro, *Formative Years of the Israeli Labor Party*.

committed to socialist-Zionism. Statism became the ideology through which Labor institutionalized its authority and attempted to socialize the new immigrants with this new interpretation of Zionist civil religion.[18]

Israel underwent a tremendous growth in population through immigration. The dynamic growth and diversification of the economy, including a stronger private sector, led to a commensurate growth and increasing complexity of government. An enormous state bureaucracy grew. Not only did the civil service grow, but the party's bureaucracy expanded with the growth of urban machines and a vast patronage system aimed at the mobilization of the immigrants.

Challenges Successfully Met

Labor maintained its dominant position for as long as it did because it was relatively successful in meeting the major challenges which Israel faced in its first three decades: defense against hostile neighbors, the absorption of masses of immigrants, and the need for economic growth. From the outset Israel's physical existence was challenged, and the leading role which Labor's leaders played in the successful defense of the nation has been one of the most important bases of their authority.[19] It was not until the shock of the surprise attack on Yom Kippur 1973 (termed the "earthquake" in the media) and the protest movements that followed that the taken-for-granted assumption of Labor's leadership of the nation and its defense establishment was seriously called into question on a significant scale.

Labor also derived considerable authority from its leading role in the integration of the survivors of the Holocaust from Europe and hundreds of thousands of Jews from Islamic countries of North Africa and the Middle East. The young nation faced an unprecedented challenge of crisis proportions in more than doubling its population in the first few years of its existence. During a period of serious economic hardship, the needs for housing, education, and welfare of these immigrants—a large proportion of whom were indigent—severely taxed the resources of the nation. Even with the considerable help of Jews abroad and foreign nations, the "ingathering of the exiles," which constituted a virtual raison d'être for the creation of the state, was a formidable accomplishment. Largely in response to this challenge, the party developed in directions which ultimately undermined its dominant position in the society.

18. For a fascinating discussion of the various versions of Zionist civil religion that dominated or nearly did so in different periods, see Charles Liebman and Eliezer Don-Yehiya, "The Dilemma of Reconciling Traditional Culture and Political Needs: Civil Religion in Israel," in Myron J. Aronoff, ed., Cross-Currents in Israeli Culture and Politics, Political Anthropology, vol. 4 (New Brunswick, N.J.: Transaction, 1984).

19. For a perceptive analysis of the relation between the military and politics in Israel, see Yoram Peri, Between Battles and Ballots: Israeli Military and Politics (Cambridge: Cambridge University Press, 1983).

As with the previous examples of the successful meeting of challenges, Labor's success in helping to achieve high rates of economic growth eventually contributed to the undermining of its dominance. As the economy became healthier and more sophisticated with high rates of employment, the dependence of citizens on the patronage provided by the government and through the party was drastically reduced. Skills and education rather than party identification became far more important in gaining satisfactory employment. The second and third generations at both ends of the economic ladder became disenchanted with Labor for different reasons.

The Loss of Labor Dominance

Duverger wrote "Domination takes the zest from life. . . . The dominant party wears itself out in office, it loses its vigour . . . every domination bears within itself the seeds of its own destruction."[20] Sometimes the successes of a dominant party can contribute to the eventual undermining of its dominance. Just as the legitimacy derived from an ideology which was central to the political culture paved the way for the political dominance of Labor, the erosion of the authority provided by ideological legitimacy undermined its political dominance. Charles Liebman and Eliezer Don-Yehiya have speculated that one of the important factors which is likely to have contributed to the decline of statism was the successful building of the nation: "As time passed the existence of the state no longer evoked such wonder."[21] Similarly, in *A Perfect Peace,* Amos Oz observed: "Once, long ago, there was a time when all things done here were done with devotion, even with a kind of ecstasy, sometimes with enormous self-sacrifice. But then the bold dreams came true."[22]

A woman of the pioneering generation who had been one of the founders of her kibbutz once confided to me: "I sometimes have to pinch myself to make sure that I am not dreaming that we actually have our own Jewish state!" For her, the creation of the state of Israel is the fulfillment of a dream, the realization of a vision which her children take very much for granted.[23] Both the realization of the dream and the sense that the reality fell short of the ideal further contributed to the end of the pioneering epoch with which Labor had been identified and from which it derived its legitimacy. "It is almost as if the very successes of the Zionist dream . . . resulted

20. Duverger, *Political Parties,* p. 312.
21. Liebman and Don-Yehiya, *Civil Religion in Israel* (Berkeley and Los Angeles: University of California Press, 1983), p. 123.
22. Amos Oz, *A Perfect Peace,* trans. Hillel Halkin (New York: Penguin, 1985), p. 177.
23. Peter Berger and Thomas Luckmann, *The Social Construction of Reality* (London: George Allen & Unwin, 1966), have called attention to the intrinsic problem involved in the transmission of culture from one generation to another. See Oz, *Perfect Peace,* for an excellent literary illustration of the same point applied to Israel.

in disillusionment because the society had somehow fallen short of its self-proclaimed utopian vision of being such a moral example for the world."[24]

Challenges Unsuccessfully Met

One area in which Labor conspicuously failed was in the socialization of succeeding generations. Studies of voting behavior indicate that Labor lost the political support of the younger generations. In most cases it failed to instill the values and ideals for which the party stood. The establishment of a Jewish Consciousness Program in the secular public schools in 1957 to counter the attraction of Canaanism (a nativist ideology which stressed the need to build a Hebrew culture without links to the Diaspora) for the youth is identified by Liebman and Don-Yehiya with the decline of statism.[25]

In other cases, though they succeeded in instilling the ideals of the party, the leaders lost the support of the youth because their actions and policies failed to live up to these ideals. Such was the case with the National Religious party (NRP), which, through its network of religious schools, succeeded in socializing younger generations who are far more nationalistic, religiously observant, and self-confident than the preceding generation. Consequently, they deserted the NRP in large numbers for the more militant Gush Emunim (Bloc of the Faithful), the political parties closest to it, Morasha, Techiya, and the Likud.[26] The leaders of the younger generation who remained in the NRP and rose to positions of power in it were instrumental in shifting the party's coalition alliance from Labor to the Likud. The failure of Labor to retain the traditional alliance with the NRP, or to replace it with an equally reliable alternative, was another challenge unsuccessfully met which contributed to its downfall.

Oligarchic tendencies that were latent from the formative years became increasingly manifest with the development of a dominant machine within the dominant party. The machine expanded as a response to the development of elaborate patronage networks designed to mobilize new immigrants. A system of indirect elections to party and Histadrut institutions through the use of appointments committees guaranteed elite domination of these institutions.

In these institutions, groups most supportive of the elite were overrepresented and other groups were underrepresented. As they became mere rubber stamps for decisions made informally by the elite, democratic pro-

24. Myron J. Aronoff, "Political Polarization: Contradictory Interpretations of Israeli Reality," in Aronoff, ed., *Cross-Currents in Israeli Culture and Politics*, 4:20.
25. Liebman and Don-Yehiya, *Civil Religion in Israel*, p. 123.
26. For more detailed discussion see Aronoff, *Israeli Visions and Divisions*, chap. 4, and the essays in David Newman, ed., *The Impact of Gush Emunim* (London: Croom Helm, 1985). The Knesset representation of the NRP declined from twelve in 1977 to six in 1981 to four in 1984. See Aronoff, "Significant Trends in Israeli Politics," in Bernard Reich and Gershon Kieval, eds., *Israel Faces the Future* (New York: Praeger, 1986), pp. 29–40.

cedures and the party constitution were increasingly put aside for political expediency. Criticism of the elite and its policies was suppressed, and recruitment and mobility to higher levels became dependent on loyalty to the elite rather than the display of independence and initiative.

The erosion of the party's responsiveness to the demands of the public coincided with a growing arrogance of the top national leaders, who became preoccupied with the perpetuation of their rule. As a result, progressively widespread feelings of political inefficacy developed among the secondary national leaders, the local leadership, and the rank-and-file membership. This disaffection contributed directly to the erosion of Labor's legitimacy and dominance.[27]

Among the alienated groups which failed to gain sufficient access to the centers of power under Labor, the most politically important were the Jews who immigrated from the Middle East, particularly those from North Africa and their offspring. As Labor increasingly came to be perceived as the party of the European-born veteran elites and their descendents, the Eastern Jews increasingly identified with the antiestablishment leader of the opposition Likud, Menachem Begin.[28] The greater militancy and religiosity of Begin also attracted the religious voters, as they attracted the NRP (under the influence of the young leaders) as a coalition partner.

Whereas in the early years of independence Labor succeeded in denying legitimacy to its main opposition, Herut, over the years it became increasingly difficult, if not impossible, to do so.[29] Although Herut began altering its policies by the mid-1950s, it was not until the resignation of David Ben-Gurion in 1963 that major changes began to take place. The decision of Levi Eshkol, Ben-Gurion's successor as prime minister, to hold a state funeral for the reinterment of the remains of Ze'ev Vladimir Jabotinsky symbolized the beginning of a process that led to the inclusion of Herut (as part of the Gahal electoral alliance with the Liberals) in the government of national unity established during the crisis preceding the war in June 1967. The participation of Menachem Begin and his colleagues in the government until their resignations in August 1970 firmly established their legitimacy and paved the way for their ascension to power in 1977.

Probably the greatest challenge which Labor failed to meet was the crisis of identity experienced by many Israelis. The sense of Jewish isolation which reemerged as symbolic of the Holocaust gained ascendancy in the late

27. Medding, *Mapai in Israel*, and Aronoff, *Power and Ritual in the Israeli Labor Party*, analyze this process in different periods and come to opposite conclusions regarding the degree of internal party democracy in Labor and the responsiveness of the party to societal demands.

28. For an excellent analysis of the appeal of the Likud to the Eastern Jews see Arnold Lewis, "Ethnic Politics and the Foreign Policy Debate in Israel," in Aronoff, ed., *Cross-Currents in Israeli Culture and Politics,* 4:25–38.

29. Ariel Levite and Sidney Tarrow, "The Legitimation of Excluded Parties in Dominant Party Systems: A Comparison of Israel and Italy," *Comparative Politics* 15 (1983): 295–327, analyze the rehabilitation of Herut, and Aronoff, *Israeli Visions and Divisions,* discusses the consequences for the more recent polarization of Israeli politics.

1950s, was heightened during the period immediately preceding the war of June 1967, and reached a peak during the war of October 1973. The process that led to a crisis of legitimacy for Labor and the political system in general was precipitated by the consequences of Israel's military victory in 1967 and was brought to a head by the widespread political disillusionment and protests which resulted from the shock of the surprise attack and the conduct of the war in its initial stages in October 1973.

Israel's lightning victory in the Six-Day War unleashed a number of different processes which had significant political repercussions. First, it ended the serious economic recession and unemployment. Although the pioneering values of voluntarism and egalitarianism had long ceased to have salience for most of the population, after 1967 the vast majority of even loyal Labor supporters ceased to pay lip service to them. Conspicuous consumption and rampant materialism typified what some came to term the Americanization of Israel.

The speed of Israel's victory, the unification of Jerusalem (including the Western Wall of the ancient temple), and the "liberation" of the areas on the West Bank of the Jordan, which had been the heartland of Jewish settlement in biblical times (including the holiest shrines in Jewish tradition), were felt by many to have been evidence of divine intervention and inspired new forms of nationalism and religious messianism. These movements offered an alternative to what they termed the moral bankruptcy of Labor's ideology of statism and the rampant materialism, which they blamed on Labor's leadership.

The conquest of the new territories posed especially significant problems for Labor as it created opportunities for the opposition (which at the time participated in the government). The government, headed by Prime Minister Levi Eshkol, decided on June 19, 1967, that in exchange for peace it was willing to withdraw to the former international borders with Egypt and Syria and would negotiate the future of the West Bank, Gaza, and the problem of the Palestinians. By August it had already modified its position.[30] In their September meeting in Khartoum the Arab heads of state explicitly articulated their policy of refusal to negotiate with Israel, to recognize the Jewish state, or to make peace with it.

The combination of pressures created by the refusal of the Arab states to negotiate, and the pressures from nationalist and religious groups to annex the territories occupied during the war, pushed the Labor-led government to increasingly tougher stands, which conflicted with many of the liberal, humanistic values held by Eshkol and other Labor leaders, who felt uncomfortable in their new roles as occupiers. With the succession of Golda Meir after the death of Eshkol, Labor moved toward more militant policies, thereby blurring the differences between it and the opposition. Rather than

30. Yitzhak Rabin, *The Rabin Memoirs* (Boston: Little, Brown, 1979), p. 130.

being apologetic about its policies, the opposition had a long-standing strong position on the territories, which had been anachronistic until Israel's victory in 1967.

Labor failed adequately to socialize a new generation of supporters and leaders, to maintain responsive party institutions, truly to integrate the Eastern Jews, to maintain its historic coalition partnership with the NRP, to prevent the main nationalist opposition from gaining legitimacy, and to prevent or resolve the crisis of identity which emerged between the late 1960s and the mid-1970s. Yet when Labor lost the 1977 election and the Likud formed a coalition government, most of the public, politicians, and pundits were shocked. Perhaps one of the most telling illustrations of Labor's dominance is that so few people had realized that the era of Labor suzerainty was over until its electoral defeat. Even then, many predicted it would be back in power in 1981, and indeed the polls showed a substantial lead for Labor until shortly before the election.

After the Likud formed its second government in 1984, it was clear to all that Labor would not accomplish what the Swedish socialists had done—to reestablish their dominant position after a parliamentary defeat. The ability of other dominant parties to revitalize and maintain their dominance (most conspicuously the Japanese Liberal Democratic party) suggests that there was nothing inevitable about the decline of Labor. Rather, most of the party's failures can be attributed to a failure of the leadership to adapt the party and its ideology to changing conditions.

The Likud's Attempt to Attain Dominance

Upon assuming the mantle of leadership of the nation, the leaders of the Likud were cautious and attempted to emphasize continuity rather than a radical break with past Labor rule. Partly in response to public anxiety created by the transition, and partly because of a lack of qualified and experienced personnel to staff many positions, the Likud government left many key Labor-appointed officials and civil servants in place. Menachem Begin even chose the former Labor defense minister, Moshe Dayan, to serve as his first foreign minister. The most significant accomplishment of the first Likud government, the peace treaty between Israel and Egypt, gained greater parliamentary support from Labor than it did from the Likud members of the Knesset.

The resignations of the most moderate members of the government, Dayan in October 1979 and Defense Minister Ezer Weizman in May 1980 (both key figures in the successful negotiation of the peace treaty with Egypt), changed the character of the government. Among other things, the government began actively to use its patronage to solidify and broaden its base of support, thereby initiating a new politicization of civil service similar to the earlier days of statehood. But because of its late start, the relatively limited number of qualified personnel loyal to the party, and the short duration of its rule, the Likud never succeeded in building institutional bases of support that were at all comparable to those of Labor at the height of its power.

The 1981 election was the most violent and polarized in recent history. It was the first Israeli election in which the outcome was not presumed to be known in advance. Early polls indicating an unprecedented Labor landslide victory produced overconfidence in the Labor ranks and high anxiety in the ranks of the Likud. Begin was particularly anxious for an additional term so that he could implement his plans for the massive Jewish settlement of Judea and Samaria, the biblical names the Likud government substituted for the area previously called by many the West Bank, the occupied territories, or simply the territories. Popular acceptance of these terms was a prelude to gaining popular acceptance of the government's settlement policies. If the territories were perceived to be the biblical heartland of the Jewish people, rather than occupied territories, the legitimacy of the government and its settlement policies would be ensured.

The Likud's electoral tactics, especially Begin's rhetoric, played an important role in the renewal of political polarization and the escalation of violence. "Begin, a master of rhetorical skills, successfully articulated the feelings of those who had been excluded from the main centers of power and from the centers of social, cultural, and ideological acceptability (or legitimacy in some cases) during Labor's long reign—his own followers from the Revisionists and Herut, the Oriental or Eastern Jews, and to a certain extent the religious Jews."[31]

The pursuit of controversial policies such as the extended war in Lebanon with its political as well as military goals provoked widespread opposition. The second Likud government, dominated by Begin, Foreign Minister Yitzhak Shamir, and Defense Minister Arielle "Arik" Sharon, attacked its critics as traitors, fifth columnists, and supporters of the Palestine Liberation Organization (PLO). These attempts to delegitimize the opposition were part of a concerted Likud effort to establish political and ideological dominance.

Having overcome the pariah image which had characterized them in the earlier period, Begin and others in his movement attempted to eliminate the last vestiges of Labor's ideological legitimacy and to establish the Likud's ideological hegemony. The government "systematically utilized the state agencies to propagate the Likud's heroes, myths, and interpretations of both history and of present realities, and to incorporate them into the framework of the national political culture."[32]

31. Aronoff, "Political Polarization," p. 11.
32. Aronoff, "Significant Trends in Israeli Politics," p. 105.

The nearly year-long events memorializing Ze'ev Vladimir Jabotinsky elevated the ideological guru of the Revisionist movement (and of Herut) to the status of one of the nation's great heroes. Unlike the leaders of Labor, who had denigrated the importance of symbols and ceremonies, Jabotinsky placed great importance on ritual. His disciple Menachem Begin used the occasion of the hundredth anniversary of Jabotinsky's birth to launch an unprecedented array of activities ranging from symposia and dissertation prizes in all universities to special programs in the schools, army units, and the media.[33] Among other things, "the celebration of Jabotinsky's birthday symbolized the rebirth of Revisionism through Herut's dominance in the Likud-led government after the symbolic death of its unusually extended period in the political wilderness."[34]

Similar events and ceremonies were designed to enshrine the heroes and martyrs of the dissident underground movements—the Irgun Zvai Leumi (IZL) and Lechi. They aimed at correcting what the government perceived to be the injustice of their having been ignored or maligned by the former Labor establishment. "Prime Minister Begin was particularly sensitive since he had been the object of Ben-Gurion's strategy of projecting Jabotinsky and Begin, Revisionism and Herut, IZL and Lechi, as pariahs beyond the pale of legitimate Zionism."[35]

The acceptance of a movement's heroes is a first step in accepting its values. One of the means by which the Likud government attempted to accomplish this was through the use of ceremonies commemorating historical figures whose heroic acts could be employed to provide meaningful guides to understanding current problems and dilemmas. The most elaborate of such ceremonies (costing approximately $250,000) was a state funeral held on May 11, 1982, in the Judean desert for the remains of what were reputedly the fighters and followers of Shimon Bar-Kochba, who led the second Jewish revolt against Rome in 132–35 A.D.

Although the bones had been discovered with artifacts in 1960, it was not until the Chief Ashkenazi Rabbi Shlomo Goren won the enthusiastic support of Prime Minister Begin that these remains were reinterred. One hundred fifty official guests, including the leading figures of the state and representatives of foreign governments, were flown by helicopter to the remote site near where the remains had been discovered.

The solemnity of the occasion was disrupted by a group of protesters wearing Roman togas and helmets, carrying spears, who charged, "You're making a laughingstock out of history." They also sang a Hannukah song

---

33. For a detailed examination of these cases, which were chosen from an analysis of twenty years of decisions of the Ministerial Committee on Symbols and Ceremonies, see Myron J. Aronoff, "Establishing Authority: The Memorialization of Jabotinsky and the Burial of the Bar-Kochba Bones in Israel under the Likud," in Myron J. Aronoff, ed., *The Frailty of Authority, Political Anthropology*, vol. 5 (New Brunswick, N.J.: Transaction, 1986).

34. Aronoff, "Establishing Authority," p. 114.

35. Aronoff, "Establishing Authority," p. 116.

about chasing darkness from the land as Rabbi Goren emerged from his helicopter before they were removed by police and soldiers. This parody of the state ceremony undermined the taken-for-granted seriousness of the event. It symbolized the widespread disagreement with the interpretation, articulated in Begin's eulogy at the funeral, which the government attempted to make of this important period and of the controversial figure of Shimon Bar-Kochba.

The Talmud refers to Bar-Kochba as a cruel, imperious leader and a false messiah, yet Begin portrayed him as a heroic freedom fighter. Critics of the interpretation of Begin and his government argued that Bar-Kochba waged an unrealistic policy that led directly to the decimation and exile of the Jewish people, and to make him a hero was tantamount to rejoicing in policies that led to national suicide.[36]

A passionate national debate ensued over the meaning of the Bar-Kochba revolt, which served as a metaphor for contemporary political choices facing the nation. This public debate, which involved prominent secular scholars, the prime minister, and the chief Ashkenazi rabbi (among others), highlighted the polarized interpretations of the Zionist vision which characterized the period. Yet, that such a diverse group of Israeli leaders seriously debated the significance and implications of events that took place two thousand years ago also indicates that they share an underlying Zionist/Israeli worldview which makes the debate over the meaning of such a root cultural paradigm both possible and significant. The challenge by respected national figures of the meanings and interpretations made by the government to explain the ceremonies is strong evidence that the Likud had failed to establish ideological dominance or cultural hegemony. I shall elaborate on this point below.

The Likud, even more than preceding Labor governments, used history and mythology to interpret contemporary political events, to gain ideological legitimacy, and to attempt to establish dominance. Its notion of Jewish statehood based on the biblical term *malkhut Yisrael* (Kingdom of Israel), stressing the sacred right of the Jewish people to the entire land of Israel, combined with a sense of Jewish isolation expressed in the biblical reference to Israel as "a nation that dwells alone," an emphasis on heroism and self-sacrifice, activism and adventurism were symbolically expressed in the burial of the Bar-Kochba bones. "The burial of the bones has deep resonance for religious Jews because it is necessary for the conservation of souls for the day of judgement. The burial site linked historical biblical rights to present political claims. The ritual associated mythical heroes to present leaders. It asserted historical continuity and justified present policies in terms of one interpretation of ancient history."[37]

36. The leading proponent of this position is Yhoshafat Harkabi, *The Bar Kochba Syndrome* (New York: Rossel Books, 1982).
37. Aronoff, "Establishing Authority," p. 126.

Although the Likud came to power as the representative of the formerly marginal elements in society, the nationalist-right, the Eastern Jews, and the religious, it did so through co-optation rather than incorporation of the latter two groups. For example, the government gave legitimacy, power, and resources to Gush Emunim (Bloc of the Faithful), the militant messianic settlement movement, and derived legitimacy and political support from it without actually gaining the affiliation of the Gush to the Likud. It gained the coalition support of the religious parties, not just through their ideological affinity, but by also paying a high price in portfolios, policy, and financial support for the independent religious institutions. None of these concessions substantially broadened the base of party support. Given the intense rivalry in Herut for succession to the top leadership position, factionalism has reached such a peak that the last party convention had to be disbanded because it deteriorated into anarchy. The proposed merger of the constituent units of the Likud has yet to take place. Menachem Begin made the same mistake as his mentor in relying too heavily on symbols and neglecting the vital organizational aspects of politics.

In addition, the Likud was in a much weaker coalition bargaining position than was Labor during the earlier period of its dominance. Whereas Labor had generally twice the parliamentary representation of its nearest rival (except in 1965 and 1973), the Likud led Labor by a narrow margin of eleven Knesset seats in 1977 and by only a single seat in 1981. This parliamentary balance severely handicapped the Likud's attempt to establish its dominance because its claims were forcefully resisted by approximately half of the members of parliament. Parliamentary representation is merely one dimension of dominance.

Evaluation of the Claim for a New Dominance

A strong element of mystical, messianic, nonrational eschatological politics that was a legacy of Revisionism in the Likud was reinforced with the co-optation of groups such as Gush Emunim into the new National Camp (as the Likud labeled itself in the 1984 election). Some scholars claimed that a new dominance had been established. Robert Paine identified the phenomenon as politics operating on totemic time.[38] Lily Weissbrod originally claimed that Religious New Zionism (or New Zionism), her term for the ideology of Gush Emunim, helped the Likud achieve dominance in the Begin era.[39] She suggested that the Likud moved to the political center of Israel by New Zionism becoming the dominant ideology. Weissbrod has since modi-

38. Robert Paine, "Israel and Totemic Time?" *Royal Anthropological Institute News*, December 1983.
39. Lily Weissbrod, "From Labour Zionism to New Zionism: Ideological Change in Israel," *Theory and Society* 10 (1981): 777–803.

fied her position on the dominance of the Likud and New Zionism by concluding that "no coherent power center has as yet crystallized that might be granted complete legitimacy."[40] She concludes that it is possible that no subsequent power center in Israel will ever attain the uncontested legitimacy and dominance which Labor achieved.

In their important pioneering work on Israeli political culture, Liebman and Don-Yehiya suggest: "The new civil religion reached a dominant position after 1967. The peak of its influence came with the Likud victory in 1977 (the Likud is more closely identified with the new civil religion than any other party). . . . Its goal was to unite and integrate the society around its conception of the Jewish tradition and the Jewish people."[41] The new civil religion is characterized by the penetration of religious symbolism in civic life.

Gary Schiff argues that "religion is and for the foreseeable future will continue to be the single most important political variable, social force, and operative ideology on the Israeli political scene." He contends that "there seems to be no viable counterideology to religion as a legitimating or motivating force within the polity today."[42]

The differences between the ideologies of Gush Emunim, Revisionism, folk or civil religion, and traditional Judaism are very significant. The national religious messianism of Gush Emunim is antithetical to the non-Zionist or even anti-Zionist interpretation of traditional Judaism of many of the orthodox Jews in Israel. The amorphous folk religiosity of even traditionalist leaders like Begin is by no means considered by the orthodox to be synonymous with, or an acceptable substitute for, their halachic (orthodox Jewish law) religious tradition. If there were a single new ideological form of Zionist civil religion it could not possibly combine at one and the same time Revisionism, national religious messianism, folk religion, and orthodox tradition.

The aforementioned scholars tend to use static approaches to political culture which fail to distinguish between the general symbolic framework of civil religion and the more specific ideological interpretations of different political movements. With the exception of Weissbrod, they fail to view dominance as a historically rare phenomenon requiring exceptional identification between a party, an ideological worldview, and an epoch in the formation or transformation of a political system.

The scholarly consensus regarding the earlier period of Labor dominance both reflected and helped reinforce the perception of Labor dominance. Most scholars identified with Labor's version of the Zionist vision and

40. Lily Weissbrod, "Protest and Dissidence in Israel," in Aronoff, ed., *Cross-Currents in Israeli Culture and Politics*, 4:66.
41. Liebman and Don-Yehiya, "The Dilemma of Reconciling Traditional Culture and Political Needs," p. 57.
42. Gary Schiff, "Post '84 Israeli Politics: The Renewed Centrality of Religion," in Reich and Kieval, eds., *Israel Faces the Future*, pp. 43–44.

accepted the authority of Labor's national leadership. They rarely questioned the assumption of Labor's legitimacy. Their writings helped produce and reinforce a historical narrative that contributed to the "consensual" dominance and legitimacy of Labor. David Ben-Gurion had a few intellectual critics, but they were the exceptions, and they became vocal only in the aftermath of the "Lavon affair." At the peak of Ben-Gurion's (and Labor's) dominance, most of "the intellectuals—some consciously, some not—became legitimizers of a messianic interpretation of social and political reality."[43]

The scholarly attention to the reputed dominance of new cultural nationalistic religious forms is related in a different way to the legitimation of a newly "invented" messianic tradition.[44] None of the scholars I have discussed would willingly contribute to the legitimation of the phenomena they analyze. In spite of their very diverse backgrounds, all are critical of various aspects of what they perceive to be a dangerous trend. Not only they but the majority of Israeli educational, cultural, and media leaders do not identify with any of the various forms of New Zionism or civil religion, which tends to contradict the assertion that there is a new dominant ideology. The leaders of the Likud, and nationalist politicians in general, have recognized this and have been highly critical of the liberal bias of most Israeli opinion leaders, whom they derisively call *yefeh nefesh* (literally, beautiful souls but freely translated as "knee-jerk or bleeding heart liberals"). A body named the Media Consumers Protection League crusades against what it calls the "leftist mafia" in the media.

Objective indicators, including the "hard" evidence of voting results and survey data on key issues such as religious identification and the role of religion in the state tend to refute the conclusion that either political dominance or ideological dominance of any party or worldview has been established.[45] Rather, the picture that emerges is of a society divided fairly evenly and tending toward polarization.[46]

In the 1981 election the two major political blocs achieved near parity (Likud forty-eight and Labor forty-seven). In 1984 Labor gained a slight edge (forty-four to forty-one). After coalition jockeying and minor party splits from and alignment with the major blocs, parity was reestablished. The new Unity Government was formed based on equally shared power and rotation of the premiership. This is hardly the arrangement one would

43. Michael Keren, *Ben-Gurion and the Intellectuals* (De Kalb: Northern Illinois University Press, 1983), p. 153.

44. For interesting discussions of the notion of the "invention of tradition" and comparative examples, see Eric Hobsbawm and Terrence Ranger, eds., *The Invention of Tradition* (Cambridge: Cambridge University Press, 1983).

45. Asher Arian, *Politics in Israel: The Second Generation* (Chatham, N.J.: Chatham House, 1985), pp. 217–18, offers survey evidence that contradicts Schiff's notion of a new religious hegemony.

46. A more detailed discussion of these and other related issues can be found in Aronoff, "Political Polarization."

expect in a dominant party system. It bears all the signs of the emergence of a competitive party system that has reached electoral stalemate.[47]

Contrary to Liebman and Don-Yehiya's assertion that Israel has had several civil religions identified with specific historical periods, I suggest that Israel has had a single core civil religion from the inception of the Zionist movement to the present. That civil religion is Zionism. Within the general Zionist framework socialist Zionism, Revisionist Zionism, statist Zionism, and religious Zionism (through the different political movements and parties identified with them) have competed with one another for power and the right to claim their version to be the *true* interpretation of *the* Zionist vision.

After Labor's socialist-Zionist version gained preeminence in the prestate period, David Ben-Gurion transformed it by inventing a new statist form which he felt was more appropriate to the postindependence period. Ben-Gurion essentially sacrificed a relatively high level of commitment among a narrower base of supporters for a lower level of commitment among a broader constituency. Whereas he and his followers claimed to be following the same Zionist vision they had followed previously, others who refused to dilute their socialism, for example, Min Hayesod, countered that Ben-Gurion had deviated from the true path.

Menachem Begin co-opted Gush Emunim and added a patina of religious symbolism, rhetoric, and rite to the official version of Jabotinsky's secular martial nationalistic version of Zionism which had become codified in Herut dogma and practice. In so doing Begin invented his own equivalent of Ben-Gurion's *mamlachtiut*. And, like Ben-Gurion, he antagonized some of his most faithful followers when he appeared to compromise the old ideology, for example, those who left Herut to found Techiya in protest against the Israel-Egypt peace treaty.

Begin's newly formulated reinterpretation of Revisionist Zionism was neither a New Zionism nor a new civil religion but a new ideological variation on an old familiar Zionist tune designed to mobilize a broader electoral constituency. Although selections were borrowed from Gush Emunim's ideology, it is far from synonymous with it. Although appealing to traditional and religious voters, it is distinct from the ideology associated with the national religious camp.

It is questionable whether the particular combination of folk religion and nationalism is sufficiently institutionalized (reified) to survive the passing of Begin as leader of the Likud. Clearly his successor, Yitzhak Shamir, lacks the ability to act convincingly as its spokesman. It depends on how long Shamir remains as the leader of the party and on who succeeds him whether this variant of ideology will survive. Among the leading contenders only

---

47. These trends are explored in more depth in Aronoff, "Significant Trends in Israeli Politics."

David Levy is likely to perpetuate Begin's ideology and rhetorical style. Whoever succeeds Shamir will certainly reinterpret the ideology to fit his style and the temper and tempo of the changing socioeconomic and political conditions.

It is considerably more difficult to create an identification with an epoch than it is to fall heir to one as did Labor through its leadership of the movement for national independence and the creation of a new state. Menachem Begin's attempt to identify the Likud with what he projected as the new era of Jewish settlement and effective (if not legal) annexation of Judea and Samaria, the "war of choice" in Lebanon, and the manipulation of symbols and ceremonies failed to establish the hegemony of the Likud for two main reasons. First, the nation was politically and ideologically divided fairly evenly into two major camps. Second, rather than subtly attempting to build unity through symbols that united the camps, Begin's conspicuous attempts to manipulate political culture called into question and undermined his efforts and even further aggravated the already existing divisions.

The Consequences of Dominance

Advantages

The stability and continuity of leadership and policy, which are characteristic of a dominant party system, may be particularly beneficial in the early stages of the development of a new society and political system. Israeli independence was won and has had to be maintained through a brutal, prolonged, and costly series of wars, both conventional and unconventional, which pose a constant challenge to the nation's survival. The mass immigration immediately following independence and subsequent waves of culturally heterogeneous immigration have compounded the normal challenges of nation building. In conditions characterized by pervasive change and uncertainty, the predictability of a political regime that results when one party dominates a polity can make a significant difference in successfully meeting such challenges.

Most relevant groups could be organized through the agency of the dominant party and its affiliated institutions, which simplified the task of national mobilization and made it more efficient. The incorporation of such diverse social forces as agricultural settlements, industrial workers, artisans, professionals, and various ethnic groups made an important contribution to national integration in a society in which the centrifugal forces have always been strong. The centralization and coordination of leadership selection, decision making, and succession in both the government and the Histadrut were major contributions of the party that helped Israel build a strong society in a relatively short period.

Disadvantages

When drawing up a balance sheet, however, one must also account for the negative effects of prolonged dominant party rule. First, prolonged dominance eventually had a debilitating effect on the party. It directly contributed to the strengthening of oligarchic tendencies, the degeneration of decision making in party institutions, and the breakdown of responsiveness of the leadership to the membership and to the public in general. Prolonged rule without serious challenge contributed to the arrogance of leadership, which in exceptional cases resulted in corruption. Whereas cases of personal corruption were relatively isolated, the phenomena of disregarding practices that violated the party constitution and principles were widespread. Recruitment and advancement through patron-client relationships deprived the party and the nation of potential leaders who displayed initiative, independence, and originality.

Prolonged dominance by one party had a serious negative influence on the main opposition party. Perpetual opposition without likelihood of gaining a share in ruling encouraged irresponsible behavior. This was particularly the case when the party and its leaders were defined as pariahs without legitimacy by the dominant party and this charge was believed by significant sectors of the general public. Lack of access to public office deprived the party leaders of valuable experience in governing and the party of a potential pool of high-caliber public servants with administrative experience.

These negative influences can lead to problems of transition when eventually the dominant party loses its dominant position. They can lead to high levels of anxiety among the public and potentially to significant problems of implementation of new policy if the civil service is too closely identified with the previously dominant party. Fortunately, Israel did not suffer from severe problems of transition. Most observers were surprised and relieved at the smooth transfer of power following Labor's defeat.

One serious problem from which Israel suffered was the polarization that partly resulted from the Likud's unsuccessful bid to delegitimize Labor and to establish its own dominance. The Likud went beyond building its own legitimacy; it vainly attempted to destroy any vestiges of Labor's legitimacy. It did so because of the need to overcome its former pariah status and possibly from the desire of certain leaders who had suffered in the past to gain revenge on their political rivals. Also, this was the model of politics which had been identified with the political system from the beginning. Consequently, the renewal of political polarization reached such a dangerous level of verbal and even physical violence that the president warned of the potential danger of civil war. This conflict was also a legacy of the aftermath of one-party dominant rule.

Whereas the benefits of single-party dominant rule outweighed the costs in the initial stages of nation building, the longer it was perpetuated the more the disadvantages began to outweigh the advantages. By the 1970s the old dominant party system had long outlived its usefulness as the dominant party failed to meet critical challenges and was discredited. The unsuccessful attempt by the Likud to replace Labor as the new dominant party indicates that the system of one-party dominance is no longer viable in the conditions that characterize Israel in the 1980s.

Conclusions

Party alignment in Israel is entering a new phase. It has evolved from a dominant party system to a competitive party system in which the two major blocs (but not their associated satellite parties and client religious parties) have moved closer to each other on a range of policy issues. This new constellation is creating a new political center that has continued to drift to the right of where it was during the height of Labor dominance.[48] This emergent system is still in flux, and there have yet to emerge clear rules of the game appropriate to the new political context. The resultant confusion and uncertainty can be seen in the responses of the Unity Government formed in 1984 to the various crises that erupted during its tenure.

It would appear that the political system and the balance of forces between the major political groups in the country have developed to a point that the return to one-party dominant rule is neither likely nor desirable. It is particularly important at this juncture in the development of the Israeli political system that the legitimacy of all parties be mutually recognized. The authority of the government and the legitimacy of the nation's institutions require the political actors to abide by the rules of the democratic game. The rule of law must be applied to all individuals and organizations, including the highest levels of government and intelligence agencies. Finally, although certainly not least important, the political culture must evolve to adapt to the changed party system. New interpretations of old Zionist themes and creative ideological innovations must emerge which meet the needs of the rapidly changing conditions. For the dialectical relations between political institutions and political culture pertain as much to competitive party systems as they do to dominant party systems.

48. For an explanation of the difficulty of collapsing the multiple dimensions of issues in Israeli politics into a highly simplified single-dimensional continuum implied in the use of the terms *left* and *right* see Virginia Dominguez, "The Language of Right and Left in Israeli Politics," in Aronoff, ed., *Cross-Currents in Israeli Culture and Politics*, 5:89–110.

9. The Dominant Party and Social Coalitions in Japan

MICHIO MURAMATSU AND ELLIS S. KRAUSS

Cases of perpetual one-party dominance among democracies in the industrialized societies are few and in the 1970s became even fewer. Of the four prime cases of one-party dominance studied in this volume, Italy, Japan, Sweden, and Israel, two lost power (Sweden and Israel) and one was forced to share power to a much greater extent than previously (Italy). In only one case, Japan, did the dominant party manage to ride out challenges to its dominance and then reemerge in the 1980s as solidly dominant as it had been two decades previously. How does one explain the singular ability of the Liberal Democratic party in Japan to survive major socioeconomic change and electoral challenge by its opposition and in the 1980s apparently enter another period of unrivaled dominance?

Undoubtedly there are many reasons why Japan has proved to be an exception among the dominant party democracies, including, as Krauss and Pierre argue in their chapter in this volume, parliamentary strategies for dealing with the opposition parties in their period of challenge to one-party rule. Beyond strategies for dealing with an opposition in the parliamentary arena, however, there are other reasons as well.

The more frequent cases in which dominance failed to be maintained offer clues as to where to search for an explanation of the unusual success of the LDP in Japan. Arian and Barnes[1] suggest that the dominant parties in

We thank T. J. Pempel, Andrei Markovits, Richard J. Samuels, anonymous readers, and other participants in the project that led to this volume, all of whom gave us very helpful comments and suggestions on earlier versions of this chapter. We alone are responsible for its final contents. We also thank Kosaka Masataka and other members of the original team that administered the survey from which our data came and the Toyota Foundation for funding the survey.
    1. Alan Arian and Samuel H. Barnes, "The Dominant Party System: A Neglected Model of Democratic Stability," *Journal of Politics* 36, nos. 3–4 (1974): 592–614.

Italy and Israel grew relatively inflexible with time, failing to respond rapidly enough to socioeconomic change. Levite and Tarrow[2] further argue that such change may have given opposition parties in these countries the opportunity to legitimize themselves and thus to mount a more effective challenge to the dominant party's rule. In Sweden, the rise of new issues and newly mobilized groups around the issue of nuclear power was associated with the SAP's electoral defeat in 1976. What these "failed cases" of hegemonic party rule have in common is the slow response by the dominant party to adapt to major social changes and the failure to accommodate the new interest groups that arise from them.

We will argue that one of the key explanations of the successful continuance of LDP dominance in Japan indeed lies in that party's flexible adaptation to change, and particularly to its ability to broaden its social interest coalition. Such an adaptation, manifested in part by the opening up of various channels of influence to the opposition social coalition, helped to perpetuate the LDP as a dominant party.

Parties, Interest Groups, and Policy Influence

The theme of the LDP's response to changing interest group structure is embedded in two more general theoretical questions of parties' relations to interest groups: the nature of the social coalition that supports the various parties in a system and the ability of opposition parties and their social coalition to influence policy. These two questions are linked in the premises of traditional models of democratic pluralist politics that most major interest groups have some influence, through parties alternating in government and/or by joining victorious, but variable, pressure group coalitions. The classical pluralist model thus made two assumptions: that interest groups are only partially and flexibly aligned with a particular party, and that the parties in the system would alternate in power.

For example, one may conceive of a system, as the American case is sometimes perceived to be, in which interest groups are only partially and flexibly aligned with a particular party. Even when a particular group is aligned with a particular party more often than not, it will nonetheless seek to advance its interests through whatever party will respond to its demands. In this case, interest groups and parties are engaged in a fluid strategic game with each other, as interest groups use their resources to bargain with parties for desired policies while parties in turn use policies as inducements to gain support from interest groups. As a result, depending on the issue and which party is in power, interest groups may and do seek influence on policy

2. Ariel Levite and Sidney Tarrow, "The Legitimation of Excluded Parties in Dominant Party Systems: A Comparison of Israel and Italy," *Comparative Politics* 15 (1983): 295–327.

through any of the major parties, and few major interest groups are permanently excluded from any influence.[3]

Few party systems, however, conform to both of these pluralist assumptions. Even when parties alternate in power, they may have a stronger relationship with some interest groups than with others. Certain interest groups and parties may be fairly permanently aligned, with groups seeking influence on policy principally through one major party and parties seeking support by policies that benefit only certain interest groups. For example, in a system like Britain's, in which ideological polarization of the parties also includes a more rigid polarization of social coalitions, unions (the Trades Union Congress) officially support only the Labour party, while major business organizations (e.g., the Federation of British Industries) support the Tories.[4] This polarized system of party social coalitions, however, need not mean that any major group is perpetually excluded from influence: most interest groups may still wield some influence as long as parties alternate in power. Fluid social coalitions as in the United States allow for the potential influence of interest groups through more than one party; but even a more polarized system such as the British allows for serial social group influence whenever parties change.

There is also a third model whereby a polarized interest group structure may be present but alternation in power is lacking. Some of the literature on dominant party systems implies that the very success of the dominant party is linked to the fixed relationship of interest groups to parties: dominant parties are parties that successfully use political strategy and their control over resources to build a permanent social coalition among some interest groups and exclude others. Thus Arian and Barnes see dominant parties as those that have managed to delegitimize their opposition and operate as organizations using patronage, co-optation of the bureaucracy, and control over the inputs of society to build their social base and to exclude the opposition and its supporting groups from influence.[5]

Even while the dominant party builds a base across the political spectrum, according to Arian and Barnes, it "mobilizes selectively and differentially," excluding some groups from political influence. "Opposition access to party and bureaucratic decision-makers is often blocked," and "opposition parties are reduced to the role of carping and sniping rather than that of developing immediate alternatives."[6] Analyzing the Italian and Israeli cases,

3. The pluralist literature on American politics, however, has been criticized for neglecting the many unorganized interests that have little or no influence on policy and the ability of elites to exclude many issues from the policy agenda. See, for example, Peter Bachrach and Morton S. Baratz, "Two Faces of Power," *American Political Science Review* 56 (December 1962): 947–52.

4. This is the case even though individual voters may cross party lines in elections and organized interests may adapt their strategies to whatever government is in power.

5. Arian and Barnes, "Dominant Party System," pp. 599–601.

6. Ibid., pp. 598–99.

they find empirical support for this dominant party model in which clear lines are drawn between the included and excluded interest groups. With one party perpetually in power, and interest groups polarized along with the party system, those aligned with the opposition are perennially excluded from any influence on policy, and those aligned with the dominant party may be the only groups with regular and significant influence on the system.

Considerations of party–interest group relations and the limited literature on dominant parties raise basic questions about the nature of influence and social coalitions in dominant party systems and about the causes of LDP success in remaining dominant: Are dominant party systems inevitably ones that perpetually exclude some interest groups from influencing policy? Or is it possible for most interest groups, even those supporting the opposition parties, to exert some influence over the policies of a dominant party regime? If so, how much influence and through what means? To what extent was the LDP's success in retaining power tied to its ability to exclude interest group segments; to what extent was it owing to a strategy of inclusion rather than exclusion?

The answers to these questions have important implications for the meaning of democracy in one-party dominant regimes. If dominant parties are able permanently to exclude a substantial number of important interest groups and the opposition parties they support from any influence on policy, then we may well question how democratic and pluralistic such regimes are. If, on the other hand, opposition parties and their social interest coalitions are able to wield some influence over policy making despite the lack of party alternation in power, then one-party dominant democracies may well be considered one variant, albeit an exceptional one, of pluralist democracies.

The Case of Japan: Excluding Opposition Social Groups?

Interestingly, although few Japanese scholars have concentrated on the phenomenon of the dominant party *qua* dominant party,[7] many of the most influential models of party politics in Japanese political science have viewed the dominant party system in Japan as one of polarized social coalitions with the opposition coalition perpetually excluded from influence on policy.

Observers of Japanese politics in the 1950s and 1960s described the limited and exclusive basis of LDP interest group support. For example,

---

7. There are some exceptions. Especially, one finds the explicit application of the concept of dominance to the LDP more frequently in very recent works on Japanese politics. For example, see Gerald L. Curtis, *The Japanese Way of Politics* (New York: Columbia University Press, 1988), chap. 2. In *Jimintō Seiken* [The Liberal Democratic Party in Power] (Tokyo: Chūō Kōronsha, 1986) and several articles, Sato Seizaburo and Matsuzaki Tetsuhisa use Japanese equivalents, such as "chōchōki seiken" (super-long period governance).

Takeshi Ishida[8] argued that the weak organizational base of many interest groups, combined with the tradition of a strong bureaucracy and a postwar polity dominated by one party (which itself had a weak organizational base) structured interest group relations in a nonpluralist way. In Ishida's scheme, the dominant party forged close ties with the bureaucracy, which in turn developed close ties with big business, the major LDP-related interest group that provided the party with funds. This theory is similar to Arian and Barnes's conception of a dominant party using the bureaucracy as a means of organizing its social interest coalitions.

Two other major interest group sectors were closely linked to the dominant party—agriculture and small and medium enterprise—but in a different way. These latter groups were dependent on government allocations controlled and used by the LDP to maintain its rule. Thus these interest groups form a dominant "subsidiary network" (*honkeiretsu*), having become clients to the ministries with supervisory responsibilities over their sector. These agencies served as patrons for the groups and as intermediaries between them and the ruling party. Alternatively, the groups were directly tied to the LDP by serving as an organized constituency for it at election time. Other interest groups that support the opposition parties, particularly labor unions, formed a separate network (*betsukeiretsu*) with very little influence on policy making. At the time Ishida was writing, in the 1950s, the most important group in this separate network was the Sohyo (General Council of Trade Union Federations) labor federation, which had close ties to the JSP, but other labor unions, student groups, and others would also be included.

Junnosuke Masumi[9] provided a similar analysis of party–interest group relations. Masumi argued that although interest groups attempt to advance their concerns through as many sympathetic Diet members or politicians as possible and though the parties are exposed to pressures from various interests, most groups succeed only partially in behaving autonomously and neutrally. He notes that in reality many important interests are tied directly to a particular party, for example, the financial world to the LDP and the largest labor federation, Sohyo, to the JSP, and that these groups will never cross over to deal with the other party. Other interest groups, even if tied less strongly, tend to gravitate to the LDP because it is the only party capable of formulating policy, and thus the dominant party regulates the arena of interest group politics.

Opposition parties and such supporting groups as labor occasionally did exert some influence in the extraordinary decision-making process involving the rare but intense conflicts over ideology, primarily through mass mobili-

8. Takeshi Ishida, *Gendai Soshiki-ron* [Modern organization theory] (Tokyo: Iwanami Shoten, 1961), esp. pp. 82–84.

9. Masumi Junnosuke, *Sengo Nihon no seidi taisei* [The postwar Japanese political system] (Tokyo: Iwanami Shoten, 1969).

zation, demonstrations, and strikes. In the much more common ordinary pattern, however, disagreements between or among such political actors as the ministries of the bureaucracy, the LDP and its factions, pressure groups, and electoral constituencies were negotiated and bargains reached without opposition participation. This typical policy-making process, therefore, was basically a pluralistic one, except that it excludes the opposition parties and their major support groups such as labor.

The analyses of party–interest group relations and influence on policy making in Japan in the 1950s and 1960s therefore portray the long-term hegemony of the LDP and the ideological-partisan fault lines of the system as creating polarized social coalitions and determining interest groups' access to and influence on government. They share a view of the Japanese system as one in which the dominant party is crucial in determining interest group relations with government; they see a close relationship between the dominant party and bureaucracy, with the bureaucracy playing an important role in mediating the dominant party's relationship with social groups; they see the dominant party pragmatically related to social groups through its control over the allocative mechanisms of government and selectively mobilizing some social groups while excluding the opposition and its supporting social groups, thus ensuring that the latter have little influence on normal policy making.

We have little quarrel with Ishida's and Masumi's characterizations of Japanese politics in the 1950s and early 1960s. The problem is that this model of Japanese politics has been adhered to even by many more recent analyses. Works on the LDP, for example, have focused primarily on the close relations of the LDP with the bureaucracy and big business and its dependence on agriculture for votes and the essential irrelevance of other interest groups and the opposition parties in influencing policy.[10] Studies of the Diet have seen the opposition and its supporting groups' ability to influence legislation as minimal, with the main decisions made by the LDP, its allied interest groups, and the bureaucracy.[11] When corporatist models

10. For example, Nathaniel Thayer, *How the Conservatives Rule Japan* (Princeton: Princeton University Press, 1969), esp. chaps. 3 and 8. More sophisticated versions of this model have recognized the heterogeneity and conflicts within these actors but have still seen these as the primary or exclusive influences on policy making. See the discussion in Ronald J. Hrebenar, *The Japanese Party System: From One-Party Rule to Coalition Government* (Boulder, Colo.: Westview Press, 1986), pp. 269–77.

11. Hans H. Baerwald, *Japan's Parliament: An Introduction* (London: Cambridge University Press, 1974). In his most recent work, *Party Politics in Japan* (Boston: Allen & Unwin, 1986), chaps. 4 and 5, Baerwald acknowledges the increased influence of the Diet and opposition parties during the "nearly equal power" period of the late 1970s and the trends toward greater influence of LDP politicians; nonetheless, he concludes that the internal factional disputes within the LDP were more important in determining policy than opposition influence and that the bureaucrats are still dominant. T. J. Pempel's "The Dilemma of Parliamentary Opposition in Japan," *Polity* 8 (Fall 1975): 63–79, is one of the few studies of the Diet in the 1970s to argue that the opposition parties had more influence than is usually attributed to them.

have been applied, the question has been raised whether Japan's corporatist tendencies constitute "corporatism without labor" because of the exclusion of that social sector from influence in the polarized Japanese system.[12] Even popular mythology in the form of the famous "Japan, Inc." stereotype takes as its basis the assumption of close consensus among the LDP, big business, and bureaucracy and the essential irrelevance of the opposition and most other interest groups.[13]

Was this depiction, so close to the more generic description of dominant parties' limited and exclusionary social coalition, still valid in Japan by the late 1970s and early 1980s? Has the system of party and interest group relations and influence on policy making established in the 1950s and early 1960s been perpetuated through the major social changes witnessed by Japanese society of the late 1960s and 1970s? We will examine these questions below, using empirical data to test interest groups' relations with and influence on parties and government.

Testing the Model in Japan: Interest Groups and the LDP

Our analysis is based on data from a systematic survey of leaders of about 250 of the most important interest groups and interest associations in Japan administered in the spring of 1980.[14]

The period in which our survey was conducted is a particularly good one to measure the relationship of social interest groups to the LDP. First, the LDP had been in power as a single party of government for almost exactly a quarter of a century. Second, for the preceding four years, the party had been in a situation of nearly equal power (*hakuchu*) with the opposition parties in the Diet. Thus the dominant party was probably most responsive to the demands of interest groups in an effort to maintain its strength vis-à-vis the opposition forces. A few months after this survey was conducted, the LDP won an overwhelming majority in the Diet in the 1980 elections and began to put greater emphasis on "administrative reform" and the politics of budget cutbacks and fiscal austerity.

---

12. T. J. Pempel and Keiichi Tsunekawa, "Japan: Corporatism without Labor? The Japanese Anomaly," in Philippe Schmitter and Gerhard Lehmbruch, eds., *Trends toward Corporatist Intermediation* (Beverly Hills: Sage, 1979), pp. 231–70.

13. See the description of "Japan, Inc." in Eugene J. Kaplan, *Japan: The Government-Business Relationship* (Washington, D.C.: U.S. Government Printing Office, 1972), pp. 14–17.

14. For details on sample selection and composition, see Michio Muramatsu, Itô Mitsutoshi, and Tsujinaka Yutaka, *Sengo Nihon no atsuryoku dantai* [Pressure groups in Japan] (Tokyo: Toyo Keizai Shimposha, 1986), pp. ii–5; also Kosaka Masataka, *Kōdō sangyō kokka no rieki seiji kado to seisaku—Nippon* [Interest group politics and public policy in industrialized states: Case of Japan] (Tokyo: Report to the Toyota Foundation, 1981), pp. 23–43. The interviews were carried out by one of Japan's most reliable survey research organizations with funds from a grant from the Toyota Foundation. The project team leader was Masataka Kosaka, a noted political scientist, and one of the authors, Michio Muramatsu, participated in the planning and administration of the survey.

If there was any time during which the LDP would be ready to use distributive politics, to reinforce its relationship with the bureaucracy, and to structure the inputs from social groups, it would be in the period when this survey was conducted. Also, with opposition parties nearly equal in parliamentary strength to the LDP, this period provides an interesting test of whether the dominant party would, and could, exclude them from the decision-making process.

In the analyses below, the prime variable for measuring the relationship of an interest group to the LDP is one we call "closeness to the dominant party." By this we mean the extent to which the interest group has close interaction with and political ties to the LDP. Closeness to the dominant party is operationalized by two indexes based on the responses to three questions on the survey: how frequently the interest group had contact with the LDP, the extent of the organization's support for the LDP, and the number of LDP Diet members the organization felt it could ask for aid.[15] We shall use these indexes to test various relationships among the interest group, the dominant party, and the bureaucracy.

The Dominant Party and the Structure of Social Group Support

To what extent is the social group's relationship with the dominant party polarized? Is there a pattern to the type of groups close to the dominant party? The answers to these questions will help us determine the extent to which the dominant party structures inputs from the society (and if so, the basis on which such inputs are structured) and also the extent to which it excludes groups associated with the opposition.

Table 9.1 provides the first indication of how the relationship with the dominant party varies by the interest group sector. The table shows first that certain interest group sectors see themselves as having a closer relationship to the dominant party than others. For example, the closest groups are professional (medical, legal, and the like), educational, and administrative (e.g., local government and public corporation groups). These are followed by the agricultural groups and, if we combine the medium and high categories, the welfare and small and medium enterprise groups. Then come large business and financial groups, and finally, with the least close relationship, labor and civic and political groups.

Clearly there is a distinct difference between the type of interest group and its closeness to the dominant party. And, as predicted by most models of Japanese politics, labor has the least close relationship with the LDP.

But other aspects of these data are not in conformity with the depiction of

15. A "simple index" assigned a single point to each interest group that responded in the two highest positive categories on each measure, thus producing an index of four categories ranging from 0 (very low) to 3 (high) in closeness. A "complex index" used the same questions but assigned points ranging from 0 to 3 for each of the discrete categories on each question, thus producing an index that ranged from 0 to 9. These scores were then divided into four categories ranging from "very low" to "high."

Table 9.1. Interest group sector by closeness to dominant party (simple index, in percent)

Closeness to dominant party	Interest group sector								
			Business						
	AGR	WELF	Lg + Fin	Mix	Sm-Med	LAB	ADM	EDCU	PROF
High	22	20	14	14	18	–	40	42	44
Medium	48	30	32	29	46	–	20	25	22
Low	13	23	24	14	18	13.5	27	25	11
Very low	17	27	30	43	18	86.5	13	8	22
	100	100	100	100	100	100	100	100	99
N =	23	30	37	21	28	52	15	12	9

a polarized Japanese system in which parties are based on narrow strata of interests. For example, the data contradict the picture presented by Ishida of narrow and structured relations between interest group and parties: an LDP with ties to only a few interest groups, its closest relationships with big business and the financial world, and its next closest with agriculture and small and medium enterprise groups. Clearly, if not in the 1950s, when Ishida wrote, then by 1980, the dominant party coalition was far broader. And, at least in terms of the percentage of groups in a sector with close, positive relations to the dominant party, professional, administrative, and educational groups saw themselves as closer to the LDP than any other groups, including those that are allegedly at the party's core.

With the significant exception of labor, a percentage of almost all categories of social groups had a politically supportive relationship with the LDP. But not all groups had even a moderately close relationship, and some categories of groups had a closer relationship than others.

If, by 1980, the LDP was a "catch-almost-all" party, the question remains whether a close relationship with the dominant party was based on pragmatic or ideological politics. Arian and Barnes's model of dominant parties and most descriptions of Japanese politics predict that for the dominant party, pragmatic politics takes precedence over ideology in its relationship with social groups. The role of ideology is primarily to justify the exclusion of certain groups.

Table 9.2 shows the reasons why interest group leaders believe Diet members have aided their group. The data show that the closer the organization is to the dominant party, the more the representatives are believed to be aiding the interest group as part of a strict exchange relationship aimed at acquiring that group's vote. On the other hand, the less close the relationship with the LDP, the more the interest groups believe they are receiving aid because of common goals and aims. Since those in the "very low" category are to a greater degree than not labor union groups, we can see the

Table 9.2. Closeness to dominant party (index) by perceived reasons why MPs help the group (in percent)

Perceived reasons for help	Closeness to dominant party			
	High	Medium	Low	Very low
For information	—	5	4.5	4
For vote	38	28	11	12
For electoral funds	2	2	—	—
Long trust relationship	21	23	18	9
Sympathy with group aims and goals	38	38	45.5	52
N =	42	60	44	106

definite influence of ideology here. In other words, groups close to the LDP are tied to it at least in part by a more pragmatic exchange relationship than groups tied to the other parties for which the relationship is based more on common values. Surprisingly, however, the influence of values and common aims is not totally absent from the groups closest to the LDP. At least as many groups in the high and medium categories in the table believe the Diet member aids them because of shared values.

The data in Table 9.3 show that the relationship of social groups with the LDP is not solely pragmatic. Interest group leaders were asked about their beliefs on the proper role of the state. Far and away the most commonly accepted role for the state was that of advancing the national economy. This was true even among groups with the most limited links to the LDP. These data indicate some basic consensus on the goals of the state in every category of social group regardless of partisan affiliation. It also may confirm Chalmers Johnson's characterization of Japan as being a developmental state in which first priority is given to economic growth.[16] But it is also interesting that there is a large disparity between those closest to the dominant party and those furthest away over their perceptions of the role of the state. The former show a strong inclination to emphasize defense and foreign policy, in Japan a major issue of ideological conflict between government and opposition, while the latter give a high priority to welfare, one of the major issues pushed by the opposition parties.

Our results thus far indicate a complicated pattern of dominant party–interest group relations. It is clear that there is a pattern of closeness of interest groups with the dominant party and that relations with the dominant party are based primarily on pragmatic exchange relationships. Further, the dominant party system in Japan ensures representation from al-

16. Chalmers Johnson, *MITI and the Japanese Miracle* (Stanford: Stanford University Press, 1982), esp. chap. 1.

Table 9.3. Closeness to dominant party (index) by perceived most important role of the state (in percent)

	Closeness to dominant party			
Role of the state	High	Medium	Low	Very low
Welfare	14	15	18	31
Public order	19	22	18	9
Public service	10	13	11	14
Economy	31	40	36	31
Defense and foreign policy	24	7	14	9
Other	2	2	2	5
NA	–	2	–	1
	100	101	99	100
N =	42	60	44	106

most all segments of society. At the same time, labor—the key social basis for the major opposition party, the JSP, and for at least one of the other opposition parties, the DSP—has the least close relationship to the dominant party.

Another finding is that the social coalition of the dominant party has broadened considerably in the last twenty years with its former major social bases, business (large, small, and medium enterprises) and agriculture, now representing only a part of that coalition.

Finally, the basis for the ruling coalition involves not only pragmatic exchange relationships but also some ideological affinity between the groups and the party. Ideology is thus not only a convenient weapon to justify delegitimation and exclusion of the opposition and certain social groups, as Arian and Barnes argued; it also forms a real basis for unity between the dominant party and its social coalition, on one hand, and for the opposition social coalition, on the other hand. The cleavages that divide Japan are not merely a reflection of the dominant party elite's political strategy but are rooted in real and relatively permanent differences in values among social groups, as shown in Table 9.3.

We find in Japan, therefore, that the dominance of one party does structure interest group relations to government, but that even groups in the opposition coalition have some representation; we find that ideology does affect party–interest group relations in an important way but that the dominant party coalition is a wide one. Value differences did not prevent the dominant party coalition in 1980 from being much broader than it was perceived to be in the 1950s.

The Influence of Social Groups on Policy

We now turn to the question of whether, as Arian and Barnes argued, a dominant party can exclude from almost any influence on policy the groups

Table 9.4. Closeness to dominant party (complex index) by perceived influence on policy making (in percent)

Perceived influence	Closeness to dominant party			
	High	Medium	Low	Very low
Very strong	25	10	10	4
Fairly strong	45	36	22	29
Somewhat strong	23	49	50	40
Little; none	7	5	16	25
NA	–	–	1	2
	100	100	99	100
N =	71	61	72	48

The simple index shows a very similar pattern of response.

that oppose it by the delegitimation of opposition, skillful building of its own social coalition, and almost complete control over the government apparatus. The same conclusion, that labor and opposition parties were denied access to the system, and thus influence, when the LDP was the perpetual governing party, formed the basis for the models of Japanese politics in the 1950s and 1960s.

Our data allow us to test this proposition directly. Table 9.4 displays the relationship between closeness to the dominant party and the perceived influence of interest groups on policy making.

It is clear that, as Arian and Barnes predicted, relationship to the dominant party determines the amount of influence interest groups have. There is a clear difference among interest groups as to their self-perception of their influence on policy, and that difference is directly proportional to how close they perceive themselves to be to the dominant party. But it is also clear that the groups furthest from the dominant party do not see themselves as completely excluded from influence. Over three-quarters of such groups claim to have some influence on policy making and about a third of them claim to have very or fairly strong influence.

A separate analysis of perceived influence by interest group sector confirms this interpretation.[17] The social interest sectors having the closest relationships with the dominant party also perceived themselves to have the greatest influence: professional groups, administrative groups, and educational groups, followed by agricultural and welfare groups. But 42 percent of labor union groups, the social interests most completely identified with the opposition and with the least close relationship to the dominant party, perceive themselves as having strong or fairly strong influence on policy making. Although this is a lower percentage than for most other groups (but about the same as found for business groups), it is by no means insignificant.

17. Muramatsu et al., *Sengo Nihon no atsuryoku dantai,* Table 4-4, p. 180.

Table 9.5. Closeness to dominant party (complex index) by actual lobbying success (adoption and veto) (in percent)

	Closeness to dominant party			
Actual lobbying success	High	Medium	Low	Very low
Yes, advantageous policy adopted	87	77	65	46
Yes, disadvantageous policy revised or vetoed	55	49	44	56

Behavioral, rather than perceptual, measures of influence[18] show the same pattern and indicate that closeness to the dominant party affects the type of influence wielded. Two questions in the survey asked interest group leaders whether their group had had a recent lobbying success in policy making, both a lobbying success in getting an advantageous policy adopted and a lobbying success in having a disadvantageous policy revised or stopped. How groups differentially close or distant from the ruling party fared on each question is shown in Table 9.5.

It is clear from the table that the extent of lobbying success in getting an advantageous policy adopted is closely related to the social group's relationship with the dominant party. Once again, the dominant party's ability to determine the pattern of interest group influence is clearly demonstrated, as is the ability of the perpetually ruling party to reward those social groups which are an integral part of its coalition.

Once again, however, this power is far from total: nearly half of even the social groups furthest from the LDP also claimed to have had a positive success. And in achieving a veto of a disadvantageous policy, the relationship with the dominant party has no influence whatsoever! Far from being completely excluded from an influence on policy making, opposition social groups seem to enjoy a fair measure of positive influence on policy and to be even better at being a veto group, preventing disadvantageous policy from being adopted by the ruling party. One of the key questions about party–interest group relations in the Japanese dominant party system is now at least partially answered: contrary to the depiction both of dominant party systems in general and the Japanese case in particular, opposition social groups do not see themselves as being completely excluded from influence on policy making.

If social interest groups with few or no contacts with the dominant party nonetheless exert influence on policy, then the question arises as to how

18. These measures are, of course, still "perceptual" even though they are perceptions of behavior. Nonetheless, by asking for specific indications of lobbying success, we have at least some indicators involving behavior to cross-check the general perceptions of influence.

Table 9.6. Closeness to dominant party (simple index) by extent to which bureaucracy seeks opinion (in percent)

Bureaucracy seeks opinion	Closeness to dominant party			
	High	Medium	Low	Very low
Frequently and quite a bit	74	62	57	18
Some extent	14	27	32	39
Not much; not at all	12	12	11	41
DK; NA	–	–	–	2
	100	101	100	100
N =	42	60	44	106

they do so. Part of the answer is found in the relation of interest groups to other parts of the state.

Relations with the Bureaucracy

In a dominant party system like Japan's, close ties have developed between the LDP and the bureaucracy.[19] The question is whether these ties to the ruling party have also determined the way the bureaucracy relates to social interest groups. Has the bureaucracy been so co-opted by the ruling party and politicized, as Arian and Barnes assert, that it has close ties only with the dominant party's supporting interest groups and excludes groups that support the opposition? We can test this relationship here in two ways: first, by the extent to which the bureaucracy takes the initiative in contacting, and second, by the general frequency of contact (on the initiative of either party) with social interest groups having different degrees of closeness to the dominant party. Table 9.6 shows the former.

As can be seen in this table, the bureaucracy is much more likely to seek out the opinion of an interest group politically closer to the dominant party, but the relationship is quite weak. The major difference is between those who are "very low" in closeness to the LDP compared to all the other groups. Only 18 percent of such groups claim to be frequently consulted by bureaucratic agencies compared to over half of those groups that rate their ties to the LDP as "low," and 74 percent of those that are close to the LDP. Yet even if most of the groups that rank "very low" in ties to the LDP are not contacted frequently, over half of them are at least consulted "to some extent" or "frequently." Furthermore, a majority of those groups of moderate or low closeness to the LDP tend to be contacted frequently. Opposing

19. For example, see T. J. Pempel, "The Bureaucratization of Policymaking in Japan," *American Journal of Political Science* 18 (November 1974): 647–64; Thayer, *How the Conservatives Rule Japan,* pp. 225–33.

Table 9.7. Closeness to dominant party (complex index) by frequency of contact with levels of the bureaucracy (in percent)

"Frequent" or "quite a bit" of contact with	Closeness to dominant party			
	High	Medium	Low	Very low
Prime minister	4	5	1	–
Minister[s]	37	20	14	19
Vice-minister[s]	30	26	15	13
Bureau chief[s]	75	75	50	58
Section chief[s]	89	92	74	63
Other[s]	68	67	58	50

groups clearly are not completely excluded from bureaucratic initiative in consulting with a social interest group.

A similar result is found if we look at access to the bureaucracy (as measured by frequency of contact with its various levels) by closeness to the dominant party. Table 9.7 contains these data. Clearly, the closer the relationship with the dominant party, the more frequent a group's contact with the government bureaucracy, especially at the highest levels of prime minister, minister, and vice-minister. But this is to be expected since the former two at least are political appointments and Diet members from the dominant party. At lower ranks of the professional civil service, however, the advantage of being a member of the LDP's social coalition diminishes, although never completely. Also, even among the groups furthest from the dominant party, from one-half to three-quarters have frequent or a fair amount of contact with bureau and section chiefs. Hence it is difficult to see these groups as completely excluded from influence in the bureaucracy by virtue of their lack of connections to the ruling party.

Thus we have a partial answer to the question of how groups opposed to or distant from the dominant party can exercise influence in policy making. At least in part they exert it through the bureaucracy. Although being part of the dominant party coalition does help a group in its relations with the bureaucracy, being in opposition to the ruling party does not exclude it from access. If this is the case, then the relationship between bureaucracy and dominant party in Japan is at least partially autonomous.

Other Channels of Influence

The opposition social groups' ability to influence the government is not confined to direct access to the bureaucracy. Separate analysis indicates that groups such as labor send representatives to the often influential advisory councils (*shingikai*). These councils are typically used by the bureaucracy to formulate policy and legitimize new policy-making ventures.

Further, a cross-tabulation measuring closeness to the dominant party measure and where the social group exercises its influence over public policy shows that both the groups closest to the LDP and those most distant choose political parties rather than the bureaucracy (those in between choose the bureaucracy). Obviously, those groups closest to the LDP are lobbying it while those most distant from the LDP are usually going to the opposition parties. As we have argued elsewhere,[20] the opposition parties' influence on policy making at both the prelegislative and legislative stages may be greater than is suggested by descriptions of Japanese politics that have emphasized the exclusion of the opposition from influence.

In data testing the extent of contact with LDP politicians, we found that opposition social groups are not completely cut off even from contact with the LDP. Social groups closest to the LDP clearly had direct access to the top party officials and to the internal policy-making body of the dominant party (the Policy Affairs Research Council), and the social groups most distant from the party had much less access to these major party organs. Still, 30 percent of the groups least close to the dominant party had contacts with LDP members on Diet committees related to their social group's interests.

Finally, opposing social groups are able to mobilize their members and the public to exert pressure on the ruling party through the tactics of mass action. Ishida argues that tactics of attempted influence vary by the type of interest group. Big business and finance do not use "pressure group" tactics but work quietly behind the scenes. Using Samuel Finer's hypothesis that "fuss, noise, mass lobbying and similar demonstrations" are signs of weak influence, he contends that the weaker interest groups in the dominant party's network, or those not in the network, would be compelled to resort to such tactics.[21] As predicted, we found that the groups less close to the LDP were more likely to use tactics such as mass rallies to influence government.[22]

We also found that such tactics can work, especially for achieving a veto or revision of policies these groups oppose. Our data showed that whereas the frequency of using such mass mobilization tactics to pressure the government did not seem closely related to success in advancing an advantageous policy, it did make a difference in revising or stopping a disadvantageous policy.[23] Groups that used such tactics frequently and those that did not were separated by a difference of 30 percentage points.

20. Michio Muramatsu and Ellis S. Krauss, "The Conservative Policy Line and the Development of Patterned Pluralism," in Kozo Yamamura and Yasukichi Yasuba, eds., *The Political Economy of Japan*, vol. 1, *The Domestic Transformation* (Stanford: Stanford University Press, 1987).

21. Ishida, *Gendai Soshiki-ron*, pp. 2–3.

22. Some groups supporting the LDP, such as Nōkyō, the federation of agricultural cooperatives representing most Japanese farmers that is closely tied to the dominant party, also use such tactics.

23. Pempel, "The Dilemma of Parliamentary Opposition in Japan," also has argued that parliamentary obstructionist tactics, which were often combined with external mobilization of supporting groups and used frequently by the opposition parties before the mid-1970s, had been an effective means by which the opposition can exercise a de facto veto over some controversial LDP policies.

Thus social groups tied to the opposition parties have numerous means for influencing policy: through the relatively autonomous bureaucracy, through advisory councils, through opposition parties and LDP members on Diet committees, and through mass action tactics. Although LDP support groups do have more access and influence, the interest groups supporting the opposition parties can exert some influence by using alternative channels, even if not to the same extent as pro-LDP groups. Having a dominant party perennially in power does make a difference in which interest groups have consistent influence on policy; but those interest groups not in the dominant party coalition are not completely excluded.

Explanation: The Development of Japan's Dominant Party System

Our empirical data on social interest groups confirm that inputs in Japan's dominant party system are determined to some extent by the dominant party and its political strategy. There is something of a hierarchy of relationships between social interest groups and the dominant party. A group's place in that hierarchy will determine, to a large extent, its influence on policy and its access to the bureaucracy. Furthermore, place in the hierarchy is based at least in part on the political consideration of what the social interest group can offer the dominant party in a pragmatic exchange of votes or other resources.

At the same time, this structuring of influence does not result in the complete exclusion, isolation, and delegitimizing of interests tied to the opposition parties. Opposition groups, especially labor, may be disadvantaged, but they are not deprived or excluded. Despite their distance from the dominant party, they do have some influence on policy. One of the major reasons for this influence, as we have seen, is that the bureaucracy's relations with interest groups in Japan is not completely politicized. Although the bureaucracy and the dominant party are close partners in governing, bureaucratic agencies also maintain relationships with social groups not in the dominant party's coalition. Opposition groups like labor in Japan have access to the bureaucracy and to advisory councils that recommend policy to the bureaucracy. Opposition groups also have various other means of influence in the system, including their ability to exercise some veto power over government policies they strongly oppose. These findings are even more surprising when we consider that one of the bases for the LDP's social coalition was not only pragmatic but also ideological and that there are major value differences between the dominant party and opposition social groups.

How do we explain these results? A starting point would be to take a cue from Levite and Tarrow's analysis of the ability of the dominant party to delegitimize the opposition and the counterability of the opposition to take advantage of historical crisis and change to legitimize itself at a later stage.

In the case of Japan, unlike the PCI in Italy and the Likud in Israel, we argue, the opposition was never fully delegitimized after the war. This was especially true for the major part of that opposition, the Socialist party and labor. During the American occupation, organized labor's role in the economy and democratic politics was legitimized, as was the existence of the Socialist party. Indeed, before any of the conservative parties controlled government, the Socialist party was the leading member of one of the first postwar cabinets (the Katayama cabinet, 1947–48). These facts made it impossible for later conservative regimes ever completely to delegitimize this part of the opposition. Unquestionably, the Socialist party's traumatic experience as a member of the Katayama cabinet raised doubts about the JSP's ability to be a governing party, which in turn aided the LDP's myth of dominance as the only effective ruling party. Still, this was not the same thing as delegitimation as an alien, dangerous, and invalid member of the polity. Indeed, even in the 1950s, many in Japan predicted a Socialist government and the development of a two-party system with alternation in power. And as the postwar period unfolded, the institutionalization of organized labor's right to exist and to advance its interests increased.[24]

The part of the Japanese opposition that was delegitimized in the same sense, for example, as the Italian PCI, was the Japan Communist party. In the immediate postwar period, the JCP emerged as a legitimate, aboveground party for the first time in Japanese history. It even had a special legitimation among many intellectuals since it was the only party to have openly resisted the prewar military regime. Its members had suffered the consequences in incarceration and sometimes worse. But then the JCP embarked—under orders from Stalin—on its "militant course" of attempted guerrilla warfare and violence from 1949 to 1952. As a result, the JCP was effectively delegitimized for almost a decade and a half. Its share of the popular vote dropped from nearly 10 percent in the late 1940s to 2 percent in the 1950s, and the JCP was eliminated as a viable opposition until the late 1960s. Then, under a new strategy of casting itself as a national and democratic party, adhering to the rules of the democratic system and increasing its effective participation in urban local governments during the environmental "crisis" of the late 1960s and early 1970s, the party was able to regain some legitimacy in the system along with about 10 percent of the vote.

The history of the Communist party in Japan, then, conforms closely to Levite and Tarrow's description of how an opposition in a dominant party system can be delegitimated and then relegitimated by a strategy that takes advantage of historical change and crisis. But as an explanation of dominant party development in Japan it is almost irrelevant because the JCP was not the main opposition as was the PCI in Italy. In Japan, the major opposition

---

24. This was the case even though in the late 1950s and 1960s the ability of labor to mobilize the vote on behalf of its JSP ally declined, and labor's political power was never to reach the peak of the immediate postwar period.

was the Socialists and labor, both of which never faced such total delegitimation.

Rather, it is our contention that the very fact that the chief opposition in Japan was *never* delegitimized and was progressively less excluded from the system has much to do with the success of the LDP as a dominant party.

For the first five to six years of its power, the LDP faced massive protests and even the resignation of a prime minister in the 1960 treaty crisis. Further, vote trends indicated that the JSP might very well take power in the future: the party reached what was to be the peak of its electoral strength in 1958 with about a third of the popular vote and Diet seats, but at that time many predicted its ascension to government within the decade. The LDP, with its narrow support base of big business and agriculture, hardly seemed a dominant party at this time. That it would remain in uninterrupted control of government for another thirty years was inconceivable.

Spurred on by the challenge of the Socialists and labor and by the massive political opposition it faced and the instability it created when it concentrated on unpopular ideological issues, the LDP embarked on its famous "income-doubling" plan (1961) under the Ikeda cabinet and devoted itself to rapid economic growth. It was only with the success of this policy in creating the "economic miracle" of the 1960s that the LDP became dominant in the usual sense of being "identified with an epoch."[25] By the end of the decade it had been in power for a generation. Of course, the LDP's success was also aided by the JSP's stubborn clinging to its left-wing ideology rather than moving further to the center to capture more votes (as did the SPD in Germany), as Otake describes in his contribution to this volume. Therefore, by the end of the 1960s it was becoming apparent that the LDP would be in power for a long time and that the opposition socialists would never come to power. By that time, the economic and distributive policies of the LDP were widening its social coalition to include such groups as professional, educational, and local government associations.

And yet, the LDP, if a dominant party, was operating in more than just a "partially pluralist" system. It confronted a continually challenging and competitive party environment: its chief opposition, the JSP and labor, had never been delegitimized; new middle-of-the-road parties like the Komeito and DSP had been created and were increasing their share of the vote even as the share of both the JSP and the LDP declined; and even the JCP was relegitimizing itself with a new strategy.

Nor was the pluralism confined to the party system. In the context of a nation with a tradition of strong bureaucratic rule and an elite, prestigious, and effective bureaucracy, the LDP did not completely control the bureaucracy. Indeed, many models of Japanese politics view the bureaucracy as the more influential of the partners in government. As we and others have

25. Maurice Duverger, *Political Parties: Their Organization and Activity in the Modern State,* 2d ed. (London: Methuen, 1959), pp. 308–9.

argued,[26] it was not until around 1968 that the LDP began effectively to influence the budget process and even later before it was able to approach policy making as an equal partner with the bureaucracy.

Beginning in the late 1960s and extending through the 1970s, the LDP faced another major challenge to its rule: the massive upsurge in public demand for improvements in welfare services and environmental protection. These demands reinvigorated the opposition parties, who championed these causes effectively at the local level: by the mid-1970s almost all the major urban areas of Japan were under opposition control. Citizen movements against pollution and welfare groups arose nationwide demanding an improvement in the quality of life rather than just the distributive benefits of economic growth.[27] Riding on the crest of these issues and the dissatisfaction they produced and on the political base they had built in the local urban constituencies, the opposition parties were able to capture almost as many seats as the LDP in the 1976 and 1979 elections and to exert even greater influence on policy through their enhanced position in the national Diet.[28]

Still the LDP was able to cling to power and even reassert itself in the 1980s. One of the major reasons it did so was the way it responded to the social change and historical crises of pollution and welfare in the 1970s. Rather than resist change, the LDP committed itself to both a "welfare revolution" and the cleanup of environmental pollution. In addition, elements of the bureaucracy (e.g., the Health and Welfare Ministry) supported the expansion of programs in these areas and aided in the pressure to respond. Welfare expenditures rose dramatically in the 1970s. And under LDP leadership, Japan adopted the most stringent antipollution laws in the world.

The LDP was thus able to co-opt the issues of the opposition and dampen their negative impact on the party. The large proportion of welfare groups close to the LDP shown in Table 9.1 indicates that such a strategy widened the social coalition of the dominant party even further. Now in coalition with the centrist parties, the LDP has taken back control of almost all the major urban local governments. In the Diet, the LDP was able to manage conflict and make the legislative process more efficient, thus reinforcing its image as the party most able to govern.[29]

26. Nakamura Akira and Takeshita Yuzuru, eds., *Nihon no Seisaku Katei* [The policy process in Japan] (Tokyo: Azusa Shuppansha, 1984), argue that the significant shift in the policy-making process toward more power for the LDP occurred after the 1973 "oil shocks" in Japan. In Muramatsu and Krauss, "Bureaucrats and Politicians in Policymaking: The Case of Japan," *American Political Science Review* 78 (March 1984): 126–46, we see that trend latent in the changes in the 1968 budget process.

27. See Kurt Steiner, Ellis S. Krauss, and Scott C. Flanagan, *Political Opposition and Local Politics in Japan* (Princeton: Princeton University Press, 1980).

28. See Ellis S. Krauss, "Conflict in the Diet," in Ellis S. Krauss, Thomas P. Rohlen, and Patricia G. Steinhoff, eds., *Conflict in Japan* (Honolulu: University of Hawaii Press, 1984).

29. See ibid.; Michael Mochizuki, "Managing and Influencing the Japanese Legislative Process: The Role of Parties and the National Diet" (Ph.D. dissertation, Harvard University, 1982); also the chapter by Krauss and Pierre in this volume.

We would argue, in contrast to Levite and Tarrow, that in the case of Japan, historical crises and social change enabled the dominant party to revitalize itself, rather than allowing a delegitimated opposition to legitimize itself. As the party identified with the era of rapid economic growth that caused the problems of neglect of social services and the environment, the LDP was certainly vulnerable in the crisis produced by its previous policies. Yet it was able not only to survive the crisis but actually to take credit for the policy turnaround and to identify itself with the new epoch of the welfare state and clean environment. This revitalization was by no means foreordained: had the LDP not responded the way it did, or responded even more slowly than it did, this crisis of social change might have resulted in more power for the opposition parties, much as happened in Italy and Israel.[30]

Our argument is that this did not occur in Japan because the LDP was able to respond in time and that the LDP's responsiveness to these new demands and its successful reinvigoration were possible only in a *competitive and pluralist* system in which the opposition was never delegitimized and excluded, and the dominant party was in only partial control of a somewhat autonomous bureaucracy. Nor was the dominant party necessarily in complete control of the political agenda. Rather, the legitimate, nonexcluded opposition, especially in times of social change, could raise its issues to the forefront of attention. Under such conditions, the dominant party had built-in incentives and institutionalized pressures to respond to change and new social demands, to shift its priorities, and to respond to social demands even from opposing groups to maintain itself in power. *The paradox of the dominant party system in Japan is that less control over the system may have resulted in more and longer power over it.* Put another way, dominant parties in a more pluralistic and competitive political market, such as Japan's, may have greater incentive to react to social change, to broaden their social coalition, and to respond even to opposing social groups' demands. In return they may acquire an even greater potential for maintaining themselves in power.

Conclusion

Our findings have shown that the relationship between interest groups and parties in Japan and the influence of interest groups on policy represent a more mixed and complicated pattern than might be expected from either classical pluralist characterizations of party–interest group relations or descriptions of Japanese politics. The more open-ended party–interest group

30. Mochizuki, "Managing and Influencing the Japanese Legislative Process," pp. 445–67, also emphasizes in a somewhat different way the importance of the party system and strategy in the LDP's relative success at maintaining its dominance compared to Italy's PCI.

relations associated with the classical pluralist system are seldom found in Japan: interest groups tend to be relatively solidly and exclusively aligned with particular parties. The parties and their social coalitions also are divided by deep-rooted ideological and value differences, as most observers of postwar Japanese politics have described. And the ability of the opposition social coalition to exert influence serially, if not constantly, has been denied by the lack of any alternation in power under the LDP's one-party dominant system.

Our data have shown, however, that by the late 1970s and early 1980s major social interest groups, even those in the opposition's coalition, had not been completely excluded from policy-making influence, in contrast to some characterizations of postwar Japanese politics. A respectable percentage of interest groups which are alienated from the dominant party nonetheless have some policy-making influence.

In Japan's dominant party system, the perpetual existence of one party in power does help determine the pattern of inputs into government from interest groups—the closer it is to the LDP, the more influence an interest group can expect to have. Thus dominant parties may make a difference; but interest group influence is not dichotomized, it is hierarchical. No major group is completely excluded by virtue of its political alliances. There is a bias in the system in favor of the ruling party's social coalition, but this bias is relative, not absolute.

We have suggested several reasons for the nonexclusionary nature of the system in Japan. One is that there are numerous points of access to influence, rather than just through the ruling party. If excluded from influence through the dominant party, they nonetheless can exert it through other means and channels, including the bureaucracy, advisory councils, and mass mobilization tactics. The other is that the LDP itself has been very flexible in responding to social change by pragmatically meeting, at least somewhat, the demands of a wide range of interest groups when it has had to, thus making itself into a "catch-almost-all" party by the late 1970s.

We have further suggested that the competitive nature of the Japanese system in which major opposition parties were never completely delegitimized provided greater incentives for the LDP to take such a responsive and flexible approach.

These considerations lead us to a final question: how typical of dominant party regimes was Japan's of the late 1970s? We do not have either comparative or longitudinal data so our suggestions here must remain speculative. We would guess, however, that all dominant parties create a differential system of access over time, with their own institutionalized social coalition provided greater access than their opposition's. Our findings and Tarrow's chapter indicate, however, that all dominant parties may be inclusive, rather than exclusive, of major social interest groups and flexibly responsive to social pressures.

It is likely, though, that some may be more exclusive and inflexible than the LDP was. In other words, though in its overall characteristics Japan's interest group system of the 1970s may be typical of dominant party regimes, it is toward the more open and flexible end of that continuum. Similarly, as we have seen, even the system in Japan was probably more exclusionary in the 1950s and 1960s than it was by the late 1970s, when our data were collected. As we have suggested, changing social and political pressures, as well as the nature of the dominant party, the extent to which the dominant party has incentive to respond to change, and the extent of autonomy of the bureaucracy and other points of access in the system, all are crucial in determining the width or narrowness of the dominant party's social coalition and the degree of access the dominant party accords to social interests in its opponents' social coalition. As these factors, and thus the strategy of the dominant party, change over time, so may the extent to which interest group influence is hierarchically organized in the system.

Clearly, nonetheless, the Japanese case in the 1970s does not simply accord with classical pluralist models of total fluidity and openness of access; but neither does it accord with some of the assertions of the dominant party and Japanese politics literature that portray the opposition's social coalition as excluded from any influence at all. Japan's interest group–policy-making system of the late 1970s was pluralist, but it was a pluralism strongly influenced by the existence of a dominant party perennially in power.[31]

And it is this special brand of dominant party pluralism that may help explain the remarkable durability of the LDP's dominance. Whereas dominant parties in Israel, Sweden, and to some extent Italy, suffered loss or diminishing of power in the 1970s, the LDP managed not only to survive similar challenges to its rule but to reemerge by the mid-1980s as more dominant than ever. In addition to other contributing causes, including electoral system and parliamentary strategy differences, we have argued that the flexibility of the LDP in responding to, and not excluding, almost all interest groups, may provide one clue to the party's ability to perpetuate its dominance.

The LDP expanded its social coalition, by responding first to the pluralization of social group interests created by the rapid economic growth and diversification of society in the 1960s and then, even if under pressure and a bit belatedly, to the new issues and demands for welfare and environmental protection in the 1970s. The ability of even opposition support groups to penetrate the system through other channels meant that almost no major interests were excluded and that pluralist social change was some-

31. We have suggested in "The Conservative Policy Line" that "patterned pluralism" would be a good name for this hybrid system with a dominant party, powerful bureaucracy, and fixed interest group–party alignments, but relatively open access to interest groups and frequent "subgovernmental" conflicts.

what matched by the pluralist political process. This very ability for both new and previously excluded interests to penetrate the system contributed to the inability of the opposition parties to move beyond challenge and actually to eliminate the dominance of the LDP. Thus social change, pluralization of interests, and partial incorporation of opposition interest groups proved not only compatible but even necessary to the continuation of one-party dominance in Japan.

10. Maintaining Hegemony in Italy: "The softer they rise, the slower they fall!"

SIDNEY TARROW

The year is 1969; the place an ugly piazza in the poor Isolotto neighborhood of Florence, downriver from the city's glorious *duomo*. A crowd gathered in the August heat watches silently as the cardinal of Florence mounts the steps of the church to say Sunday mass in place of the parish priest. The priest, Don Enzo Mazzi, has been deprived of his pulpit—ostensibly for issuing statements in support of radical students, but actually because he has been spreading a radical social doctrine among the poor of his parish. Mazzi is absent this Sunday morning, but he is supported by a coalition of left-wing Catholics, radical students, and local people, who, in an ancient Florentine tradition, are ready to believe that the authorities are against them.

The cardinal says mass to a nearly empty church, and outside, Mazzi's supporters read a statement criticizing the church for authoritarianism and for complicity with capital. They vow to follow their pastor into the wilderness. The following Sunday, a priest from Turin says an unconsecrated mass outside the church. Every Sunday since, either Mazzi or one of his associates has held an assembly and a mass in the ugly piazza outside the church of the Isolotto.[1]

All over Italy in these years, Catholics were leaving the church in droves and protesting abuses in its practice. In Milan the Catholic University of the Sacred Heart was a center of student agitation; in Parma a group of students who occupied the cathedral were ejected with the pope's blessing; even in

For comments on an earlier version of this essay I am grateful to Giuseppe Di Palma, Stephen Hellman, Ariel Levite, Peter Katzenstein, and T. J. Pempel.

1. This incident and the events that led up to it are related in detail in my "Old Movements in New Cycles of Protest," in Bert Klandermans, Hanspeter Kriesi, and Sidney Tarrow, eds., *From Structure to Action: Comparing Movement Participation across Cultures* (Greenwich, Conn.: JAI, 1988), chap. 10.

the traditional south the social mobilization of the period affected parishioners, who protested their priests' transfer to other parishes.[2]

Practicing Catholics like these contributed to a major cycle of protest that culminated in the student movement of 1967–69 and the labor strife of 1968–69. Many moved from these events into "extraparliamentary" groups of the left and into the Catholic trade union confederation (CISL); some with backgrounds in Catholic Action, like Trento student Renato Curcio, would even gravitate into terrorism. The Catholic subculture on which the power of the country's dominant Christian Democratic party (DC) was based appeared to be crumbling.

The DC was acutely aware of this threat to its power; the crisis of the late 1960s and early 1970s led a leader of Italy's dominant party to ask: "Where have we fallen short? It seems to me that reforms have been at a standstill, and that the structures of civil society have aged further and the whole fabric has deteriorated. Social forces have not found suitable challenge for the expression of their sense of freedom. . . . The moment of pluralism in our society is becoming a moment of disorder."[3]

The party, never robust, had based its power on a combination of religious faith, political anticommunism, and the skillful allocation of patronage. But without a charismatic leader or even an effective party organization, the DC was ridden by factionalism and, from the 1950s, was obliged to share power with a widening coalition of center-left and moderate right-wing parties. During the late 1960s this model was threatened both by an increasingly powerful communist (PCI) opposition within the party system and by extremists of left and right outside the party system.

These trends gathered force in the mid-1970s as the whirlwind of mass protest stimulated an electoral wave that brought the communists to the brink of power. But by the end of the decade, the tide had receded, the communists and the unions were in retreat, and the DC was still in power. It was only in 1983 that the DC suffered a serious decline. The major puzzle of Italian politics is therefore, How could so uncharismatic, factionalized, and shakily based a party maintain a system of one-party dominance in so divided a country and for so long? If one-party dominant democracies are "uncommon democracies," this is one of the most uncommon of them all.

Soft Hegemony: Maintaining Dominance within Opposition

A contrasting example will underscore the theoretical problem posed by the Italian case. The year is once again 1969; the place is Paris. After months

2. These examples and others will be found in chapter 8 of my *Democracy and Disorder: Protest and Politics in Italy, 1965–75* (New York: Oxford University Press, 1989).
3. Quoted in Bob Lumley, "Social Movements in Italy, 1968–78" (Ph.D. dissertation, Centre for Contemporary Cultural Studies, University of Birmingham, England, 1983), p. 133.

of political wrangling within the government, the charismatic President de Gaulle has placed on the ballot a referendum that will, if passed, greatly reduce the powers of the Senate, the last institutional outpost of the anti-Gaullist forces.[4] Confident after its massive electoral victory of June 1968, the Pompidou government is unenthusiastic about de Gaulle's tactic: if the referendum loses, the power of the opposition will be consolidated in the Senate; if it wins, it will tilt the balance of power within the government toward the presidency.

But de Gaulle, who saw his personal power eroding during the previous May, insists on reasserting it by forcing this referendum onto the ballot and threatening to resign if the referendum fails to pass. To most peoples' amazement, the referendum *does* fail to pass, and de Gaulle resigns as president of the republic he founded in 1958. With his disappearance from the political scene, the glue holding together the once proud Gaullist party is gone and the party goes into a tailspin. Gaullism's ideological mission to unite the French and reassert France's international position is reduced to mere conservatism. (*"Enrichissez-vous!"* says the Pompidou government to businessmen.) Factional squabbling breaks out in the conservative bloc. When Pompidou disappears from the scene in 1974, the Gaullists lose the presidency to Valéry Giscard d'Estaing and then, in 1981, to socialist François Mitterrand. They gain the premiership briefly in 1986, but under a system of *cohabitation* with the socialist president; after the elections of 1988, they are once again back in opposition. "Hard" hegemony is impressive while it lasts, but it is difficult to maintain.

Why did the charisma of a de Gaulle fail to be institutionalized in the party that bore his name, while the weak and divided DC continued in power for another ten years under far greater strains? The twists and turns of French politics since de Gaulle's resignation would require a separate essay.[5] In this chapter, I shall focus only on the DC. In contrast to most interpretations of the Italian governing party, I will argue that the uncertainty of its hegemony was actually a sign of its flexibility and a source of its political strength.[6] It is this pattern that I call "soft hegemony." If it was hard to establish, as Giuseppe Di Palma maintains in his contribution to this volume, it was even more difficult to contest.

4. See Peter Gourevitch, "Reforming the Napoleonic State: The Creation of Regional Governments in France and Italy," in Peter Katzenstein, Luigi Graziano, and Sidney Tarrow, eds., *Territorial Politics in Industrial Nations* (New York: Praeger, 1977), chap. 2.

5. For a preliminary sketch, see Peter Gourevitch, "Gaullism Abandoned, or the Costs of Success," in William G. Andrews and Stanley Hoffman, eds., *The Impact of the Fifth Republic on France* (Albany: State University of New York Press, 1981), chap. 5.

6. Most of these interpretations stress the anticommunism, the patronage system, and the religious bases of DC support, underestimating its leaders' strategic acumen and the requisites of a centrist strategy. For two exceptions, see Gianfranco Pasquino, "Italian Christian Democracy: A Party for All Seasons," in Peter Lange and Sidney Tarrow, eds., *Italy in Transition* (London: Cass, 1980), chap. 5, and Giuseppe Di Palma's contribution to this volume, as well as the other papers by this author cited in note 13.

Soft hegemony is a pattern of political relationships based on a flexible centrist governing formula, an interclass social base, friendship to business but solicitousness to marginal groups, and a governing style that is based heavily on distributive policy. Previous interpretations of the DC have stressed the corrupt and clientelistic elements in its governing practice; but these interpreters often miss the point that corruption and clientelism are only the extreme expressions of a system of governance based on political exchange.

The advantages of such a system for the governing party are that it creates a common and divisible political currency, disarms the opposition, and leaves few actors with the conviction that they will lose absolutely from the dominant party's rule. Based on service to the interests of a variety of social groups, it reduces polarization by forcing the opposition to deal in the same currency. Finally, in newly democratized systems, it gives the governing party a crucial position in the consolidation of democracy, not because its constituents are inherently democratic but because their interests are identified with the party's survival in power. It is only when that consolidation is completed, as had occurred in Italy by the end of the 1970s, that the dominant party loses this strategic advantage.

Before analyzing the strategy and consequences of soft hegemony in Italy, I will first outline three alternative explanations, all based on voting behavior and clearly inadequate, before turning to a fourth—Giuseppe Di Palma's—which is based on institution building and will lead us in a more promising direction. The first three explanations are unconvincing because they leave out political strategy, whereas Di Palma's, which is about the institutional strategy he calls *garantismo,* must be extended to the strategic interaction between government and opposition, to the political economy, and to the social forces on which both are based to explain party hegemony.

Focusing on these variables, I will sketch the conditions within which the DC evolved the political strategy that made it so hard to topple as a dominant party. The remainder of the chapter will illustrate how the strategy was adapted during the 1960s as major changes swept across Italian society and how well it stood the party when, in the mid-1970s, it faced its gravest challenge.

Three Inadequate Explanations

There are three models that are normally used to explain DC hegemony, all of them based on assumptions about voting behavior and lacking assumptions about political strategy:

The Tactical Voting Model. Italian scholars and journalists often find it humiliating that a political class like the DC has run their country for the better part of forty years.[7] For example, they explain the DC's electoral success in turning back the communist vote in 1979 by arguing that moderate voters "held their noses" and voted Christian Democratic defensively to keep the communists out of power. Tactical voting is the major analytical key used by these interpreters.

The Religious/Subcultural Voting Model. Others have used religion and subcultural identification to explain voting behavior in Italy.[8] From this standpoint, the long continuation of DC power results primarily from its voters' deeply embedded Catholic faith, and the inability of the opposition to unseat it comes from the inability of the opposing Marxist subculture to convince Italians of its democratic credentials.

The Economic Performance Model. From the political business cycle literature comes the hypothesis that voters punish incumbents for poor economic performance and reward them for economic growth. From this point of view, continued DC dominance would be the result of the country's economic performance; it would follow that during economic crises, voters would punish the governing party.

Each of these hypotheses has some explanatory power, but each of them presents some problems:

Tactical Voting. Beginning from rational choice assumptions about partisan competition, some have argued that the DC's survival in power was the result of defensive tactical voting by moderate swing voters against the communist electoral threat. As that threat receded, so this argument goes, DC hegemony was no longer necessary and swing voters, who had previously "held their noses" and voted DC, would be free to allocate their votes to other parties.

The problem with the tactical voting model is that it is based on a strong but unstated assumption of collective electoral rationality. For moderate voters to "hold their noses" and vote DC because the PCI was a serious electoral threat, they would have to have some idea of how others like themselves were likely to vote. Such an image of collective rationality has not been borne out in careful empirical studies of the electorate.[9]

Religion and Subcultural Voting. That the religiosity of many Italian voters explains a large part of DC support has long been obvious, but so has

7. For an examination of this negative view and an alternative interpretation of *la classe politica*, see Joseph LaPalombara, *Democracy, Italian Style* (New Haven: Yale University Press, 1987), chap. 5.

8. Giorgio Galli and Alfonso Prandi's *Patterns of Political Participation in Italy* (New Haven: Yale University Press, 1968) is the classical statement of this view. Joseph LaPalombara refines but essentially accepts this view in his *Democracy, Italian Style*, chap. 3.

9. See Giacomo Sani, "Le elezioni degli anni settanta, terremoto o evoluzione?" *Rivista Italiana di Scienza Politica* 7 (1976): 261–88.

the religious basis of conservative voting in France, which did not prevent the Gaullists from losing ground through the 1970s.[10] The most striking thing about religious practice and politics in Italy is how much earlier the religious basis of the vote declined than the DC's support base.[11] If the decline of religiosity was the major cause of decline in DC dominance, then the ruling party ought to have lost power much sooner than it did.

Economic Performance. The performance of the Italian economy in the 1970s does not help us to understand the survival of the DC's hegemony either. Indeed, an authoritative account—that of Michele Salvati—shows that, though the economic crisis of the late 1960s was being skillfully handled by the French Gaullists—who were to lose power a few years later—the Italian government responded poorly to the crisis, yet the DC remained dominant through the 1970s.[12] If economic performance was the cause of one-party dominance, the Gaullists ought to have been rewarded by the voters while the DC was being cast into opposition. That the opposite happened casts serious doubt on the economic model.

A Better Explanation: Institutional Structuring

By returning to rules established in the founding of democracies, Giuseppe Di Palma opens up a more plausible explanation for DC hegemony than any of the voter-based models do.[13] He argues that the party's dominance was rooted in the very institutions of the republic founded in 1946 and in the broad norm of *garantismo* that it established. Di Palma claims that the DC gave not only democracy but its own hegemony a solid start by granting other groups and parties open access to the political process. This was done "by means of arrangements such as accentuated

10. In France, even as the Gaullists lost their hegemonic position, social scientists were finding a close connection between religion and politics. See Guy Michelat and Michel Simon, *Classe, religion et comportement politique* (Paris: Fondation Nationale des Sciences Politiques at Editions Sociales, 1977).

11. In a summary of changes in religious behavior based on a 1975 survey, Sani reports that 25 percent of older voters, 31 percent of intermediate cohorts, and 51 percent of younger voters attended church less often in 1975 than they had five years earlier. Sani argues that such increases in secularization may help to explain the loss of DC electoral support; my point is that, based on secularization alone, one might have expected a greater decline. See his "The Italian Electorate in the Mid-1970s: Beyond Tradition," in Howard Penniman, ed., *Italy at the Polls, 1976* (Washington, D.C.: American Enterprise Institute, 1981), p. 118.

12. See Michele Salvati, "May 1968 and the Hot Autumn of 1969: The Responses of Two Ruling Classes," in Suzanne Berger, ed., *Organizing Interests in Western Europe* (New York: Cambridge University Press, 1981), chap. 11.

13. I base my summary of Di Palma's theory mainly on his contribution to this volume because it is the most accessible to our readers. For more fully developed versions, see his *"Tout se tient:* Constitution-Making and Constitutional Culture in Italy," paper presented at the 1987 Annual Meeting of the American Political Science Association, Chicago, September 3–6, 1987, and his "On Reforming the *Grundnorm,*" paper presented at the Conference on Italy: Political, Social and Economic Change since 1945, Woodrow Wilson International Center for Scholars, Washington, D.C., February 1–4, 1988.

parliamentarism, proportional representation, procedural guarantees protecting the oppositions." In this way, the DC gained two objectives: first, it constitutionalized the extremes; and second, it assured its own dominance through their cooperation.[14]

If Di Palma is right, then the same process that initiated Italy's transition to democracy also assured the DC the bases of its hegemony. The DC would have permanently profited from the image of "democratic sturdiness" that it showed to an electorate anxious for democracy. It would also have profited from the support that opposition groups were willing to lend a political system that protected their survival through constitutional guarantees. The DC emerges from Di Palma's analysis as an institutional engineer that proposed a mechanism which allowed opponents to participate in a system they could never take over or subvert.

The empirical basis of Di Palma's model is largely correct. He is correct when he writes that the postwar Italian republic was founded as a democracy with a strong leftist opposition whose popular support had to be taken into account in the institutions that were created. Hence a constitutional charter with strong guarantees for individuals and an established role for political parties was adopted. Proportional representation was established to protect the place of smaller parties, and both they and the PCI became devoted advocates of *garantismo*. The DC, as heir to the postwar settlement, profited from these accommodations to remain in power as their guarantor.

But Di Palma oversimplifies. First, the DC did not "grant" the opposition accentuated parliamentarism; it was but one actor in a complex political game in which others—including the silent partner of the DC, its American ally—held many of the cards.[15] From the point of view of the form of the new political system, DC leaders agreed on the establishment of a republic but invited their supporters to vote their consciences because they knew how divisive the issue would be. The role of the party system in the emerging political system was imposed by the strength of the left and by the legitimacy of the parties that emerged from the armed resistance to fascism.[16]

Second, Di Palma's model is a good one if we wish—as he does—to explain the transition to democracy. But as he is quick to recognize,[17] hegemony must often be "re-invented." If we use the institutional rules established at the founding to understand the consolidation of the DC's

---

14. In this volume.

15. Recent research has produced a far more subtle and differentiated view of the constitution-making process. For an example, see Roberto Rufilli's "Quel primo compromesso: I contrasti e le mediazioni all'origine della Repubblica," in *Il Mulino* 37 (1987): 99–112.

16. Ibid., pp. 104–5.

17. "Once that stage [the transition], comes to a close," he writes, "and even more as a new democracy enters and proceeds beyond the phase of institutional consolidation, party dominance can and sometimes must be 'reinvented'" (in this volume).

system, we run the risk of the genetic fallacy (e.g., the way things are established determines how they will develop). Di Palma counsels that the state apparatus and the practices of political exchange may become the key resources in the reinvention of hegemony. I will add to these the purely political choices of the actors and their strategic interaction.

Third, in theorizing about the transition to democracy, Di Palma points out that the left-wing opposition shared in the basic institutional choices that he calls *garantismo*.[18] But he deals with the PCI's strategy in largely institutional terms, when it had origins that were prior to the transition and went beyond institutional rules. The left made independent social and political choices that concorded with the DC's social and political strategy and were crucial, I shall argue, in permitting the DC to establish the pattern of hegemony that will be described below.

Fourth, Di Palma's model proceeds along the lines of a certain school of Italian political science which focuses on the political actors and leaves their social and economic bases in the shadows. This may be appropriate for understanding the insulated process of constitution making that he studies (although even there, it is useful to keep in mind the social forces that each party hopes to represent). But when we try to understand the consolidation of a democracy, we must try to establish how parties appeal to these social forces and how the latter respond to their appeals. Otherwise, how are democracies different from dictatorships?

This injunction to look beyond the political actors and institutional rules is particularly true when we turn to the political economy, where the basic choices are made which shape the social coalition that supports a dominant party and determine what social bases are left to its opponents. In trying to understand how DC hegemony was maintained for so long, therefore, the party's governing strategy, the concordance between it and that of the PCI, its relation to social forces, and its role in the political economy will prove to be the crucial variables.

The Postwar Political Settlement

Di Palma has given us a good sketch of the conditions in which a "guarantist" transition to democracy was established in Italy. But we need to return to the historical conditions in which the transition occurred and trace the reasons for the strategic choices that were made. Three major charac-

---

18. Although he deals little with the role of the opposition in this volume, in *Tout se tient* (p. 4), Di Palma writes: "A measure of *garantismo*'s attractiveness to the Communists is that, being left with no other immediate options, they quickly converted to, and exacted it during the tenure of the Constituent Assembly." He is thus far from unaware that *garantismo* was embraced by the PCI, but he accounts it only to its institutional vocation and ignores the party's broader strategy.

teristics of Italy's postwar settlement which conditioned the transition to democracy were the reproduction within its domestic politics of the international Cold War, a domestic cleavage structure that pitted a communist-led working class against a Christian Democratic–led conservative bloc, and weak and inefficient political institutions. Each of these left a heritage of conflict and instability, but among them they also provided the bases for the DC's future political dominance.[19]

The International Settlement

Italy entered the postwar world with the influence of the United States guaranteed internally by its major ally, the DC, but with a strong presence of the Soviet Union through the communists and the General Confederation of Italian Labor (CGIL) that they controlled, along with their Socialist ally (PSI). The contest between the victorious wartime allies in the presence of predominant American influence mirrored international tensions within the political system and helped consolidate the party system around its communist and Christian Democratic poles. It also led the new government to choose a centrist political and social strategy.

International polarization soon became more important for the party strategies it permitted than for the direct interference of the superpowers in domestic politics. Attention has focused far too much on the American role in installing the DC in power and on the anticommunist tactics it mandated. But although incidents of American pressure were many in the late 1940s, they became increasingly rare during the 1950s and were soon secondary to the main function of anticommunism, which was the construction of a political-economic bloc based on Christian Democratic power and capitalist reconstruction. Although American influence was paramount, it was also liberal, making the choice of any institutional structure but a pluralistic one impossible.

The purely political benefits that the American connection gave the DC are obvious: it divided the unions and isolated the communist-socialist CGIL, created an anti-Marxist Social Democratic party (PSDI), and provided the DC with the economic resources to establish its autonomy vis-à-vis the Vatican. But more important in the long run were the gains to Italy's newly liberated economic managers. For them liberation had brought free-

19. The interpretation offered in this section is a synthesis of a number of previous papers and articles that, for the sake of brevity, I will cite here and then draw upon without further citation. The major sources are *Peasant Communism in Southern Italy* (New Haven: Yale University Press, 1967); the concluding chapter in Donald L. M. Blackmer and Sidney Tarrow, eds., *Communism in Italy and France* (Princeton: Princeton University Press, 1975); the Introduction to Luigi Graziano and Tarrow, eds., *La crisi italiana* (Turin: Einaudi, 1979); the Conclusion to Peter Lange and Tarrow, eds., *Italy: Crisis and Consensus* (London: Cass, 1980); "Three Years of Italian Democracy, in Penniman, ed., *Italy at the Polls, 1979*, chap. 1; and "The Crisis of the Late 1960's and the Transition to Mature Capitalism," in Giovanni Arrighi, ed., *Semiperipheral Development* (London: Sage, 1985), chap. 12.

dom from the economic constraints of the former corporate state, as was obvious in the breath of fresh air that the liberal "Einaudi line" afforded business expansion. But it also brought the threat of working-class insurgency and indiscipline.

American influence assured that in economics as in politics, reconstruction would follow liberal-capitalist lines and that the working class would learn who was boss in the factory. After the declaration of the Truman Doctrine, the DC took a harder line against its former communist allies and closed both the PCI and the socialists out of government. The exclusion of the working class and its political representatives from the government in 1947 reinforced the strength of the liberal economic model, for it divided the working class between its Catholic and socialist-communist components and permitted reconstruction to take place under managerial prerogatives.

But American influence was a double-edged sword, for although it sanctioned tough anticommunist tactics, it was liberal in politics as well as in economics. The Americans conspired to exclude the PCI from government and to isolate communists and socialists within the unions, but they also gave the DC the signal that it was expected to govern through essentially democratic means. This helped willy-nilly to resocialize a generation that had grown up under fascism into the novel idea that you defeated your enemy, not with clubs and castor oil but at the ballot box. And it allowed the left to survive at the local and trade union levels to fight again another day. Ironically, just as American politics was entering a McCarthyite phase, American tutelage conditioned the DC to construct a centrist political strategy and create a moderate welfare state.

This is important, not because the DC, left to its own devices, would have moved in a confessional direction, but because there was no solid constituency for democracy in 1945 in Italy—either on the left or the right. Future support for democracy could thus not be based on the DC's "democratic sturdiness," as Di Palma argues, but on the concrete benefits the party provided to its social bases. Centrism was the DC's formula for sharing benefits among a broad constituency and avoiding the polarization that would result from a clear choice of capital over labor or of confessional Catholicism over tolerance.

At the same time, and for reasons of its own, the PCI was adopting a rough analogue to DC centrism. This was the joint result of the geopolitical dictates of the Yalta settlement, the party's attempt to appeal to non-proletarian groups, and Palmiro Togliatti's own strategic preferences. In a country with an underdeveloped south and a large Catholic peasantry, which found itself within the American sphere of influence, the PCI would have to compete with the DC for a coalition of lower- and middle-class supporters. It would do this through a strategy of "presence" within the institutions and by downplaying the supremacy of the proletariat in the array of social forces that the party wished to mobilize.

This set up a strategic concordance between the two major political actors in Italy, which—underneath the harsh polemics of the Cold War—produced a pattern of seeking support among the same social groups, not through ideological outbidding, as has been claimed, but through policy competition. In the short run, there were irresponsible claims, outbidding, and fierce ideological language. But the DC's strategy and the PCI's response eventually led the two parties to speak the same political language— a language of interest and social coalition—and to cooperate in subtle but significant ways.

Domestic Alignments

By internalizing the international cleavages of the Cold War, Italian politics was frozen for a generation in approximately the form in which it had emerged from the war. The socialists lost their early leadership of the left to the PCI and a monarchist and neofascist extreme right soon reappeared. But the left and moderate right retained roughly the same share of the vote from 1948 onward. The DC was never able to recapture the near-absolute majority (48.5 percent) that it had gained with American assistance in 1948 and was forced to govern through a series of multiparty coalitions. The communists inched upward in the electoral tolls, but their gains were mainly made at the cost of the PSI, and their symbiotic relationship with the DC remained.

Each electoral bloc at first consolidated around itself a closely woven network of party and mass organizations, unions and professional associations to accommodate the needs of their supporters. Their relationship was truly symbiotic; neither party could risk a major strategic change without provoking a competing move by the other. But the degree to which these party subcultures actually enjoyed the active participation of their supporters should not be exaggerated. Both on the left and in the DC, partisan involvement became a flexible and more or less open affair.

Though party conflict was intense, polarization was limited by the interclass strategies of the two major parties and by their policy competition. The DC had always had a populist orientation deriving from Catholic social doctrine and the heritage of antifascism. To this was added Alcide De Gasperi's shrewd preemption of the political center, which avoided isolating the DC into a confessional or right-wing ghetto. As for the PCI, its strong rural base, its relative weakness in the northern Industrial Triangle, and its ambition to organize the south and the middle class led to a strategy of alliances which was eventually to result in Togliatti's undoctrinaire "Italian Road to Socialism."

The competition between the DC and PCI was thus never a raw conflict between capitalists and workers. Had it been, a strong lay center probably would have developed and political change been facilitated. But just as the Catholic CISL and ACLI (the Catholic Workers' Association) organized

Catholic workers on behalf of the DC, there were thousands of peasants, artisans, and members of the middle strata to balance the tough old Resistance cadres in the PCI. The interclass nature of both Marxist and Catholic subcultures left them open to a variety of forms of activism and quickly eroded the civil war atmosphere of the early Cold War.

The evolution of this loose and open partisanship—so frequently castigated by Catholic integralists and Marxist purists alike—served an important function for the character of political exchange. In a political system in which reconciliation was blocked at the summit, negotiation could still take place at the base, not only within the two main subcultures but, increasingly, between them. This was tantamount to an unofficial, subterranean consociation in which elites made deals at the base of the system that were not politically possible at the summit.[20] By the early 1960s, for example, it became clear that parliamentary *leggine* (e.g., committee bills) were passing with votes that approached unanimity. In distributing the patronage of the political system, Marxist left and Catholic center-right had learned to work together.

The costs of interclassism also became apparent in the 1960s. Despite challenges from the Liberal party (PLI) under Giovanni Malagodi, the DC was clearly the main party of business. But business had to share government largesse with other groups in the party's constituency, especially the independent middle strata, which provided the bulk of the votes to the Catholic party. Thus reform of the tax system, for example, was held up for years by the DC's unwillingness to tap the income of its independent middle-class supporters.

Similarly, although the PCI was the main workers' party, its rural base and its attempts to woo the middle class put radicals in some doubt as to the durability of its commitment to the working class. Thus the party-led "struggle for the land" in the South had braked its elements of class conflict through its leaders' fear of offending its putative middle-class supporters. In the end, the party never acquired the votes of the southern middle class, and the DC-administered land reform produced a new class of small farmers in debt to the governing party.

Although neither the DC nor the PCI became "catchall" parties, in the jargon of the 1960s, both were trying to catch more support than in the past, to some extent from among the same electorate. The long-run effect of this joint appeal to the political center was to moderate their competition, reduce polarization, and reinforce the status quo. The DC did not remain in power because of institutional structuring or even because of its "democratic sturdiness," but because it governed from the center, disarmed the communist opposition, and became an essential linchpin in political exchange.

---

20. For evidence on this point, see my *Between Center and Periphery* (New Haven: Yale University Press, 1977), chap. 6. For a similar, more general interpretation see LaPalombara, *Democracy, Italian Style,* chap. 4.

The Institutional Framework

Postwar Italy was born a democracy. But like the early French Third Republic, its republican constitution was not the system most people would have preferred but the one that divided them the least. Even many of its most salient characteristics—including a weak executive and a constitutional court—were not the result of the preferences of the electorate or of the political class but were reactions against the last regime or imitations of the practices of foreign friends. The most innovative characteristics such as the creation of regional governments were put on the shelf for years, and many laws from the fascist era were never taken off the books.

Installing a weak executive is a prudent practice in a country just beginning life as a democracy, but it was not devotion to balance-of-power principles but fear of authoritarianism that constrained parliament from providing the prime minister with more effective power. What was most obvious about the consequences of this decision was the lack of decisional capacity that it produced. Governments changed frequently and ministers seldom remained in power long enough to see their policies carried through. Public authorities could not keep track of, let alone direct, the changes that were rapidly transforming the economy.

But there was another effect of the weak executive powers that were enshrined in the republican constitution; it consolidated the power of the parties over policy and politics. Cabinets were almost invariably coalitions of parties, factions, and notables. Parliamentary groups controlled the parliamentary agenda and made and unmade prime ministers. Government crises were resolved by long and elaborate negotiations between president and party leaders and among the latter. Although the society was bursting with energy and developing in a variety of directions, the weak institutional framework directed the expression of demands to the party system and, as its rule continued, primarily to the DC.

In the context of Catholic centrist-populism, weak decisional capacity, and a left that was too strong to be ignored but could not be excluded, the only policies on which governing coalitions could agree and which did not require detailed implementation were distributional ones—in simple terms, policies of patronage. Since the DC lacked the electoral strength to govern on its own after the earliest years of the Cold War, governments were formed and maintained as coalitions for patronage.[21] Opponents might rail at corruption, clientelism, and waste, but underlying the frequent scandals that became the daily fare of the newspapers, the system ran on patronage because it was the only currency that could be distributed proportionally among competing coalition partners.

21. For the concept of the coalition for patronage, see Martin Shefter, "Party and Patronage: Germany, England and Italy," *Politics and Society* 7 (1977): 403–51.

Soft Hegemony

It was the DC's affiliation with the United States, the requisites of its centrist strategy, and the distributional policies that followed from these that created the foundation for the party's hegemony. Because it lacked an overall majority and depended on distributive deals to stay in power, the DC's hegemony was "soft"; but because it provided the necessary glue to fuel the country's extraordinary economic growth, the softness was hegemonic, although to journalists and to the untrained foreign eye, it looked like chaos.

Di Palma is correct in that it was Italy's accommodative institutions that provided the institutional bases for this pattern of hegemony. But it was the initial choice of a centrist strategy because of the weakness of the DC, its populist traditions, and American tutelage that allowed this structure to be used to the DC's advantage. The DC allowed other parties a share of patronage—if not of power—if only because any other strategy would have increased polarization and undermined its position at the center of the political spectrum.

The DC was never *only* a party of patronage; it was also a party of devout Catholics, which explains why for so long its electorate tolerated its actions, and it remained a party of defense against communism, which explains its American allies' unending patience with its failings. But both religious values and anticommunism became increasingly weak political supports as fear of a Red Menace retreated and voters became restless with the rhetoric of 1948. Despite its spiritual and ideological ties, the DC needed to construct governing coalitions against opponents who were both skilled and determined, and this made patronage the most useful common denominator of its relations with allies and supporters.

But the DC's strategy left the country without the capacity for programmatic planning that it would need when the infrastructural needs of an advanced capitalist economy began to grow. One does not need to moralize against patronage to grasp its potential dangers. In a country undergoing rapid social change, regulative, redistributive, and constitutive decisions would sooner or later have to be made. Some—like tax reform, decisions on such social issues as divorce or abortion, and especially the reform of industrial relations—would not be made until the insistent pressure of popular protest forced them onto the public agenda, as it did in the 1960s.

The DC in the Political Economy

Italy's political economy was not organized along the classical lines of business versus labor, first, because such an alignment would have been disastrous to the DC's hegemony and, second, because the party was trying to contest so many sectors of social terrain with the left for votes. Nor did Italy possess a state apparatus capable of implementing either a neo-capitalist or a Keynesian model of economic growth. Growth was market-led but politically assisted. As long as it proceeded, DC political control was convenient to business and critical to the party's populist constituency. It was only when the growth model slowed and new social actors appeared that strains occurred within its diverse social and political coalition.

The period of greatest testing of DC hegemony began after the economic "miracle" of the 1950s had ended. Economic growth in this period had been truly spectacular. But the monument of prosperity had feet of clay. First, it was based on exploitation of domestic labor that was possible only as long as reservoirs of cheap labor and divisions between the trade unions remained. Second, even at the height of the miracle, there was significant structural dualism in both industry and agriculture and north and south. Third, the economy had a small internal market that left it susceptible to recession at every international downturn. Fourth, and most important, the government failed to develop a programmatic capacity for steering the economy in either a neoliberal or a Keynesian direction.

Inactive State Intervention

Insofar as the state was called upon to intervene in the economy, it did so by providing interest-free export loans to industry, constraining demand whenever a general rise in wages threatened to overheat the economy, and supporting the rapidly growing public sector. But once used in this facilitative way, the tools of economic management were rapidly set aside and complementary tools—increasing employment, supporting domestic demand, or addressing structural problems—were never employed.[22] The central role in managing the economy fell not to the government but to the Bank of Italy.

But this was not a classical liberal economy, nor even the kind of government-enforced market economy we have come to know in the Reagan-Thatcher era. For if business had ready access to political influence, there was no central vision of an identity between business and government, nor even a mechanism for formulating politically the interest of capital. The government lacked the policy instruments to advance business interests or even a civil service that envisaged an activist role. Industrialists enjoyed free range for exploiting opportunities for economic expansion not because of but despite the state's role in the economy.

The absence of instruments for implementing a capitalist project did not mean that planning was exercised on behalf of other classes or groups, for

---

22. See Michele Salvati, *Il sistema economico italiano: Analisi di una crisi* (Bologna: Il Mulino, 1975).

the state had little planning capacity of *any* kind. The Mezzogiorno, for example, was a region in which the DC had a major political stake; its economic needs were genuine, and possibilities for social and territorial planning abounded. Yet the Cassa per il Mezzogiorno that the government created to coordinate development in the south was never more than an instrument for distribution of resources, many of which found their way into the coffers of northern firms.

An Interclass Social Coalition

The availability of state resources for investment meant that business had close ties with particular ministries, but it lacked confidence in the government's capacity to produce economic growth. In addition to the lack of central direction, one reason was that resources were generally channeled through political party or clientele contacts that business regarded as particularistic; what businessman would trust a government as susceptible to pressure as they knew the Italian one to be?

But business distrust does not imply that the working class had a solid base in the governing party. Despite the DC's professions of devotion to the world of work and the advantages it offered the CISL in the state-run sector, the party rejected the notion of representing the workers as a class. Whenever wage inflation threatened—as it did in the early 1960s—a freezing dose of monetary and fiscal constraint was applied to cool off the economy. And until the late 1960s, when it was forced to do so, the governing party failed to institute a modern industrial relations system.

The DC also had ideological and electoral commitments to a variety of other groups. For example, because of their privileged position in Catholic social ideology and electoral calculations, the peasants gained protection and unheard-of access to credit, social insurance, and more secure title to the land. After the brief and explosive land occupations of the late 1940s, they relapsed into political silence (far more so than in France, for example). This was a remarkable development in a country that had known rural class warfare as recently as 1919–22.

For much the same reason, the independent middle strata of city and province were politically favored, in part through a tax system that failed to tap their incomes but more basically because they were most advantageously placed to prosper from the climate of "individualistic mobilization" that marked the postwar atmosphere.[23] Shopkeepers, small businessmen, and artisans were favored by law and policy and formed the core of the provincial voting strength of the DC.

A new and important constituency was added with the growth in the state

23. Alessandro Pizzorno, "The Individualistic Mobilization of Europe," in *Daedalus* 93 (Winter 1964): 199–224. Pizzorno intends by this term the decline of group and class mobilization and the increase of individual orientations toward consumption behavior.

sector. Although planning played little part in the postwar political economy, employment grew rapidly in public administration, in the public sector firms, and in the *parastato*.[24] The DC became the natural electoral bastion of these public sector employees, especially in the south, where the public sector outstripped industry as a source of jobs.[25] The electoral importance of the public sector would make it difficult for the DC to cut public expenditures when inflation hit in the 1970s.

New Social Actors

There were two growing social groups that were marginal to the DC's social coalition—the educated middle strata and the immigrant workers of the northern cities. Each of these was to prove the Achilles' heel of the DC's social coalition and of its entire governing strategy.

The New Middle Class. According to estimates made by Paolo Sylos-Labini, the new middle strata increased from 10 to 17 percent of the population between 1951 and 1971, an increase that corresponded closely to a simultaneous decline of the traditional middle class.[26] Thus the country's transformation to an industrial economy was producing a major new population group in the centers of economic growth, the cities of the North.

This new middle class was not only the most rapidly growing social group produced by the economic miracle, it was also a potential threat to the DC's continued political dominance. First, it was physically replacing the independent middle class and peasants who were still the governing party's most reliable postwar base. Second, it was an articulate and educated class with professional ambitions that produced a set of demands going beyond those of its predecessors—demands for civic modernization, educational reform, and urban planning. It produced something else as well: a postwar boom of children. Many of these would crowd into institutions of higher education in the 1960s; few, when they started to vote, gravitated naturally to the DC; many more were socialized politically as insurgents against the government in the student movement of 1967–69.

The Immigrants. One other group occupied an equivocal position in the DC's social coalition—immigrants from the rural areas and the south. Between 1951 and 1971, even as the birth rate was declining, the large cities of the north nearly doubled in population. This increase was largely the result

24. According to Paolo Sylos-Labini, the number of people working in public administration grew from 595,000 in 1951 to 980,000 in 1971. See his *Saggio sulle classi sociali* (Bari: Laterza, 1975), p. 155.

25. In the south, according to Sylos-Labini, the number of jobs in industry increased from 2,300,000 to 3,220,000 from 1951 to 1971, and jobs in public administration increased from 288,000 to 400,000 in the same period (ibid., p. 158).

26. Ibid., p. 155.

of the mass migration of southerners and peasants to the cities. Most of the unskilled and semiskilled workers taken on by northern factories in the 1950s and 1960s were immigrants who lacked both a tradition of industrial discipline and a tie to the trade unions.

Many of these new workers came from Catholic backgrounds, and their vestigial ties to the church might have been expected to foster new Christian Democratic strength in the working-class periphery of the northern cities. But the lack of urban services—even decent housing—to welcome them, the low salaries and poor working conditions that many of them found, and the discrimination they encountered from northerners—added to the organizational weakness of the DC in the cities—guaranteed that this would not occur. Some of the most militant workers in the protest wave of the late 1960s and early 1970s would be recent rural migrants from the Veneto and the south.

Thus the governing party organized an interclass coalition based on patronage, religion, and anticommunism whose roots were deepest among two declining groups—the peasants and the independent middle class—and shallowest among the workers and two growing population groups—immigrant workers and the new middle class. Although it officiated over the greatest economic expansion in the country's history, its particularistic policies, its inefficiency, and its failure to attract these latter groups deprived it of "hard" legitimacy. The party could respond only by adding new political allies to its governing coalition, which is what helped to produce the crisis of the late 1960s and 1970s.

The Crisis of the DC System

Some political systems are challenged by unbearable strains caused by forces outside their control, as was the case for the French Fourth Republic. Others, like the Israeli Mapai,[27] are eroded through the evolution of their internal characteristics. It was the latter process that eroded—but failed to destroy—the DC's system of power. The international situation that had placed the party in power was no more; the power of anticommunism and religiosity to hold together the DC's coalition had declined; and the party's centrist strategy obliged it to add new supporters to its coalition whose appetites and policy demands stretched the capacities of the country's weak political institutions and helped trigger a cycle of protest.

The Coming of the Center-Left

The first signs of crisis were intellectual and industrial. In the early 1960s, a widespread debate developed on both left and center-right over the transi-

27. See Michael Shalev's contribution to this volume.

tion to mature capitalism and its costs and promises. In government circles it focused on planning, on the technical needs of a modern society, and on the defects of the existing industrial relations system. On the left there was an open debate on the tendencies in modern capitalism and on the growing role of the new middle class—what the PCI was beginning to call by the early 1960s the "productive middle strata."

The academic tone of these debates disguised the important fact that they bridged political subcultures. In government circles, debates on the economy were stimulated by a small but influential group of liberal thinkers around the Republican party (PRI) leader Ugo La Malfa, who would be budget minister in the first center-left government. But it also had expressions in Catholic circles, particularly in a group of younger economists who had come out of Catholic Action and were active in the Interministerial Commission for the South and in the semipublic Association for the Development of the South (SVIMEZ).

Arguments turned in part on the lack of a modern industrial relations system, which leaders of the Catholic CISL joined CGIL leaders in wishing to reform.[28] Although much of management was reluctant to change its paternalistic and repressive labor relations, there were outcroppings of modernism in the Olivetti empire in the private sector and among younger technocrats in the public sector. While the private firms represented by the manufacturers' association, Confindustria, continued to try to keep the unions out of the workplace, the public firms represented in the Institute for Industrial Reconstruction (IRI) and the National Hydrocarbons Trust (ENI) wanted to institute bargaining with the unions at the level of the firm. When a wave of industrial conflict developed in 1961–62, it was clear that a new industrial relations system had to be created.

On the left, the debate was more theoretical but was no less important. The communists, through their Gramsci Institute in Rome, held an important conference on tendencies in Italian capitalism, which put them ten years ahead of their French comrades in recognizing the effects of economic change.[29] A strategic debate on the role of the productive middle class began in the party at the same time, as—sensing the decline of its traditional rural supporters—the party looked for new electoral allies in parts of the middle class that were created by advanced capitalism.

These debates, together with the economic and social changes that had stimulated them, made Italians conscious of the profound changes under way in their country, traced the rough boundaries of a potential constituency for modernization, and sketched the axes of future confrontations. In the

28. See Gino Giugni, "Critica e rovesciamento dell'assetto contrattuale," in Aris Accornero, ed., *Problemi del movimento sindacale in Italia, 1954–1973* (Milan: Feltrinelli, 1976), pp. 779–808.

29. See Istituto Antonio Gramsci, ed., *Tendenze nel capitalismo italiano* (Rome: Editori Riuniti, 1962).

circles of power, they made clear that a realignment was necessary if the DC was not to follow the decline of its traditional social groups with its own political decline. Unless the DC could construct a coalition for modernization that would isolate the PCI, it was in danger of losing power altogether.

The Center-Left Governments

This was the atmosphere in which the DC brought the socialists into government in 1963–64. The opening to the left was neither the first nor the last stratagem the Christian Democrats would use to hold on to power. The DC had always been willing to share resources with other political groups, first with the conservative Liberals and then with the moderate Social Democrats and Republicans. When coalition politics was extended to the PSI, it became a much more risky undertaking—as the journalistic literature at the time underscored—but it also allowed the DC to extend its basic strategy to new social actors.

The period of center-left governments was marked by continual crisis, not only because of the unsteady nature of the PSI but for two more fundamental reasons: first, broadening the coalition to a party with close to 15 percent of the vote placed new burdens on the reservoirs of available patronage; and, second, the center-left coalition incorporated new issue agendas within the government that could be adopted and radicalized by those who were left outside.

As a coalition expands it becomes more difficult to manage, as could be seen in the increasing time it took to resolve government crises and in the growing delays in getting government business done. With the entry of the PSI, which had lacked access to national power since 1947, into the government, patronage needs expanded just as the rate of economic growth began to decline. A good sign of this growth is that the number of parliamentary bills by private members mushroomed.[30] This both increased public expenditure and took the initiative for distributive spending out of the control of the government, but it addressed none of the structural problems of the political economy.

The expanding coalition and the absence of a strong executive also encouraged the proliferation of factions within the parties of government, particularly in the DC, just as major reform issues—pensions, education, industrial relations—were coming up. If a group of parliamentary notables could count on the unhampered delivery of resources through a given ministry, they could ignore government policy and even undercut its majority, hoping in subsequent negotiations to enhance their own power. The period

---

30. See Giuseppe Di Palma, *Surviving without Governing: The Italian Parties in Parliament* (Berkeley and Los Angeles: University of California Press, 1977), pp. 50–52, for evidence on the increase of parliamentary *leggine* from the first to the fourth legislatures.

of the center-left governments not only increased the number of factions in the DC; it also made possible cross-party alliances between factions in the two major coalition partners.

This factional growth and the corresponding weakness of the center-left governments helps to explain why the coalition experiment failed in its major political goal—the isolation of the PCI. Although the center-left strategy kept the communists at bay for several years and drove them out of many municipalities that they had jointly governed with the PSI, it left the PCI's position in the unions and in the working class unscathed. PCI electoral gains accompanied the start of the center-left experiment in 1963 and continued in the 1967 elections.

But factions had a positive function for the DC and for its capacity to adjust to the changing political tides. As the French Gaullist experience shows, a rigidly ideological and unified party has difficulty adapting to a radically changed situation. But soft hegemony provides greater scope for adaptation; as political crises succeeded one another, the faction-ridden DC could find leaders of the moderate right or the moderate left (or those, like Giulio Andreotti, who migrated from right to left) to respond first to one and then another change in the political wind. It was this flexible property of the DC's strategic model that allowed the dominant party to survive in government through the crises of the late 1960s and 1970s.

The Cycle of Protest

But first there was a major crisis to overcome: what Emilio Colombo had called the "moment of disorder." The greatest cost of the center-left governments to the DC was to have placed issues on the agenda that these governments could not resolve and that provided a policy agenda for groups outside the political system to exploit. The center-left governments triggered a period of widespread social and political mobilization based on the accumulation of old grievances and on the new political opportunities that it opened up.[31] It was through such a process that new social actors and their demands exploded onto the political scene.

For example, the 1967 debate over pension reform, which began in parliament, soon led to widespread mobilization of the workers, far outstripping the expectations of the unions. The controversy over divorce that resulted in a 1974 referendum and a decided defeat for the church began with a campaign for a modest divorce law in parliament. The famous Gui bill for the reform of higher education began in the Education Ministry but eventually mobilized both educational interest groups and college students and triggered the rise of an extraparliamentary social movement sector.[32]

31. I have made this argument at greater length in my *Democracy and Disorder,* chap. 2.
32. For this issue, see ibid., chap. 6.

Finally, it was largely because of the initiative of the center-left government that a modern industrial relations bill, the *statuto dei lavoratori,* was passed in 1970.

The center-left governments not only placed issues on the policy agenda that stimulated radicalization; they also encouraged insurgent groups to believe that they could protest and get away with it. For whatever the defects of the socialists, their claim to be part of the left limited the state's options for repressing dissent as long as the PSI was in government. Neither the old recessionary solution to wage increases, nor unleashing the forces of order against demonstrators, nor the use of political anticommunism was a viable political option for the DC after 1964, with the PSI attempting to preserve its claim to a share of working-class votes and gain support from the new middle class. The result was that the DC was forced to deal with dissent mainly by political means.

These political means led to long, costly, and involved negotiations with social actors and their representatives, spreading outward from parliamentary corridors and ministerial offices to interest group headquarters and to the streets and piazzas. For example, educational reform, which had been on the agenda since the late 1950s, was never really removed from the agenda until the mid-1970s—nor were the protests in the schools and universities that fueled the debate. Industrial relations were another continuing bone of contention, especially after inflation began to erode the wage gains that the workers had made in the "Hot Autumn" of the 1970s.

One after another, new social actors—tenants, women, prison inmates, doctors and lawyers, the unemployed—tried to force their demands on the political agenda through "collective bargaining by riot." The response was a combination of occasional brutal repression and constant negotiation with their representatives and with those who took up their cause from within the political system. The DC used a strategy of disaggregation of the various strands of the crisis to deal with it.

In the conservative wake of the movements of the late 1960s and early 1970s, public and scholarly attention focused on the costs of the government's accommodation to dissent. From the mid-1960s on, public sector deficits began to rise steadily, especially in the nationalized industries. Challenged by the socialists and by the left, DC leaders responded to problems by throwing money at them, keeping uneconomic public sector firms open and encouraging the Bank of Italy to pay the costs by printing more money, thus fueling inflation.

It was not simply that new claimants were demanding public support or that the unions were putting pressure on management that increased social costs, but that the government undertook these new costs while continuing to subsidize the older components of its social coalition. And how could it have been otherwise, given the DC's electoral dependence on these groups? As the government became increasingly paralyzed by competing demands and skyrocketing costs, the political system seemed to be dissolving in a centrifugal logic of left- and right-wing extremism.[33]

The Survival of DC Hegemony

Yet through all these years of Italy's long and "sliding May," not a single major split developed within the DC. Its electoral losses were gradual and small,[34] and it remained in control of every government coalition—including the government of national solidarity of 1976–79, which depended on the PCI's support in parliament. Despite inflation, corruption scandals, terrorism, and the growing restiveness of its allies, the party maintained control of the premiership until 1981.

There is no ground for concluding that DC hegemony is somehow natural to Italy; indeed, the long premiership of Bettino Craxi in the 1980s has demonstrated that the country could survive—and even prosper—with another party at the helm. The real question is, How did the DC extend its hegemony from the politics of the Cold War and the economic miracle through the center-left governments, the crisis of the late 1960s, and the stormy 1970s? It is not enough to point to anticommunism, which lost its electoral appeal with the end of the Cold War, or to the religious basis of the vote, which began to decline long before the DC vote did. It was soft hegemony—the DC's basic strategic decision to govern from the center, to share power, and to balance support for business with service to its other constituency groups—that continued through all these changes and allowed the party to adapt to changes in society and in the political situation.

Through the 1950s, the DC had stayed at the helm of government by co-opting first one and then another of the smaller parties into coalition governments. This system was made possible by both its centrist position and its skilled use of political patronage to defuse ideological policies and satisfy the needs of a variety of different social groups. In the 1960s, under the new ideology of the center-left, the DC did essentially the same thing, with the difference that its partnership with the socialists unleashed a broader set of claims that were much harder to fulfill. In the early 1970s, the stratagem of centrist political brokerage was threatened as social tensions increased and economic performance plummeted. As workers, students, tenants, extra-parliamentary leftists, and militant Catholics—not to mention a violent

33. The term is Giovanni Sartori's, who, however, seems to have intended it to mean the spatial extension of the existing party system and not its expansion to include new groups of extreme left and right. See his "European Political Parties: The Case of Polarized Pluralism," in Joseph LaPalombara and Myron Weiner, eds., *Political Parties and Political Development* (Princeton: Princeton University Press, 1966), chap. 12.

34. The Christian Democrats gained 35.2 percent of the vote in the national election of 1946 and had fallen to 32.9 percent by 1983. See Samuel Barnes, "Secular Trends and Partisan Realignment in Italy," in Russell Dalton, Scott Flanagan, and Paul Alan Beck, eds., *Electoral Change in Industrial Democracies* (Princeton: Princeton University Press, 1984), p. 213.

extreme right backlash against them—began to mobilize against the government, the DC's days as a dominant party seemed numbered. In the divorce referendum of 1974, the local and regional elections of 1975, and the parliamentary elections of 1976, the popular tide became electoral, and the left inched toward numerical parity with the DC.

The most worrying feature of this electoral threat was that it was largely based on the vast majorities of recently enfranchised young people, who voted disproportionately for the left.[35] Many came from the very social groups—the new middle strata and the children of southern immigrants—that the DC had been unable to accommodate to its system of political exchange. As older voting groups disappeared from the scene, would the new generations of voters mathematically displace the DC's electoral plurality with a majority for the left?

Yet the DC's capacity to organize coalitions survived these crises and piloted the country through the international oil crisis, the collapse of the lire, and the rise of organized terrorism. By the parliamentary elections of 1976, the left-wing tide had stopped rising and DC notable Giulio Andreotti was able to form a government of national solidarity with external communist support. As a concession to the PCI, its policies were hammered out, not in the cabinet or in parliament, but in meetings among the secretaries of the participating parties. The DC was even willing to take the final step of including the communists formally in the coalition, when the architect of the DC-PCI entente, Aldo Moro, was kidnapped and murdered by the Red Brigades.[36]

The DC's supporters, both in Italy and in Washington, feared that the communists would never be extruded, once given the legitimacy of supporting a government. But this extension of the strategy of soft hegemony worked; the most concrete achievement of the governments of national solidarity was to force an austerity policy on the reluctant unions and to gain communist support for a repressive strategy against terrorism. The PCI was so compromised on the left by its support for the government that it lost the bulk of the youth vote that had produced its major electoral victories. The Christian Democrats emerged from the 1970s shaken but renewed, with their major electoral bastions untouched.

Conclusion

Before the year 1968, many of those who paid attention to French and Italian political developments were awed by the powerful hegemony of the Gaullists and sent into paroxysms of laughter at the frustrated efforts of the

35. See Sani, "Le elezioni degli anni settanta, terremoto o evoluzione?"

36. See Peter Lange, "Crisis and Consent, Change and Compromise: Dilemmas of Italian Communism in the 1970s," in Lange and Tarrow, eds., *Italy in Transition*, chap. 6.

DC to patch together coalition governments of short duration and of little consequence. The years after 1968 created some tremors in gallophile *suffisance* but no letup in the hilarity engendered by the apparently feeble Italian efforts to respond to the country's interminable crises. It has been only in the last decade, as the cracks in the monolithic Fifth Republic have become apparent, that Italy has been taken more seriously as a functioning liberal democracy.

The delay in recognizing Italy's successful establishment as a democracy is in part the result of its enduring social inequalities; in part of the outrage of its entrepreneurs at their only partial domination of its governments; and in part of its intellectuals' penchant for putting forward an image of a colorful little *Italietta* composed of mafiosi, terrorists, fashion designers, bourgeoisified Marxists, and corrupt politicians.[37] But a more basic reason has been our inability to recognize that Italy has had a hegemonic party—the DC—which maintained its hegemony precisely because its leaders knew how to avoid the self-glorification, the sectarianism, and the arrogance that destroyed the Gaullists' power.

Not easy to establish, soft hegemony was even harder to disestablish, for it allowed the dominant party to avoid bipolar ideological duels and to shift its social and political bases in response to change in a way that a harder strategy of domination would not have permitted. Its defects were its incoherence in policy making, its enduring corruption in government, and the alienation of large parts of the public—even those parts that had profited from DC largesse—from the government.

The party's hegemony declined only after Italian democracy had survived its greatest crisis, in the late 1970s. This decline was symbolized by the kidnapping and murder of Aldo Moro—and for a paradoxical reason. Moro had been a key symbol and linchpin of DC hegemony. As premier of the first center-left government in 1964, he was repeatedly called upon to stitch together coalition governments at crucial stages of the party's wobbling course. Moro's death not only deprived the party of its most representative leader; it also showed that the republic could survive such a devastating blow without succumbing either to anarchy or to repression.

There is a lesson here that goes back to the founding of the Italian republic but may be extended to the founding of other new democracies as well. A party that emerges at the helm of a new democracy is often identified with the survival of the system. The dominant party often self-consciously plays on this identity, condemning the opposition as antidemocratic and warning the electorate that it needs guidance if it is to avoid the pitfalls of extremism or anarchy.

But the strategy of wrapping the dominant party in the founding flag of the republic does not always work and is insufficient in itself to retain

37. For a penetrating treatment of the image that Italians give of their own political culture, see LaPalombara, *Democracy, Italian Style,* chap. 2.

hegemony for very long, as other founding parties have discovered. Christian Democratic hegemony had three advantages that the French Gaullists and other hegemons lacked.

First, in contrast to the Gaullists, it was never more than soft hegemony—so soft that some observers assumed it was little more than accidental that a party like the DC happened to occupy the political center, and others doubted that it constituted a true party at all. By governing with an inclusive strategy, the DC gained access to an interclass voting bloc, making itself essential to the system of pluralistic patronage on which many groups depended.

Second, the DC had an unintended partner in the establishment and maintenance of its hegemony—the PCI, which, with its strategy of institutional presence and social alliances, unwillingly participated in a system of political exchange based on distributive policy and policy competition. A PCI that followed a harder strategy of its own might not have forced its way into power, but it could have forced the DC to the right and created space for a stronger independent lay center as an eventual ally.

Third, Italy—unlike France— was undergoing its first real transition to democracy after the long hiatus of fascist rule. It was not clear in 1948 that Italy would remain a democracy. By cooperating in the institutionalization of a representative political system, the DC both gave opponents a stake in the system and made itself central to future political coalitions. Its identification with the country's dramatic economic takeoff was particularly significant; through it, an industrial bourgeoisie, and those influenced by it, gained the conviction that democracy was not necessarily inimical to profits or to economic stability.

As long as Italian democracy remained in transition, the DC was guaranteed a central role within it. But by the late 1970s it was clear that the mobilizations and conflicts of the decade that was ending had extended and tempered—but not destroyed—Italy's democratic institutions. New social groups had gained the right to be heard and were using new modes of political expression to exercise it. New issues were placed on the political agenda; some of these even resulted in reform. Though the top echelons of the political elite remained largely unchanged, a substratum of new activists entered political life through the unions, movements, parties, and increasingly active interest groups that rejected party attachments.[38]

Even terrorism demonstrated the country's capacity to resist violence and the relative strength of its institutions. Although a repressive law, the *legge Reale* was passed to facilitate prosecution of terrorism, the Italian government never controlled its press or excluded people from the public service for their political affiliations, as did West Germany during the same period. Terrorist outrages endangered security, making government offices and

38. See Peter Lange, Sidney Tarrow, and Cynthia Irvin, "Phases of Mobilization: Social Movements and Political Party Recruitment," *British Journal of Political Science,* forthcoming.

even party headquarters resemble armed camps. But they also triggered a mass movement against violence and led the unions and parties to rally around the symbols of constitutional legitimacy. Long before the kidnapping and assassination of Aldo Moro, it was clear that the political class was squarely united against violence and in favor of democracy.[39]

By the early 1980s, Italy's economy had once again begun to revive. Public life, which for much of the previous decade had tumbled into the streets and piazzas, moved back into parliamentary corridors and ministerial offices. At an epochal strike at Fiat in 1980, the unions were badly beaten, signifying the end of a decade of protest. DC hegemony, which had seemed crucial to the survival of democracy, no longer was so, and a new, more competitive form of politics developed between the parties of the governmental arc. But that is another chapter in the history of this uncommon democracy.

39. For the best existing empirical study of Italian left-wing terrorism, see Donatella della Porta's "Organizzazioni politiche clandestine: Il terrorismo di sinistra in Italia durante gli anni settanta" (Ph.D. dissertation, European University Institute, 1987).

Conclusion. One-Party Dominance and the Creation of Regimes

T. J. PEMPEL

One-party dominance occurs infrequently among the advanced democracies. The cases explored in the preceding essays, along with many other examples that might come to mind, show how unusual it is for any single political party to form the core of a national government for three decades or more. The chapters in this book suggest that the principal cases are those of the Labor party in Israel (preindependence until 1977), the Social Democratic party in Sweden (1932–76), the Liberal Democratic party in Japan (1955–present), and the Christian Democrats in Italy (1945–80, or present). The exceptional nature of these four cases is doubly apparent from the numerous instances of what might be termed "failed dominance," cases in which a political party seemed to enjoy many of the same advantages that favored one or more of the parties that achieved "successful dominance" but never managed to translate these assets into continued control.

The CDU/CSU in West Germany and the MRP in France, for example, enjoyed many commonalities with Japan's Liberal Democrats or Italy's Christian Democrats, yet neither was able to hold on to power with the tenacity of the latter two. The Social Democrats in both Denmark and Norway had many of the same assets as their Social Democratic neighbor in Sweden; so did the British Labour party. But only the Swedish SAP ruled for forty-four years and in the process became the model of social democratic dominance. Labour in Australia and New Zealand shared many assets with Mapai/Labor in Israel, but the Australasian parties spent far more time out of power and opposing electorally successful right-of-center coalitions than they did controlling the government themselves. Yet during the same period in Israel, the left seemed to have an unshakable hold on power.

Post-hoc analysis of dominance may inadvertently imply the operation of an ineluctable teleological process. When a party is in office for so long, its dominance may appear to have been historically foreordained. But in reality, as the limited number of examples would suggest, dominance is exceptionally rare, involving a serendipitous congruence of effort and luck. And inevitable as each of these cases might appear with hindsight, the specific conditions that fostered one-party dominance in each one typically involved the interplay of highly idiosyncratic factors different from those in the others. Their differences suggest few readily identifiable commonalities to explain just why these four countries, or these four political parties, and no others in the contemporary period, enjoyed such similar experiences of long-term rule. The peculiar mixtures of effort and luck that worked for each party are highly individualized. What benefited one rarely worked for all four. At the same time, as will be explored below, the bewildering cascade of historical detail is not without several streams of analytic commonality that run through each of the different cases of one-party dominance. Despite the myriad details involved in each country's and each party's complicated history, it is possible to identify a cycle of dominance through which each has passed. All four dominant parties are, in this regard, similar in the conditions surrounding the origins, maintenance, and consequences of their long-term rule.

In addition to this cycle of dominance, the experience of long-term dominance is also similar in that all four cases involve more than simply a series of hard-fought electoral victories strung together sequentially. The significance of one-party dominance extends far beyond the who-beat-whom of media headlines and election night celebrations, even when the victor has run up an impressive streak of wins. The weightiest political consequence of long-term dominance lies in the ability of the dominant party to shape, over time, the nation's nexus of public policies, its rules of political conflict, and the benefits and burdens imposed on different socioeconomic sectors of the society. With each successive victory, the dominant party gains increased resources with which to reshape the country's politics and society. Used wisely, these resources allow the dominant party to remake the country in its own image and likeness, in ways designed to benefit its supporters and weaken its opponents. Such power is not unlimited in a functioning democracy. The ruling party is by no means unfettered in its ability to carry out its policies; formal rules and informal norms, combined with the countervailing weight of political and societal constraints, all set limits within which such changes can occur. But the fruits of a long-term series of electoral victories are by no means insignificant, and the major consequence of one-party dominance lies in the great leeway that the dominant party has in reshaping a nation's politics and policies to achieve its own historical project. In this sense, the very dominance of government by a single party affords the opportunity, though by no means the guarantee, of using the powers of office to benefit its own electoral fortunes. In this regard, dominance has the potential to beget further dominance or to spiral upward in a virtuous cycle for the long-term ruling party.

These two points, the establishment and continuance of dominance on one hand, and the consequences of dominance on the other, form the core of this concluding chapter. Examining both, it becomes clear, first, that below the surface-level differences there are several important commonalities to all the cases that set them off from nation-states that did not experience long-term dominance by a single political party and, second, that the causes and consequences of one-party dominance are interrelated in reinforcing ways. This reinforcement process provides the possibilities for a virtuous cycle of ongoing dominance.

This concluding chapter first examines the causes and consequences of dominance in isolation and then moves on to show the positive interaction among them and how in each of the four cases, they have operated to generate that virtuous cycle of continued dominance.

The Commonalities of Dominance

The greater the detail in which any case study is examined, the greater its uniqueness appears to be. This is certainly true of the main cases of one-party dominance examined in the preceding chapters. The specific circumstances in each country are unusual in numerous important ways. All the countries have different historical experiences and political structures. The dominant parties and their major opponents exhibit similar structural and historical differences. The support bases of the dominant parties are distinct. They often fuse unlike socioeconomic coalitions. Their electoral appeals are based on uniquely blended symbols, ideologies, and payoffs. Some stayed in power immune to serious challenge for long periods of time; others seemed to survive only by miraculous or supernatural intervention. In at least two of the four cases, Israel and Sweden, dominance by a single party ended abruptly in the late 1970s, while the other two parties held on to the reins of government, possibly even more securely than before. In the case of Sweden, an even more complex experience occurred as a once dominant party was deposed and then returned to rule after a six-year interregnum with national support and internal self-confidence almost as solid as if it had never left office. Conversely, in Israel, the Labor party, which once seemed indomitable and treated officeholding as a natural right, suddenly was replaced by a coalition of its former opponents, and as of the late 1980s Labor showed only pale shadows of its former strength. These and other differences were explored in the Introduction and have been underscored by the analyses in the individual chapters.

At the same time, the experiences of one-party dominance are not without important commonalities. An inductive examination of the cases suggests that several conditions are common to all four cases of one-party dominance. These conditions seem to be necessary contributors to long-term rule by a single party. None of these individually could be said to have actually *caused* single-party dominance; rather, in combination, they operated to keep dominance the prevailing possibility.

I will argue that there are three important commonalities to the one-party dominant regimes. First, each has a common structural trait, namely an electoral system that fosters a multiparty system. A second major similarity among all the cases is what might be termed a cycle of dominance, a historical evolution marking the origins, the maintenance, and the possible ending of dominance. Finally, the third major similarity involves the consequences of long-term dominance, namely the ability of the ruling party to use government office to its own benefit, not just in the simple distribution of patronage usually associated with the power of office, but beyond that in the ability to reshape the entire political profile of the country—including its symbols, its values, and its public expectations—in ways that fundamentally recreate the political climate of the country. This re-creation, in turn, *can*, but need not necessarily, benefit the party in power. Thus these last two points are interrelated, with the origins of dominance providing, for example, certain assets in the subsequent maintenance of dominance, and with the control of office allowing dominant parties to use such powers to maintain themselves in power for even longer periods.

Electoral Systems and Dominance

Common to all the cases of one-party dominance is that they occur under variants of proportional representation and electoral systems that foster multipartism. As Esping-Andersen points out in his chapter, electoral systems do little to explain one-party dominance. And as was seen in the Introduction, Italy, Israel, Japan, and Sweden all operate under electoral systems that differ in important details from one another. Moreover, other countries that never experienced long-term rule by a single party have electoral systems that resemble those in one or more of these countries. Thus no specific electoral system can be said to cause one-party dominance. At the same time, a system that fosters and encourages multipartism is certainly a precondition for the emergence of one-party dominance.

The essential reason why this system encourages dominance is that under a multiparty system, one party typically needs far less than 50 percent of the seats in parliament to be dominant. In a system with four, five, or more parties, the party that can gain 35 percent or so of the seats in parliament is in a preponderant bargaining position to become the core of any government. This is doubly true when the political system is ideologically fragmented and certain theoretically possible coalitions offer no practical likelihood for the development and implementation of a coherent policy agenda. In such cases, the plurality party enjoys a particularly favored bargaining position vis-à-vis other parties. Forming a government without the plurality party is extremely difficult; including it is almost essential; its position as the largest partner gives it the potential to dominate its partners and to be the ongoing element in a series of governments.

Conversely, it is relatively easy to see why first-past-the-post and/or majoritarian systems work against one-party dominance.[1] Such systems work against larger numbers of parties gaining representation, thereby raising the threshold for long-term dominance from a continual 35 percent or so of the votes or parliamentary seats to much closer to 50 percent. The core voting constituency required to dominate is typically much greater in such first-past-the-post systems than in systems of proportional representation. And in ideologically divided systems, bargaining power and the power to head a series of coalitions is greatly enhanced for the party that can control a relatively secure one-third or so of the electorate.

Thus of the four cases under examination here, only Japan's LDP comes close to having enjoyed the support of 50 percent or more of the voters over the entire period of its rule, and it fell below this margin on several occasions. Sweden's SAP received 50 percent of the popular vote only once (1968) during the thirteen elections from 1932 to 1976. From 1949 to 1965, Mapai typically won between one-third and two-fifths of the seats in the Knesset. In Italy, the DC typically won around 38 percent of the vote.

Indeed, one of the important conclusions to emerge from Pontusson's comparison of Britain and Sweden is precisely the way the British electoral system has operated to reduce Labour's ability to translate a 40 percent or so core of popular support into long-term control over government. At the same time, and in conjunction with other factors, the Swedish electoral system made a major contribution to SAP rule by allowing the party to govern continually even though it generally received only 42 to 46 percent of the total votes cast.

The electoral system was relevant as well in that the 4 percent cutoff for parliamentary representation in Sweden has prevented the proliferation of the small splinter parties that have been far more common in Norway and

---

1. Indeed, one of the more interesting experiences of dominance within first-past-the-post systems concerns the long-term rule by the Democratic party in the U.S. South. Key to such dominance was that the Democratic party's wide-open primary system allowed multiple candidacies from which the victor was almost assured victory in the actual election against the Republican challenger. In effect, the primary, not the general election, was the true contest (V. O. Key, *Southern Politics in State and Nation* [New York: Knopf, 1960]). A second interesting feature can be seen in Australia, and to a lesser extent New Zealand, where a first-past-the-post system combined with preference ballots has allowed the Liberal and Country parties to compete as separate electoral entities but to combine in governing, thus blocking the stronger Labor parties from holding power.

Denmark and have worked against the Social Democrats in both of these countries. And finally, the electoral system reforms of 1971 worked against the possibility of a Social Democratic majority in the Riksdag by making representation somewhat more strictly proportional than it had been in prior years and thereby penalizing the SAP.

The Japanese electoral system for the House of Representatives, which fosters multiple candidates from the same political party within a single electoral district, was an important ingredient in facilitating the merger of the Liberal and Democratic parties in 1955. It minimized the need for zero-sum competition among candidates from the two parties. It also helped the party to stay in power by reducing the capacity for electors to vote systematically against the ruling party. And finally, by the facility with which new political parties can gain representation under its provisions, the electoral system has often worked as well against the unification of opposition parties.[2]

The list system of proportional representation combined with the relatively large electoral districts in Italy helped the DC compete as an electorally "unified" party despite the strong personalist and factional divisions within its ranks. The simultaneous existence of the preference vote within the list system allows individual candidates to seek to improve their chances of election without undermining the list as a whole. It could also be argued that the system has allowed the parties, including the DC, to adapt over time to changing circumstances in ways that have remained far less visible to the public eye than would have been true under first-past-the-post or other one-on-one systems.

Multipartism, an electoral system that favors it, or both by no means guarantee single-party dominance, as should be clear from the many instances to the contrary throughout Europe. In many, it as easily works against dominance by a single party and in favor of the shifting coalitions that predominate in many of the Benelux countries. Although these countries have multiparty systems, with shifting balances of power, a single party has never been in a long-term position of dominance (although the Dutch Catholic party or the Danish Socialists may show more similarities to dominance than not). The electoral system in itself guarantees nothing specific about the actual outcomes of elections. But as is well established, proportional representation militates toward greater stability in representation than does the simple-majority, single-ballot system.[3] It is significant for one-

2. Some of these points are explored in greater detail in T. J. Pempel, *Policy and Politics in Japan: Creative Conservatism* (Philadelphia: Temple University Press, 1982), chap. 1, and Ronald J. Hrebenar, "Rules of the Game: The Impact of the Electoral System on Political Parties," in Hrebenar, ed., *The Japanese Party System* (Boulder, Colo.: Westview Press, 1986), pp. 32–54.

3. See, for example, Douglas W. Rae, *The Political Consequences of Electoral Laws* (New Haven: Yale University Press, 1967), esp. chap. 5.

party dominance primarily in concert with several other features elaborated below.

At least four points are worth stressing. First, a proportional representation system often allows divisions within a dominant party to be papered over at election time, preventing intraparty fratricide and zero-sum competition among competing tendencies or candidates within the party. Because proportional representation frees a political party from the need to garner 50 percent plus one vote to govern, the party is less compelled to dilute its own program, to alienate its core supporters, or to choose among its competing internal tendencies.

Second, such a system can work against the unification of parties opposed to the ruling party by, at a minimum, allowing them to compete and do well as independent, even if minority, elements. Organizational integrity need not be compromised for electoral competitiveness. This point affects the individual opposition parties in the same way as it does the governing party. But when multiple opposition parties exist, the opposition as a whole lacks a single focal point of serious challenge to the dominant party. And when multiple opposition parties cannot unite, the ability of the dominant party to stay in office is often reinforced.

Third, particular electoral systems often work to prevent voters from acting systematically against the party in power. This is seen most explicitly in the Japanese case but was true as well in the pre-1971 Swedish system. In all multiparty systems in which the opposition is divided the voter opposed to the governing party has great difficulty knowing precisely which opposition party to vote for to maximize the likelihood of defeating the party of government.

And fourth, as was noted above, multiparty systems allow a dominant party to rule with less than a parliamentary majority. Only Japan's LDP, for example, of the four dominant parties examined, rather consistently received more than 50 percent of the votes cast. For most of its history Mapai/Labor was well below the 50 percent mark; it remained in power largely as a consequence of the votes received by its allies. More striking still is that only once in its history did the Italian Christian Democratic party come even close to a majority (48.5 percent of the votes cast in the 1948 election). More often it received fewer than 40 percent of the votes in the Chamber of Deputies elections. This ability to dominate with less than a full majority of the votes and/or seats in parliament is especially true in situations of ideological polarity or high programmatic conflict. In such cases, a "well-positioned" party with a substantial plurality enjoys a high degree of bargaining power vis-à-vis smaller parties and the system as a whole. The end result of all of these features is that, in a multiparty system, long-term rule is rarely contingent on keeping a majority of the electorate happy all of the time; far more often it is at least a partial artifact of the rules of the electoral game.

The Cycle of Dominance

All of the cases of one-party dominance reveal a historical cycle of dominance, a clear beginning, a process of maintenance, and then one or more historical crises which the dominant party must deal with successfully if it is to continue its rule. Four components are common to all of the cases, and hence suggestive as necessary conditions for long-term rule by a single party. The first is related to the origins of dominance and involves a mobilizational crisis and/or new mobilizational opportunities. The second, third, and fourth are related to the continued maintenance of dominance, namely relatively fixed patterns of electoral mobilization based on major historical blocs as opposed to discrete voters and a pattern of ideological distancing maintained by both the dominant party and its principal opponents. This last, in effect, works to prevent the initial mobilization from coming unglued and often prevents the formation of effective majoritarian counter-coalitions. Finally, and somewhat paradoxically, the fourth element is that the maintenance of dominance requires an intellectually fuzzy but nonetheless important combination of flexibility and rigidity by the dominant party. This combination is essentially a matter of skill, judgment, and leadership, and it revolves around continually resolving the tension between the dominant party's ability to retain its core of support for long periods of time but gradually to move beyond that core (which almost inevitably shrinks with time) so as to garner new blocs of support. In essence, the party must be rigid enough to hold on to its key supporters for long periods but flexible enough to replace this loyal core, at least in substantial part, as socioeconomic changes reduce its overall importance within society. In short, the party that is successful over time will almost certainly have become so through a Machiavellian repudiation of one or more of the groups critical to its initial ascent to power or an overall watering down of its original ideological fervor; in the process of so doing it will have become in its maturity a broader, more inclusive party than it was in its infancy.

In this sense, prolonged dominance is somewhat like a long-distance race: the outcome is almost impossible to predict at the starting gun or even after the first few laps, though many of the most important contests take place well before the finish line. The tactics that lead to victory may well be invisible to the unseasoned bystander. Yet, as with the race, ultimate victory is clearly the consequence of sustained effort and not a little bit of luck and involves more than a quick spurt of energy before each electoral finish line.

As with electoral systems that favor multipartism, each of these components can be found in many specific instances in a number of countries that have never experienced one-party dominance. In isolation, no one of them offers sufficient intellectual leverage to explain such one-party dominance. But in combination, they provide a reinforcing syndrome of conditions that separates the cases of dominance from those of nondominance. Indeed, they are particularly useful in differentiating the dominant cases from those of near dominance or failed dominance. Each deserves elaboration.

The "Mobilization Crisis" and the Origins of Dominance

One-party dominance is a political creation. It has an identifiable beginning and, usually, an end. All dominant parties can trace the origins of their long-term rule to a major event or series of events that stimulated what might be called a mobilizational crisis, that is, a major reorientation of the political dispositions of key socioeconomic groups. In this sense, the creation of one-party dominance resembles the big bangs of geophysicists. Yet though there are many such big bangs in political history, only a few lead ultimately to one-party dominance. Most political big bangs involve moments that contain an infinity of possibilities, only a small number of which might be long-term dominance. Thus if all dominant parties can trace their origins to some such big bang, they are not alone. Far more distinguishing is that their ultimate success resembles the evolutionary biology of Darwin. The dominant parties are those that emerge victorious from a long-term battle that reduces to the survival of the fittest.

Rarely can one predict long-term dominance at the time of a party's first ascension to power. Dominance is more easily recognized in the cycle of its continuance than in the seeds of its generation. Only with hindsight do the particular events that mark the beginnings of one-party dominance take on greater clarity.

One of the first things to note is that in three of the four cases, the dominant party's rule can be marked from its origin as a political organization. If nothing else, the parties' very creations offered new mobilizational opportunities for socioeconomic groups and new stimuli to mobilization on the part of political parties. In these cases, the party's origin and its dominance began simultaneously. Thus Japan's Liberal Democrats began their reign in 1955 following the deliberate creation of the party by leaders of its two major components, anxious over the possible electoral threat posed by a newly fused socialist party. Mapai's dominance also began with a merger when, in 1930, the two leading Zionist parties joined forces. Although the Italian Christian Democratic party had prewar roots in the Popular party of 1919–26, it was created in 1943, and its rule continued from the first postwar Italian election held in 1946. Only the Social Democratic party in Sweden had been an unsuccessful competitor in numerous elections before sufficiently outdistancing its opponents to win its epoch-starting victory in 1932.

As Di Palma has shown in his comparison of various new regimes that emerged from authoritarian pasts, there is an inevitable tension between achieving dominance and creating democracy. To the extent that democratic norms are biased against long-term rule by a single party, it is doubly surprising that Italy and Japan in particular (and Israel to a lesser extent) were able to maintain and develop one-party dominance and political democracy simultaneously. More probable would have been the loss of power by such parties even though they seemed to start with tremendous advantages that might have led to long-term rule. The experiences of the MRP in France, the CDU/CSU in West Germany, Nea Demokratia in Greece, or the UCD in Spain would appear to have been far more common experiences for parties that emerged strong for one or more elections following an authoritarian period but faded from strength as the requisites of democracy seemed logically to usher in an alternative party.

Most important, the mobilizational crises in all of the instances under examination involve more than simply the creation of new political organizations. Indeed, such organizational changes are far more often the consequences than the causes of new mobilizational opportunities. In all of the instances in question, one-party dominance can be traced to a historical period when preexisting patterns of politics were drastically shattered, when old solutions lost their appeal, when new problems and new social, political, and economic groups were at the fore, when old alliances were broken. In effect, dominance traces to a time when the nation's political dice were given a good hard shake and a new roll.

Such a mobilizational crisis is analyzed by Gourevitch in his study of the political reactions within different industrialized countries to three periods of major world economic crises: the late nineteenth century, the 1920s and 1930s, and after the oil shock of 1973. Within each country, important historical blocs allied or divided in ways that gave each a unique confluence of interests and set the country's politics on a consistent trajectory for subsequent decades.[4]

Within the cases of one-party dominance examined here, such mobilization crises occurred in Italy and Japan at the end of World War II and with the superimposition of democratic institutions by the Western occupying powers. Possibly more important in each case than the actual end of the war, however, was the emergence of the Cold War. With the DC and the LDP's predecessor conservative parties closely linked to the U.S. government and its foreign policies, political mobilization around the bipolarizing issues of capitalism versus communism and pro-Soviet versus pro-Western policies was inevitable. International tensions became a principal axis for domestic political mobilization. In the Japanese case, these initial divisions were further stimulated by the end of the U.S. occupation and still another opportunity for national rethinking about competing political priorities. From the end of the war until the early to mid-1950s both countries witnessed divisive and polarized political mobilizations around issues linked to each country's authoritarian past, its postwar reforms, the Cold War and foreign policy, and the future course of the nation's political economy.

4. Peter A. Gourevitch, *Politics in Hard Times* (Ithaca: Cornell University Press, 1985).

In the Swedish case, new mobilization opportunities were provided for the blue-collar working class primarily as a consequence of mass male suffrage in 1919, as well as by the world depression of the late 1920s and early 1930s, the consequent threat felt throughout the country by the violent labor-management conflicts at home, and the specter of fascism on the nation's southern flank. The conservative order of the late nineteenth and early twentieth centuries was unalterably eroded by its collective inability to deal with any, let alone all, of these changes. The mobilizational crisis was less immediately identifiable in the single year or two before the SAP gained office; rather, it was a long-term historical shift in political powers that occurred over a decade or so but eventually crystallized in the early to mid-1930s and was similar to, although more exaggerated than, that of many European countries at about the same time. Particularly relevant, there was massive labor-management strife that traced from the general strikes of 1902 aimed at securing the franchise to the strike against the law on collective bargaining of 1928. Thus the 1930s began with fierce labor-management battles that included numerous lockouts, which in the words of Walter Korpi "led to a change in the front lines" of politics and economics in the election of 1932.[5]

In Israel, the mobilizational shakeup traces back to Israel's prestate immigration and to conflicts within the Zionist movement and the Yishuv, the Jewish community in Palestine during the decades before statehood. As Gregory Luebbert phrases it, Israel's prestatehood community was "born democratic" with the result that the liberal democratic format and universal suffrage were never the burning issues they had been in Europe, including Sweden.[6] Yet because many of the new Israeli immigrants had already been partially mobilized into different ideologies in the lands they left, each successive wave brought with it new challenges to the prestate parties in Palestine. In effect, each major wave of immigration catalyzed a new mobilizational crisis. It was into this well-stirred pot that Mapai dipped for its support when it was formed in 1930. At that time Israel had experienced three major waves of immigration, the latest of which had taken place from 1919 to 1923.

What is clear in all four cases is that no instance of dominance can be traced to beginnings clearly rooted in "normalcy." Each traces far more explicitly to a crisis. Obviously, war and the formation of a new state are less normal than are economic crises. And undoubtedly there is a component of subjectivity in the identification of historical opportunities for the major realignments of key socioeconomic blocs. Most political democracies undergo many apparent crises during their histories, and in only a few

5. Walter Korpi, "The Historical Compromise and Its Dissolution," in Bengt Ryden and Villy Bergstrom, eds., *Sweden: Choices for Economic and Social Policy in the 1980s* (London: Allen & Unwin, 1982), p. 131.

6. Gregory M. Luebbert, *Contemporary Democracy* (New York: Columbia University Press, 1986), p. 93.

instances does long-term rule by a single party result. All the same, a party that can take power following such a crisis and deal with that power effectively enjoys particularly long-lasting benefits in the popular memory. A party that forges a historical compromise among important socioeconomic sectors in the crucible of crises enjoys a halo effect for some period thereafter. A party perceived as a national savior is hard to oppose.

Moreover, how citizens initially view such a party is principally a function of their position as farmers, business people, union members, exporters, small shopkeepers, and the like. In these moments of mobilizational crisis, voters line up to support or oppose a political party, far less as individual voters and far more as members of specific socioeconomic blocs. When the issues facing a country are deep and divisive, it is the major cleavages in the society that define the electoral fault lines.[7] Such an initially fixed pattern of mobilization leaves its legacy on political identification for a long period of time, providing either a plus or a minus to the subsequent adaptability of the entire party system. This is particularly so, as shall be explored below, when the ideological bases for the initial division are sharply and distinctly drawn. And in addition, it is so when the electoral system tends to recreate an existing pattern of mobilization.

Regardless of the form of creation, a final point is that few political observers of any one of these countries predicted decades of uninterrupted rule following what became the dominant party's first taste of victory. Only with time and consistent retention of office, as well as the consequent ability of the dominant party to implement its historical project, did the prediction of each successive victory become easier. Even then, in all four cases, it was almost as common to predict the loss of office as its retention. For a political party to dominate government over several decades an advantageous beginning is not enough. To stay in power, it is necessary for such a party to institutionalize its initial mobilization.

Maintaining Political Distance

Following each of these mobilizational crises, the domestic politics of all four countries was marked by a relatively fixed pattern of mobilization involving major historical blocs. In the Japanese case, organized agriculture, the major business and financial sectors, and small and medium-sized shopkeepers formed the organizational core of the LDP's support. Organized labor, urban dwellers, and, in a less formally structured way, the general intellectual community provided the key ingredients of support for the socialist and communist opposition.

7. This line of logic is explored in broad historical terms in Seymour M. Lipset and Stein Rokkan, "Cleavages, Structures, Party Systems, and Voter Alignments: An Introduction," in Lipset and Rokkan, eds., *Party Systems and Voter Alignments* (New York: Free Press, 1967), pp. 1–64.

A similar pattern occurred in Italy, with the key economic supporters of the Christian Democracy being bolstered by the Catholic church and segments of the trade union movement associated with it. In addition, though lacking any organizational framework, the DC benefited systematically from greater support among female voters.

In Sweden, it was organized labor, primarily in the form of LO, that provided the principal support base for the SAP while organized agriculture, major businesses, and the urban middle class were divided into support patterns gravitating around each of the three major parties in the so-called bourgeois bloc.

It was also labor, organized through the Histadrut, that was the organizational heart of Mapai, and then later, as Shalev has shown, Eastern Jewish immigrants, Arabs, and the new Jewish middle classes, also mediated by the Histadrut, afforded Mapai additional support. Meanwhile, the religious blocs and the old petit bourgeoisie, agriculture, and business found it difficult to unite into a single party and divided their opposition to Mapai/Labor in several directions.

These major socioeconomic orientations remained in place for long periods following the dominant party's ascension to power. Clearly such coalitions did not remain intact automatically. If dominance emerges from a particular beginning it also requires certain steps to allow it to continue. Dominance, like any well-functioning machine, requires systematic attention to maintenance. One of the most valuable assets in such maintenance of dominance by the parties investigated here was the existence of the ideological polarity within society and within the party system that emerged from the mobilizational crises discussed above.

In many historical situations, one can point to events that led to major reshuffling of historical blocs. In very few, however, do such alliances remain intact and in constant control of government power for such lengthy periods of time, particularly given the incentives many such groups would have under a system of free association and free elections to break the original alliance. Why do they not? One of the major reasons is that these different blocs would find the theoretically plausible option of joining the opposition to be totally ludicrous ideologically.

Polarizing issues by definition leads to radically competing solutions. But as these take institutional form in the programs of competing parties and in the loyalties of major socioeconomic groups, such issues can easily become frozen in time and political rhetoric. The incompatibility of alternative solutions becomes manifested organizationally in the mutual exclusivity of the parties that offer up these competing programs. Free traders cannot readily compromise with mercantilists; only an ideological contortionist could be procapitalist and procommunist simultaneously; deeply religious and avowedly secular solutions to problems rarely blend. Certainly for long time periods following major mobilizational crises, each of our four parties of dominance worked hard to maintain the ideological cleavages from which it was benefiting electorally and politically. And in most instances, the opposition party, or parties, did the same, loudly proclaiming the superiority of their solutions over those of the government in power.

Throughout such a process, dominance can be maintained by material or symbolic means. Typically, both are employed. But the symbolic battle should not be ignored in the focus on the material. Thus, Levite and Tarrow have made a particularly compelling case for the importance in both Italy and Israel of the delegitimization of the opposition as a basis for continued one-party dominance.[8]

In Israel Mapai and later Labor, for example, relied heavily on the symbols of the initial pioneering efforts by the vanguard of Zionism (*chalutziut*), voluntarism through the kibbutz movement, and egalitarianism. Later the new ideological glue of statism (*mamlachtiut*) was superimposed onto the initial prestatist values. Throughout its rule, such symbols added cultural weight to Mapai/Labor's claims to some peculiar right to rule. But at the same time, ideology was bolstered by the practical payoffs of politics in the forms of, among other things, an urban machine, a state-created middle class, and housing, jobs, and cash subsidies to new immigrants. Through these mechanisms, Mapai and later Labor were able to hold on to old supporters and to socialize new ones in a recurring cycle of party maintenance. Meanwhile, the principal opposition bloc, Herut, later Likud, was subjected to a systematic campaign of delegitimation and political isolation. David Ben-Gurion, in particular, was relentless in his efforts to discredit the Herut movement, which he accused of being an "antidemocratic, repressive, fascist type of movement that posed the gravest threat to the core values of Jewish society and the Israeli state."[9] It was only with time, counter symbols, a revived nationalism following the 1967 war, and inclusion in a wartime coalition cabinet that the Likud was eventually able to shed its scabrous image.

Similar ideological distancing can be seen in Italy and Japan. In both instances, traditional symbols, those of the Catholic church and freedom of the individual in Italy, and of cultural nationalism, the emperor, and group harmony in Japan, were mustered by the two dominant parties to solidify their own voting support and to undermine potential support for their opponents. In Italy, De Gasperi mirrored Ben-Gurion's hostility to Likud by "opposing the extremes of left and right as threats to the Italian democratic system and maintaining the DC in some kind of centrist position by stressing its 'centrality' as the protector and keystone of Italian democracy. In other words, 'Her Majesty's Loyal Opposition' has not existed because many both inside and outside Italy have perceived the major opposition

---

8. Ariel Levite and Sidney Tarrow, "The Legitimation of Excluded Parties in Dominant Party Systems: A Comparison of Israel and Italy," *Comparative Politics* 15 (April 1983): 295–327.

9. Ibid., p. 300.

party as not 'loyal' to the democratic system and not a legitimate or acceptable alternative to, or possible coalition partner of, the DC."[10] A similar delegitimizing effort was attempted by Prime Ministers Yoshida and Kishi in Japan.

Yet such symbolic appeals were given substantial economic underpinnings because in both Italy and Japan the state (and the ruling party) was able to use the state treasury to provide a wide array of assistance to major industries and to numerous individual communities in the form of pork barrel programs.[11] And as in Israel, the practical payoffs of patronage, state spending, and the pork barrel provided tangible reinforcement for the more ephemeral cultural and ideological appeals that in Israel were rooted in ancient Zionism and contemporary social democracy.

In Japan, the communists were a much smaller party and hardly the major opposition, but they were systematically subjected to the same sorts of delegitimation as were their counterparts in Italy. And the Japan Socialist party, if not fully delegitimized in the sense that Levite and Tarrow use the term, was certainly subjected to political isolation and withering ideological criticism by the ruling LDP. As but one example, a prominent LDP leader stirred controversy but not much surprise by a statement to the effect that the LDP handled the entire budget process and the only thing the JSP members did during the process was to raise their feet to warm them by the heaters.

In Sweden, the division between the three major parties of the so-called bourgeois bloc and the ruling Social Democrats was clear and more or less unbridgeable during the bulk of the SAP's rule, though it lacked the constancy of verbal vitriol found in the other three political systems. Positions for or against the social welfare state and the planned economy provided the main line of division, and for the SAP there was no middle ground in its commitment. This acute division was perhaps most noteworthy during the years immediately following World War II, when the business sector launched its PHM (opposition to the planned economy) drive, generating a climate of spiteful rhetoric over tax policy, the social welfare state, and private ownership. The main lines of debate reopened in subsequent policy battles over the supplementary pension controversy and the wage earner funds, among other issues.[12]

10. Douglas A. Wertman, "The Christian Democrats: Masters of Survival," in Howard R. Penniman, ed., *Italy at the Polls, 1979* (Washington, D.C.: American Enterprise Institute, 1981), p. 67.

11. In the Japanese case, see Hirose Michisada, *Hojokin to Seikentō* [Subsidies and the ruling party] (Tokyo: Asahi Shimbunsha, 1981). On Italy, see Stepard B. Clough, *The Economic History of Modern Italy* (New York: Columbia University Press, 1967); Joseph LaPalombara, *Democracy, Italian Style* (New Haven: Yale University Press, 1987), pp. 73–83.

12. On wage earner funds, see Jonas Pontusson, *Public Pension Funds and the Politics of Capital Formation in Sweden* (Stockholm: Arbetslivscentrum, 1985); Walter Korpi, *The Democratic Class Struggle* (London: Routledge & Kegan Paul, 1983); and Gøsta Esping-Andersen, *Politics against Markets: The Social Democratic Road to Power* (Princeton: Princeton University Press, 1985).

In all these cases, strong symbolic and ideological divisions continually reinforced the initial patterns of party mobilization of key socioeconomic groups. The issues and values around which the major party divisions were first formed received regular and systematic injections of new vitality, certainly by the dominant party and often by its opponents as well. The major political parties periodically remobilized their initial followings, made new appeals on old grounds, and distanced themselves from one another by these regular reincantations of slogans and promises left over from the formative period. Key social groups were reminded on a regular basis of why they had come to support the political parties they did, of what values, norms, and expectations kept them together (and separate from their opponents). In effect, each successive beat of the ideological drum helped the various parties' marchers to remain in synchronous step with one another as they paraded on through time.

Rigidity, Flexibility, and Subsequent Crises

There is a curious irony to the problem of maintaining dominance over time. A dominant party must be rigid enough in its beliefs and program to hold on to its core supporters. At the same time, no modern democracy has a society that is fixed in stone. With time, new issues, new social groups, new generations, and new orientations all emerge. It was in this context that Maurice Duverger warned that "domination takes the zest from life. . . . The dominant party wears itself out in office, it loses its vigor . . . every domination bears within itself the seeds of its own destruction."[13] The party that puts together a cohesive bloc of supporters and a committed body of true believers willing to work hard for a set of common goals has a great advantage in gaining and holding political power. All the same, over time, it faces great difficulty in adjusting to new conditions. Rigidity ensures the continued loyalty of the already committed, but often with negative electoral consequences, as Otake showed for the Japan Socialist party and as Tarrow showed for the Gaullists in France. Thus, as Duverger notes, the party that does not change to keep up with the society it governs is doomed to lose power. That is the perennial tension faced by any governing party: how to be rigid enough to retain its core support while staying flexible enough to attract newer, potentially more politically important support. Most political parties at some time go through processes of self-criticism and reorientation. Typically, however, these follow some stunning defeat— the U.S. Republican party following the Goldwater debacle of 1964; the Bad Gödesberg program of the German SPD following a series of defeats in the 1950s. Far less common are instances in which a party *in power*

13. Maurice Duverger, *Political Parties: Their Organization and Activity in the Modern State* (London: Methuen, 1967), p. 312.

transforms itself; the incentives to do so are far less pressing. The prevailing wisdom seems to be "Why fix it if it ain't broke?" And the longer a party is in power, the more difficult it becomes to see the necessity for change. Indeed, when a party initially gains office through fixed support blocs and rigidity of ideological appeals, the probability of transformation while in office is lessened even further.

Yet for the dominant party to retain continued control it has, in effect, to abandon the very tactics and patterns of mobilization that brought it victory. It must become something very different from what it was, despite being spared the stimulating heat found in the crucible of defeat. In the phrasing of Tarrow, its hegemony should be "soft."

Certainly, there is nothing automatically self-perpetuating about control of government. This was evident in the losses of office by all our cases of failed dominance. It was also seen in the case of the Israeli Labor party's loss in 1977 and the Swedish Social Democrats' defeat in 1976. Furthermore, in Italy, the Christian Democrats lost their hold on the prime minister's office in 1980 though they remained the largest party and the most well-represented in the number of cabinet seats held. And though it did not actually lose control of parliament and the cabinet, during the 1970s in Japan the LDP was expected by most analysts to be forced into coalition if it were not forced out of office completely. Such experiences underscore both the tenuousness and the political character of one-party dominance.

If a party is to stay in power for several decades, it cannot rest on its original claims to victory. Nor can it typically rely exclusively on the original coalition that brought it to power. With time, old rigidities must be superseded by new flexibilities if the party is to continue its rule. In this sense, the maintenance of dominance is clearly a political art, one that relies on the skills of the dominant party's leadership.

Two possible dimensions of flexibility seem particularly relevant. One involves the Machiavellian capacity to betray some portions of the party's original support group in order to attract newer, more vital support. Typically this involves dropping a component of the party's governing coalition when that component becomes less numerically, economically, or politically significant because of changes in the overall political economy of the country. The agrarian population shrinks; blue-collar workers give way to computer technicians; protected industries lose international competitiveness and political muscle; certain geographical sectors become more populous or economically critical than others; new generations bring with them different political values; small shopkeepers, once the economic heart of a country, lose sway with the arrival of department stores and shopping malls. Such changes and others make it highly unlikely that a political party can continue to retain power by the simple expedient of continuing election after election to rely on its original support groups for campaign contributions, party workers, programmatic ideas, and votes. The rigidity that keeps such supporters loyal in the short run leads to political sclerosis and loss of office for the party in the long run.

This scenario occurred perhaps most clearly in Israel, where Labor's loss in 1977 was heavily attributable to the party's inability to attract support from the successive waves of Sephardic immigrants. Nor did it do well in socializing succeeding generations of Israeli youth into the values on which the party's appeals had originally rested. It also did poorly in creating a national consensus about how to deal with the new territories Israel had gained as a result of the Six-Day War. It also failed to maintain its long-standing partnership with the NRP. And finally, it did little to revitalize the role of the Histadrut as a political support vehicle for the party. In short, its loss of power was overdetermined, but almost all of the causes could be traced to its inability to adapt to new socioeconomic circumstances.

An interesting contrast is provided by the wholesale jettisoning of a major support bloc by the Social Democrats in Sweden. Originally in power on the basis of a red-green coalition of blue-collar unionists and agricultural groups, the SAP in the late 1950s broke with its agricultural supporters and moved to attract additional support from white-collar unionized wage earners. This shift was vital to the SAP's retention of office and its regeneration as a political party.

Yet even the supple SAP was not invulnerable, as its defeat in 1976 made clear. Then, the issues of nuclear power and the wage earner funds left the party internally divided and temporarily unified the opposition parties. Krauss and Pierre suggest that the SAP's early willingness to reach across the long-standing divide between itself and the bourgeois parties may have undercut some of its core ideological support and contributed to its loss of the 1976 election. At the same time, these new issues did not reflect or generate massive socioeconomic shifts in Swedish society. As a consequence, the SAP was able to regain power after six years out of office. (And, indeed, when it came back into office, its social democratic agenda had hardly been tampered with.)

The Liberal Democratic party in Japan has been subjected to less close scrutiny on these matters of flexibility and rigidity in the preceding chapters, although Muramatsu and Krauss make it clear that the party and the government have been increasingly open to once hostile interest groups; Inoguchi identifies explicit policy efforts in the late 1970s and early 1980s designed to hold old supporters while appealing to new constituencies. During the late 1970s, the LDP began moves to appeal to new urban voters and blue-collar unionists, even if this meant alienating its core support from farmers and small business people.[14] The LDP's stinging defeat in the 1989 Upper House elections revealed the hazards of this tactic.

14. T. J. Pempel, "The Unbundling of 'Japan, Inc.': The Changing Dynamics of Japanese Policy Formation," *Journal of Japanese Studies* 13 (Summer 1987): 271–306; Pempel, "Japan's Creative Conservatism: Continuities under Challenge," in Francis G. Castles, ed., *Comparative History of Public Policy* (London: Polity, 1988).

If one major source of flexibility by a dominant party involves the overt switching of support groups, there is a second dimension of flexibility that is also possible for the dominant party. This involves less overt betrayal, requiring only that the party, while continuing to make appeals from a clear ideological position, and with due respect to well-entrenched political values and norms, in fact govern far more pragmatically from the political center.

Muramatsu and Krauss (and Muramatsu in another context)[15] provide a good deal of evidence to show how different political interest groups once completely alienated from the Japanese power structure, including organized labor, environmental groups, citizens groups, and others, were gradually able to gain access to the power structure that prevailed under the ruling LDP. Tarrow has shown in several contexts just how the Christian Democrats in Italy proved themselves to be far more flexible in their appeals to different socioeconomic groups through a system of political exchange than were their conservative French counterparts, who tried to govern through a system of political hegemony. The result was that the more flexible Italians retained power whereas the more ideologically consistent French did not.[16]

Long-term rule gives a party numerous opportunities to broaden its electoral appeal. It can generate policy measures explicitly aimed at garnering new loyalties; it can use its power over the instruments of political socialization from schools through the national media to develop a new generation of loyalists. The party in power also benefits from the growing awareness on the part of all social actors that to accomplish their ends they must somehow learn to deal with the government of the day. The party also occasionally benefits from the vague positive aura associated with long-term rule: duration of rule readily contributes to a climate in which such rule is taken as logical, inevitable, and in the nature of things.

Under such conditions, the dominant party has numerous incentives to become flexible and absorptive in its outreach to individual citizens and social groups. It has strong incentives to move beyond any ideologically cohesive but narrowly based blocs of supporters and to become what Kirschheimer and others have called a "catchall party." Consequently, if exclusivity is an asset in the early stages of dominance, inclusivity becomes the watchword of the successfully dominant party in later years.

In many respects, this mixture of flexibility and rigidity comes dangerously close to tautology: the party that succeeds had the "right" mixture; the one that failed did not. And what is "right" or "wrong" is definable essentially in terms of the party's ability or failure to retain office. Yet in thinking about a cycle of dominance, the mixture, though perhaps not

15. Muramatsu Michio, *Nihon no Atsuryoku Dantai* [Interest groups in Japan] (Tokyo: Toyo Keizai, 1987).
16. See Sidney Tarrow, "The Crisis of the Late 1960's in Italy and France and the Transition to Mature Capitalism," in Giovanni Arrighi and Immanuel Wallerstein, eds., *The Political Economy of Southern Europe* (Beverly Hills: Sage, 1985); Tarrow, *Between Center and Periphery: Grassroots Politicians in Italy and France* (New Haven: Yale University Press, 1977).

subject to easy analysis, is nonetheless important to underscore. In all the cases under examination, the dominant parties were subjected over time to a series of widely recognized challenges to their continued rule. In several instances, the attraction of new supporters revitalized the dominant party; in other instances the inability to make policy shifts led to its loss of office. In either instance, however, it is clear that holding office provided at least the potential for creating the dominant party's own historical project, in the course of which the dominant party also enjoyed numerous opportunities to reinforce and expand the basis of its electoral power.

The Consequences of Dominance: Ideological Hegemony and the Creation of a Regime

Perhaps the greatest commonality among the dominant party systems, and probably the most important aspect of long-term rule by a single party, is that the dominant party, by the longevity of its rule, acquires the opportunity to reshape the nation's society and politics to its own liking. All parties in government seek to do this, but in a democracy, longevity of rule may be the most valuable asset in achieving this goal. In effect, one-party dominance by its very persistence over time permits the recreation of the political regime. Long-term rule by a single party allows the party and its core elements to shape a nation's politics through public policy choices and to move the country along a trajectory different from that which might have occurred had its opponents been in power. In this sense, long-term rule has the potential to shift the ideological balance in society.

Having used the social and economic mobilization of key sectors to gain control of the instrumentalities of the state, a party is then able to use these instruments to reward its socioeconomic support groups and to punish or isolate its enemies. To the extent that it does so in ways that are tactically wise and politically without major backlash, these actions can bolster and expand the base of the ruling party. At the same time, they can reconstruct the major outlines of the nation's society, politics, and economy to accord with the party's political agenda. Over time, this process shifts the ideological axis of the country and the terms of political debate. Through this entire process, policies that were once highly volatile and nationally divisive become institutionalized and accepted as natural components of the nation's political agenda. Long-term rule thus affords a political party the possibility of unleashing a virtuous cycle in which, by the fulfillment of its political agenda, it continually reinvigorates itself electorally and becomes increasingly perceived as the logical party of government. In this sense, Duverger is only partly correct in his judgment that the dominant party contains within itself the seeds of its own destruction. Those seeds indeed are there, but the party also has within itself the potential to recreate the society it governs in ways that reinvigorate itself.

Incumbency is not automatically an advantage. An incumbent must frequently deal with political issues that are almost guaranteed to hurt, rather than help, its chances for survival. Witness only the widespread defeats suffered by most incumbent parties following the world economic downturn in the late 1970s, as pointed out by Inoguchi. At the same time, incumbency carries with it untold advantages that, used astutely, can provide the incumbent with an ever-upward spiral of political support.

Few observers at the beginning of the various long reigns in the four countries studied could have envisioned these societies several decades later, unless it was by projecting forward into time the policy proposals of the parties that eventually became dominant. This is perhaps most clearly seen in the case of Sweden. The SAP turned Sweden into the prototype of the social welfare state and a regime whose foreign and security policy is based on the principle of neutrality. Swedish state spending and Swedish social welfare programs were not dramatically more developed, and indeed in many instances were actually less comprehensive when the SAP came to power than they were in other European countries. Labor's organizational strength was also not greater than in the labor federations of other countries. And following World War II, there was considerable debate over whether to join NATO. Yet over the course of their forty-four years in power, the Social Democrats put into place taxation, housing, social welfare, and labor-management policies that transformed the country's political economy, the size of the Swedish state, and business-labor relations. Political neutrality was nationally accepted as a given in foreign and security policy. And perhaps most important, the political base of the SAP had been bolstered by the programs that expanded the organizational appeals of LO, the peak labor federation, so that by the 1980s over 90 percent of the Swedish work force belonged to the unions (and a large portion were ipso facto SAP supporters), and by additional programs that expanded the cooperative movement, a second key prong in the support base of the party. Indeed, by the time the bourgeois coalition government toppled the Social Democrats in 1976, most of these elements were so well institutionalized that the coalition found itself more committed to the social welfare agenda than the Social Democratic government it had replaced. Furthermore, the inability of the new government to create a new political identity for itself led in 1982 to the return of the Social Democrats, quite possibly stronger electorally, if not internally, than when they left office.

From the opposite side of the ideological spectrum, the LDP in Japan also managed in time to transform both the economic agenda and the defense and security profile of the country, though in a very different direction. In the process, the party virtually destroyed the credibility of its opponents on the left, the JSP and the JCP. Issues of alliance with the United States and the legitimacy of the Self-Defense Forces, which had led to politically rocking demonstrations in 1954 and 1960, were by the 1980s largely irrelevant to the practical political agenda. The LDP's use of state power to break the most radical trade unions in the late 1950s and early 1960s contributed to its hegemony and security in office. On the left, banners continued to reaffirm old slogans, but their capacity to generate broad-based political action was vastly diminished. Moreover, the high economic growth agenda pursued by the LDP led during the thirty-odd years of its rule to the widespread creation of a self-assured middle class, an economically well-off rural population, and even a less militant blue-collar work force, all of whom by the late 1970s saw little appeal in the histrionic calls by the major opposition party, the JSP, for a "dictatorship of the proletariat." The increased electoral strength of the LDP in the 1979 through 1986 elections was but the most tangible payoff of these successful transformations made in Japan's political economy as a result of LDP dominance.

Mapai/Labor carried out a somewhat parallel, though by no means as comprehensive, transformation of Israel. Nationalism, social democracy, and Zionism became the political umbrellas under which the country and the party moved forward together. The Histadrut in particular, and the kibbutz to a lesser extent, became entrenched institutions in the simultaneous service of the Israeli state and the dominant party. Labor in Israel reached levels of organizational strength only slightly below those in Sweden and far ahead of most other industrialized countries, and the Histadrut was the main force in institutionalizing labor relations at workplaces throughout the country. During the same period, it expanded its own enterprises while simultaneously gaining increasing control over larger and larger sectors of the modern and dynamic sectors of the private economy. Moreover, most of Israeli agriculture came to be incorporated into the state system through the collective farms, rather than remaining a source of private power. And what Shalev has called the "state-created middle class," that is, the vast number of public sector workers, also owed their economic well-being to the political program of the dominant party.

At the same time, despite all these assets, Labor lost power in 1977. And in an interesting contrast to the bourgeois coalition that replaced the SAP in Sweden a year earlier, when Likud took power in Israel, rather than respecting and accepting the seemingly entrenched Labor arrangements, it sought to undermine the cultural and political basis of the Labor regime. Likud's actions showed both the weaker institutionalization of the program of Labor and the greater ideological commitment of the Likud to its own competitive agenda. But one interesting measure of the power of office, as Aronoff has demonstrated, has been the ability of the Likud, in its ten-plus years in office, to reshape radically the ideological and symbolic basis of Israeli politics in ways that suggest it seeks not simply to replace Labor as the party in power but also completely to restructure Israel in ways that suggest a completely different form of one-party hegemony.

Finally, in Italy, one finds still a fourth case of dominance under the Christian Democrats. Much like its conservative counterparts in Japan, the

DC managed to take issues of alliance with the United States and the general orientation toward an economy based on capitalism out of the realm of serious party debate and to move them into the realm of accepted and nondebatable givens. It also took much of the sting out of earlier problems between the Catholic church and the Italian state, although largely as a consequence of the party's gradual moves to separate itself from the church, rather than through an institutionalization of church-state ties. In so doing, the DC bolstered its own electoral base, particularly among organized Catholics for whom such issues were central. But on matters of political economy, the regime created under the DC would appear to have been less hegemonic than those in either Japan or Sweden. Rather than the hegemonic implementation of a clear-cut program, the DC set in place a system of organized clientelism.[17] Under this system, various regions and socioeconomic groups loyal to the DC, or potentially supporters of the party, were woven into a patchwork coalition for patronage based on benefits from the state treasury.[18] As part of this process the DC government bought up various sectors of the private economy and sold off segments of state-run enterprises, both on terms beneficial to Italian capitalists. As Joseph LaPalombara has described it, Italy's business sector knew that when its propensity to risk vanished, when managerial intelligence or luck in the market ran out, or when an enterprise was on the brink of bankruptcy, the state would always be willing to buy it out at a nice profit. In this way, the DC created a system of economics under which the business community could unload its "losers" on the state.[19] Conversely, profitable public sectors were sold off on terms desirable to the private sector business community.

Yet, supportive as the DC was of its business allies, it was less willing or able to bludgeon Italian labor into quiescence than the LDP was able to do in Japan during the late 1950s and early 1960s. This was seen in the ability of the Italian labor movement to carry out the "Hot Autumn" of 1969 and the *svolta sindacale* (union turning point) in 1977–78. Both showed the inability of the DC to subjugate the unions to its own agenda; the unions continued to retain an independent voice in policy formation, despite being outside the official DC orbit.[20]

17. This term is that of Luigi Graziano, *Clientelismo e sistema politico: Il caso dell'Italia* (Milan: F. Angeli, 1980), as cited in Sidney Tarrow, "Political Exchange, Hegemony, and the Transition to Mature Capitalism," unpublished ms., Cornell University, 1984.

18. Martin Shefter, "Party and Patronage: Germany, England and Italy," *Politics and Society* 7 (Spring 1977): 403–51.

19. LaPalombara, *Democracy, Italian Style*, p. 199.

20. Marino Regini, "Changing Relationships between Labor and the State in Italy: Towards a Neo-Corporatist System?" in Gerhard Lehmbruch and Philippe Schmitter, eds., *Patterns of Corporatist Policymaking* (Beverly Hills: Sage, 1982); Regini, "Labor Unions, Industrial Action and Politics," in Peter Lange and Sidney Tarrow, eds., *Italy in Transition* (London: Cass, 1980), pp. 49–66; Michele Salvati, "May 1968 and the Hot Autumn of 1969: The Responses of Two Ruling Classes," in Suzanne Berger, ed., *Organizing Interests in Western Europe* (Cambridge: Cambridge University Press, 1981).

The DC was also less successful in socializing Italian youth into support for the party than might have been expected given its long-term rule. Thus younger voters by the late 1970s were consistently providing a growing advantage to the political left, above all to the PCI. Such fluidity among voters and failures of political socialization left the DC in the mid-1980s with less sanguine long-term prospects than either SAP in Sweden or the LDP in Japan. In this sense, the DC would appear to have been less hegemonic in several ways than the ruling parties in these other two countries. Indeed, most contemporary projections of electoral and party politics in Italy suggest that the DC, while continuing to serve as an essential fulcrum in national politics, will no longer be the inevitable provider of the prime minister and the national policy agenda. In the meanwhile, even the PCI has come to accept many of the fundamental components of the DC agenda of the 1950s and 1960s, including membership in NATO and a capitalist economic system. Considering the controversial nature of these issues two decades ago and the DC's rare acquisition of more than 40 percent of the popular vote, however, this would appear to have been a remarkable achievement.

The Future of One-Party Dominance

What, if anything, is the future of one-party dominance in democratic societies? Is it a passing phenomenon, the wave of the future, or something in between? Looking at the four countries given the greatest emphasis in this volume—Sweden, Japan, Italy, and Israel—it would be hard to make a case for some inevitable logic to continued dominance. The Swedish Social Democrats lost control of the government in 1976; Israel's Labor party was defeated in 1977; and though the Christian Democrats remain the largest party in the Italian parliament and cabinet, they lost their monopoly over the premiership when Republican Giovanni Spadolini and then Socialist Bettino Craxi took office in 1980. Only the Liberal Democratic party in Japan remained comfortably in uninterrupted control of the national government by the late 1980s, and internal dissent, political scandal, and an Upper House electoral loss in 1989 made even its continuation in office problematic.

The Swedish case, however, provides an important check on the temptation to dismiss long-term dominance as an interesting but passing phenomenon. As was noted earlier, the bourgeois interregnum from 1976 to 1982 led to little fundamental change in the public policies that had been put into place by the Social Democrats over their forty-four years of rule. For many Swedes, including many of their opponents, the return of the Social Democrats in 1982 was simply a return to normalcy. And certainly, several years under the prime ministership of Craxi put an end to any notion that only the Christian Democrats could create a noncommunist government in Italy, even as it left the DC with the bulk of the cabinet seats, control over subsequent prime ministerships, and the principal influence over public policy.

Predicting the end of LDP rule had become a growth industry comparable to autos or consumer electronics in Japan through the late 1960s and the bulk of the 1970s. As the electoral strength of the LDP continued to slip steadily toward, and then slightly below, the 50 percent margin, journalists, political analysts, and general pundits all put forward their specific scenarios for the "inevitable" demise of Japan's single-party rule. Yet in the 1980 and subsequent elections, the LDP reversed its seemingly inexorable slide, and by the late 1980s, the prevailing theme among both serious and topical writers in Japan had been transformed into the inevitability of LDP hegemony. The 1989 election created yet another wave of expectations of LDP decline.

Only in Israel by the late 1980s could one cite a relatively definitive end to one-party rule. There the Likud bloc had clearly gained if not superiority to, at least parity with, the once invincible Mapai/Labor bloc. Indeed, with Likud in power for the decade following Labor's defeat, there was good reason to consider the possibility that Labor dominance might well be replaced by Likud dominance, a situation quite different from the much more fragmented oppositional governance in Sweden or Italy. In any event, it seems clear that if Labor regains control of the Israeli government through something more than a joint coalition with the Likud such as prevailed in the mid- to late 1980s, it is not very likely that its rule will ever be as hegemonic as it was in the 1940s, 1950s, and 1960s. The competing power bloc, Likud, has escaped the taint of illegitimacy or irrelevance that opposition parties or blocs in Italy, Japan, and perhaps Sweden have found difficult to shed. Likud has shown it can govern, and it has moved quickly to dismantle elements of the Labor government's policies and to introduce its own political regime. This has been especially true with regard to the West Bank and Gaza Strip settlements.

Thus, for the future of one-party dominance in Italy, Israel, Japan, and Sweden, the picture would appear to be mixed. In Japan, Sweden, and possibly Italy, there seems to be a reasonable expectation that the long-dominant parties will continue to be the principal axis of government, particularly in control of most cabinet offices, the policy agenda, and the maintenance and reinforcement of the prevailing ideology and regime. Possibly of even more importance, it also seems apparent that the long-term rule by these parties has enabled them to shift fundamentally the basis of politics in their respective countries in ways that are unlikely to be quickly reversed even by the loss of one or more elections or even if control of cabinets no longer continues to be the exclusive monopoly of the once dominant parties.

Are there any likely prospects for political systems outside these four developing into one-party dominant regimes? No single party in any of the industrialized democracies currently appears to be close to thirty-five or forty years of uninterrupted rule. Yet with the left in Britain so divided and with Margaret Thatcher apparently so firmly in control of a strong Conservative party, there is ample journalistic speculation about the prospects of one-party dominance in Britain. American Republicans seem enamored of similar possibilities for their party in the United States, at least for the presidency. Yet Thatcher came to power only in 1979, and the American Democratic party held the White House as recently as 1980 and never fully lost control of Congress. Indeed, the House of Representatives has had Democratic majorities since 1954. As should be clear from the cases of Norway, Denmark, West Germany, or Ireland, or even Labour in Britain or the American Democrats in the 1930s and 1940s, it is one thing for a party to appear dominant for ten or fifteen years; it is more than double the problem to stay in power for twice that time period.

If the above analysis concerning the peculiar mixture of a favorable electoral system, a mobilizational crisis, strong ideological divisions, and subsequent flexibility are at all close to being necessary conditions for the creation and maintenance of one-party dominance, there seems little likelihood that there will be a significant increase in the number of one-party dominant regimes emerging from the ranks of contemporary democracies in the near future. At a minimum, social, political, and economic conditions would appear too "normal" to catalyze such a development.

The one thing that might change this situation would be a massive mobilizational crisis affecting large numbers of the current industrialized democracies, a crisis comparable to the economic depression of 1929–40 or to World War II and the Cold War. As Inoguchi showed in his chapter, the economic downturns of the second oil shock of 1979 certainly offered at least a mini-crisis of mobilization and support which toppled most of the major governments within the industrialized world. Yet the political reorganizations and recombinations that followed in most countries appeared more ad hoc than permanent. Value changes and the redefinition of political interests had little of the fundamental character that they took on when the choice seemed reduced to Marxian versions of socialism and liberal versions of capitalism. If one-party dominance is to emerge in one or more of the contemporary industrialized democracies, it would appear to be likely only after a far more drastic reshuffling of the intellectual, ideological, political, and economic deck.

The Israeli case suggests one other important possibility, namely the emergence of one-party dominance in a relatively new nation. Even here, however, as Di Palma's treatment of Spain, Portugal, and Greece suggests, the establishment of one-party dominance is never very easy in democracies, particularly when the prior regime has been authoritarian and democratization is a major national goal. No party, however favored in the first years of postauthoritarian rule, has an easy job of simultaneously creating a climate for democracy and one in which it becomes the logical and preeminent party of government.

Nonetheless, with the single mobilizational party so prevalent in the less industrialized world, and with several such countries giving signs of increasing the levels of domestic political democracy, it is not unreasonable to imagine that one or more such countries might evolve toward both industrialization and democratization without surrendering single-party control. Despite the incredible barriers to such an evolution, countries such as Mexico, India, South Korea, Singapore, or Taiwan could conceivably do so with time. In a similar vein, within much of Latin America and sub-Saharan Africa, if the power of the military and other sectors to topple elected governments is ever permanently arrested, an evolution toward one-party dominance under conditions of industrialized democracy might occur. Prime candidates might well include Brazil, Argentina, or Peru, Kenya or the Ivory Coast. Speculative as such comments must be, the evolution of one-party nondemocracies toward industrialization and democracy under single-party rule would surely seem at least as important a possibility as that of competitive party systems within the industrialized world giving birth to single dominant parties.

Regardless of future developments, the phenomenon of one-party dominance within industrialized democracies has indeed left an important legacy and posed important questions. The legacy continues largely in the context of the ideological repolarization and the regime creation made possible under long-term one-party rule. In this sense, the four countries are clear testimony to the proposition that "parties matter." It would be hard to imagine any of the four cases having evolved as they did over the past four to five decades without giving primacy of place to the parties that dominated politics within these countries during those years.

Just as important are the questions thus posed for democratic theory. By examining how certain democratic political parties have been uncommonly adept at forging historical social coalitions and then mixing recurring electoral support with long-term control over governance and policy agendas so as to reward their supporters and to perpetuate themselves in power, these essays and the book as a whole redirect empirical attention to the interaction between socioeconomic blocs, elections, and state power. To the extent that these uncommon democracies force more systematic attention to such interaction, they provide an important window on industrialized democracies as a whole. Many recent studies have been based on a dichotomization between "state" and "society." Our analysis has shown how integrally the two are in fact connected within industrialized democracies. Others have emphasized elections in isolation from the socioeconomic coalitions behind them. This study has addressed the interrelationship between both, underscoring in particular the role of political parties in maintaining such an interrelationship. Too often public policy has been studied as a product of government. This book makes it clear how such outputs can function as well to reward friends, punish enemies, remain in power, and redirect a nation's political trajectory. As a result of the analysis of such relationships within the world's "uncommon democracies," it may be more easy to assess such complex interactions among the remaining, more common, democracies.

Index

Library of Congress Cataloging-in-Publication Data

Uncommon democracies : the one-party dominant regimes / T. J.
  Pempel, editor.
    p.   cm.
  Papers from a conference held in London and sponsored by the Joint Committees on
Japanese Studies and Western Europe of the American Council of Learned Societies and the
Social Science Research Council and the Japan Society for the Promotion of Science.
  Includes bibliographical references.
  ISBN 0-8014-2367-8 (alk. paper). — ISBN 0-8014-9696-9 (pbk. : alk paper)
    1. Political parties—Congresses.   2. Opposition (Political science)—Congresses.
3. Representative government and representation—Congresses.   4. Comparative govern-
ment—Congresses.   5. One party systems—Congresses.   I. Pempel, T. J., 1942–   .
II. Joint Committee on Japanese Studies.   III. Joint Committee on Western Europe.
IV. Nihon Gakujutsu Shinkōkai.
JF2011.U53   1990
324.2′04—dc20   89–22111